Awakening
The Feminine Path of Power

Divine Feminine Initiation Path

By Megan Wagner, PhD

Veriditas Publishing
Redwood City, California

Dedication

This book is dedicated to all the women and men who are actively embodying the Divine Feminine as She floods our world with unconditional love and radical compassion.

Table of Contents

Introduction – Awakening the Divine Feminine

Dear friend and sister,

For many years now I have been initiating women who are living amazing lives - women like you who are passionate about their families, relationships, healing the planet, healing themselves, diving deep, and opening to spirit in their own unique ways.

As the world is changing and paradigms are shifting, we need to show up in the world with confidence, integrity, strength, compassion, and creative vision. We need a path of awakening that is tailored to the feminine way and encourages us to trust our spiritual knowing.

Our feminine visions, feminine dreams, and feminine knowing are so important to bring to the women's circle at this time. We need to support one another on this incredible journey of awakening that is happening around our beautiful planet at lightning speed. The time is right for us to gather as communities of women and initiate each other into the Divine Feminine Way as we did in the ancient days. We haven't forgotten how to do it. The memories are there, right below the surface.

I remember well the day those memories opened for me. I was traveling to Crete to lead my first women's group on that beautiful Greek island. As soon as I set foot on the land, it was as if a door swung open inside my heart and I began *to remember*. I could smell, see, taste, feel, hear, and sense deep in my bones the ancient initiation rites we performed in other times and places. I remembered being part of a vital women's circle. I remembered being initiated by elders who held me in sacred, unconditional love.

I remembered being connected to my body, to my sexuality, and to nature in a way that was joyfully, shamelessly sensual. I remembered being connected to my sisters in a way that was deeply nurturing and healing. I remembered being connected to the stars and the sky and the cosmos in a way that made me feel, without a shadow of a doubt, that *I belonged.* I felt connected and part of this world in a way I had never experienced before. It was the most profound feeling of *coming home*.

The Divine Feminine was now living inside me as a felt reality. Her message of unconditional love, deep compassion, profound acceptance of what is, and interconnection with all living things, was quickening in my life. I felt more accepting of my body as a beautiful Goddess Temple. My heart opened to let in more love. My mind cleared and I trusted my intuition more. I had more access to my will and clarity about what I wanted to do with my life. I felt less bound to and affected by my early childhood wounding and conditioning.

The most profound shift came for me when I connected to other times and places where women's spiritual authority and spiritual knowing was honored, trusted, and welcomed. Honored. Trusted. Welcomed. I had certainly felt my share of being dishonored, mistrusted, and unwelcomed when it came to my own spiritual authority - as an Associate Minister and as a woman Kabbalah Teacher. And so I was filled with excitement when I realized that the Feminine Spiritual Way wasn't just a reality in the past - *it is a reality in the present* - when I embody this truth within my being, stand in my spiritual knowing, and trust and honor myself profoundly. I realized the only way to awaken this truth in the here and now, was to be it, to live it, and to share this living reality with my sisters.

Embodying our spiritual authority, our feminine knowing and intuition, our feminine ideas, visions, and solutions is exactly what the Divine Feminine is calling us to do and be in the here and now. *She is calling us home.*

This miracle and this blessing of finally feeling home inside myself continued to grow and I became ever more curious about how to cultivate this deep connection for myself and for my sisters. I was already studying various psycho-spiritual paths such as Kabbalah, Shamanism, Jungian and Archetypal Psychology, Astrology, Tarot, Alchemy, Fairy Tales, and world Mythology and I was deeply immersed in a Kabbalistic Mystery School. All of these were transformative and tremendously healing for me.

What was missing, however, was the Women's Initiation Circle. I longed for a circle of women to guide me on my path. And so it felt vitally important to create rituals and initiation practices designed specifically for women that profoundly call women home to themselves. I wanted to bring forward our ancient initiation rites into a modern form so that we, like our ancestral mothers and grandmothers, could take our place around the women's circle and feel connected once again.

This inner knowing propelled me to explore how the Divine Feminine was expressing Herself in the ancient world. Being based in England at the time, I began to research ancient Priestess traditions around the Mediterranean and then traveled extensively throughout England, Wales, Scotland, Ireland, Western Europe, Morocco, Greece, Turkey, and Israel. I then began gathering women to experience life-cycle rituals and rites of passage. We explored many different kinds of Divine Feminine rituals to bless pregnant mothers, to celebrate the moon phases, to heal from wounding to the feminine, elder ceremonies, first blood rituals, seasonal rituals, birthing rituals, ancestral healing rituals and so on.

And then something profound happened in my early 40s. My son was just starting school and I had a bit of space to breathe, think, and create. I began to write a series of women's initiation stories to take women through a full feminine initiation process. As I wrote, five beautiful Divine Feminine Guides presented themselves to me, and the stories unfolded. The five Feminine Archetypes or Spiritual Guides who emerged were the Wise Woman, Warrioress, Queen, Visionary, and Manifestor. As I worked with these sacred guides, it was clear each corresponded to an element and essential part of our being. This guided me as I wrote the stories and developed the various steps of initiation for each Divine Feminine Guide.

FEMININE ARCHETYPE	ELEMENT	ESSENCE
Warrioress	Earth	Body
Queen	Water	Heart
Visionary	Air	Mind
Manifestor	Fire	Will
Wise Woman	Ether	Spirit

After the stories were written, I created a series of Sacred Robes to depict the Goddess/Priestess of each story so that women could have a visual representation to help embody the Archetypal energy even more. Women can get into the Sacred Robes and try them on, step into new possibilities, and animate that particular Divine Feminine energy. At the end of this process, my women's initiation program called *The Feminine Path of Power* was born.

As I write this book, we have been offering this women's initiation program for over 10 years. We gather in circle, both virtually and live for weekend retreats. I drum and tell the women's initiation stories and then throughout the weekend, we reenact Divine Feminine rituals. For the Wise Woman, we do rituals together to connect with our deep spirit. To embody the Warrioress, we do communal rituals to establish healthy boundaries and conquer our fears. To embody the Queen, we do rituals for emotional cleansing, opening the heart, and activating self-compassion. To embody the Visionary, we do rituals to open the third eye and increase our Visionary powers. For the Manifestor, we do rituals to align with our own will and create an action plan to manifest our dreams.

The rituals are suited to us as modern women and are designed to help us get grounded, open the heart, clear the mind, access the will, and connect with spirit. These modern initiation rituals are designed to connect us to our deepest nature, feel welcomed into the women's circle, and value the gifts we bring to the "village". There's nothing quite like experiencing ritual with other conscious, healthy, joyful, open women. I feel it's the best way to reconnect with our wise feminine being. Experiencing ritual together is fun, playful, deep, enriching, profoundly moving, adventurous, and always surprising.

If you are ready to step into your wisdom of body, heart, mind, will, and spirit, then welcome! If this book inspires you, I invite you to join our *Feminine Path of Power* community and seek your Divine Feminine initiation - which is your birthright. With inspiration, encouragement, and support, you will identify your mission and purpose and create an action plan to manifest your goals and dreams. You will feel fully empowered to create healthy boundaries, balance your emotions, clear your mind, focus your will, and trust your spiritual knowing.

I am so pleased that you are here and ready and willing to go on this amazing journey together. Welcome Priestess. Welcome Goddess. Welcome Divine Feminine Woman. You have something very important to contribute to the women's circle. I look forward to discovering this with you!

Many blessings,
Megan

Chapter 1
Women's Initiations

Divine Feminine Initiation

The Divine Feminine is emerging into our world with a force we can no longer ignore. For many of us, the Divine Feminine consciousness is breaking through in our dreams, in our cultural awareness, and right inside our own hearts. Many women are taking action according to what their hearts are telling them – to save the planet, stop violence, envision change, and create peace! Many women want to feel empowered to usher in this new Feminine Awareness. How do we do this as a community of empowered women?

The surest way to accomplish this is for you to *become the Divine Feminine yourself.* This means becoming your true self and BEING who you truly ARE. When you, as a woman, embody your feminine wisdom and power, you usher in the new feminine paradigm within your own heart. To do this, you need to feel supported, seen, validated, loved, nurtured, and encouraged. You also need to be initiated by women who are already being their Divine Selves, women who love who they are and want you to love yourself just as profoundly.

So how does this feminine initiation happen for us as women? How can we become our true Divine Feminine self and BE who we truly ARE? How can we claim our full power and have self-confidence? How can we gain a sense of self? How can we trust our intuition? How can we develop our own will and use our power of choice? In other words, how do we, as women, get initiated?

The simplest answer is that we need to come into contact with women who are already empowered and initiated. We need to spend time with women who claim their power and trust their own inner guidance. We receive feminine knowledge from women who are already empowered and we get initiated by women who have themselves been initiated.

Women's Initiation goes back thousands and thousands of years. In the ancient days, we naturally gathered in women's circles and had daily contact with women who possessed powerful skills - women who embodied their self-confidence and power. By being with these women over time, we would internalize the qualities we saw in our mothers, aunties, older sisters, and the wise women of the village.

Not only did we spend a lot of time with already initiated women, we were invited to begin our initiation training when the time was right. This was usually during adolescence, when our curiosity about the world was growing and we were ready to receive more feminine knowledge. We were then guided systematically through the initiation process, through stages of learning, to become the empowered women we were meant to be.

In the ancient days, there were traditional, well-thought-out initiation rituals, called rites of passage, which were perfectly designed to help a woman trust her intuition and knowing. In the ancient days, there were initiation rituals to help a woman find her true power and claim it. There were sacred exercises to help a woman connect with her natural powers of body, heart, mind, will, and spirit.

It is important to recognize that a woman naturally has a powerful connection to the Earth and a natural connection to her body and her sexuality. She has a natural connection to her emotional power. She has a natural connection to her intellectual power and to her will power. A woman has a strong connection to her spiritual power and spiritual knowing. But often her primal instincts to connect with the earth, her body, emotions, mind, will, and spirit becomes dulled and she falls asleep to her natural powers.

I know for me, when I was in my teens and twenties, I wanted to feel deeply connected to myself and to the world, but I had fallen asleep to myself. I felt deeply disconnected from my intuition and disconnected from my emotions. I was hungry for feminine guidance and really suffered because I couldn't find a way to be initiated and guided by empowered women. So after years of research, study, training, and traveling around the world, I developed an initiation path just for women. I wanted to resurrect these ancient initiations rites and rituals so that modern women could experience feminine initiation.

I have distilled my years of learning into a women's initiation path called *The Feminine Path of Power*. This path features five dynamic feminine guides to activate a woman's sacred relationship to her body, heart, mind, will, and spirit. These five guides – the Warrioress, Queen, Visionary, Manifestor, and Wise Woman - teach women of all ages how to become empowered.

These Divine Feminine guides are designed to provide women with a step-by-step initiation into full feminine wisdom. It is so important at this time in our history to reclaim what has always been ours - our right to feminine leadership, feminine wisdom, feminine power, and feminine spiritual authority. As we reclaim our women's initiations and feel fully empowered, we can pass on these gifts and empower our sisters, nieces, cousins, and daughters.

A feminine path of awakening supports our physical, emotional, and spiritual development. When we are initiated, we can see and recognize how powerful and beautiful we really are. We recognize that each of us has a unique gift we bring to the "village of women" - a gift that is crucial to the functioning of the whole village.

Initiation is an important way to ensure the highest functioning of the "village" (any community of women you are involved with), because it ensures that everyone's gift is being optimized. It's like a beehive; if everyone is expressing their gift to their highest level of functioning, the hive works together to accomplish tremendous things!

The Priestess Path

For millennia, women have gathered in sacred circle to initiate women into their full feminine wisdom. In ancient times, these sacred circles were often connected to a particular Priestess Path, which was also connected to a different Goddess, Archetype, Myth or Story, depending on the place and cultural tradition.

For example, in ancient Minoan Crete, Priestesses followed the Myth of Ariadne, snake priestess and guardian of the labyrinth. These initiation rites involved working with snake energy (Kundalini / vital life force energy), developing visionary and oracular gifts, and celebrating the beauty and bounty of nature. During her Labyrinth initiation, A Cretan Priestess met Asterion, her mythological star consort, with whom she entered into the cosmic dance of life.

In ancient Sumeria, Priestesses were connected to the Goddess Innana, Queen of Heaven. Their initiations involved a descent into the underworld to meet the shadow sister, Ereshkigal. They would descend, both physically and psychologically, through seven gates (7 Chakras) and strip themselves of worldly possessions and emotional attachments to arrive at a truer, deeper sense of identity.

In ancient Greece, the Priestesses of Demeter, (Earth Goddess and mother of Persephone) re-enacted the story of Pluto and Persephone in the great Eleusinian Mysteries. In these Mystery rites, Persephone was abducted into Pluto's underworld, where she learned to transmute grief and loss to be reborn to new, expanded life. The Priestesses drank a "medicinal potion" to induce visions of the worlds beyond. This shamanic rite of drinking plant medicine allowed women to see multi-dimensionally and to lift the veil into the archetypal and spiritual worlds.

In ancient Egypt, the Priestesses of Isis also learned to lift the veil, called the "Veil of Isis". Using intensive breath work, sound, and meditation techniques, they opened their third eye to experience unified consciousness in the cosmic realms where all things are connected.

In ancient India, Dakini Priestesses followed the stories of the Dakinis or "Sky-dancers", working with tantric/sexual/Kundalini/life force energy to purify and activate powers of self-renewal and regeneration. Their practices penetrated the veil of physical reality to "dance in the sky", the cosmic realm of spirit.

In ancient Israel/Judea, the Magdalene Priestesses excelled in Sacred Marriage practices, activating their inner masculine and feminine energies to cultivate unconditional love and unitive states of consciousness.

It seems that no matter what the tradition, the Priestess Path aims to connect a woman intimately to herself, others, the natural world, and the cosmos. A woman who is in a sacred relationship to these realms – Herself, Her Community, Nature, and Cosmos – is a woman fully alive.

When a woman steps into her Divine Feminine wisdom, she lives in the physical, psychological, and spiritual worlds at the same time. She walks between the worlds. She transcends time. She brings knowledge from the spirit world into practical, physical reality. She heals. She teaches. She speaks her truth without fear. She changes what needs to change and allows things to die that need to be reborn. She is connected to her center of power. She is compassionate and generous. She loves herself profoundly. She knows. She is a Wise Woman. The Priestess Path awakens this Mystery deep inside us.

The Feminine Path of Power

How then do we, as modern women, come into sacred relationship with our self, community, nature, and cosmos? This was the burning question in my own mind and heart when I was searching to create a modern day Women's Initiation Path and Mystery School for women.

When I compared various ancient Priestess traditions, I began to see common threads. Most included teachings, exercises, and rituals to align a woman's body, heart, mind, will, and spirit. This made perfect sense to me because all Priestess paths aim to harness a woman's physical, emotional, mental, and spiritual gifts. Many traditions included rituals and exercises to heal wounds from the past, cleanse and balance our chakras (energy centers), and rewire our physical and emotional systems through breathing, toning, chanting, meditating, dancing, communal ritual, healthy diet, healthy sexual expression, and radical self-care.

Even though many of the specific ancient initiation practices and rituals have disappeared from our conscious awareness, we *can* access our ancestral memories by tuning in with our deep intuition and spiritual knowing. This happened for me over many years as I opened my ancestral memories and together with my own deep knowing as a therapist and spiritual teacher, I created a women's initiation pathway relevant and useful for women today.

This initiation path, called *The Feminine Path of Power* is designed to help you, as a modern woman, step fully into your Divine Feminine wisdom and to align your body, heart, mind, will, and spirit.

Archetypes: Warrioress, Queen, Visionary, Manifestor & Wise Woman

On *The Feminine Path of Power* there are 5 Divine Feminine Archetypes to guide you through the process:

1. **The Warrioress**
2. **The Queen**
3. **The Visionary**
4. **The Manifestor**
5. **The Wise Woman**

The **Warrioress** awakens your physical senses and connects you to your sacred body. The **Queen** awakens your powers of heart and compassion and helps you balance your emotions. The **Visionary** awakens your natural intuition and intellectual powers and sharpens your mind. The **Manifestor** awakens your will to manifest your dreams into the world. The **Wise Woman** awakens your spirit and invites you into self-mastery and spiritual knowing.

As you deepen into this Divine Feminine Initiation Path you will be able to embody the powers of each Sacred Feminine Archetype. Each Archetype or Divine Feminine Guide walks a particular Path of Power.

The Warrioress walks the **Path of Strength**. When she is present within, you possess healthy boundaries and you feel grounded and present.

The Queen walks the **Path of Compassion**. When she is present within, you love yourself profoundly and offer deep compassion to others.

The Visionary walks the **Path of Change**. When she is present within, you are clear-minded and ready for positive change.

The Manifestor walks the **Path of Action**. When she is present within, you focus your will for decisive action.

The Wise Woman walks the **Path of Mastery**. When she is present within, you honor your deep spiritual knowing and feel aligned in body, heart, mind, will, and spirit.

When you walk confidently on the 5 Paths of Power - Strength, Compassion, Change, Action, and Mastery - you utilize your body, heart, mind, will, and spirit to shape the world around you. You command attention and create positive change. You create a loving and compassionate atmosphere wherever you go. You are masterful, awake, aware, shining, and radiant. These are the gifts of awakening the Divine Feminine energies within you.

I have been working with these 5 Divine Feminine archetypes for many years now and I continue to find correspondences with many different traditions. I look forward to your contributions to this sacred path. Perhaps your own spiritual tradition or area of study can shed some light on these archetypes, paths, and elements. The following is a table of correspondences that I have created so far. I'm sure there's more to come…

ARCHETYPE	ELEMENT	ESSENCE	PATH	WORLD	TAROT
Warrioress	Earth	Body	Strength	Physical	Pentacles
Queen	Water	Heart	Compassion	Emotional	Cups
Visionary	Air	Mind	Change	Spiritual	Swords
Manifestor	Fire	Will	Action	Divine	Wands
Wise Woman	Ether	Spirit	Mastery	Integration	Major Arcana

Feminine Empowerment

When women hear the word **empowerment**, many different responses bubble up. Here are some common responses from the women in my groups and trainings:

- *When I think about women's empowerment I think of believing in my free will.*
- *I think of having choice.*
- *It reminds me that I have the ability to receive, not only to give.*
- *For me, women's empowerment is about trusting my inner guidance and my intuition.*
- *Traditionally women have been taught to serve others and even be subservient. So women's empowerment reminds me that women can own their own power.*
- *I think of claiming my own power and moving with it.*

As I discuss this topic with women who have been my clients, students, and group participants, we have concluded that a woman's path to empowerment looks very different than a man's path to empowerment. As women we must claim our own way and see it as a valid way for us to be empowered.

A woman's empowerment comes when she achieves self-confidence and personal mastery. It is crucial that each woman develops the capacity to deeply value and validate her true self. Every woman has a birthright to healthy self-esteem. Our world will be an amazing place when every woman feels self-confident and self-assured. We will trust our intuition, own and claim our power, and exercise free will and choice. The world will be transformed.

In order for you to feel initiated as a woman, several things need to happen. First, you need to feel welcomed into the village of women. Second, you need some feminine guidance. Third, you need your gifts to be recognized. And finally, you need to experience the power of choice available to you.

An important aspect of Divine Feminine Initiation is feeling welcomed into the "village of women". It feels wonderful to be welcomed into any circles of women you belong to: your family, your peers, your co-workers, or your spiritual community. It's so satisfying to be celebrated as an important part of the circle. Your gifts and talents are needed for the highest functioning of the circle of women. It's important to feel that your feminine power and your unique gifts are honored and welcomed.

In order to feel like an initiated woman, you also need some feminine guidance so that you feel powerful in body, powerful in heart, powerful in mind, powerful in will, and powerful in spirit. Through training you can master your emotions, your mind, and your will. You can receive this through feminine initiation.

Your gifts also need to be recognized. This begins with you, when you recognize the value of your unique gifts and talents. When you value yourself, you will gladly contribute your gifts to the village. Then your gifts can be recognized and you can experience how important your contribution is to the entire village of women.

Lastly, for you to feel initiated as a woman, you need to experience the power of choice available to you. When you feel empowered, you notice how many choices you have in any given situation. When you feel disempowered you probably feel downtrodden, trapped, or hopeless. The initiation process empowers you to move out of habitual hopelessness and out of feeling trapped or frozen. Feminine initiation gives you access to all the tools you need to choose a positive outcome for yourself and your loved ones.

Many of you grew up in families where there was very little feminine training and guidance. You didn't feel welcomed into your family and you didn't feel welcomed into any communities of women. You didn't feel your gifts were recognized and you may not have felt empowered to make positive choices for yourself. This is a common experience so please do not lose hope! There are new opportunities for you to feel part of the village of women and to feel welcomed, appreciated, seen, and embraced. This is what Divine Feminine Initiation is all about.

What Disempowers women?

When a woman is disempowered, she can easily fall into negative, addictive behaviors. She can feel frozen, fearful, or silenced to speak her own mind and heart. She can feel isolated and alone. She may give her power away to others. She may undervalue or undermine herself. She may harbor secret feelings of self-loathing and self-hatred. She may be deeply self-critical. Does any of this feel familiar?

In my workshops, I ask the question, "What disempowers women?" Here are some common responses:

- *Not having any healthy feminine role models.*
- *Isolation! Having to do everything alone, everything by myself.*
- *Not getting any support.*
- *Gossiping about other women and negative talk undermines other women.*
- *Criticism - being criticized for what you feel, think, for what you do.*
- *Envy and jealousy coming from other women.*
- *When nobody has your back, nobody's looking out for your best interests.*
- *I hate it when women are so competitive with other women. It's the opposite of support and encouragement. It's so painful when other women compete with you instead of encourage you.*

Women often do destructive things to other women to disempower them: competition instead of cooperation, envy instead of support, judgment and criticism instead of encouragement. This is the opposite of supporting a woman to recognize her beauty and her gifts. I don't know about you, but I grew up in a family and culture where I didn't feel very seen or heard. As a result, I spent my youth competing intensely with other girls until I woke up one day (when I was 12) and was horrified at my own behavior.

I made a conscious choice when I was a young teenager to walk on the path of truth and co-operation. I could see very clearly how destructive it was to compete rather than cooperate and pull together our joint resources. I could see how destructive it was when girls and women were not seen and heard.

I've made it my life's work to see and hear other women because I know how important it is to be positively mirrored in this way. If you are the type of person who encourages and supports other women, remember that you need it too! You need to get this kind of support for yourself.

What you need to be Initiated

In order to be empowered and initiated, you need support, containment, a positive environment, and encouragement. You need physical support, emotional support, and spiritual support. You need to feel safe and held by a circle of elders and trustworthy women. You need a positive environment where other women really listen to you. You need women to really see you and encourage you.

You also need healthy mirroring from your initiated elders and from your peers. When you are mirrored in the initiation process, other women can see certain feminine qualities in you. When someone says to you, "I see you have this amazing quality or ability, please share it with us", then you begin to really understand what feminine power looks like. Receiving the mirroring you need is important because it supports you to grow and develop far beyond your perceived capacity.

The Feminine Way vs. the Masculine Way

It is certainly true that the feminine way of empowerment is different from the masculine way of empowerment. Our culture tends to support a more masculine way of empowering - encouraging us to set goals, go after what we want, and push to get things accomplished. As a result, we feel frustrated and impatient most of the time.

An important aspect of the feminine way is to set our intentions clearly and then *wait patiently*. The feminine way includes learning to rest in the process of waiting. This is difficult for many of us because we set our intentions and then we want everything to happen right away. Feminine, organic growth usually takes longer than we expect. We're conditioned in our culture to want things to go fast and to want things to go in the way we want them to go. But the feminine way is the way of organic growth, which is about slow, steady, step-by-step growth.

A baby grows organically in the mother's womb, with daily nourishment and sacred holding and gestating. This kind of powerful, feminine holding and daily nurturing can feel deeply satisfying when we give it to ourselves. We need to patiently hold sacred space and take each day to nourish and incubate our projects along. As soon as we start pushing for growth to happen too quickly, what happens? We might sabotage the project or it falls apart or it is birthed prematurely.

Organic timing is natural timing - however long it takes something to grow and develop. Of course it's important to set goals, and yet it is also valuable to learn to rest and to stop controlling the timing of the cooking process. Things need to cook, incubate, and stew - this is the feminine way.

My Personal experience of Feminine Initiation

I remember feeling fairly "out of it" when I was in my teens and twenties. I felt disconnected from my true self and my real feelings. I felt disconnected from my intuition. Then, in my late twenties I became interested in initiation rituals and rites of passage in ancient cultures and I became really excited. Here were women who seemed to be deeply connected to themselves and their feminine power. My mantra became, "I want to be initiated!"

Then, when I lived in London during my thirties, I trained with some amazing women teachers, shaman, and healers who taught me about the power of feminine initiation. Soon I was leading my own initiation rituals and began taking women's groups to Crete for feminine initiation. Since 1995 I've been taking women to Crete to experience the powerful feminine mystery tradition that lasted for 1500 years on that ancient Mediterranean island.

All that I have learned and intuited and remembered about women's initiation I am passing on to you, because I want you to experience being seen, heard, and received in a powerful circle of women.

My desire is to bring forward and modernize these ancient initiation traditions to women today so we can recreate the women's circle. We need to re-establish the circle so that every woman understands her essential role to complete the circle. In ancient times, we were immediately welcomed into a women's circle and shown how to ground and connect deeply with our body, how to balance our emotions, how to clear our mind and open our intuition, and how to manifest our gifts and dreams into life.

Women's Initiation Stories

I find the best way to teach the initiation process is through the power of story. Imagine sitting around a campfire, bundled up against the night chill and hearing your favorite story. Storytelling is an ancient art, a sacred tool that captures our imagination, transports us to far-flung places, and teaches us important life lessons.

When we hear a story and empathize with the characters, we feel we're not alone. When we watch the protagonist struggle for a solution or resolution to their conflict, we feel somehow connected. Their struggle is our struggle. We can relate.

Stories help us find creative solutions and encourage us to be resourceful, ingenious, and inventive. They call us to be ethical and do the right thing. Stories encourage us to be soulful and full of spirit, overcoming odds and fighting adversity. Stories live in our bones, in our hearts, and in our spirits.

But where are the women's stories? How do we embody the Divine Feminine if we can't hear our own stories being told? As women we often feel disconnected from OUR stories, our heroic women stories. Imagine being initiated by our elders around our own campfire and hearing our stories once again. This is what inspired me to write initiation stories for women because we want to know how to step into our full feminine wisdom. We want to know how to live a soulful and spiritually rich life.

Throughout this book, you will meet five heroic female characters with their own initiation story. During their adventures, they overcome obstacles and find creative solutions to real life problems. They guide us in our own initiation journey as we follow their story. These five protagonists have powerful names – names that actually mean "female shaman" in different languages. The Five Initiation Guides are:

1. Majah, The Wise Woman (pronounced *Ma-jah*)
2. Chiman, The Warrioress (*Chee-mon*)
3. Oyuna, The Queen (*Oh-you-nah*)
4. Pujai, The Visionary (*Pooj-eye*)
5. Salima, The Manifestor (*Sah-lee-ma*)

In the first initiation story, we journey with **Majah** to a magical land where women's power has always been honored, where women are seen as powerful in body, powerful in heart, powerful in mind, and powerful in will. We follow her adventure as Majah meets her destiny to unite the 4 Sacred Clans of Women and integrate the wisdom Paths of Strength, Compassion, Change, and Action.

In the second initiation story, we journey with **Chiman** as she trains to be a powerful Warrioress, mastering the Path of Strength. She becomes an Earth Clan Woman, powerful in body, focused and strong. We follow her wilderness adventure as Chiman battles the Shadow Path of Fear, breaks the spell of the Victim, survives the Cage of Bones, and activates the Sacred Boundary around her Soul.

In the third initiation story, we journey with **Oyuna** as she trains to be a powerful Queen, mastering the Path of Compassion and becoming a Water Clan Woman, full of emotion and big of heart. We follow her ocean adventure as Oyuna celebrates in the Sacred Grotto, drinks love potions in the Temple of Self-Love, luxuriates in the Tent of Healing Touch, swims with the dolphins, and tells stories by the fire near the cove.

In the fourth initiation story, we journey with **Pujai** as she trains to be a powerful Visionary, mastering the Path of Change and becoming an Air Clan Woman, powerful in mind, full of vision. We follow her high mountain adventure as Pujai flies with Falcon, hangs upside down in the trees, learns the art of Swordcraft, masters the Winds of Change, confronts the Veils of Illusion, and awakens her visionary powers in the Dream Dome.

In the fifth initiation story, we journey with **Salima** as she trains to be a Manifestor, mastering the Path of Action and becoming a Fire Clan Woman, powerful in will, ready for action. We follow her hot desert adventure as Salima connects with the fire in all living things, tames her wildfires, learns to shine her big light, receives her Cape of Fire, and masters the art of Wandcraft, ready to manifest her dreams into the world.

Each guide follows a different path of initiation to awaken a different feminine power. Majah, the Wise Woman, walks the Path of Mastery and awakens your power of choice and deep spiritual knowing. Chiman, the Warrioress, walks the Path of Strength and awakens your physical senses and connects you to your sacred body. Oyuna, the Queen, walks the Path of Compassion and awakens your natural powers of the heart and helps you balance your emotions. Pujai, the Visionary, walks the Path of Change and awakens your natural intuition and sharpens your mind. Salima, the Manifestor, walks the Path of Action and awakens your will to manifest your dreams into the world.

Through the five initiation stories you are guided to awaken your innate feminine gifts. The Wise Woman teaches you to embody your own spiritual authority and become a true master of your life. The Warrioress teaches you to ground, be present, and to embody your unique strength. The Queen teaches you to express and balance your emotions and offers profound compassion. The Visionary teaches you to clear your mind and envision the change you want. The Manifestor teaches you to manifest and create your life according to your own will.

Sacred Initiation Robes

Over the years, I've been mindful of making the initiation path more accessible for my students. So I decided to follow a vision I had years ago to create a series of Sacred Robes to teach the path of initiation in a more embodied way. I wanted to give women the opportunity to step into a Sacred Robe and receive the wisdom and healing available from the spiritual guide on the Robe.

For *The Feminine Path of Power*, I created 5 special Goddess Robes, depicting the Wise Woman, Warrioress, Queen, Visionary, and Manifestor. During live workshops, women can wear the Robes to embody each Goddess and activate their powers of body, heart, mind, will, and spirit. Each Robe is designed, created, and hand-painted by me in my studio in California.

The Robes travel with me on my round-the-world adventures and I invite people to try them on and "step into a new possibility". It is truly amazing to watch people transform as they step into the Robe of their choosing. Women say, *"When I step into the MASTERY Robe I feel I can better control and master my life." "When I step into the COMPASSION Robe I open to love and compassion for myself." "I want the VISIONARY Robe to activate my creativity and vision." "In the MANIFESTOR Robe I feel I can manifest my desires." "In the WARRIORESS Robe I feel the strength to stand my ground."*

Trying on a Robe activates particular initiations for each woman. She steps into a new possibility for herself and begins to imagine what her life could be like if she were more free or masterful or compassionate or creative. She can feel the energy of the Robe as it imparts some of its wisdom and magic.

Many people ask me how I came to create these Sacred Robes. Here is a brief story about how I became involved with sacred art....

Sacred art has always fascinated me. In my home as a child I was surrounded by sacred images from Africa, Asia, Oceania, North and South America. This beautiful indigenous art, depicting mystical journeys, unconscious dream states and shamanic cosmology became gateways for my imagination, transporting me to other times and other places. It was only later, when I trained in depth psychology and mysticism, that I understood the deeper function of sacred art – to induce altered states of consciousness to access our higher self and connect with the divine.

Traveling the world and witnessing sacred initiations and rites of passage from various cultures inspired me to find a new medium to teach the path of initiation. I wanted to find a creative approach to help my students and clients experience the initiation process in a more embodied way. This led me to create a series of Sacred Robes that would tell a visual story of the initiation journey, Robes that could be worn in ritual as well as contemplated as sacred art.

Now I travel around the world and teach with my Initiation Robes. Many people have tried them on, performed rituals and sacred ceremonies, danced, drummed, and chanted in the Sacred Robes. They have been to sacred sites in Crete, Italy, England, Scotland, Spain, France, Turkey, USA, Morocco, Hawaii, Mexico, Thailand, Indonesia, Japan, and West Africa so far.

It's hard to describe the feeling when you wear the Robes. During ritual, I have heard amazing wisdom come forth from the most ordinary people. The archetypal image on the Robe begins to speak and ancient wisdom comes pouring forth.

Each Initiation Robe has a unique design and color scheme, which I carefully choose over time with the help of dreams, prayer, and meditation. The images on each Robe are influenced by my years of personal therapy and dream work, alchemical study, world mythology, and extensive traveling. Some of the designs come fully formed in dreams. Some designs evolve over time as I work with them.

The Feminine Path of Power Initiation Robes are designed to empower each woman to activate her own initiation. She can literally step into any new possibility. She can choose to embody a certain quality she wants to call into her life. She can be the strong, capable woman she wants to be. She can channel new love and compassion to herself. She can feel her ability to manifest her dreams into real life.

Remember what it was like to play dress up when you were a girl? Remember how fun it was to try on your mother's clothes or your sister's clothes? Remember how fun it was to pretend to be a fairy princess? When you step into one of the Goddess Robes, you feel young again, you feel beautiful. The whole world of possibilities opens once again and you can access your divine child, ready to take on the world. We play with the Sacred Robes in our live *Feminine Path of Power* workshops.

Chapter 2
The Wise Woman: Walking the Path of Mastery

It is time now to hear *The Story of Majah,* the first Initiation Story introducing Majah, the Wise Woman feminine guide who walks the Path of Mastery and Magic. *The Story of Majah* also introduces us to the Feminine Paths of Power available to us: The Path of Strength, The Path of Compassion, The Path of Change, The Path of Action and The Path of Mastery.

In this story, you will journey with Majah to a magical land where women's power has always been honored, where women are seen as powerful in body, powerful in heart, powerful in mind, powerful in will, and powerful in spirit. Let's follow her adventure now as Majah meets her destiny to unite the four Sacred Clans of Women and integrate the wisdom paths of Strength, Compassion, Change, and Action.

Through Majah's initiations, you learn to awaken the powers of each clan and acquire their greatest magic: from the Warrioresses you gain strong boundaries, from the Queens you gain emotional balance, from the Visionaries you gain clear vision, and from the Manifestors you gain the power to manifest your dreams. As you complete initiation you discover the Majah within you, the Wise Woman who masters your life, walking with strength, compassion, change, and action.

You will also be introduced to the shadow paths of each clan, which pull women off their paths of power. The shadow path of the Warrioress is the path of fear. The shadow path of the Queen is the path of self-sacrifice. The shadow path of the Visionary is the path of chaos. The shadow path of the Manifestor is the path of manipulation.

Through the initiation process, your inner Wise Woman is activated and helps you master the shadow paths and get back on your path of power and back into alignment and integrity with your true self. You'll be able to identify where you get stuck in disempowered behaviors - whether it's fear, self-sacrifice, chaos, or manipulation. You can overcome the fears that hold you back from being your true self. With the gifts of the Wise Woman, you can reclaim your own power, align with your true self, and focus your will.

When you embody the Wise Woman, you live your life with strength, compassion, vision, and power. You are spiritually centered and fully awake. As the Wise Woman you are master of your own life and destiny. You follow your calling and know your life's purpose. You have a powerful inner light like a beacon or compass, pointing to your true north each day of your life. The Wise Woman awakens your true feminine power and helps you embody your true feminine essence. She can help you unlock your creativity and full potential.

Let's go now on the Journey with Majah …

Majah Part 1: The Story of Majah

Once upon a time, in an ancient time, a time so long ago that some women have forgotten…But a long time ago in a far away land there was a place where women's power was honored, a place where women were seen as powerful in body, powerful in heart, powerful in mind, and powerful in spirit. There was no question of this, no doubting of this. And so no woman grew up questioning her worth or going into existential despair. No, in this ancient land Great Temples were built to honor the clans of women who all held positions of authority in every avenue of life.

And according to the ancient ways, when mothers were pregnant and full of life, the elders would gather round and ask the unborn child, "Are you a male or female child? What is your name? And to what clan do you belong? The elders needed to know the destiny of each child so they could prepare accordingly. Now, if it was a boy child, the male elders would take charge. And if it was a girl child, the women elders would take charge and there was always much rejoicing in the women's village because here was another great soul coming into the community to bring new power and new gifts to the clan of women.

Now in this ancient land there were many types of women. There were the singers and the dancers, the ritual keepers, the lovers, the fools and tricksters, the ones who loved the day and those who loved the night. There were women powerful in mind and sharp as a blade and women powerful of heart. There was every variety of woman you could imagine and there was always a place for the gifts that each woman brought. But arching over all this diversity were the 4 Great Clans of Women that all women were sorted into at birth. There was the Warrioress Clan, those who walk the Way of Strength. And the Queen Clan, those who walk the Way of Compassion. And the Visionary Clan, those who walk the Way of Change. And finally the Manifestor Clan, those who walk the Way of Action.

And for thousands of years the women lived in this way. They had well-established initiation rites for each clan. They had their traditions, their ways of working, their ways of awakening each woman to her essential beauty and awakening each woman to her deepest self so that every woman learned to love and respect herself and learned to serve her community with her highest and most excellent gifts.

But the clans were very secretive and protective of their initiation rites and so it happened that the Warrioresses did not know what the Visionaries did to awaken their powers. And the Manifestors did not know how the Queens were instructed to open their powers. And no one really questioned it. It's just the way it was. But even though there was a lot they did not know about each other, here is what everyone did know…..

It was common knowledge that the Warrioress Clan followed the Way of Strength. They defended and protected the land and the people. They were the earth clan women, powerful in body, focused and strong. They were skilled in hunt, confrontation, and strategy of all kinds. And it was common knowledge that the Queen Clan followed the Way of Compassion. They were the water clan women, full of emotion and big of heart. They fed and nurtured all the people with their generosity and love and were skilled in diplomacy, right speech, and random acts of kindness.

And it was common knowledge that the Visionaries were altogether different. They followed the Way of Change. They were the air clan women, powerful in mind, who envision new ways, new ideas that breathe life into the village. They were skilled in shape-shifting, attitude changing, and knowing when things need to die to be reborn. And it was common knowledge that the Manifestor Clan followed the Way of Action. They were the fire clan women, strong of will, who knew and understood what needed to be done…where, when, and how. They were skilled in manifesting, leading, guiding, and accomplishing whatever was set before them.

And so for thousands of years the 4 clans lived in balance and in harmony and year after year each girl child was sorted into her clan and no one questioned it. Until one day something very strange happened……

Majah Part 2: The Birth of the Majah

One day a woman in the community who was ripe with child went before the circle of elders to receive the sacred message from her unborn child. Now this woman was always a bit odd, a bit strange it seems. For she had some funny ideas about the clans and how she believed they should share their knowledge with each other. But this was so outrageous, so preposterous that most women would just roll their eyes when she would carry on with one of her speeches about the way things ought to change. But in her defense she was in the Visionary Clan and she was setting about trying to change something she had seen in one of her great visions. But I suppose the community wasn't quite ready.

So on this strange and unusual day our Visionary woman gathered in the circle of elders to receive the sacred message from her unborn child. The wise elders gathered round and held their ears close to her big belly and they closed their eyes for deeper listening and after a long pause one of the elders said, "It's a girl!" and there was much rejoicing in the circle of elders. A shout went out and soon the entire community of women was shouting enthusiastically, "It's a girl!" "It's a girl!" "A new gift is coming!"

And then there was quiet once again and they all waited to hear the name. The elders bent low over the woman's belly and after a long silence, the elder who could hear whispered something so that only the circle of elders could hear. Their eyes widened and they stood there stunned, shocked, like a giant meteor had just fallen out of the sky. "What? What is her name?" asked the mother. And the oldest of the wise women stepped forth and in a whisper not unlike when a person has just seen a premonition she said, "Majah. Her name is Majah."

Now to you and me this just sounds like an ordinary name, a beautiful but ordinary name. But not to the women of this ancient land. NO. There had been a prophecy years and years ago that one day a woman would come to the clans, a woman who would have the power to unite the clans, a woman who would be able to learn the Mysteries of each clan and she would break open the secrets that had been held close by each clan over the centuries. It was said that this liberator would carry the name of MAJAH. And that is why this day the circles of elders stood in stunned silence while Majah's mother smiled secretly to herself and whispered a blessing right then and there that her baby would come forth steady and strong.

You see in this ancient land, the name Majah came from the ancient word "maj" which means TO BE ABLE and "maj" gives birth to "Magus" "Magi", "Magic" and Mastery. And the people knew that the Majah would be a great master, a great Magus Magician, she would be able to master the powers of each clan, which no other woman had ever done before. But this caused some to believe that Majah would be all-powerful and so women held fear around the coming of the Majah.

And so you can understand the great anticipation when the elders bent down a third time and held their ears over Majah's mother's belly and asked, "And what then is your clan, what is your destiny?" And here was Majah's reply, "I belong to all the clans. My destiny is to unite the women and empower all women in self-mastery."

Loud gasps could be heard in the circle of elders as this never-before-heard-pronouncement was made. And then laughter penetrated the silence, laughter from the oldest of the wise ones and it grew louder and louder and the contagion of laughter spread far and wide until one way or another the entire community got wind of the Majah's imminent arrival and all fear was banished from their hearts and all doubt dashed from their minds and there was celebration for 13 days and 13 nights.

And soon after the celebrations, Majah was born and the Clan Leaders honored her by bringing her gifts. The Warrioresses gave Majah a sacred shield, a shield to banish fear and empower the self with boundaries, protection, and worthy defense. And the Queen Clan brought Majah a sacred crystal heart, a crystal heart to speak truth with compassion, master emotions, and free the heart from pain and sorrow. And the Visionaries gave Majah a sacred sword, a sword to cut though confusion, clear away self-doubt, and obtain clarity of mind. And the Manifestor Clan gifted Majah with a sacred wand, a wand with a fiery tip to focus the will, accomplish the task, and light the way for others. And so it was that Majah grew in body, heart, mind and spirit, surrounded by her sacred shield, crystal heart, sword, and wand, surrounded by the love of the people and nurtured in the old ways. And as the years passed, the Elders watched and waited………..

Majah Part 3: Into the Shadowlands

So Majah was raised in the village in the normal way and did her chores and made friends and lost friends and had her heartaches like every other child in the village. But as the years went by and Majah was approaching her coming of age, she began to have disturbing dreams, dreams that would wake her at night, dreams that took her far away into an unknown land. And when the Elders heard of these dreams they agreed it was time for Majah to begin her training at last. So the Elders of the Clans gathered and brought Majah out of the village to the faraway land that she had seen in her dreams, the place called the Shadowlands.

Now the Shadowlands was a dreadful place, a desolate land with few living creatures, muted sunlight, and no laughter, a place where women are trapped between the worlds where they are neither living nor dead. The Shadowlands was a place where women go who have strayed off their path of power and forget the true light at the center of their being. And the Clan Elders brought Majah here so she would see with her eyes wide open how women become disempowered – how women get ensnared and spellbound into the negative ways of fear, self-sacrifice, chaos, and manipulation.

It was the Great Warrioress who stepped forward first, holding the Sacred Shield, which was infused with the powers of the Warrioress Clan. "Come with me." She said to Majah, "Come see a woman who walks the Way of Fear." And suddenly they were in the Shadowland of Fear and there was a woman whose back was bent and looked as if she had been scared for a long, long time. And Majah saw a hideous creature hovering around this woman following her wherever she went. And the Great Warrioress told Majah this was the Demoness of Fear and her name was VICTIM. She stalks women on the path of fear and tempts them to remain victims by blaming others and staying small.

And Majah saw how this woman lived, how she was fearful to speak up, fearful to defend herself, scared of men and women who had authority over her. And because she had no shield to protect herself, people abused her body and soul, they intimidated her and she gave into their demands and slowly she became downtrodden and gave up her goals. She heard cynical voices inside her head "you can't do this, you're not capable of that." And she isolated herself, secretly drowning herself in strong drink until finally she became a victim. And the Demoness of Fear feasted off her negative energy growing stronger and more frightful.

And it was at that moment the Demoness of Fear turned her terrible face towards Majah and came towards her fixing her eyes upon hers and through her dreadful gaze she sent powerful waves of ice cold fear into Majah's being. Shivers crawled up her back, her body contracted, her guts tightened, and she thought she might turn to stone. But in that second before she lost herself to Fear, Majah seized the Sacred Shield of the Warrioress Clan and blocked the ice cold fear from penetrating her and she sent the fear flying back to the Demoness who instantly turned to stone. And coming back to herself, Majah breathed and sighed and the Warrioress Elder smiled and gently took back the Sacred Shield and said, "You have done well my daughter. Now it is time to go with the Queen to the Shadowland of Self-Sacrifice."

And the Great Queen stood before her holding the Sacred Crystal Heart, which glowed with the powers of the Queens. "Come with me." She said to Majah, "See a woman who walks the Way of Self-sacrifice." And suddenly before Majah there was a woman who looked exhausted and drained of energy, as if she had sacrificed her life-blood giving to everyone but herself. Her faced was etched with bitterness and resentment. And Majah saw the hideous creature hovering close by this woman and knew this to be the Demoness of Self-Sacrifice. And the Queen Elder said, "The name of this evil spirit is MARTYR. She stalks women on the path of Self-sacrifice and tempts them to give and give, never allowing themselves to be vulnerable and doomed to remain forever disappointed in love."

And Majah saw how this woman lived, how she sacrificed for her family, rescued her friends, and chose lovers who were needy. And she thought if she just kept giving she would get love in return for that is what she truly craved. But no one could ever break through her façade of self-sufficiency or penetrate her heart that was locked and caged. And she heard cynical voices in her head "You'll never get what you want, no one will ever love you or give to you." And the blood in her veins flowed with resentment and she poured bitter tea to others and fed them sugar-coated cakes toxic with poison. And over the years her heart shattered, shriveled, and hardened until she became a martyr. And the Demoness of Self-sacrifice feasted off her negative energy growing stronger and more dreadful.

And it happened faster than lightning that the Demoness who delights in broken hearts ran towards Majah and with an almighty force, hurled a poison arrow straight into Majah's heart. The world split open and a flood of grief filled Majah's soul, she felt the despair of never knowing love. But in that second before she drowned in grief, Majah seized the Sacred Crystal Heart of the Queens and held it to her own bleeding heart. And she felt warm, deep, penetrating love seep back into her wounded heart. And this gave her the courage to pull the poison arrow from her heart and with all her might she threw it into the heart of the Demoness who dissolved into a pool of water and blood. And coming back to herself, Majah clutched her heart and the Queen Elder smiled and gently took back the Sacred Crystal Heart and said, "You have done well my daughter. Now it is time to go with the Great Visionary to the Shadowland of Chaos."

And Majah walked over to the Visionary Elder, who was holding the Sacred Sword, which was infused with the Powers of the Visionary Clan. "Come with me." She said to Majah, "See a woman who walks the Way of Chaos." And now Majah saw a woman who was almost a blur, she was moving so fast and doing so many things there was a tornado of energy circling around her. And Majah saw the hideous creature swirling beside her and the Visionary confirmed, "This is the Demoness of Chaos and her name is SABOTEUR. She stalks women on the path of Chaos and tempts them to sabotage themselves through confusion, procrastination, and holding on to old ways that don't work."

And Majah saw how this woman lived how she was constantly distracted, scattering her energy in a hundred directions. And how she threw up elaborate smokescreens and made every excuse why things weren't changing, she became a master of self-deception. And because she had no sword of truth to cut through the chaos and gain clarity of mind, she forgot things and lost things and couldn't make good decisions. And in her relationships she stirred up chaos, gossiping and betraying confidences. And she had lots of ideas, lots of plans but they never came to fruition. And she heard cynical voices saying, "You'll never step into your wisdom and power." And over the years her chaos drove her loved ones away and they threw up their hands in frustration. And the Demoness of Chaos cackled in triumph and feasted off her negative energy, growing stronger and more terrible.

And when the Demoness of Chaos turned to Majah and sped towards her like a wild tornado, Majah was ready and she seized the Sacred Sword of the Visionary Clan and flung herself forward to meet Chaos head on. And she raised the sword of clarity high above her head and when Chaos was upon her with confusion and self-doubt she sliced the Demoness in two, cutting and slashing until the Demoness disappeared in a cloud of putrid yellow smoke. And Majah steadied herself and regained her balance. And the Elder of the Visionary Clan smiled and gently took back the Sacred Sword and said, "You have done well my daughter. Now it is time to go with the Elder of the Manifestor Clan to the Shadowland of Manipulation."

And Majah drew a deep breath and walked to the Manifestor Elder, who held in her hand the Sacred Wand possessing all the powers of the Manifestors. "Come with me." She said to Majah, "See a woman who walks the Way of Manipulation." And now Majah saw a woman who walked with purpose and direction and whose desire to get what she wants was like a powerful force field that pushed aside anything in her path. She manipulated people and things like puppets. And Majah saw the hideous creature hovering close by whom she knew to be the Demoness of Manipulation and control. "Her name is MANIPULATOR" said the Manifestor. "She stalks women on the Path of Manipulation and tempts them to seek power, domination, and control over others."

And Majah saw how this woman lived how she was outwardly successful and accomplished but inwardly lonely and isolated. There was a hole in her belly filled with a lack of self-confidence and insecurity. She hated that she secretly felt invisible and powerless but when she could manipulate others, it felt so good, it filled the hole in her belly and made her feel important. And the fire she had, which was supposed to be used not for self-gain but for the good of the community, a firelight to lead others out of the dark and into the light, had turned into a wild fire, a consuming fire that destroyed everything in its path. And she heard cynical voices in her head saying, "It feels so good to get what you want. This food tastes better than love." And over the years her manipulation choked the life out of all she loved and her life was barren and empty. And the Demoness of Manipulation feasted off her negative energy growing stronger and more terrible.

And at that moment, the Demoness turned her ghastly face towards Majah and in a whoosh of fire and heat bore down on her, filling her body with enormous power. And for a moment Majah felt she could manipulate life to get anything she desired. But in that second before she was consumed by power, Majah seized the Sacred Wand of the Manifestor Clan and commanded the fire enter the wand and with all her will power she focused the flame into a laser beam of light that hit the Demoness of Manipulation, who exploded in a shower of light and heat.

And Majah came back to herself and took a deep breath. And the Elder of the Manifestor Clan smiled and gently took back the Sacred Wand and said, "You have done very well my daughter. Today, in the Shadowlands you have seen how women stray off their path of power and get trapped in the negative ways of fear, self-sacrifice, chaos, and manipulation. And now we ask you, will you commit your life to transforming the 4 disempowered paths? And Majah said with all certainty in her heart, "Yes, I will." And will you surrender all the ways you have disempowered yourself, releasing and letting go of the negative energy that has flowed through your body and soul, robbing you of your power? And Majah said with all certainty in her heart "Yes, I will."

Then come with us to the Place of Liberation. And they left the Shadowlands and traveled to a dense forest, where the Elders had dug a fresh grave and instructed Majah to lie down and remain in the grave covered by the earth until she had released all toxins, all poisons, all ways she had allowed herself to be disempowered. And as she lay there in the grave Majah surrendered her fears and let them seep into the earth. And she surrendered her bitterness and disappointment that kept her heart locked away. And she surrendered any chaos and confusion that kept her from seeing the clear, stark truth. And she let go of all the ways she manipulates and controls.

And for 3 long days and 3 long nights she stayed in the Place of Liberation until the Elders decided she was done. And when she arose from that grave, Majah felt the liberation in her body, heart, mind, and spirit beyond anything she had ever felt before. And they drummed and danced and sang and celebrated Majah's triumph in the Shadowlands and release in the Place of Liberation. And the Elders nodded at one another for they knew the second part of her initiation was drawing near...............

Majah Part 4: Awakening the Powers of Each Clan

And when the release and celebration in the forest of Liberation was complete, the Elders gathered in a Sacred Circle to hear Majah recount her adventures in the Shadowlands, and she described how she battled the negative energy of each path of Disempowerment, how she faced each Demoness and broke the spells that capture so many women and swallow them in misery. And after her tales of bravery the Elders knew the time had come for Majah to learn the secrets of awakening the powers of each Clan.

And so Majah journeyed far to the wilderness training ground of the Warrioresses to begin her initiation and awaken the powers of the Warrioress that lay deep within her being. And they took her to the wild far country where the granite mountains stand strong and the red earth smells rich and ripe with life. And the Great Warrioress said, "We follow The Path of Strength. Our empowerment comes through STRONG BOUNDARIES."

And so Majah was thrown into the wilderness without food or water, without clothing, tools or comforts of any kind. She was forced to survive, to let go of the cravings of her body and she learned to listen to the earth, to the animals and plants. She learned to fashion tools and find food and her body became strong, instinctive, alive.

And the Warrioresses threw her into situations that roused her worst fears so she could face and conquer fear. And through this training she was skillfully prepared for confrontation and adversity, ready to defend and protect. And then they taught her their greatest secret of all, how to activate the Sacred Boundary that surrounds the soul, the Sacred Boundary that protects the inner self from violations and frees the soul to live in its birthright of potency and strength.

And after some time had passed, Majah journeyed to the training ground of the Queen Clan to awaken the powers of the Queen that lay deep within her being. And she traveled to the place of the waters, where the streams and rivers flow into the lakes, and the waters pour into the sea. And the Great Queen told Majah, "Our path is The Path of Compassion. Our empowerment comes through EMOTIONAL HONESTY."

And so Majah learned from the mighty waters about the human heart and how the emotional waters flow too little or flow too fast or don't flow at all because the heart's been frozen through grief and neglect. And she learned all the ways women keep their hearts caged and small and hidden and she learned a thousand and one techniques to release pain, grief, and sorrow.

And the Queens threw her into situations that aroused her most intense emotions so that her heart grew strong. And they made her step into other people's shoes until she could feel what they feel, understand their perspective, empathize and forgive even her enemies. And she became skilled in the art of diplomacy, negotiation, and right speech. And then the Queens taught her their greatest secret of all, how to love the self with profound compassion, compassion so powerful it banishes all self-loathing and casts out all hatred so that the heart can do nothing but love.

And after some time had passed, Majah traveled with the Visionary Clan to their training ground in the high country to awaken the powers of the Visionary that lay deep within her being. And she found herself on the highest mountain, where the winds blow cold and the trees grow tall and majestic. And the Great Visionary said, "We follow The Path of Change. Our empowerment comes through CLARITY OF MIND."

And without warning the shape shifters flew down and seized Majah and hung her upside down in the trees and she was forced to see everything from a brand new perspective. And as she hung there disoriented, her mind split open and suddenly new possibilities appeared, new ways of thinking and imagining. And the fierce gusting winds showed Majah how to move energy for change, to blow out the cobwebs of old beliefs, and break the madness of negative thoughts. And she gazed into the cauldron of inspiration to arouse inner sight, inner vision, and creativity.

And when she mastered the art of sword craft the Visionaries threw her into chaotic situations where she cut through confusion, made swift decisions, banished all self-doubt, and trusted herself completely. And then the Visionaries taught her their greatest secret of all, how to liberate the mind for change and transformation so that women can bring forth their powerful, revolutionary feminine vision into the world.

And after some time had passed, Majah traveled with the Manifestor Clan to the land of the Desert Fires to awaken the powers of the Manifestor that lay deep within her being. And she found herself in a vast desert scattered with crackling fires, some contained and some burning wild, and in the desert night they were bathed under the radiant light of the stars. And the Great Manifestor said, "We follow The Path of Action. We awaken the spirit of fire. Our empowerment comes through FOCUSING THE WILL."

And when Majah befriended the desert fires and the light from the sun and the stars, she awakened the flame of spirit in the core of her being. And following the wisdom of this flame she became skilled at inspiring, motivating, and leading. And from the wild fires Majah learned the power of destructive will, will used for selfish gain without concern for others.

And the Manifestors threw her into situations that demanded action, where her life and other's lives were in danger and she could not hesitate by thinking it through or wondering how this might affect everyone else's feelings. No! She had to act, swiftly, clearly, and cleanly. She had to mobilize resources in the flash of a second. And finally the Manifestors taught her their greatest secret of all, how to focus the will to manifest feminine values, feminine dreams, feminine knowledge, feminine leadership, feminine truths, feminine perspectives, and feminine solutions.

And now Majah's Initiation was complete. She had awakened the powers of each clan and learned to walk The Path of Strength, The Path of Compassion, The Path of Change, and The Path of Action. And when she returned from the training grounds of her Initiation, there was great rejoicing in the village of women. For all the women knew that now the clans could be united, now all women would have access to the ways of strength, compassion, change, and action. All knowledge could be shared and all women could become like Majah, a Magus, a Magician, and a Master of her destiny.

And so the ways of women transformed on that day and from that time forward women affirmed their own beauty and loved themselves deeply and served their community with their highest and most excellent gifts. And Majah lived long amongst the people - serving and loving and giving and receiving and celebrating each new woman child that blessed the village of women……………………….

Majah Part 5: Majah's Prayer

One day Majah called the sisters together and spoke these words of encouragement, and the women etched these words on their hearts and it became their manifesto whenever they gathered in circle…..

And this is what Majah said…
"Arise, proud bringer of feminine knowledge and wisdom.
Share your beauty with your sisters.
Do not fear that your wisdom will be shunned or dismissed,
We are eager to hear what you bring to us from the other land, the land of spirit.
Your opinion matters to us,
What you think and feel is essential to our survival and well-being.
Take your place around the women's circle,
Trust yourself completely.
Do not hold back if you sense there is untruth here or falsehood or deceit,
We need you to be strong and honest.
We need your insight, expertise, understanding, intelligence, perception, originality, good judgment, creativity, observation, astuteness, cleverness, ingenuity, talent, and skill.
Without your contribution our circle is less colorful, less diverse, less vibrant.
So I urge you sister to value what you bring to the women's circle,
However crazy, however outrageous, however unusual.
For what you bring completes our circle.
And we are proud to know you,
You bless our circle,
You, proud bringer of feminine knowledge and wisdom."

Chapter 3
The Four Clans

WISE WOMAN OVERVIEW

Archetype: **The Wise Woman**
Path: **The Path of Mastery**
Essence: **Powerful in Spirit**
Element: **Ether**
Tool: **Circle of Empowerment**
Symbol: **The Rainbow**
Qualities: **Spiritually centered, wise, fully awake, confident, self-responsible, integrates and aligns with your life purpose**
Affirmation: "**I choose responsibly, I am Master of my life.**"
Motto: **"I am a Wise Woman aligned in body, heart, mind, will, and spirit."**
Empowerment: **comes through choice**

The Village of Women

The first part of the Majah story tells us that women are initiated and empowered by other women - not by men. This is a crucial part of the story. In the village of women, the women are empowered by the women and the men are empowered by the men. This is important because so often women turn to men to find their empowerment, but it doesn't work. A woman needs women to initiate her into feminine empowerment.

One of the most striking aspects of the story is that each girl child is totally welcomed at birth. Isn't this an amazing concept? Each girl child is welcomed into the village and each girl child is appreciated for the gifts she will bring to the village.

Imagine what it would be like for you to be welcomed into your village of women. Imagine the whole village waiting for you, the next magnificent soul coming to bless the village. For most women, this never happens. They do not experience being celebrated by their community. Sometimes they are not even celebrated by their parents. This is a very sad situation for a child, when they don't feel welcomed by a village.

In western culture, we rarely experience being part of a village anymore, with extended families around us. Rather than being supported by a whole group of adults, parents feel a burden of responsibility to raise children by themselves. Usually the entire burden of initiating the girl child falls entirely into the hands of the mother. But what if that mother is not initiated? How can she then initiate her girl child? Isn't this where many of us find ourselves - with a mother who was not initiated?

This is why it's so crucial for you, as a woman, to be initiated into a circle with women elders present, because only initiated elders can hold a sacred space the way the elders do in the story. Only initiated elders can welcome you so wholeheartedly because they know exactly why your gifts are important to the village of women. They hold the bigger picture and the larger perspective. Rather than seeing you as competition, they already know you as a co-creative member of the village.

In the story, the initiated elders know how to listen to a woman before she is born. They know what her name is, what her purpose is, and to what clan she belongs. The elders in the story ask the name of the soul, what clan or tribe she belongs to, and what her particular purpose is. They affirm that every soul coming into the world has a destiny. Without a village of elders, it might take you a long time to figure out what your destiny is. Wouldn't it be amazing to have an elder carry the knowledge of your destiny until you are ready to receive it?

Put yourself in the story for a moment. Let's pretend that you (while in your mother's womb) tell the elders you are part of the Queen Clan, the water clan. Immediately they know that you are strong in heart and that your Queen gifts will benefit the whole village. Then, as you grew older, you would be trained by the Queens to balance your emotions and to be a diplomat for the village. If the elders knew you were coming to be part of the Warrioress Clan, the earth clan, they would know you were strong in body and gifted at grounding and holding effective boundaries. You would be trained to defend and protect the village.

If the elders knew you were part of the Visionary Clan, the air clan, you would be respected for your different views. You would be trained to open your third eye and utilize your gifts of dream and vision. You would learn to be clear-minded and sharp-witted. If you said you were part of the Manifestor Clan, the fire clan, your fiery will would be encouraged. The Manifestors would train you to be a leader in the village. You would be trained to manifest and be a way-shower.

When I tell the story of Majah, women get very excited about the beginning of the story because it introduces some powerful concepts that many women are looking for. Here are some common responses when I ask, "What strikes you about the first part of the Majah story?

- *What strikes me is that every person has value. Wow! What a concept. I never felt that.*
- *There's excitement for each new girl soul. There's an assumption in the village that every soul coming forward is great. I wish there had been excitement at my birth.*

- *There are so many different kinds of women: healers, dancers, tricksters, women strong in body, women sharp in mind. I feel like there is a place for me.*
- *We know there are four clans and everyone can find a place in their clan. The clans are equal and they don't know much about each other because they keep their secrets. I wish they were not secretive about their clans.*
- *It is a secret how they awaken their powers. So the Warrioress clan doesn't know how the Visionaries gain their powers. They have secret initiation rites for each clan.*
- *They know what each person does in the village but they don't know how to awaken the powers of each clan. It's a mystery.*

Just talking about a "village of women" is foreign to many women, for they have never felt safe in a circle of women. Some women were hurt by the women in their family, which makes it difficult to feel safe and supported in a circle of women. Some women feel their birth was neither wanted nor celebrated. Some women have never felt valued for their natural gifts and so don't even recognize they might be part of a "clan" with those particular gifts.

Each Girl Child is Celebrated

According to the ancient ways, when mothers are pregnant and full of life, the elders gather round and ask the unborn child, "Are you a male or female child? What is your name? And to what clan do you belong?" The elders need to know the destiny of each child so they can prepare accordingly. If a boy child comes to the village, the male elders take charge. And if a girl child comes into the village, the women elders take charge. There is always much rejoicing in the women's village because here is another great soul coming into the community to bring new power and new gifts to the clan of women."

What would it be like to have elders interested in you even before you were born? What would it feel like to be celebrated by the village of women? What would it be like to be recognized for the gifts you bring?

This part of the story is so powerful because the elders can actually receive a soul's name and purpose before the child is born. This often resonates deeply with women when they hear the story, but they don't know how or why. I believe it is because we do carry our purpose deep within us, but it often goes completely unrecognized and unacknowledged in our family of origin. Most of us know somewhere deep inside that we do carry the knowledge of our purpose and when we imagine ourselves in the story, it sparks a deep longing to be recognized.

It would have saved us years of therapy, pain, and frustration if our gifts had been seen and nurtured from the beginning of life. So the story helps us to re-imagine a life in which our higher purpose is known and held sacred by the initiated women of our village.

The Four Clans

In the first part of the Majah Story, we learn there are Four Clans in the women's village. The Four Clans are: the Warrioress Clan, the Queen Clan, the Visionary Clan and the Manifestor Clan. (As each clan is described, you will notice images that accompany each clan. These are the images from the Sacred Robes that correspond to that clan.)

We begin with the beautiful **Warrioress** (above) who walks the Path of Strength. The Path of Strength calls you to ground yourself in the here and now and create healthy boundaries. The Warrioress rules the Earth Clan.

Next we meet the beautiful water goddess the **Queen** (above). She walks the Path of Compassion. The Queen awakens your heart so you learn to give and receive love. The Queen rules the Water Clan.

The next Divine Feminine guide is the **Visionary** (above). She walks the Path of Change. The Visionary brings you clarity of mind and innovation for change. The Visionary is ruler of the Air Clan.

The next guide is the **Manifestor** (above**)**. She walks the Path of Action. She helps to align your will to manifest your dreams in the world. The Manifestor rules the Fire Clan.

And then there is the **Wise Woman**. Her name is Majah. Majah walks the Path of Mastery and she is the part of you that masters your own destiny. She unites all the clans together so you feel a sense of your own power and purpose. The Wise Woman knows that in any given situation you have the power of choice. This brings tremendous freedom, so you don't feel trapped in your old patterns of behavior.

If you find you feel disempowered, you may feel you have no choices and you may feel a victim of circumstance. Majah, your Wise Woman, can move you out of the victim stance so you can see available choices. With your Wise Woman you can choose a tool from one of the 4 paths: strength, compassion, change, or action, depending on what the situation requires. Majah brings all the clans and all the paths together. She stands right in the center of herself and asks, "What path am I going to choose in this situation? Do I need to bring some change right now? Do I need compassion? Do I need to ground myself and create healthy boundaries? Do I need to take action?"

It is important to notice how you're feeling towards each Divine Feminine guide. At different times in your life, you may be drawn to one of the guides and may even feel intimidated by one of them. For example, you may notice that you are drawn to the earth guide, the Warrioress. Others will be naturally drawn to the Visionary because that energy comes easily to them. Others may feel attracted to the fire guide, the Manifestor. Some women are drawn to the Queen, because they are naturally big-hearted and generous.

Astrology and the Clans

As you contemplate which clan you are attracted to, you can look to your astrology to see which of the guides corresponds to your astrological sun sign (based on your birth date). For instance, if you are a fire sun sign, you may be drawn to the Fire Clan and to the Manifestors. If your sun sign is in air, you may be naturally drawn to the Air Clan and the Visionaries. If your sun sign is in water, then you may very well be drawn to the watery Queen Clan. If you are an earth sign, you may feel an immediate affinity for the Warrioress and the Earth Clan.

- The Warrioress Clan corresponds to the Earth signs: **Taurus, Virgo, Capricorn**
- The Queen Clan corresponds to the Water signs: **Cancer, Scorpio, Pisces**
- The Visionary Clan corresponds to the Air signs: **Gemini, Libra, Aquarius**
- The Manifestor Clan corresponds to the Fire signs: **Aries, Leo, Sagittarius**

Some women find they are drawn to a clan other than their sun sign clan. This is often because a woman has her rising sign, her moon, and other planets in another elemental sign. This may cause her to feel drawn to a clan that is not her "sun sign" clan. For example, I have both my sun and moon signs in air, so I am naturally drawn to the Visionaries and the Air Clan. I also have several planets in fire, so I have an affinity for the Manifestors and the Fire Clan as well. I know another woman who has an earthy sun and yet has many planets in water, so she relates to the Warrioresses and also to the watery Queens.

Getting to know your personal astrology chart is very helpful because you can see clearly which clan gifts you already possess. Your Astrology chart will show how many planets you have in Earth, in Air, in Water, and in Fire. Knowing what elements are strong in your birth chart helps you see where your natural connections and gifts already exist. So if you have a lot of water and earth planets, you will most likely be a strong Warrioress, sturdy and reliable, and deeply feeling like a Queen. If you have a lot of fire and air, you may be more creative and dramatic (fire) and able to communicate well (air).

Whatever natural gifts you bring to the village of women, you can affirm them and explore how they are useful to you and your village. You can also see which clans you may feel less comfortable with, if you don't have many planets in a certain element. For example, you may discover you have no water represented in your astrological birth chart. Lacking water, you can seek initiation with the watery Queen Clan to access your emotions and increase your self-compassion. You may have few planets in earth and therefore feel uncomfortable in your body or sometimes ungrounded. You can then work with the Warrioress guide to help ground you more and stay present in the here and now.

The most important aspects to look at in your birth chart are your rising sign, your moon sign and your sun sign. These three aspects form the core of your personality and point you to the clans for which you already have a natural affinity. Playing with your personal astrology helps you to identify which clans you are strong in and which clans you can strengthen through the initiation process.

The Functions of the Clans

Let's review each clan so we get a good idea of their differences and what function each plays in the village of women.

The Warrioress Clan

What do we know about the Warrioress Clan? What path do they walk and how do they contribute to the village of women? Here are some responses from my students:

- *The Warrioress walks the Path of Strength. She's the Earth Clan woman.*
- *She has healthy boundaries.*
- *The Warrioress provides strength and protection.*
- *She's fearless and courageous.*
- *The Warrioress is skillful in communication.*
- *She's grounded. She connects you with your animal nature.*
- *She's a healer and medicine woman.*

These are many of the great qualities of the Warrioress. She walks the Path of Strength. She is embodied - strong in body and strongly in her body. She's fully present. She's physically alive and connected to nature and she can access the gifts that come from the plants and animals. Because she is connected strongly to physical reality, she has no fear when it comes to surviving in the wilderness and being in the natural world of stones, earth, plants, and animals.

She communicates with the physical world and does not separate herself from it. The Warrioress feels at home in her body and deeply connected to nature. Many women feel disconnected from their bodies and from the earth, which makes it hard to be fully present. When a woman is not fully present she cannot be very effective in the world. The Warrioress helps a woman connect strongly with her sacred body and sacred earth.

Here is an observation about the Warrioress clan from one of my students: *"I observe when I'm in nature, that plants and animals live at their natural vibration. They naturally vibrate at their highest level of functioning and they give off a real vitality. We humans don't really vibrate at our highest state! So I noticed in last few weeks being in the high mountains and being with all the creatures and plants and land, that it recalibrates me. It reminds me that the Warrioress helps me to be grounded and embodied."*

The Warrioress also helps us to create strong and healthy boundaries to protect what we love. With the help of the Warrioress, we learn to protect ourselves and learn to draw appropriate boundaries around ourselves. This helps us feel grounded and contained. Then we learn to face our fears and become the strong, courageous, fearless Warrioress who is rock solid.

You can always trust a Warrioress to be unflappable, grounded, and present during a crisis. She really is the salt of the earth! Do you know any women like this - women who you feel instantly safe around? You know when you are around a

Warrioress because she is strong in many ways, and not just physically strong. She is composed and levelheaded. She is great in an emergency. A Warrioress is fearless and bold and not intimidated by fear.

The Queen Clan

What do we know about the Queen clan? What path do they walk and how do they contribute to the village of women? Here are some responses from my students:

- *The Queen walks the Path of Compassion. She's part of the water clan.*
- *The Queens are emotionally honest.*
- *A Queen is diplomatic. The Queen is always called in when there are arguments or disputes.*
- *A Queen exercises right speech, conscious speech.*
- *A Queen is empathetic and compassionate.*
- *The Queen nurtures and feeds the village. She nourishes the people.*
- *Her chalice is full. She is abundant and gives to others out of abundance.*

These are all great qualities of the Queen. She walks the Path of Compassion. The Queen helps us express the full range of emotions we possess. The Queen helps us to be diplomatic and skillful with our words because words carry such emotional power. The Queen helps us to open our heart, even when it's been caged or closed or shut down.

Over the years of being hurt, let down, and betrayed, we often build a large cage around the heart. If our hearts have been broken and have gone through very painful losses, separations, and disappointments, we are in need of much healing. Once we've dismantled the cage around our hearts, then our hearts can open fully.

The Queen, in her full glory, is full of love. If we love ourselves first, we can then be emotionally honest and can be balanced with our emotions. On the other hand, when we give our love away to others first, we walk down the shadow path of the Queen and begin to feel depleted. The true Queen fills up her inner cup first, full of love until it is overflowing. Then she can easily give to others without depleting herself. When caught in the shadow side, we lose a sense of ourselves and give our emotional power away to others.

Another important aspect of the Queen initiation is becoming aware of the negative emotional entanglements we have with others. When we are negatively connected, the relationship is not life giving to us or to the other person. By dissolving any negative connections we have with others, we gain back our own emotional power.

We can become empowered as a Queen by being in a place of abundant giving. To do this we need to be strong and centered in our true heart and true self. In order to be emotionally strong and centered, we need to love ourselves profoundly. This is the absolute key and linchpin of the Queen initiation - loving ourselves so profoundly that we banish all self-loathing from our heart. When we love ourselves profoundly, no negativity can live in our heart – no negative voices and no negative feelings.

The Visionary Clan

What do we know about the qualities of the Visionary Clan? What path do they walk and how do they contribute to the village of women? Here are some responses from my students:

- *The Visionary walks the Path of Change. She's the Air Clan woman.*
- *Visionaries are very different because they always envision change. They think creatively.*
- *A Visionary uses the power of her mind to find creative solutions.*
- *The Visionary doesn't get caught up in feelings, because when you have to conjure energy for change, you can't worry about everyone's feelings.*
- *The Visionary knows when it's time to let go, if something's no longer working.*
- *They are called into the village when things need to change! They come in when energy is stuck and they cut through illusion or old beliefs.*
- *They have clarity of mind.*

These are great qualities of the Visionary. She walks the Path of Change. The Visionary represents the Air Clan so she utilizes the powers of the mind. A Visionary needs to be clear-minded and cannot afford to feel everyone's feelings. She can't get bogged down by feelings and hesitate when change is demanded. There's no time to vacillate and falter when change is necessary, because a whole village could be in danger if a Visionary doesn't act swiftly and decisively.

In order to embody the skills of the Visionary, we clear out our inner chaos and confusion and become very, very crystal clear with our intentions. The Visionary uses the power of the mind to cut through the smokescreens of confusion. She takes her Sacred Sword and cuts through any distractions that stop her from being clear-minded and clear-sighted. She's also the master of change. She knows how to master the element of air to gather the mighty winds of change.

It takes a mighty wind to change people's attitudes. It takes a stupendous effort, so the Visionary calls in the tornado and hurricane force winds to change collective beliefs. When a community needs to change their attitude or shift their paradigm, the Visionary mobilizes her wind power. She is a shape-shifter and attitude-changer.

The Visionary pays attention to her visions and dreams and the knowledge that comes to her from beyond the sky and stars. This is why the Visionary clan ushers in the new paradigms. As we all know, we are in a great era of change. Many old belief systems are crumbling, institutions are falling, and old patterns are transforming. So as we all embody our Visionary, we participate in the emotional, mental, and spiritual changes needed to breathe new life into the village and shift into the new paradigm.

The Manifestor Clan

What do we know about the Manifestor? What path do they walk and how do they contribute to the village of women? Here are some student responses:

- *The Manifestor walks the Path of Action. She is in the Fire Clan.*
- *She executes the change or executes whatever needs to be done in the village.*
- *The Manifestors are the leaders. They show healthy leadership. They lead the way.*
- *The Manifestor mobilizes resources and gets things done.*
- *She's the light bringer, the torchbearer.*
- *She magnetizes what's needed for the village through her magic and her magnetic will.*
- *She has a powerful and focused will. Her will is fire and her fire is her will to do, to act, and to manifest.*

These are great qualities of the Manifestor. She walks the Path of Action and makes her desires real in the world. She knows how to manifest and her manifestation depends upon her initiation into the other clans. When she is grounded and present with the Warrioress, openhearted with the Queen, and clear-minded with the Visionary, then she can easily manifest what she desires.

The Manifestor is powerful in will. This can be truly magnificent when the will is used properly and disastrous when the will is used inappropriately. We all know someone who is powerful in will, but uses that will to crush others or push them willfully aside. When a Manifestor is disconnected from her heart, it can be catastrophic because then she controls and manipulates people without empathy. This is a true misuse of will. An untamed, fiery will that is unleashed into the world as a wildfire and can burn down the village!

The Manifestor helps us align first with our own will and second, with our highest will for all concerned. In this way the Manifestor helps us come into right relationship with our higher, spiritual will. When we are able to manifest the will that considers everyone's highest good, then we have the capacity to lead others, empower others, and enlighten others.

When the Manifestor has tamed and harnessed her will, she can become a light unto the village; she can light the way. A Manifestor gets things accomplished by mobilizing resources and delegating responsibilities so that a big project can come to life.

We spend a good deal of time in the Manifestor initiation learning how to align with our own will. If we are living under anyone else's will, we must do the work of getting out from under that person's will, control, and power. As Manifestors, we must feel firmly connected to our own, sovereign will. Once we align with our own will, then we learn to focus our fire, radiate our fire, and command our fire to manifest what needs to be done. As Manifestors, we learn the path of Right Action.

Majah's Magical Name

Let's take a look now at the significance of Majah's name. How does it reflect who she really is? How does it reflect the Wise Woman Archetype?

Before Majah is born, the village elders gather to hear what the new soul has to say. Usually the unborn soul tells the elders what her name is and what clan she belongs to and what her purpose is. On this special day, what happens? The new girl soul indeed tells the elders her name and her purpose. She tells them her name is Majah and then she says, *"I belong to all the clans. My destiny is to unite the women and empower all women in self-mastery."*

Here are two stunning pieces of information: Majah's name has a special meaning and is also a name surrounded by a powerful, ancient prophecy. The name itself comes from the root word "maj" which means TO BE ABLE and "maj" gives birth to Magus, Magi, Magic and Mastery. So Majah's name implies her destiny, which is to be a woman of Mastery. She is destined to master her life, to live out her true purpose with focus and self-knowledge.

Another important part of her destiny is to become a woman of Magic. What does this mean? It means Majah will resonate with her own magical feminine power. A woman's own magical feminine power is her ability to create her own life, create her own destiny, and be the author of her own life. It doesn't mean casting spells to get what she wants. A woman of Magic is a Magus, a Master. A woman of Magic is able to command her life, claim her power, and create the life she chooses for herself, her family, and her loved ones. A woman of Mastery cares for the good of all humanity.

What does it mean to be the Magus? The Magus is in control of her thoughts (Visionary) and feelings (Queen). The Magus is in control of her physical body and her sacred boundaries (Warrioress). The Magus is in control of her will (Manifestor). The Magus is in control of her circumstances with the power of choice (Wise Woman). In other words, the Magician/Magus is a fully initiated, integrated woman.

This is a far cry from the old view of a Female Magician. In the last few thousand years, a powerful woman with intuitive, feminine knowing was labeled as a witch, a dark magician, and spell-caster. But we know that a woman who is in command of her body and boundaries, her thoughts, feelings, actions, will, and circumstances, is a woman of power.

Majah also means, "to be able". What does it mean to be able or to "be"? Being is the opposite of doing. If you look at the image of Majah on her Sacred Robe, she is radiating BEING. She is relaxed. She is supremely herself. She is resonating a deep quality of being that is connected to her divine origin. She is who she is, not what she does. So the Wise Woman can just be. She is able to show up and BE HERSELF. Doesn't that sound so relieving to just show up in the world and be you, rather than being what everyone else wants?

Here's another secret about Majah's magical name - "maj" is also related to the root words "mag" and "magda". So Majah is related to the name Magdalene and Magdalene is of the same spiritual lineage as Majah. This makes perfect sense because the Wise Woman archetype is related to the High Priestess, the Initiated One. In ancient times, the title *Magdalene* was given to a High Priestess, an Initiated Wise Woman. So Mary the Magdalene is related spiritually to Majah the Wise Woman. They are spiritual sisters because they have been fully initiated. So Majah comes to the village of women to bring full initiation to all women. She is the Wise Woman, the Initiated High Priestess within each of us. She is the Magdalene in all of us.

Majah's birth: Overcoming Fear

In the village of Women, there was an ancient prophecy that one day a soul would be born who would unite the clans and her name would be "Majah". People held fear around the coming of this soul because she would be able to master the powers of all the clans. She would learn the Mysteries of each clan and she would break open the secrets.

So why was there fear if she was to be a liberator, setting the women free? Why did they fear a powerful Liberator and Savior? What was so scary about Majah's potential feminine power? Perhaps we are similar to the women in the story, fearing our full power. Sit with this a moment and see what arises within you. Are you aware of any fear or hesitation about coming into your own full power? Do you feel any fear around being fully liberated?

Embodying the Wise Woman, the master within us, requires a full initiation training so that we can banish all fear from our body, all hatred from our heart, all doubt from our mind, and all selfishness from our will. Embodying the Wise Woman means mastering the body, heart, mind, will, and spirit. Even though this sounds amazingly positive, we may hold some fear around this radical liberation because we are not used to it.

In the story, the women in the village have fear when they hear Majah is coming, until the laughter vibrates through the village and cuts through the fear. This laughter comes from the oldest and wisest of the elders because she is ready for the coming of Majah. She is ready for the time when all women will awaken the powers of the clans and share this great knowledge.

That time for us is now. We can embody the Wise Woman and learn the secrets of all the clans. It is our time to be fully initiated. It is time to step onto our Path of Power and BE the Divine Feminine powerful beings that we are.

How to birth the Majah

How are you to birth the Majah within yourself? To understand how, let's talk a bit about Majah's mother because she is the one in the story who is strong enough to birth Majah. Majah's mother knew that the TIME had come. How did she know this? Why did she know that things were going to change? She knew this because she was a Visionary. She could see the future. She could envision the change that needed to come. This is a very important part of the story because it speaks to your own readiness to birth your inner Wise Woman. Majah's Mother, the Visionary, was internally ready to conceive, gestate, and birth Majah.

Majah's mother represents the Good Mother in you who can contain the birth of your true self. She is ready and able to nurture, incubate, and hold your full power. In the story, everyone in the village made fun of Majah's mother because she was always going on about how things needed to change. She envisioned the time when a woman would be able to awaken her full powers, the powers gained in all the clans.

What happens when you envision something or when you have a dream or a vision for what needs to change? Do people laugh at you? Are you afraid they might? In a way, Majah's mother was an outcast in the village. People didn't take her seriously. They rolled their eyes and put up with her like she was one of those "weirdo new age" people.

So here's the lesson - if you have an idea or a vision that could improve your life or the lives of others, don't be discouraged by the "nay-sayers". Keep moving ahead with your vision and be like Majah's mother. Your vision may be exactly what's needed to unite the village. Do not give up on yourself. It means you are ready to birth your Wise Woman, the Majah within yourself.

The Female Mysteries

Majah came to the women's village to unite the women and to open the gates of the Female Mysteries. What are the Female Mysteries? The Female Mysteries are teachings that help women open to their feminine way of knowing and being in the world. These teachings lead women down a path of knowledge, to awaken their full feminine powers - physical, emotional, intellectual, spiritual, and divine.

For us as women today, we can embark on this path of self-discovery by awakening the Wise Woman archetype within our deep selves. The Wise Woman is the part of us that can unite and integrate our physical, emotional, mental, spiritual, and divine awareness. In times past, this archetype had different names. The most common name was the High Priestess. This name is often intimidating or off-putting because it conjures up fear or negative energy. I chose to use the name "Wise Woman" because it feels more modern and has fewer religious labels attached to it.

This is important for a few reasons. First, many women have been deeply wounded by religious institutions that have refused to recognize their spiritual authority. In ancient times, a woman would have been readily accepted into the initiation path and would have been trained into her particular "clan" according to her gifts and talents. Her spiritual authority would never be questioned - of course a woman has powerful physical, emotional, intellectual, and spiritual authority! When the Female Mysteries were the norm, a woman's power was welcomed and not questioned. A woman's power was valued and held in high esteem. Imagine living freely in that time.

What occurs in initiation training is that a woman begins to live in a time frame where she remembers this reality. By that I mean she learns to live outside of normal, linear time. She shifts into spiritual time where she can fully remember being seen for her spiritual authority. This paradigm shift happens through the initiation process, so that our modern paradigm - where women's power and authority is undervalued and unseen - dissolves.

What comes forward in a woman's consciousness is another dimension of reality, the spiritual dimension, in which her spiritual authority and spiritual gifts are supremely valued. So let's shift into that time right now and continue our discussion of the Female Mysteries.

Feminine initiations are designed to awaken our female essence and to awaken our Wise Woman or High Priestess deep within our being. When these archetypes are mirrored and activated, we blossom and come to know, feel, and experience our true divine essence.

A New Female Paradigm

Majah is the Wise Woman whose name means Magus, Master, and To Be Able. We could say that Majah is able to be herself and able to BE. Interesting that this is not about doing, but being. In many spiritual traditions, the goal of enlightenment is to radiate Being and move out of chronic Doing. Majah, the Wise Woman, helps us to **be** who we really are, not **do** who we really are.

We have already discussed the fact that in other times, the Wise Woman archetype was called the High Priestess and was imbued with spiritual authority and divine sovereignty. In other times and places, the Wise Woman would also have been known as the Female Christ, the Female Anointed One. To our modern ears it sounds strange to put female and Christ together in one phrase. We rarely speak of a feminine Christ figure because for a long time, Christ consciousness has been thought of as exclusively "male".

A "male-only Christ" would sound ridiculous to our ancient ears. Of course a woman can reach this level of spiritual awakening and awareness. In ancient Crete for example, a woman who had reached this level of awakening, enlightenment, or initiation would become the High Priestess. She would of course be seen as a female "Christ" figure or enlightened spiritual teacher.

Our modern, collective understanding around the Christ energy has been connected with a male figure. So whenever I present this idea to women, they inevitably look dumbstruck. "Female Christ energy, what's that?" Well, Majah, the Wise Woman embodies Feminine Christ Consciousness and represents the level of spiritual development that truly liberates us to be and live our soul's purpose. The High Priestess or Female Christ energy embodies a woman's highest spiritual authority. It is similar to the Divine Feminine awareness that is flooding our world.

We are witnessing a time of great shifts. One of these shifts is a coming of age for the Wise Woman, High Priestess, Divine Feminine, and Female Christ Consciousness. We are ushering in a new paradigm, where women embody and hold their own Female Christ awareness. We do this by being fully initiated so that we can hold this level of spiritual awareness with dignity, strength, power, emotional balance, and inner integrity.

The old paradigm tells us as women that it is not possible to liberate ourselves totally. The old (Western) paradigm holds up a male Christ figure as our role model. Our new, empowered feminine paradigm says that it is perfectly possible to embody the gifts and powers of all the clans and to become the master of our own body, heart, mind, will, and spirit.

The outdated female paradigm is based on *linear time, limited truth, and a one-dimensional worldview.* In the old paradigm based on *linear time,* we are used to hearing things such as, "Only men have spiritual authority. This is the way we have always conceived of self-mastery." We know this is not true because in other times and places a woman's spiritual authority was honored in equal measure to a man's spiritual authority. A woman's power was valued equally. A woman was seen as masterful when she had completed her feminine initiation.

The old paradigm is based on *limited truths* such as, "Only men can assume spiritual authority or spiritual wisdom". We know this is not true because men and women are created equal, with equal access to inner development and equally qualified to attain great spiritual wisdom.

The old paradigm is based on a *one-dimensional worldview* such as, "Women are limited by the dominant cultural views". We know this is not true because a woman is multi-dimensional and is not bound by how the dominant culture defines her. A woman lives simultaneously in the physical, emotional, spiritual, and divine worlds. She is free, unlimited and not bound by cultural beliefs. Initiation opens a woman up to a vast, multi-dimensional worldview so she can experience her versatility and know her vast inner territory.

In the story, the elders ask Majah to let them know who she is while still in her mother's womb. The elders trust that the soul coming into incarnation knows her purpose, knows who she is and knows what she is coming to do and accomplish. Majah tells them she belongs to all the clans, and that her destiny is to unite the women and empower all women in self-mastery. Think about Majah as the Wise Woman inside you. She is an indwelling feminine guide within you who has the power to unite all the gifts and qualities you possess, and to empower you in self-mastery.

The Wise Woman is familiar with your deepest self. She awakens your timeless self, your multi-dimensional self. You know Her and she knows You. She's known you since the beginning of time. The Majah in you knows your past, present, and future. She helps you move out of linear, limited time and moves you into timelessness, eternal time. She is the bigger, higher self within you.

The Wise Woman as your spiritual self knows what to do. Remember, the Wise Woman activates your power of choice. When the Wise Woman within you sits in the center of your being and makes a conscious choice in the moment to do the right thing and to choose the best solution for the situation, you become a master of the circumstance.

Think about that - being the master in every circumstance. This brings the power back within you, rather than giving your power over to others or over to the situation because you feel powerless. The Wise Woman knows without a doubt that in every single situation you have choice. This locates all the power within you and not "out there" with others.

Majah, the Wise Woman, gives you the patience and the presence to carry through with your choice and your truth every step of the way. She helps you climb up every rung of the ladder of initiation. She helps you do the work. She brings the spiritual presence of self-mastery. The Wise Woman is your multi-dimensional self, in touch with so much more than just the physical plane of existence. She helps you gracefully navigate the physical, emotional, mental, and spiritual worlds so that you can be in all the worlds at the same time.

We do this naturally, it's just we don't think about it this way very often. Women multi-task all the time: we do our mundane chores to keep the family moving forward, while at the same time negotiate with our children, solve complex emotional problems, and take decisive action. We are aware of everyone's feelings, and at the same time give tough love, make healthy boundaries, say no, and say yes! Women do it all, all of the time. So we are multi-dimensional beings naturally and the Wise Woman helps us make our multi-dimensionality more accessible and more integrated.

The Clan Tools and Gifts

When Majah is born, the Clans honor her with sacred gifts. Let's look at why each gift is significant and what it means to each clan.

"And soon after the celebrations, Majah was born and the Clan Leaders honored her by bringing her gifts. The Warrioresses gave Majah a sacred shield, a shield to banish fear and empower the self with boundaries, protection, and worthy defense. And the Queen Clan brought Majah a sacred crystal heart, a crystal heart to speak truth with compassion, master emotions, and free the heart from pain and sorrow. And the Visionaries gave Majah a sacred sword, a sword to cut though confusion, clear away self-doubt, and obtain clarity of mind. And the Manifestor Clan gifted Majah with a sacred wand, a wand with a fiery tip to focus the will, accomplish the task, and light the way for others. And so it was that Majah grew in body, heart, mind, and spirit, surrounded by her sacred shield, crystal heart, sword, and wand, surrounded by the love of the people and nurtured in the old ways. And as the years passed, the Elders watched and waited.........."

So the Warrioress Clan gives Majah a Sacred Shield. The Queen Clan gives Majah a Sacred Crystal Heart. The Visionary Clan gives Majah a Sacred Sword. The Manifestor Clan gives Majah a Sacred Wand.

The Sacred Shield - The Magic Tool from the Warrioress Clan

The Warrioress Clan honors Majah with a Sacred Shield. We know the Warrioress Clan walks the Path of Strength, so the tool has something to do with honoring your inner strength. Think for a moment about a shield. What's the first thing that comes to mind? Why is the Shield the sacred gift of the Warrioresses?

Perhaps you thought of a shield for protection, keeping safe, holding off, defending or staving off. Certainly the Sacred Shield of the Warrioress Clan is designed to create healthy boundaries. A shield does indeed protect what is near and dear to you.

If you had a Sacred Shield, what might you want to support and protect? You may want to support and preserve your truth and what you believe in. You may want to secure your core values. You can also use the Sacred Shield to banish your fear. The shield can help you face fear and empower you with healthy boundaries.

So imagine when you're feeling fear, you can utilize your Shield of protection. Imagine holding your Shield and utilizing your Shield in your everyday life. How might it assist you as you move through your day? The Shield helps the Warrioress remain strong and brave. It makes sense that the Shield is the sacred tool on the Path of Strength.

The Crystal Heart - The Magic Tool from the Queen Clan

The Queen Clan gives Majah a Sacred Crystal Heart. The Queen Clan walks the Path of Compassion, so the tool has something to do with honoring your heart and giving yourself compassion. Think for a moment about this Sacred Heart. What's the first thing that comes to mind?

Perhaps you thought of courage and openheartedness. Maybe you thought of compassion. I love the image of a Crystal Heart because it reminds me of a strong, robust heart and at the same time, a soft, transparent, open heart.

As a Queen you need to give love and compassion to yourself first - to all areas of your life. As a Queen you learn to love your body, your emotions, your mind, and your strong will. As a Queen you love every single cell in your body, every part of yourself, every perceived flaw – everything! When your Queen's Crystal Heart is full of love, then you can also be abundantly loving and compassionate towards others.

The Crystal Heart of the Queen Clan helps you speak your heart's truth with diplomacy and right speech. It helps you to master your emotions. So when you get triggered with rage, frustration, or hurt, you can master your emotions and speak your truth with love and compassion.

The Crystal Heart also frees your heart from pain and sorrow. It cleanses your heart from the hurts of past wounds. If you carry pain, betrayal, and wounding in your heart it can become closed and hardened. The Crystal Heart helps you cleanse any hurt and melt any glaciers of grief so that the waters of your heart can flow once again.

Imagine holding your Crystal Heart and utilizing it in your everyday life. How might it assist you as you move through your day?

The Sacred Sword - The Magic Tool from the Visionary Clan

The Visionaries honor Majah with a Sacred Sword. The Visionary Clan walks the Path of Change, so the tool has something to do with honoring your inner vision and your ability to create positive change. Think for a moment about a sword. What's the first thing that comes to mind?

Perhaps you thought of cutting, swishing, and moving. The Sacred Sword is utilized to cut through confusion, to clear away self-doubt, and to move energy for change. As a Visionary you need to be clear minded, straight forward, and full of vision. You can't be a Visionary with your head full of confusion, self-doubt, and clutter! The Sword cuts through bewilderment, clears away self-doubt, and helps you obtain clarity of mind.

The Sword also helps you to master the Winds of Change. The Sword can move energy necessary for a change in beliefs, a change of attitude, or a change of behavior. You may become stuck in old beliefs and attitudes. You may become stuck in addictive, repetitive patterns. The Sacred Sword is designed to swish and stir the Winds of Change and to liberate you by moving the energy necessary to break through any blocks or any negative thought patterns.

Imagine holding your Sword and utilizing it in your everyday life. How might it assist you as you move through your day?

The Sacred Wand - The Magic Tool from the Manifestor Clan

The Manifestor Clan honors Majah with a Sacred Wand. The Manifestor Clan walks the Path of Action, so the tool has something to do with honoring your will and taking decisive action in your life. Think for a moment about a wand. What's the first thing that comes to mind?

Perhaps you thought of spell casting or manifesting what you want to happen. The Sacred Wand of the Manifestor Clan is used to focus your will. The Wand is not only designed to manifest what you want for yourself, but helps you to accomplish the tasks at hand. The Wand also lights the way for others who may be in darkness. It is a tool of leadership. It illuminates the way forward. It is a tool to help the entire village.

The Manifestors walk the Path of Action so the Wand is a tool for conscious action. This means you must learn to tame your will and focus it through the tip of your wand and then learn to hit your target perfectly with your conscious will. Then you can act consciously and manifest whatever is needed for the project to be completed. There is great responsibility when you utilize the Sacred Wand.

Imagine holding your Wand and utilizing it in your everyday life. How might it assist you as you move through your day?

Majah's Magic Toolbox

With the clan gifts of the Shield, Heart, Sword, and Wand, Majah grows in body, heart, mind, and will. These are the sacred tools in Majah's magic toolbox. She is reminded each day that:

- Her body is sacred and she possesses a Shield of fortification to support her sacred boundaries.
- Her heart is sacred and she possesses a Crystal Heart to cleanse and balance her emotions.
- Her mind is sacred and she possesses a Sword of Clarity.
- Her will is sacred and she possesses a Wand to direct her will towards conscious action.

You also possess this magic toolbox. Receiving these gifts is your birthright. You're created with a beautiful body, a heart, a mind, and a will. It's your human design. The gift of your sacred body connects you to the Earth Clan of the Warrioresses. The gift of your sacred emotions connects you to the Water Clan of the Queens. The gift of your sacred mind connects you to the Air Clan of the Visionaries. And the gift of your sacred will connects you to the Fire Clan of the Manifestors. As you integrate these gifts and develop your body, heart, mind, and will, you can utilize the gifts in your toolbox and pull out the right tool for any given situation.

Majah is held by the elders and by the community in a holistic way so that she can fully develop and be fully initiated by these feminine guides. The four sacred tools are designed to initiate her into all four clans and they are all necessary to become a true, enlightened, full human being.

Imagine what it would be like for you, to come into life and be gifted with these four sacred treasures. What would it be like for you to be surrounded by elders who held the knowledge of all the clans, telling you that you deserve to have the gifts and the initiations at each of these levels so that you can be fully empowered to do what your soul came to do?

Think about your own family and community of origin. Maybe you came from an intellectual family that encouraged the mind but really didn't encourage you to feel your emotions. In this case, you may know how to use the Air Clan Sword but not the Water Clan Heart.

Maybe you came from a family that valued the strength of the physical body but didn't help you develop your will. In this case, you may know how to use the Earth Clan Shield but not the Fire Clan Wand. Or perhaps you came from a family that valued feelings but neglected the body. Maybe your family encouraged the development of your will but not your intellect.

Depending on the nature of your particular family and cultural education, you will probably find it easier or more comfortable to use certain sacred tools. Think about what tool or gift of the four clans is easier for you to use. If you came from an airy, mind, intellectual family, perhaps you feel more comfortable with the Sacred Sword. If you came from a watery, emotional family you may find it easier to use the Crystal Heart. Maybe your family was fiery and entrepreneurial and you like to use your Sacred Wand. Or maybe you came from earthy, practical stock and find it easy to use the Sacred Shield of the Warrioress Clan.

We all come into this life born on a particular day, which determines our astrological sun sign. Your sun sign corresponds to the elements of earth, water, air, or fire and the tools of Shield, Heart, Sword, or Wand. So you will naturally be drawn to the clan and tool that reflects your particular element. So fire signs will naturally have some of the fire qualities of the Manifestors and will enjoy using the Wand; air people will naturally be drawn to the Visionary and the Sword. Earth signs will already possess some of the Warrioress qualities and enjoy using the Shield and water signs will naturally be drawn to the Queen Clan and the Heart tool.

This is helpful because it gives you a clue about your soul's purpose, what you came to do. As a fire sign, did your soul come to light the way for others and use the Wand for enlightened leadership? As a water sign, did you come to be a diplomat in the village and use the Heart for emotional balance? As an air sign, did your soul come to envision new ways and use the Sword to change attitudes and beliefs? As an earth sign, did your soul come to protect and defend the good in the village with your Shield? Your particular astrological sun sign holds a clue to the gifts you bring to the whole community. In the Majah story, Majah is given access to all the clans and all the gifts. We live in a time when all the empowered ways of being are needed.

Another thing to consider is that you may sometimes overvalue one of the clans and undervalue another one. For instance, you may overvalue the Queen, your powerful emotions, but undervalue the Warrioress, who creates healthy boundaries. When this happens you may find your life out of balance. You may have a big Queen Heart but give too much of your love away to others because you lack the boundaries and Shield of the Warrioress Clan.

Or perhaps you overvalue the creativity and change of the Visionary but undervalue manifesting your ideas with the help of the Manifestor. You may end up spinning your wheels and not manifesting your ideas. You can see why it is so important to be able to integrate all the paths and tools together. For you need healthy boundaries (Warrioress Shield) and self-compassion (Queen Heart) to be able to envision change (Visionary Sword) and then put it into action (Manifestor Wand).

Many women feel discouraged in our culture because we value certain tools and clans and undervalue others. In our modern age, we tend to overvalue the Air Clan and our intellectual education and undervalue emotional intelligence, the territory of the Water Clan. We tend to overvalue the Fire Clan, manifesting and getting what we want, and undervalue the Earth Clan, making appropriate boundaries. So how do we change our culture to allow all the clans to be equally valued? We do like Majah does and learn to utilize all the sacred tools and learn to awaken the powers of each clan.

So right now, as you think of these tools - the Shield, the Heart, the Sword, and the Wand - what are you most attracted to? What tool feels unfamiliar? What tool do you need right now?

It's helpful to understand your own relationship with the tools and to ask Majah, your inner Wise Woman, to help you integrate your entire toolbox. Your inner Wise Woman is the master of all your tools. She knows how to utilize each one in each particular circumstance. She will help you choose the right tool for the right situation. Majah is very handy in that way. She is master of your inner toolbox.

The Circle of Empowerment

Let's turn now to Majah's Sacred Tool, called the Circle of Empowerment. We know that Majah walks the Path of Mastery, the path of integration. She brings all of the clans together and unites all the powers; strong body, open heart, clear mind, focused will, and awakened spirit. Her element is ether or spirit. As she walks the path of mastery and integration she also gathers all the sacred symbols: the Shield, the Heart, the Sword, and the Wand. The Wise Woman has her own sacred tool called the Circle of Empowerment.

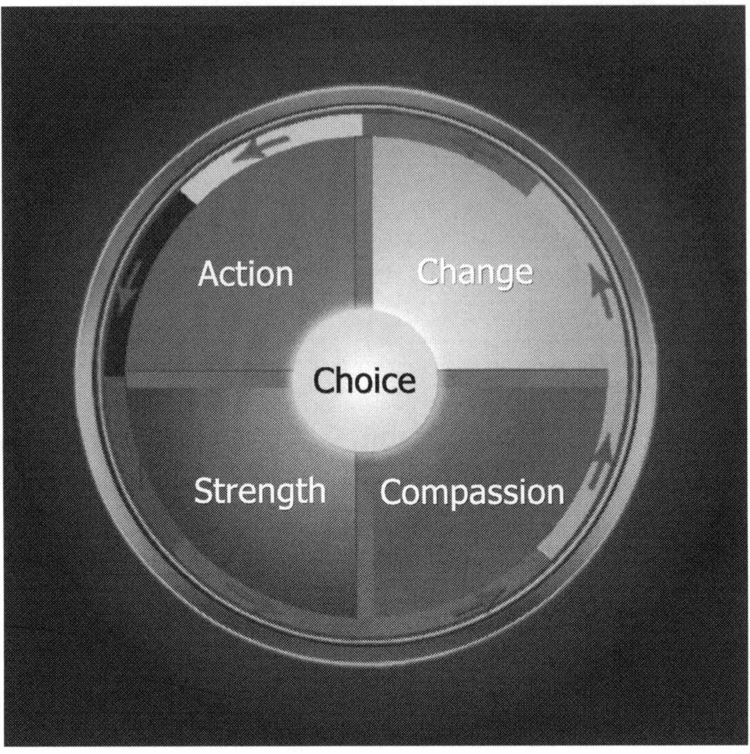

The Circle of Empowerment is an integrative tool that is a circle divided into the four quadrants of Strength, Compassion, Change, and Action. In the very center is a circle called CHOICE. As the Wise Woman, you can stand in the center, in the center of yourself, and choose which path you want to take.

As you stand in your own Circle of Empowerment, you can ask yourself these questions: Do I need the Path of Strength in this moment to stand my ground? Do I need my Warrioress Shield to employ healthy boundaries? Do I need a compassionate response from the Path of Compassion? Do I need my Queen Heart to offer diplomacy and right speech? Do I need to clear my mind and make some changes here, utilizing the Path of Change? Do I need my Visionary Sword to cut through some chaos? Do I need the Path of Action in this situation? Do I need my Manifestor Wand to focus my will on the task at hand?

No matter the situation, the Wise Woman sees your power of choice in every circumstance. She stands in the center and chooses responsibly. You may find yourself in a situation where you feel trapped or frozen. You may not know what to do because you are being triggered. In these situations you may believe you have no options because you are caught in your habituated responses that don't work very well.

Your Wise Woman sees CHOICE. She knows there is always a creative solution and that in every moment you can choose what path to take. Part of her gift is perspective. She takes the biggest picture of the scenario into account. When you can see you have an option and a choice, this empowers you to find a creative solution in the moment.

You can utilize this amazing tool whenever you are faced with a choice in your life. You can call up Majah, stand in the center of your Circle of Empowerment, and feel where you are internally. You can ask yourself, do I feel frozen, intimidated, confused? Do I feel fearful or trapped? Get a sense of where you are and what you need to make a positive decision.

You may need some self-love in the moment, so you step onto the Path of Compassion, the domain of your Queen. There you can call up your Queen to deliver some self-compassion. If you feel confused, step onto the Path of Change and call up your Visionary to give you clarity of mind. If you are fearful, step onto the Path of Strength and call in your Warrioress to hold your Sacred Shield to banish your fear. If you feel powerless to make a decision, step onto the Path of Action and call your Manifestor to help you connect with your will to take decisive action.

When you step into the center of the Circle of Empowerment, you can breathe deeply and connect with your Wise Woman and connect with your power of choice. Stand for as long as you need in the center and look around at the 4 great choices you have. You can choose strength, compassion, change, or action. You can connect with the elements of earth, water, air, or fire. You can call in your Warrioress, Queen, Visionary, or Manifestor. You can affirm your wise body, heart, mind, and will. And you can call upon your higher spiritual self.

You have so many wonderful choices when you remember to *stand in the center of yourself.* You can even create a magic Circle of Empowerment in your sacred space where you live and actually stand in the center of your circle. You can make it with scarves or a small rope to create a circle on the floor. When you stand in the center, you will actually feel your power of choice and the liberation your inner Wise Woman brings to your life.

Some affirmations for the Wise Woman are:

- I am committed to align my body, heart, mind, will, and spirit.
- I am masterful and confident.
- I align with my higher self.
- I follow my calling and step into my destiny.
- I have choice in every situation.

The Wise Woman Sacred Robe

Let's take some time and look at the Sacred Robe of Majah, the Wise Woman. When you look at her image what comes up for you? Here are some responses from women in my trainings:

- *When I look at the Majah robe she says to me, "I'm ready and I am always ready."*
- *Majah lives between the worlds, she lives between veils, she's multidimensional and she brings all multidimensional understanding into the present, now and ready.*
- *Majah is saying, "Come to me, I'll show you how to make peace."*
- *For me she is the I Am, she is connected with the I Am, connected to God or Spirit.*
- *To me Majah is supremely serene!*
- *For me she brings a deep feeling of inner knowing.*
- *Majah is sitting on her throne and taking her royal place. She seems to be in command of herself and her destiny.*
- *I like that her chakras are open. I can see her hand chakras open and relaxed. I think she can heal me with her hands and her spiritual power.*
- *For me too Majah has great spiritual power. Her rainbow headdress is radiating out such amazing light and power. She is enlightened!*

Majah, your inner Wise Woman, also has a powerful rainbow light that she is radiating out in all directions. When you are fully centered in your deep core self, when you have aligned your body, heart, mind, and will, you bring a spiritual presence to every situation. You vibrate out into the world your inner light, your inner song, and your inner beauty.

What I love about Majah is her radiant beauty. I'm not talking about standard forms of beauty or even external beauty. I'm talking about her inner beauty that shines into the outer world. I think you know the kind of radiant beauty I'm talking about. If you've ever been in the presence of a spiritual teacher or a Wise Woman, you know what I mean.

Majah walks the Path of Mastery and Magic and this comes through in the Sacred Robe. She is exuding self-mastery and a magical quality that is mysterious and wondrous. When you look directly into her eyes, she can give you a direct transmission of the mystery of your mastery and she can connect you with your spirit or higher self. You have an inner Magic that is unique to you. When you are willing to express it, you bring your own brand of magic into the world.

You can use the image of the Sacred Robe to contact your inner Wise Woman. Meditate in front of her. Allow her image to melt inside you. Become her. Sit with your hands out and imagine radiating out a rainbow headdress. Breathe and relax and feel your magic radiating out from your head and your body. Imagine a purple flame enveloping your entire body. Feel the magical properties of the purple flame. Allow her image to inform you about your own mastery and about your own brand of magic.

Chapter 4
The Shadowlands

The Shadowlands and the Shadow Clans

When Majah is ready, the elders take her to the Shadowlands to see what happens to women who wander off their Path of Power. It's important for her initiation that she sees with her eyes wide open the devastating effects of negative choices. When a woman continues to disempower herself through negative choices, she ends up losing her power, giving it away, or misusing it. This has devastating effects on her self-esteem, her truth, her heart, her mind, and her sense of purpose. She ends up in the mythological "Shadowland".

What is the Shadowland? The Shadowland is a place where there is no joy and no laughter. It is a place where women are neither dead nor alive. It's a strange "in between" world where women aren't really living, but they're not really dead. The Shadowland is a place where women go who have wandered off their Path of Power. They have lost their way. They are disconnected from source. All the joy has gone out of life.

The Shadowland is also a place where there aren't many living creatures. There is not much light at all. In other words, there are not many sources of enlightenment. There is not much consciousness. There are no elders showing us the way to be initiated. There are no sisters helping us out of our misery.

Imagine what it is like to be caught in the Shadowland. Perhaps you have experienced this "place". Maybe you have experienced times in your life when you were in despair or fear. Have you ever felt stuck or emotionally paralyzed? Have you been confused or fallen back into addictive and destructive patterns? Maybe you know exactly what it feels like to wander off your Path of Power. Many of us have experienced the Shadowland and we know how horrible it is. When we fall onto a disempowered path and lose our way, we can feel deep misery and loneliness. We can feel deep sadness and grief.

Let's review the different Shadowlands and discuss what each disempowered path looks and feels like.

The Shadowland of fear is the shadow of the Warrioress Clan. When a woman is on the path of fear, she feels small and contracted, paralyzed with anxiety. She lacks the Sacred Shield of the Warrioress to protect her and give her strength.

The Shadowland of self-sacrifice is the shadow of the Queen Clan. When a woman is on the path of self-sacrifice, she gives away all her compassion and love energy to others and has no juicy heart left for herself. She becomes bitter and hard-hearted. She lacks the Crystal Heart of the Queen to give her access to self-love.

The Shadowland of chaos is the shadow of the Visionary Clan. When a woman is on the path of chaos, she is confused and unclear. She runs in circles of addiction or distraction, never changing. She lacks the Sacred Sword of Clarity to cut through the illusions and confusions of her mind.

The Shadowland of manipulation is the shadow of the Manifestor Clan. When a woman is on the path of manipulation, she controls others and the world around her for selfish gain. She has a hole inside her that she tries to fill by grasping and manipulating. She lacks the Sacred Wand of the Manifestors to align her will and illuminate her path.

It's interesting to notice which Shadowland you relate to or which Shadowland you have experienced. For example, I recently worked with a woman who was outwardly successful but she was driven by fear. So she looked as if she was a strong Warrioress and successful Manifestor, but the fuel that drove her core self was fear - fear of not being good enough.

Fear is the shadow quality of the Warrioress Clan, whereas strength is the positive quality of the Warrioress Clan. If you are caught in the shadow energy of a clan, it's hard to accomplish what you want and difficult to make the changes you desire. In the Shadowlands you live your life with less consciousness and less power.

So my fearful Warrioress sister had a hard time standing up for herself. She had lost the strength to do so. Even though she had successes in the world, she felt overwhelming anxiety and fear. This caused her to feel like a fraud and fake and she contracted and retreated even more into herself. She worked on calling her Warrioress and working with her Sacred Shield and this helped her get back onto her Path of Power.

What happens when you are caught in self-sacrifice, the shadow side of the Queen? It means your access to self-compassion is greatly diminished or cut off. You may be doing kind things for others, but when it is infused with the energy of self-sacrifice, it is laced with poison and may have strings attached. You are most likely not getting any of that love back for yourself. This causes your heart to shrivel or become hardened.

I worked with a woman caught in the Shadowland of self-sacrifice and she appeared to be the sweetest, most loving person in the world. However, inside she was enraged and deeply embittered. She ended up never getting the love she needed and this pushed her further into misery and grief. It was so hard for her to love herself first because of the many beliefs she held around self-love being *selfish*. We worked on calling in her powers of heart so she could open the floodgates of self-compassion.

What happens when you are caught in chaos, the Shadowland of the Visionary? When caught in chaos you cannot see clearly and cannot envision the changes necessary to move on. You may be caught in self-illusion or self-delusion. You may be completely numb to your real feelings. You may stir up chaos wherever you go and get so distracted that you get very little accomplished. This is the classic scene where you have lots of ideas, but never really do anything about it. When caught on the path of chaos you create elaborate smokescreens and become defensive when confronted with procrastination. You may end up spinning in circles and your life never changes.

When I worked with a woman caught in the Shadowland of chaos, it was hard to create a coherent treatment plan for her. She was late to her appointments and she distracted herself (and me) by the chaos in her life. She would forget to do her assignments and would over-commit herself and get sidetracked. In her life in general, she would gossip and turn friend against friend and then couldn't understand why her friends wouldn't return her calls or spend time with her. To help cut through her chaos, we worked on visualizing her Sword of Clarity and clearing her mind of all her chaotic, inner clutter.

What happens when you are caught in manipulation, the shadow of the Manifestor? You dominate and control others. Whatever you accomplish and manifest is most likely laced with toxic energy. For if you are aligning with your will-full-ness rather than your higher will, your fiery nature becomes like a wild-fire, burning out of control. This kind of willful pushing to manipulate and get what you want without regard for others creates a toxic wasteland all around you. People move away from you for they don't want to be controlled. They don't want to be caught in your web of manipulation.

One woman I worked with who was caught in the Shadowland of manipulation looked like a masterful Manifestor on the outside but she was terribly lonely and unfulfilled on the inside. She would cry and cry in my office because she was so unhappy. She never seemed to have the love she wanted and it was hard for her to see how she manipulated her relationships. She pushed her lovers away because she controlled them from a very unconscious, needy place. Together, we worked to align her will with her higher will first so she was no longer manipulating and controlling others. With her Manifestor Sacred Wand, she learned to control only her will and not her relationships.

Shadow Creatures: Victim, Martyr, Saboteur and Manipulator

In the Shadowlands there are terrible creatures of the darkness. These "creatures" represent the negative shadow archetypes of each Path of Power. In the story it says these negative archetypes "feast off a woman's negative energy". What does that really mean? When a woman is caught in the shadow aspects of a clan and engages in fear, self-sacrifice, chaos, or manipulation, she gives her power away to the negative archetype. If you can imagine the negative archetype as a hungry creature who is nourished by a woman's fear or resentment or anger, you begin to get a picture of how the negative archetype works.

Have you ever noticed a woman who walks around with a dark cloud around her? You can bet that she is caught on one of the disempowered paths and has attracted one of the "negative creatures" - the creature of fear, the creature of self-sacrifice, the creature of chaos, or the creature of manipulation.

In the Shadowland of fear, when a woman indulges her fear and contracts her energy, over time she becomes invisible and loses her strength. Imagine the negative creature hovering around this woman, feeding off of her negative energy.

In the Shadowland of self-sacrifice, when a woman continually sacrifices herself for others, over time she spreads hate and an ugly distortion of love into the world. Again, imagine the negative creature of self-sacrifice who pushes her further into misery and sadness.

In the Shadowland of chaos, when a woman continues to engage in chaos and scatters her energy, over time she becomes less and less conscious, unable to envision what she wants. The hideous creature of chaos continues to distort her thinking and confuse her further.

In the Shadowland of manipulation, when a woman engages in manipulative behavior over and over, she loses her light and falls into darkness. The negative shadow creature of manipulation feeds off of her energy and continues to disconnect her from her own will.

The Shadowland creatures take us away from the initiation process, so instead of evolving and becoming more and more conscious, we lose energy and become extremely downtrodden. We lose hope and the light begins to fade from our eyes.

When we feel disconnected from source and disconnected from our Wise Woman community through abuse, trauma, or isolation, we can encounter the negative archetype of each path. I have seen many women stuck in a Shadowland because they do not have a woman's community to pull them out or keep them accountable to the ongoing initiation process. A good therapist, a good spiritual guide, and a good community can prevent a woman from wandering off her Path of Power and into the Shadowlands. One of the worst things a woman can do is isolate if she finds herself slipping onto a shadow path.

But this is often exactly what we do. When we engage in shadow behaviors we feel so ashamed and we retreat into ourselves. We stop asking for help. Our energy contracts and we play small. We insulate ourselves. We drink too much. We become addicted to substances and relationships. We have terrible personal boundaries. We let people take advantage of us. The Shadowlands dull our senses and our joy and our passions. We feel alone and isolated in the Shadowlands. This is why the Shadowlands are so toxic to our body and soul.

Let's look more closely now at each of the hideous creatures that lurk in the Shadowlands. When you can identify and recognize these creatures of shadow, you are less likely to fall prey to them. In the story, they are called creatures and so you can imagine them with a body and a character. This is actually a helpful way to think about them because these negative archetypes are real and are indeed powerful energies that really do zap your precious life energy. Let's take a look.

The Victim

If a woman is prone to fear and continues to indulge her fears over time, eventually she will encounter the Victim, the negative archetype of the Warrioress Clan. The Victim delights when she remains powerless and fearful. This negative archetype then grows stronger and more terrible.

A woman caught on this shadow path may feel in the grip of this negative energy and find it even harder to break away. She is plagued by inner voices that make her feel small and terrified. She is overwhelmed by anxiety – and this anxiety may not be connected to anything obvious, making it all the more scary. When the Victim is at work in her psyche, she feels victimized by every situation. Her "story" of being a victim colors all her interactions. She attracts people into her life that do indeed treat her like a victim. So the woman caught in the Shadowland of fear is in great danger, for she may be victimized in a very traumatic way.

The Martyr

If a woman walks down the path of self-sacrifice and chronically sacrifices her needs to care for everyone else, she will eventually encounter the Martyr, the negative archetype of the Queen. The Martyr delights when she continues to give her heart energy away to others without giving compassion to herself.

A woman caught on this shadow path may give her heart away without filling it back up with love and compassion. The shadow creature, the Martyr, then feeds off her negative energy. When the Martyr is at work in a woman's psyche, she feels emotionally depleted. She may become physically ill. Her heart hardens and shrinks. Maybe her heart breaks and shatters. So the woman caught in the Shadowland of self-sacrifice is in great danger, for her heart may close for good and she may be martyred in a very traumatic way.

The Saboteur

If a woman walks down the path of chaos and gets befuddled and confused about her core identity, she will eventually encounter the Saboteur, the negative archetype of the Visionary. The Saboteur feasts off her energy when she gets stuck and continually sabotages herself and fails to change her life.

A woman caught on this shadow path may hear inner voices that tell her she'll never make anything of her life and that she'll always fail. Each time she procrastinates or distracts herself from her true path, the Saboteur takes her precious life energy. The Saboteur delights in making sure a woman sabotages her plans with disruptions, distractions and mishaps. The woman caught in the Shadowland of chaos is in great danger, for she may very well sabotage her life in a traumatic way.

The Manipulator

If a woman walks down the path of manipulation and dominates and controls others to get what she wants, she will eventually meet the Manipulator, the negative archetype of the Manifestor Clan. The Manipulator delights when she continues to control and push everyone away.

A woman caught on this shadow path may remain forever isolated and lonely. Instead of having her own source of light and lighting the way for others, she remains in the dark and so does everyone around her. She may feel totally driven to work harder, consume more, and accomplish more, while disregarding what is happening to her inner life. She may feel that if she doesn't manipulate to get love or material things, her life will be completely bereft. So the woman feeding the Manipulator is in great danger, for she may very well cause lasting trauma to herself or others by snuffing out her own light of consciousness.

Unhealed Wounds from the Past

When these negative creatures grip us, we literally become paralyzed to make other choices. We feel we have no other choice than to continue the negative behavior, thought, feeling, or addiction. I have certainly been there. It was a horrible place to be, when I felt stuck and trapped. What really helped me to break free of the paralyzing grip was recognizing the reality of the shadow archetype and choosing to say, "NO! I'm not going to give energy to you anymore!"

Why do we get entangled with these archetypes in the first place? Why do we end up giving energy to them? There are many reasons and the most common one is because we get caught in unhealed wounds from the past. Here are some examples from my own practice as a therapist and spiritual guide.

I worked with a woman whose father was abusive to her when she was young. When she got into adult relationships she recreated this abuse by "attracting" men who did not respect her. She became more and more downtrodden and felt victimized by these men. Over time she aligned herself with the Victim energy and allowed this energy to overtake her. She had fallen off her Path of Power and was now on the path of fear. Her unhealed wound from childhood created an internal story that then played out over and over like a broken record.

Most of the time we don't consciously want to be aligned with this terrible negative energy. We align with these shadow energies mostly unconsciously because we have been wounded, abandoned, or betrayed and we don't see another way out. These are all legitimate reasons why we fall onto the disempowered path. When we are traumatized as children, as my client was with her father, we don't have the emotional resources to cope. When no one is around to help us resolve the wounding, early trauma can create a crack in the fabric of our tender psyche. Then the wounded part aligns with fear or self-sacrifice or chaos or manipulation.

When we are aligned with our pain body, we move towards behaviors that are destructive. We align with the negative archetype and it begins to feed off our life energy. We literally give our power away. Then we are propelled towards repeating these patterns until we have enough resources, self love, help, and support to move into a whole different pattern.

If a woman aligns with the shadow creature, like the "Demoness of Fear" or the "Demoness of Martyrdom", she often gets a kind of strange pay-off from it. She may feel aligned in a distorted way with the negative archetype and then move further and further into the Shadowland. Perhaps this is the only connection she feels. Perhaps she is so identified with her story as a victim or loner or manipulator, it gives her satisfaction. Some women align with the shadow creatures to take vengeance or enact retribution for a perceived wrongdoing or betrayal. Of course, this hurts the woman herself and not the other person. These are all reasons why it's so important for a woman on a shadow path to get hold of her willpower to choose something different.

There has been some interesting research done on addictive patterns and the releasing of chemicals in the neurological system that perpetuate our addictions to the negative behaviors. For instance, when a person feels fear, it releases certain chemicals that create feelings of shame and guilt, which then increases the fear. A person on the shadow path is used to these chemicals in her system and it feels familiar and safe. She can hide there and stay in shame.

This perpetuates a woman's journey in the Shadowland and paralyzes her. She becomes disconnected from the light and from her power of choice. So if she recognizes, sees, and perceives that she is addicted to fear or to being a victim, or addicted to being a martyr, then it gives her a chance to break the addictive cycle and move out of the Shadowland.

Many of us who are caught in the Shadowland want to get out and want to resolve the dilemma. We want to have resolution because we don't want to live this way. When someone betrays us and hurts us, we know that there's something innately wrong with the relationship. But we falsely believe that if we can just make this person understand, if we can just be more compassionate, if we can just be different, then our efforts will resolve the negative cycle. But it is not so. The problem is that we are choosing people to recreate our trauma and there we are, back on the wheel of addiction and trapped in the Shadowland.

The Shadow Paths: Fear, Self-Sacrifice, Chaos, Manipulation

The Shadow Path of Fear

The shadow path of the Warrioress Clan is the path of fear. What does a woman feel when she walks the path of fear?

When a woman walks the path of fear she ends up feeling denigrated. She fears other people having power over her and feels she has no strength to stand up for herself. She feels downtrodden. If she has no Sacred Shield to protect her basic rights, she may feel totally disempowered. When a woman feels weak, it can really eat at her soul. She may feel stuck or frozen and unable to care for herself in very basic ways. In the Majah story, the woman on the path of fear goes completely numb and begins to drink to numb herself down even more.

She begins to play the role of the Victim. When you feel like a victim, your body and soul contract, shrink, and become small. From this shrunken place, it is easier to blame others and stay focused on others instead of yourself. You feel as if life is happening to you and that circumstances are conspiring to put you down even more. All the power that was inside you is seen to reside in others. You have lost your power. "It's not my fault! I am the victim of my circumstances!"

When you are caught on the path of fear, you tend to project everything outside yourself. You contract and get smaller and smaller. The path of fear is the path of contraction. You move further and further away from your source, further and further away from your center. It's crippling.

What about the shadow creature - the Demoness of Fear? She wants you to get small and to continue blaming others because she wants to feed off your victimhood. She is insatiable and will try and keep you downtrodden as much as possible. "Victim" wants your life to be ruled by fear. Every shadow archetype has this kind of greedy energy.

As a therapist, I have experienced clients when they are in the grip of this energy. When they are feeling victimization, hopelessness, and despair, I can feel the tight grip of the negative energy/archetype.

Early in my therapy practice, I would often feel hopeless when a woman was telling me her heart-wrenching story. But I realized early on, that if I gave any energy to this negativity, I would lose my objectivity and healing capacities. Now I know, very clearly and powerfully, that these negative archetypes cannot have any power over me if I stay strongly in my Wise Woman and my center of power.

It is important to remember that the shadow archetype often attaches to your wounded inner child. Your adult self however, has more resources to break free of the horrible grip from the "Demoness".

For example, an adult woman feels victimized by her mother. She is caught on the path of fear and cannot stand up to her mother to make appropriate adult boundaries. In this case, her wounded inner child is running the show and she continues to blame her mom for all her problems. On the one hand, her inner child needs compassion and healing to move out of the wounded position. Her adult self and her Warrioress can help her in this process, but the inner child must be willing to stop feeding the shadow archetype.

In this example, the inner child fears being alone, being abandoned, and being hurt again by the mother. But the only way out of this negative grip is to begin helping the wounded child let go of blame and anger. It is a difficult road. Sometimes the wounded inner child gets gripped by the shadow archetype of Victim and befriends the Victim. This way she has company inside herself - miserable company - but at least she is not alone.

Another example of someone who is caught on the path of fear is the woman who has a hard time saying no and has a hard time protecting herself. If someone is treating her badly, she doesn't feel the power to say, "Stop, you can't talk to me like that!"

The antidote of course, is to receive the initiation into the Warrioress Clan. During the Warrioress initiation you learn to use the Shield to stand your ground and activate your inner Shield to protect yourself from hurt. With the Shield, you can use words or actions to stop the abuse coming your way.

The Shadow Path of Self-Sacrifice

The shadow path of the Queen Clan is the path of self-sacrifice. What does a woman feel when she walks the path of self-sacrifice?

A woman who walks the path of self-sacrifice is consistently giving her power away to others. The more she gives, the more drained she feels. It's as if her lifeblood is draining out to feed everyone else. A woman possessed by the Demoness of self-sacrifice can look exhausted and drawn. Her face can be etched with bitterness and resentment. Even though this woman starts out in life with a big heart, she ends up with a shriveled heart. Her heart has been broken or disappointed far too many times.

When a woman closes her heart but continues to give, she becomes entangled by the shadow archetype of the Martyr. The Martyr then stalks her on the disempowered path of self-sacrifice and tempts her to give and to give, never allowing her to be vulnerable. Thus she remains disappointed in love and doomed to despair at ever knowing true love.

A woman caught on this path is addicted to rescuing people and consistently chooses people who are needy. Of course she is hoping for love in return but it is very difficult to penetrate through her defense of "self-sufficiency". She has locked away her heart and it is unavailable, closed for business. She can't be vulnerable. A woman on the path of self-sacrifice hears cynical voices telling her she'll never get what she wants and no one will ever give her love.

Think of a time when you have given so much, you forgot to think or feel about yourself. Have you ever felt yourself sacrificing so much that you stopped considering your own needs? This compulsion to give away your love is a compulsion that comes from a very wounded part of the personality - probably from the wounded inner child.

When you get to this point, you don't know what else to do but to keep martyring yourself. You don't feel you have any other choice. "If I can just keep giving then maybe he/she will love me. If I just keep sacrificing, then someone will notice me and my needs."

Look how helpless you are when you don't acknowledge your own needs. You become depleted and exhausted. Your cup is empty. No one around you knows how to care for your needs because they don't consider your needs. Perhaps you have never allowed them to even see your needs. Do you see the trap?

A woman on this shadow path keeps addictively running this pattern because she doesn't want to be rejected. Her heart is so tender, so sensitive to hurt, so unprotected, and so beaten up. She has to defend her heart by becoming the Martyr. Underneath this, is an enormous craving and a desperate hunger to be loved in return.

The defense mechanism of the Martyr is to close the heart. "I can't let myself be vulnerable. I cannot be needy. I can't be like a child. I cannot be the wounded child because it makes me feel too small and vulnerable. If I can just get myself in the position of being the giver to everybody else, then I never have to be the needy child." Here is the classic co-dependent dilemma - being the giver/good mother but never the receiver/needy child.

How do you learn to be vulnerable if your heart is closed and bitter? What's the antidote to this path of self-sacrifice? You have to face the pain of the original wound and feel the feelings. But this is the shadow path of the Queen, the most emotional, feeling of all the clans - yikes! It's hard to feel all those feelings that make you feel small, vulnerable, weak, helpless, hopeless, and wounded.

The antidote to this dilemma is to receive the initiation into the Queen Clan. During the Queen initiation you learn to love your inner child and love your whole self profoundly. You gain access to great and powerful love. This dissolves the Martyr and brings you back to the Path of Compassion.

The Shadow Path of Chaos

The shadow path of the Visionary Clan is the path of chaos. What does a woman feel when she walks the path of chaos?

The woman who walks the path of chaos may look very familiar to you! She is a multi-multi-tasker. She shops, cooks, cleans, mends, talks, organizes, texts, leads, coaches, negotiates, decides, supports, cares, helps, visits, writes, repairs, completes, pays, emails, teaches, drives, and then she falls into bed at the end of the day.

She is almost a blur. She is moving so fast and doing so many things, there is a tornado of energy circling around her. Many of us in this culture are taught that this is normal. But this is very *abnormal*. It is the path of chaos and leaves us vulnerable to the shadow archetype of the Saboteur. The Saboteur stalks women who are busy, busy, busy, and tempts them to sabotage themselves through confusion and procrastination.

Women on the path of chaos also tend to hold on to old ways that don't work. They end up spinning their wheels and never changing because they don't allow themselves to move through the wheel of change, which takes a woman through birth, death, and then rebirth. When a woman gets stuck on that wheel and remains in a perpetual additive pattern of thoughts, feelings, or actions, she never experiences the renewal that comes when she lets something go and lets it die, so that new life can be reborn within.

A woman on the path of chaos is constantly distracted, scattering her energy in many directions. She makes excuses for why things aren't changing, rather than taking responsibility for her actions. She creates smokescreens to camouflage and conceal her inner chaos. A woman on the path of chaos is a master of self-deception. She can be a "scatter brain" - forgetting things, cancelling appointments, losing things, changing her mind, and not keeping her commitments. Her "big plans" never come to fruition. She stirs up chaos in her relationships, by either gossiping about others or betraying confidences. She hears cynical voices telling her she'll never step into her wisdom and power.

Women on the path of chaos often don't see there is a path at all. They are too busy being distracted to notice anything is wrong. However, they create amazing chaos all around them that other people do indeed notice. Sometimes this chaos can be internal - like when your mind goes spinning and spinning and you can't think straight. Other times the chaos is very external and there is disorder and disarray all around you.

When you are under the influence of this shadow archetype, the Saboteur, you become distracted and chaotic and lose your power. The Saboteur makes sure you don't go on your vision quest to find your vision. She makes sure you don't find your wisdom and power. Your third eye shuts down and you don't trust your intuition.

When you try and clear your mind and try to get out of your bad pattern, the Saboteur will confuse you and spin your mind around. You become befuddled and confused about your gifts. You start to procrastinate. You get distracted and scatter your energy. "I'm too busy. I have to get this done first. I have so many important things to do, etc. etc. etc."

The antidote is to receive the initiation into the Visionary Clan. During the Visionary initiation you learn to use the Sword, which cuts through the confusion and the illusion. It is the Sword of Clarity after all. When you wield the Sacred Sword of the Visionary, you can easily cut through the chaos and confusion. You are finally willing to see it and face it head on. No more smokescreens and no more self-deception.

Notice energetically how very different this is from the path of fear (the shadow of the Warrioress) and the path of self-sacrifice (the shadow of the Queen). The path of fear and the path of self-sacrifice constrict your energy. The path of chaos expands your energy to the extent that it becomes a mighty tornado or hurricane! Watch out! The energy moves all around in a chaotic wind pattern. When you feel this you need to grab your Sword of Clarity and focus your energy.

The Shadow Path of Manipulation

The shadow path of the Manifestor Clan is the path of manipulation. What does a woman feel when she walks the path of manipulation?

The woman who walks the path of manipulation walks through life with purpose and direction. She definitely looks successful and might be quite intimidating. She wants what she wants and she wants it now! Her desire body is strong. She is fiery. Her desire to get what she wants is like a powerful force field that pushes aside anything in her path. She manipulates people and situations as if she is a puppet master and other people are the puppets.

She is in the grip of the Shadow archetype called the Manipulator. This "Demoness" stalks women on the path of manipulation and tempts them to seek power and domination and control over others. Every time this woman disregards others, she feeds the shadow Demoness and moves further along the disempowered path of manipulation. What's the trap? She's trapped in the illusion that outward success gets her what she really wants. It does not!

We need to see past the outward success and look inside this woman. What we will find is a hole in her belly filled with a lack of self-confidence and insecurity. This woman secretly feels invisible and powerless and so she manipulates others to feel the buzz that comes with control. This temporary buzz fills the hole in her belly and makes her feel important.

The core of this problem is that the Fire Clan woman is supposed to use her fire for the good of the entire village, not just for her own self-gain. In modern psychological language, we say that her ego is getting in the way. Her ego is attaching to the outcome. Her ego is getting inflated and she is enjoying the control and domination over others.

Her fire is supposed to be used to enlighten herself and to lead others out of the dark and into the light. Her inner fire is her inner will. So a woman is supposed to use her will by being *willing to lead others*. But the woman caught by the Manipulator archetype is willful, pushing, and controlling with her will. Then her fire turns into a consuming fire that destroys everything in its path.

The woman on this disempowered path hears cynical voices inside her head such as, "It feels so good to get what you want. This food tastes better than love!" When she achieves success based on manipulation, she feels a temporary high of the success, but it's not connected to her core fire, which is her will to become enLIGHTened. Her continued attempt to achieve success is a defense against loneliness and isolation and does not bring the light of illumination.

Manipulators stay in the darkness and get trapped by their own willfulness. The path of getting what we want is so seductive. It tricks us into thinking we are on the right path! And we can become consumed by the fiery, intoxicating power of domination over others. For the Manipulator, the desire is there to be creative, to see what she can manifest, but the drive to create and manifest is generated from a hole in her belly. It's coming from the ego, which "wants what it wants now!" The hole wants to be filled up.

The most effective way to work with this fiery, creative, willful energy is to be grounded with good boundaries (Warrioress), heart-centered (Queen), and clear-minded (Visionary). Then this intoxicating manifesting power is far less seductive.

The woman on the path of manipulation fears that she is invisible and powerless. That's what is motivating her on this negative path. So if you've been wounded and your will has been crushed, then this is going to be a tempting shadow path to take. Every woman is here to create something of her life, to manifest something, however big or small. So you need to be able to tame your fire and not get caught on the path of manipulation, caught by your insatiable need to be seen.

The antidote to balancing and taming your will is found when you receive initiation into the Manifestor Clan. During the Manifestor initiation, you learn the art of Wandcraft – how to control your will and align your will with your higher purpose. With your Wand, you also learn to focus your will to manifest what is good for you and the whole the village.

The Place of Liberation

After Majah triumphs over all the Demonesses and destroys all the shadow archetypes, the elders take Majah to the Place of Liberation. They are so proud of her ability to vanquish the negative energies. Majah has liberated herself from the grip of all four negative paths.

In the Shadowlands, Majah saw with her eyes wide open what happens to women when they wander off their Path of Power. She witnessed how women get trapped in the negative ways of fear, self-sacrifice, chaos, and manipulation. The elders were pleased with her progress, but her initiation was not over yet. The elders had another initiation for her to experience. But first they want her to let go of all the ways she has disempowered herself.

In the Place of Liberation, the elders ask Majah a series of important questions: Will you commit your life to transforming these four disempowered paths? Will you surrender all the ways that you have disempowered yourself? Will you release and let go of the negative energy that has flowed through your body and soul, robbing you of power?

Like Majah, it's very important that you answer these questions as well. Are you willing to transform these disempowered paths? Are you willing to surrender all the ways you have disempowered yourself over the years? Are you willing to let go of all of the toxic energy that you have engaged with over the years? During initiation you are asked powerful, direct questions that you need to answer truthfully in order to move to the next level of your initiation.

After Majah answers that she is willing to let go and surrender, the elders bring her to the Place of Liberation and she is buried in the earth for 3 days and 3 nights. She is asked to lie down in a personal grave and remain covered in the earth until she has released all the toxins and all the poisons and all the ways she has allowed herself to be disempowered.

This is a crucial part of her initiation. She comes into intimate contact with the earth and must trust the earth to hold and receive and absorb all the toxins she has taken into her body and soul over the years. She surrenders her fears. She surrenders all the ways she has been disappointed in love. She surrenders the chaos and confusion that keep her from seeing the clear truth. She surrenders any ways that she manipulates and controls.

In other words, she surrenders her body, her heart, her mind, and her will to the initiation process, to be cleansed and purified. It's not that she is surrendering to the elders or to anyone in particular. She is surrendering *to the process* and *to herself*. She must trust that the initiation process will cleanse her of toxins and purify her energy field, both inside and out. The result of this surrender is the recovery of her sacred body, her sacred heart, her sacred mind, and her sacred will. Now she is liberated to be her full, true self.

Following Majah's example, when you decide to detox yourself, to surrender all the ways you have fed these Demonesses - eaten toxic emotional food, exchanged toxic energy, and engaged in toxic behaviors towards self and others - you are in for a wonderful surprise. It might be an intense detox for sure, but you will definitely experience liberation.

Consider now all the ways you have walked the path of fear. How have you remained a victim? What fears bind you? How have you kept yourself unshielded? How do you stay small? How can you liberate yourself?

Consider all the ways you have walked the path of self-sacrifice. How have you sacrificed yourself? Is your heart closed with bitterness or pain or disappointment? How would you like to release your wounded heart? How can you liberate yourself?

Consider all the ways you have walked the path of chaos. How much chaos have you engaged in? How do you sabotage yourself? How do you procrastinate? How do you avoid change and growth? How can you liberate yourself?

Consider all the ways you have walked the path of manipulation. How have you manipulated and controlled? Where are you pushing too much in your life? Where do you dominate others? How can you liberate yourself?

Imagine now what it feels like to let go of all your fears. Imagine letting go of all the ways you have been disappointed in love. Imagine surrendering your chaos and confusion about yourself and your purpose. Imagine letting go of all the ways you have controlled and manipulated. Imagine lifting up your body, heart, mind and will for total detoxification. Imagine recovering your sacred body, sacred heart, sacred mind, and sacred will. Imagine reclaiming your birthright.

And when you are finished surrendering and releasing, experience the true liberation that detox brings. When Majah is finished, the elders dance and drum and celebrate. You can do the same.

Chapter 5
Awakening the Powers of the Clans

In the final part of the story, Majah learns to awaken and master the gifts of each clan. To do this, she must learn the secrets of each clan and empower herself with the essential power each clan possesses.

Majah journeys to the four initiation training grounds in order to awaken the powers of each clan. In her role to unite and integrate all the paths, she must experience the different initiations, master each path, and awaken the powers of each clan.

Majah is initiated by being thrown into the classroom of life. She must experience each initiation firsthand. She does this by traveling to the training grounds and experiencing the different terrains and exercises that awaken each clan power. She becomes masterful by going through the death and rebirth process that each initiation demands.

Who holds her through the initiations? Who holds space for her when she is thrown into the process? It is the elders who hold the sacred space so that she can go through her initiations without getting hurt. This is how it should be for us. We need trustworthy elders holding space around us as well.

It says in the story that Majah goes to the training grounds to awaken the powers that are *already deep within her being*. What does this mean for you and me? It means that we, as women, already have the clan powers innately embedded within our being, but they need to be awakened and unlocked through the initiation process. Initiation calls our inherent powers forth. Let's look now at what powers are called forth in each of the training grounds.

Awakening the Powers of the Warrioress

When Majah travels to the Warrioress training ground, she finds herself in a wilderness place full of rocks, mountains, plants, trees, and animals. It's the wild country with granite mountains and forests. It's a place where the earth smells rich and ripe with life. We know also from the story that the Warrioresses walk the Path of Strength and their empowerment comes from creating strong boundaries.

In the Warrioress training ground, Majah is thrown into the wilderness without food or water, without clothing, tools, or comforts of any kind. She learns to fashion tools and find food and her body becomes strong, instinctive, and alive. So the beginning of her Warrioress initiation involves being alone and learning to fend for herself. She must survive in the wilderness with no food, shelter, or help of any kind.

Have you ever had your basic comforts taken away? It is challenging at first because you are used to having your physical and emotional needs met and met fairly quickly. This makes you feel safe and protected. When you are thrust into the "wilderness" – whatever that is for you – you suddenly feel naked and unprotected. Maybe you feel unsafe and very uncomfortable. So when you are thrust into your own wilderness place, it toughens you up. The wilderness wakes up your instincts and your senses and eventually you start to *feel alive*. Your physical senses awaken and you see, hear, and smell things in a new way. A Warrioress is strong because she has awakened her instinctive body and her physical senses are vitally sharp and alive.

Next in her Warrioress initiation, Majah is forced to let go of the cravings of her body, which helps her to listen to the earth, to the animals and plants. When you let go of your physical and emotional comforts and the cravings of the body for food, drink, and whatever other substances you are addicted to (sugar, alcohol, chocolate?), you can begin to connect with nature in a more profound way. Like Majah in the wilderness, you can tune into the earth and hear earth's heartbeat. You can observe and listen deeply to the animals and learn from their unique gifts. You can appreciate the beauty and vitality of the plant world and make a strong alliance with the trees and flowers and plants.

Why does a Warrioress need to be so in tune with the natural world? A Warrioress walks the Path of Strength so she draws her strength from nature and all creation. Connecting with nature grounds her and brings her firmly into the present moment. It gives her a profound anchor so she can respond to life with a grounded presence. Have you noticed how soothing, calming, and centering it is to be in nature? Connecting with the wilderness and allowing your instinctive body to attune with nature, you can be solid like a tree, aware like a panther, strong like a horse, and present like a mountain. There are many gifts from nature that a Warrioress taps into in order to be an effective guardian of the village.

As a Warrioress, Majah must learn to rely on her own inner resources and trust herself completely. She becomes self-reliant and able to survive physically. Her body becomes strong and she manages to quell and control the cravings of her body. This means she is no longer enslaved to the body but a master of her physical longings, desires, and passions.

In the Warrioress initiation, Majah must also face her worst fears so that she can conquer her fears. Conquering fear is one of the most important exercises of the Warrioress initiation. When you feel fear, you contract and shrink away from whatever is in front of you. A Warrioress is trained to not shrink away from a challenge but to stand her ground in the face of adversity. A Warrioress learns to face her fears with bravery and strength. Bravery doesn't mean we don't *feel* fear, it means we keep going ahead *despite* the fear we may feel. A Warrioress trains to stand, hold, be present with, and face her worst fears.

All of these initiation exercises out in the wilderness bring out Majah's own innate strength and prepare her to awaken the greatest power of all. The greatest power of the Warrioress Clan is the power to activate the Sacred Boundary that surrounds the soul. This Sacred Boundary protects the inner self from violations and frees the soul to live in its birthright of potency and strength.

What does that really mean? The Warrioresses know that each soul has the right to be fiercely safeguarded. This safeguarding occurs for a girl in the ancient village when the elders activate the Sacred Boundary around her soul. This is an invisible and potent circle of energetic protection that surrounds each human being. It is not designed to keep people out, rather to give a woman a sense of her own sacred space. Then she can choose when she wants to interact, share her energy, and exchange herself freely with others on her own terms. The Sacred Boundary allows her to have her own independent thoughts and feelings and her own sovereign physical, emotional, and spiritual space to be herself.

This Sacred Boundary may not have been activated for you as a girl growing up. Did the elders in your family activate your Sacred Boundary? Did they recognize you had one? Did they respect your sovereign rights?

Indeed we know that in our culture, many girls have their boundaries violated - physically, sexually, emotionally, and spiritually. We need the Warrioresses' secret weapon - the knowledge of how to activate this Sacred Boundary around the soul to counter all the boundary violations we have experienced. We learn exactly how to do this in the Warrioress Initiation.

If, when you were young, your elders did not help you activate the Sacred Boundary around your soul, you may very well have been violated. You may have lost the power to say NO if someone came too close for your comfort. You may have allowed people to invade you emotionally because you didn't know how to shut the door, stand your ground, say no, or consider your own feelings. If your elders did help you activate your Sacred Boundary, then you felt your own power to say no (or yes if you wanted to). You felt OK about having your own thoughts and feelings, separate and independent from the rest of your family.

During initiation, the elders are there to teach you how to recognize where your Sacred Boundary actually is and to recognize when people get too close either physically or emotionally. Then you learn to hold your own boundary by educating others as to where it is. You learn phrases such as, "That is close enough, no closer please." "Do not speak to me that way, I will listen when you speak to me with respect." "No." "Stop." "That is not how I feel, this is how I feel." Knowing and holding your own boundary gives you a wonderful sense of strength and self-confidence. As a woman, you have a right to determine your own personal boundaries.

Imagine now that you came into this life with a birthright to be free to live in your potency and strength. This is your core self. This is the golden nugget and central core of the Warrioress initiation: to activate the Sacred Boundary and to free your soul to live in its strength. When your personal boundaries are intact and you know exactly how to support them, you then feel safe, protected, secure, and shielded from harm.

Awakening the Powers of the Queen

On her next adventure, Majah journeys to the Queen's initiation training ground, which is located near the sacred waters - water being the Queen's element of power. So Majah travels with the Queens to the place of the sacred waters, where the streams and rivers flow into the lakes and the waters pour into the sea. We also know from the story that the Queens walk the Path of Compassion and their empowerment comes through emotional honesty.

In the Queen training ground, Majah learns from the sacred waters all about the human heart. She learns how the emotional waters flow too little or flow too fast or don't flow at all because the heart's been frozen with grief and neglect. When your emotional waters flow too little it means you are emotionally constricted or cut off from your true feelings. This can happen when you experience trauma, hurt, or neglect in your relationships. One way of coping is to cut off from or dissociate from intense feelings because they are too overwhelming. Of course, this shuts down your heart and then you are unavailable for love and healthy relationship.

Sometimes your waters flow too fast and you find yourself acting out intense emotions on the people around you. You might erupt with anger or rage. You might blurt out sarcasm or cynicism, which pushes people away. You may end up crying at inappropriate times, making it hard to articulate what you want or need. Acting out your emotions without containment releases the emotions without resolution or understanding. When your waters run too fast, you need some inner containment and restraint on acting them out all the time so that you can offer yourself compassion and understanding and eventual resolution.

Sometimes your waters don't flow at all because they are frozen through grief and neglect. This is when a deep-seated grief takes over and freezes your emotions. You may feel nothing, you may feel numb, or you may feel empty. You may feel disoriented or alienated from others and from yourself. When you don't know how to process grief, you can get stuck for years in this frozen state. When your waters stop flowing altogether, your heart can hide away and even disappear. During the Queen initiation you learn how to thaw the places within you that are trapped in the frozen wasteland of grief and recover some of your tender heart.

In the next part of the Queen initiation training, Majah learns all the ways women keep their hearts caged and small and hidden. This part of your initiation involves a deep exploration of all the ways your heart responds to the sorrows of life and relationships. Tallying up your betrayals, traumas, and ordeals is not about blaming others, but serves to help you come to terms with what has happened. Your heart is very tender and sensitive and when you get hurt, you often build a cage around your heart to keep out any further hurt. Sometimes you allow your heart to shrink, shrivel, and virtually disappear because you think if it can disappear then it won't get hurt again. Or you hide your heart in your work, in your caretaking of others, or in a thousand different ways. Acknowledging how your heart became caged, small, and hidden can be tremendously healing and validating.

Next in the Queen training, Majah learns a thousand and one techniques to release pain, grief, and sorrow. This is good news! For we need so many techniques to release the heart from its cage. This also brings tremendous hope that our hearts really can recover from trauma. We often hold onto grief, pain, and sorrow because we believe it keeps us connected to the ones we have lost. But staying connected in this way drags us down into an underworld place where we don't really resolve the loss. Or we hold onto pain because it keeps us tied to the rage or blame we still hold over that person. Unfortunately this only serves to wound our hearts even more profoundly and never releases us from the suffering. The Queen within us can release the hold these energies have over us so that our hearts can dance and sing and be free once again.

The Queens then throw Majah into situations that arouse her most intense emotions so that her heart can grow strong. Imagine this part of the initiation. What would arouse your most intense emotions? I remember doing a powerful ritual once where we were invited to concentrate on the thing we most dreaded - the thing that would cause us most grief or pain. Everyone had his or her own version of this. Mine was the loss of my partner and son. So I allowed myself to dwell on this for many hours, during which we had to continue a fairly grueling breathing technique. When the Shaman/Ritual Leader came to me to activate my inner sight, I actually experienced the loss of my partner and son – vividly and in full color. My emotions were very intense. I was in deep grief and it was overwhelming. I allowed myself to cry and wail and grieve. I must say, that when the grief was released from my body during the ritual, I had the most profound sense of love and connection to the universe. Afterwards I felt far more connected to my beloveds and my heart felt cleansed in a powerful way. This was truly a Queen-like initiation and my heart opened and grew strong!

In the next part of the Queen initiation training, Majah must step into other people's shoes until she can feel what they feel and understand their perspective. Now, I have to say that women are usually fairly good at this already. Nevertheless, it is part of our Queen training to really feel what it is like to walk in another woman's shoes. As a therapist, I have heard the most heart-wrenching stories and I can deeply empathize with what that person feels. But what does it mean to really, really step into another person's shoes?

The Queen training invites you into a deep, intimate participation in the suffering of the world. When you can feel the suffering of your sisters, something profound happens, both to the one who is being witnessed *and to you*. For the one you empathize with, she feels a profound sense of being heard, mirrored, and validated. This is deeply healing. For you it breaks down any false illusions you have of being separate and different. It draws you closer to your sisters and washes away divisions and prejudices. As a Queen, you realize that we are all one. This is crucial to a Queen, whose heart is open to all beings.

Next in the Queen training, Majah practices compassion and forgiveness even for her enemies. It seems obvious that a compassion practice is fundamental to the Queen, but what about the forgiveness part, even for your enemies? Forgiveness is a tricky business, because you can't force yourself to forgive someone who has hurt and wronged you. You can offer yourself time to let go and release. However, often women hold onto their hurt and anger and don't want to forgive someone because they feel it lets the other person off the hook for the crime they committed.

An initiated Queen knows that holding onto the hurt only inflicts further wounds to her own heart. So an important part of the Queen initiation is your willingness to release your own heart from suffering because of your deep and abiding compassion for self. "I love myself so much that I am willing to release this hurt from my heart. I forgive myself for hanging onto this. I release the other person or persons and visualize them going on their own way."

In the next part of Majah's initiation with the Queens, she becomes skilled in the art of diplomacy, negotiation, and right speech. A Queen has a big, cleansed, open, supple, strong heart! She is the diplomat of the village and knows the power of words to either wound or heal. As a Queen, you learn to deliver good news, bad news, and difficult news with diplomacy and grace. When your emotions are triggered and you are angry or enraged, you find ways to communicate this with tact and clarity. A Queen can alchemically change the charge of intense emotions so they can become palatable and able to be metabolized by others. This is truly a gift and skill.

All these initiation experiences prepare Majah's heart to be full, strong, open, and generous. In order for your heart to be open like a Queen, it's important to allow yourself to feel any grief and sadness that has blocked the waters of your heart from flowing. This is not easy. It can feel very painful to go deep into the feelings of grief and loss, especially when it seems these feelings will never end. However, when you allow yourself to be emotionally honest you can cleanse your heart from grief and sorrow so that it can become open and supple once again.

When Majah opens her heart and is sufficiently prepared, the Queens teach her their greatest secret of all. This secret is the power to love the self with profound compassion. The Queen's magical compassion is so powerful it banishes all self-loathing and casts out all hatred so that the heart can do nothing but love.

Can you imagine living a life where you love yourself profoundly each day? Can you imagine banishing all self-loathing from your heart? Can you imagine casting out all hatred so that your heart can do nothing but love? This can be done through initiating your inner Queen.

For many of us, we are not taught nor are we shown how to love ourselves profoundly. We are taught to give love and compassion to others but we do not know how to give it to ourselves. Most of us have had experiences that shut down our heart so that we are cut off from essential self-love and self-compassion. This is a major problem! For if we cannot love ourselves profoundly, then we cannot unleash the power of our Queen.

Unleashing the power of your Queen means unleashing the power of love into your heart and into the world. This means having no blocks to loving and accepting all of yourself. This is a world where you and others are cherished and appreciated, valued and esteemed. This is a world where only encouraging words are heard. Go ahead and imagine that world and allow your Queen to live and shine.

Awakening the Powers of the Visionary

When Majah travels to the Visionary training ground, she finds herself in the high country, in the high mountains, where the winds blow cold and the trees grow tall and majestic. This makes sense because the Visionaries are masters of the element air. So they train their initiates in the high country where they can take advantage of the fresh air and the Winds of Change. We also know from the story that the Visionaries follow the Path of Change and their empowerment comes through clarity of mind.

Something interesting happens when Majah arrives at the Visionary training ground: she is immediately seized by the shape-shifter falcons, who fly down and hang her upside down in the trees. Majah is then forced to see everything from a brand new perspective. When she is hanging upside down, she becomes disoriented and her mind splits open and suddenly new possibilities appear. Suddenly, her inner Visionary is activated and she sees new ways of thinking and imagining.

In order to embody the Visionary, we must find ways to open our minds and open our perspectives. Most of the time, our minds think in very narrow and limited ways because of our cultural conditioning. We think the way we are taught to think. Our minds often don't explore outside the parameters given by our family, our culture, our education, and our upbringing. For example, when I was a teenager, I was part of a youth group that believed Astrology was “wrong” and “bad”. It didn’t feel that way to me, but I didn’t dare say anything because I wanted to belong and not “rock the boat”. It took me several years after leaving that group to allow myself to think outside that box and explore Astrology. This stretched my mind, my values, and my perspectives and opened my mind to new ways of thinking.

The same thing happened when I left my formal education at Stanford University. My education was wonderful in many ways and I was aware it was focused on a rather scientific, medical model of the human body and psyche. In graduate school and beyond I studied mysticism, shamanism, and the sacred arts and broke through some of my own barriers of limited thinking. I began experiencing the realities of what some call the dream world, the unconscious, the astral plane, the etheric realms, and traveled into a whole new world of ideas and perceptions. I felt like Majah upside down in the trees. It was mind-boggling when a whole new perception of reality opened up to me.

During the Visionary training, Majah's perceptions are changed and broadened. She opens her mind to new ways of thinking, perceiving, and imagining. This is profoundly liberating. Imagine unleashing the powers of your own mind, to think in new ways - outside the boxes of your conditioning. Your mind is an incredible tool for higher consciousness, creative thinking, and intuition. These powers can be tapped into when you are willing to suspend judgment and open your mind.

The next phase in the Visionary training is when Majah is shown how to move energy for change by the fierce gusting winds. Moving the Winds of Change is needed when you, as an individual, need to change something in your life, like a habit or behavior. The *mighty* Winds of Change are needed when a collective way of life needs to change. You can feel the great Winds of Change now, as people are protesting all kinds of inequalities and injustices in the world. Next time you turn on the news, notice the Winds of Change sweeping through our culture and all over the globe.

When a woman gets stuck in a habit or a habitual pattern of thinking or feeling, energy gets locked up in the pattern. The Visionary knows how to move this energy and how to change the pattern. One way to do this is through your breath. The Visionary is a master of the element air, so using the breath to change a pattern is a powerful Visionary tool. You can focus on the pattern you want to change and begin breathing right into that pattern. You can imagine it as a ball of energy that you want to send out of your body. As you breathe deeply, you can move this stuck pattern out and free your energy. Then breathe some fresh, new air throughout your system and allow your energy to flow freely through your body.

In the next part of the Visionary training, Majah learns how to blow out the cobwebs of old beliefs. You know that feeling inside your mind when you have old beliefs gathering dust? Or when you find yourself saying things and doing things that sound like your mother, grandmother, or some ancient version of yourself? The Visionary within you clears out the cobwebby attic or basement where you store old beliefs that really don't work for you anymore. When you do a thorough housecleaning inside, you clear your mind of unwanted clutter so you can live with beliefs and principles that feel more authentic to who you are now.

Another crucial part of Majah's initiation with the Visionaries is when she learns to break the madness of negative thoughts. Many of us are plagued with the shadow side of the Visionary and get stuck in obsessive, negative thinking. We loop around a problem over and over and never find a creative solution. Or we continually think a negative thought because we have carved a powerful, neural groove in our brain and nervous system. There we go again thinking, "I don't deserve." "What is wrong with me?" "I'm so stupid I did that again!" "I hate myself."

During the Visionary training we learn to still our minds and break the hold of negative thinking. This is one of the most difficult aspects of the Visionary training because we must be willing to stop these negative thoughts and open our minds to something totally new. The mind is a powerful tool when harnessed to think *positive* thoughts.

There is fascinating research being done on the human brain that shows when we stimulate a new part of the brain with a new thought, feeling, or behavior – our nervous system actually grows new neural pathways to accommodate the new learning. Think about that for a minute. By calling up your inner Visionary to create a new thought or new creative solution to counter your old thought patterning, your brain sends out new impulses and a new branch of a neuron begins to grow. This is a wonderful demonstration of how the body responds and accommodates to the initiation process. When you desire to break the hold of negative thoughts, your brain will assist you by creating new neural pathways to carry new, positive thoughts to your entire system. This means that your mental and emotional systems are being renewed as well as your physical body.

I've been experimenting with an initiation exercise, imagining my Visionary's Winds of Change literally blowing through my brain. You can try to imagine this yourself when you want to clear out an old voice or belief. Identify the old beliefs that you are still connected to. Maybe do an active imagination and go into your attic or basement to find whatever is collecting dust. You begin to see how these old beliefs or old voices weigh you down and suck tremendous energy from your life. You store these patterns within your brain and nervous system. So if you can imagine blowing out the cobwebs and clearing your mind/brain with the wind of the Visionary, you are clearing the slate for a fresh new start. You can then re-pattern your nervous system with beliefs and thoughts and feelings that support you. Picturing the Visionary winds clearing your mind is a powerful process.

In the next part of the story, the Visionaries show Majah how to gaze into the Cauldron of Inspiration to arouse her inner sight, inner vision, and creativity. One way to open your third eye and arouse your inner sight is to find a practice that stills your mind, allowing it to play and discover. You can create your own version of staring into the Cauldron of Inspiration. This could be meditating with a burning candle, or getting a toy cauldron and filling it with water and breathing while you gaze into it. Or you might put on some music and dance or move and sway to awaken your inner sight. Through the initiation process, you will find a spiritual practice that works for you to open your third eye.

When women are able to awaken their inner sight, they find ways to help and heal others and they find creative solutions to problems. I know women with amazing psychic gifts who minimize and downplay their abilities to see, feel, hear, and sense what is going on for others. They receive pictures, images, impressions, and sensations but don't know what to do with them so they repress or dismiss them. In the Visionary training, we learn to value our inner sight and to stop behaviors of dismissing, minimizing, downplaying, and devaluing our amazing Visionary gifts. Sit by your own Cauldron of Inspiration and see what happens. See what opens within you and begin to trust your inner sight!

The next step of Majah's training with the Visionaries is when they throw her into chaotic situations where she cuts through confusion, makes swift decisions, banishes all self-doubt, and trusts herself completely. We know that life itself is a wonderful initiation process! I guaranty that your life will inevitably throw you into chaotic situations so you can practice being a Visionary who can make swift decisions, cut through confusion, and trust your intuition.

One thing I have noticed is that women tend to get confused easily and stop trusting their intuition. Many of my women clients over the years have said things like, "I had an intuitive hit that I should have done this or that but I didn't listen to my intuition." Or they tell me they were confused in an emotionally charged situation. However, when I ask them to quiet their mind and see exactly what was going on, they usually know exactly what was going on. This "confusion smokescreen" as I call it, comes from years of not trusting our intuition. We often dismiss our knowing either because our intuition was dismissed in childhood, people around us didn't want us to know what was going on, or we were punished for our psychic gifts. It is so important as a Visionary to trust our intuition and act on it when we get an intuitive "hit". It's equally valuable to stop being confused or foggy in a situation and to engage our clear sight and SEE what is really going on.

The next stage in Majah's training is when the Visionaries teach her their greatest secret of all - how to liberate the mind for change and transformation so that women can bring forth their powerful, revolutionary feminine vision into the world.

Why is liberating your mind so important? Because your mind is a powerful tool when it is not locked up with negative thoughts, chaos, and confusion. When your mind is still and calm, you can step beyond your limited beliefs and see all the possibilities open to you. With a liberated mind you can envision whatever you want and you can bring about that change through the power of your vision.

Imagine liberating your mind completely. Imagine your life without negative thinking. Imagine your life without obsessive thoughts swirling in your mind. Imagine being free of any self-doubt and self-illusion. Imagine being crystal clear about who you are. Imagine trusting your own intuition. Imagine trusting your visions, however crazy and unusual. Imagine envisioning the change you want and seeing it come to fruition. Imagine commanding the Winds of Change. Imagine using your mind as a tool of consciousness. These are the powers of the Visionary!

Awakening the Powers of the Manifestor

For her last initiation, Majah travels to the Manifestor training ground, to the land of the desert fires. Here she is to awaken the powers of the Manifestor that lie deep within her being. The Manifestor training ground is a vast desert scattered with crackling fires, some contained and some burning wild. This makes perfect sense, for the Manifestors are masters of the Fire Clan. The desert is hot, sun-drenched, and parched, often without water. The desert is the Fire Clan sanctuary for awakening the element of fire. The desert is also a perfect place to bathe under the night sky and see the radiant light of the stars. If you've ever been to the desert at night you know what I mean! Without light pollution from the city, you can actually see the Milky Way and the millions of stars and various planets of our own solar system. (I've been twice to the Sahara Desert and I can tell you that the stargazing is really quite inspiring.) We also know from the story that the Manifestors walk the Path of Action and awaken the spirit of fire within us, which is our inner, personal will. The Manifestors gain their empowerment through focusing the will.

In the first part of her initiation, Majah befriends the desert fires and the light from the sun and the stars. In doing this, she awakens the flame of spirit in the core of her being. This is an important part of the Manifestor initiation because it reminds us that everything in creation has a spark of light, a spark of consciousness deep within. When we know this at the core of our being, we have a great respect for every person, every plant, every animal, and every precious piece of creation. When we know that everything is alight with consciousness and that every part of creation is connected, we will use our will more consciously. We will manifest not only for ourselves, but also for the good of others.

What do the stars have to do with the Manifestor initiation? When we look up at the stars on a clear night, especially when we can see the Milky Way, a great mystery unfolds. The stars twinkle and sparkle and seem to be alive with a vitality that is awe-inspiring. During the Manifestor initiation, we are reminded that we too are self-generating stars. Stars are continually combusting and exploding, generating their own light, heat, and radiance. Each one of us is a star, a self-generating being full of light. As a Manifestor, we learn to awaken this internal flame of life to find our inner radiance.

When a woman is not connected to her self-generating core, she often feels she must "borrow" energy from others. She might be envious of another woman and try to take her light or take some of her energy. Have you ever had this experience, either wanting someone else's light or feeling someone trying to take some of yours? It is a horrible feeling either way! I remember an experience when I could actually feel another woman trying to take my light and energy at a retreat I was leading. She didn't feel comfortable in her life and in her own skin. She was envious of me because she perceived my life as "perfect, charmed, and easy." She may have observed my happiness and my enthusiasm for life and interpreted or projected that I had an easy, charmed life.

She couldn't have known how much I had struggled and how many emotional obstacles I had overcome in my life because I had not shared this with her. She gave me a really hard time during the retreat, criticizing me and diminishing my leadership. Then at night, when my energy was low and I was tired, I could feel her wanting my energy. It felt like she was sending out energetic tentacles wrapping around me like octopus arms. This was a significant "Manifestor moment" for me, for I realized she was attempting to take my light and my energy precisely because she wasn't connected to her own inner light. When self-generating our own light, we don't feel the need to take light from others. We can stand in our own radiance and connect, engage, interact, and have intimacy with all other beings in the universe. Rather than stealing light we can play and engage with the light in all life! This is a crucial part of the Manifestor training.

The next step Majah takes in her Manifestor initiation is to become skilled at inspiring, motivating, and leading. A Manifestor masters her leadership skills, for she is manifesting not only for herself, but also for the world. So she must learn to inspire and motivate others to take action. The Manifestor holds her own light in a way that encourages others to find their own inner light, so that eventually they can become authors of their own destiny.

Imagine Majah holding up her Sacred Wand to light the way for others. When a woman's wand has gone out, she may be disconnected from her own will. It is helpful to have someone lighting the way, pointing to your own wand so you can take it up once again and find your own will. I know when I feel my "light has gone out" or when I feel depressed, grieved, or lost, it really helps when I hear an inspiring talk or see an inspiring movie. It motivates me to rekindle my fire and find my light once again.

I have also witnessed some powerful magic and miracles when I have inspired and motivated others and pushed them beyond their perceived capabilities as a workshop and ritual leader. I have encouraged a lot of women to go on some pretty crazy adventures with me, in my round-the-world travels and in the initiation rituals I have cooked up over the years! We have crawled into caves, hiked into dark forests, kayaked into sea caves, sung to the stars, been buried in ritual graves (below the neck), released in grief rituals, trance danced blindfolded, hiked to the top of volcanoes to do sacred ritual, crawled into sacred burial chambers, dressed in ridiculous costumes, and so much more. When my Manifestor is on and leading, inspiring others to go beyond their comfort zone, I have seen many women grow and transform.

Next in her Manifestor initiation, Majah is shown the destructive nature of the "wild fire", the fire of a woman's will that is untamed and running wild. The wild fires represent the life force energy when a woman uses her will in a way that is out of control or destructive. Because we have free will, we can focus our will to create and manifest anything we choose. This means that sometimes we use our will for destructive purposes and/or for selfish gain. This would be when a woman harnesses the power of her will to get what she wants for herself without regard for others. That kind of wild fire might damage or hurt or push someone aside. A Manifestor keeps her wild fire in check.

I worked in a women's group many years ago with some very enthusiastic women who wanted to promote women's initiations in the wider world. We had a good team with a lot of fire and wholehearted passion. There was one woman who really had her heart in the right place, but her fire was a bit wild and out of her conscious control. She made suggestions that sounded more like commands than proposals. When she didn't get her way, we could feel this woman's will pushing and almost railroading over the collaborative process. After many months of her manipulating, pushing, and wanting her agenda to be followed, we asked her to leave the group. She was devastated because she was fairly unconscious of her powerful will. Her wild fire was sabotaging our cooperative effort to manifest this important project into the world.

The next stage in Majah's Manifestor initiation is that she is thrown into situations that demand action, where her life and other's lives are in danger. She learns that as a true Manifestor, she cannot hesitate by thinking it through or wondering how this might affect everyone else's feelings. She has to act swiftly, clearly, and cleanly. She has to mobilize resources in the flash of a second.

To be an effective Manifestor, you can't focus on feelings, thoughts, or other people's comfort levels. Obviously a good Manifestor will be aware of all these things. However, in order to mobilize resources and go into action, a true Manifestor must focus her will on the tasks at hand and on motivating and leading others.

I remember one Crete trip when there were 12 women following me into a cave that I always venture into on my women's retreat. There was one woman who was very afraid of the dark, one who was claustrophobic, and one who was scared of the climbing because she was not very fit. When we got to the cave, I focused my will and mobilized my resources. I chose my 2 most solid Warrioress types and asked one to be in the middle of the group and one to be at the very end. I asked the most confident climber to go directly after the women who felt unfit so she could give her a few pushes and pulls along the way.

I asked a Queenly type woman to sit next to the woman afraid of the dark so she could hold her hand when I blew all the candles out and we sat in total darkness. The claustrophobic woman was directly behind me as we hiked in so I could talk her through the cave as we went along. We all had a great experience because of the way I had organized the hike and made sure we utilized everyone's gifts to their greatest abilities. When we manifest well - mobilizing resources, motivating, and inspiring - we can accomplish great things!

When Majah comes to the end of her initiation, the Manifestors teach her their greatest secret of all, how to focus her will to manifest feminine values, feminine dreams, feminine knowledge, feminine leadership, feminine truths, feminine perspectives, and feminine solutions.

Why is this so important? One reason it is crucial for us as women to manifest our feminine dreams, leadership, and feminine ways is because feminine solutions are going to heal and change this world. When feminine solutions are applied to practical problems, we feel more connected, more compassionate, and more sensitive to the planet; we feel more cooperative, more generous, and more peaceful. When women manifest for themselves, their loved ones, and the planet, they usually find brilliant resolutions to complex problems.

Awakening the Powers of the Wise Woman

How do you awaken the powers of the Wise Woman? The Majah story says that your Wise Woman has the power to awaken the gifts of all the clans and unite all four clans within you. Your Wise Woman has the ability to align and coordinate your Warrioress, your Queen, your Visionary, and your Manifestor. Your Wise Woman can align your body, heart, mind, will, and spirit.

When you awaken your Wise Woman, you begin using your great power of choice. In any given situation you have the power to choose the Path of Strength, the Path of Compassion, the Path of Change, or the Path of Action. Your Wise Woman gives you the versatility of many choices and many possibilities. She walks the Path of Mastery so that you become masterful in your use of the Four Clan tools and masterful in making wise choices.

When you awaken your Wise Woman you also unlock the power to discover your true destiny. Your inner Wise Woman knows without a doubt what your calling is and what your true purpose is. As you exercise choice each day and free yourself from all fear and from all limiting beliefs, thoughts, and feelings, your mind and heart will open. When your mind and heart are open, your spirit is free to "come online". Your ego-needs fade into the background and your spirit rises into ascendency. Your spirit becomes the dominant force in your life and you have more internal space to discover your true purpose.

How do you discover your true purpose? How do you tap into your spirit? It really helps to start each day centering in your Wise Woman. You can imagine sitting on your purple throne as Majah does on the Sacred Robe. Then you can call in your Warrioress, your Queen, your Visionary, and your Manifestor so they are there, ready with their tools and their different paths for you to choose. I also find it helpful to call in each clan's gift – your Shield, Heart, Sword, and Wand.

With the help of your Warrioress you can choose healthy boundaries every day. This makes you strong and capable of confronting whatever life brings you. You can stand strong in the face of adversity and rather than checking out or escaping, you can stay present and grounded. You can activate your Shield and feel strong within your Sacred Boundary.

When you choose to activate your Queen and give yourself love and compassion each day with your Crystal Heart, your emotions will balance and your heart will be filled with love. This love will then overflow to others and you can bring a sense of harmony, comfort, and joy to the world. You can practice diplomacy and right speech and settle disputes and arguments wherever they occur. You can also quell the inner critic and other inner characters that can be divisive to your sense of well-being and equilibrium.

When you activate your Visionary, you take your Sword of Clarity to clear your mind of all the daily clutter and feel a sense of creative spaciousness. You are prepared to tackle whatever Winds of Change are blowing your way. Like a Ninja Priestess, you move flexibly with the chaos around you. You listen to and trust your intuition, which guides you in the right direction.

When you activate your Manifestor, you take your Wand of light and connect with your will and your higher will. You pull in your fire and focus your will on whatever you want to accomplish. With your Sacred Wand you can illuminate your path and bring conscious action into each decision. Rather than procrastinating or thinking or feeling too much about something, you act on what is important.

When your body, heart, mind, and will are awake and connected through your Wise Woman coordination, you are far more prepared to identify your life's true purpose. You begin to get glimpses of it day after day when you are aligned and awake. Then more of your purpose will unfold because you are able to handle, contain, and act on it.

Majah, your Wise Woman, activates the clans and unites the clans within you, presenting you with choices throughout your day. In each and every circumstance, your Wise Woman knows you have a choice. You observe, you evaluate, you assess, and you wait patiently until the right choice presents itself. "I need a strong boundary here. I need to be diplomatic there. I need to cut through the confusion here. I need to manifest and act now."

I love the visual of Majah in repose on her purple throne. She is relaxed, hands out, heart centered, mind clear and open to new possibilities. She is radiating her supreme and sovereign self. And here is a secret about the magic of your Wise Woman – when you resonate with your true self and embody your Wise Woman, you send a vibration out into the universe that powerfully attracts exactly what you need. Some call this synchronicity. This is when you are sounding your note, vibrating your sound, and resonating with your higher self.

Think of a radio station finely tuned so that it plays clear, beautiful music. When there is static and interference, you can't quite hear the beautiful song or symphony. When you allow distortions within yourself, such as negative thinking or destructive inner voices, it creates static and interference. When you vibrate out static and interference, you may not receive back exactly what you want! So if you are willing to center yourself and sing out your true note to the universe, your energetic field will come into more harmony. There will be less static and your song will sound out to the universe. The magic of your Majah will bring things, people, and events into your field to help you unfold your mission and purpose even more. This really is the way magic works.

Your Wise Woman walks the Path of Mastery and Magic. She helps you to be the master of your life. When you master your emotions and thoughts each day, you have a lot more energy to devote to your life purpose. When you are the author and co-creator of your life, you make decisions and choices that are good and beneficial for you. When you are doing this consistently in your life, you will be happier, more fulfilled, and more available for your relationships. You will feel a sense of inner mastery and self-confidence.

Your Wise Woman also helps you claim your own spiritual authority. For thousands of years, women have been discouraged from seeing, feeling, and experiencing their own spiritual authority. It's time to claim that back. You must trust your inner knowing and your unique brand of spirituality. You know spirit through nature, through devotion, through singing and dancing. You see spirit everywhere. You are spirit when you smile at a stranger, help a friend, do the right thing, and love yourself. Women's spirituality is one of the most powerful forces in the world. It's time for you to claim your own spirituality and to be your own spiritual authority. It is time to unleash the Divine Feminine into the world.

The shadow side of the Wise Woman is activated when you feel you have lost your power of choice. This is when you are faced with a situation and you feel paralyzed, triggered, stuck, frozen, enraged, or blocked. Instead of feeling calm and seeing possible choices and solutions, you may feel hopeless and helpless.

Observe yourself and notice how and when you lose your power of choice. Are there certain people with whom you seem to lose your power of choice? Are there situations in which you feel powerless to choose for yourself? What situations trigger you into past trauma? What circumstances stop you in your tracks and you feel frozen and paralyzed? What triggers you into rage? When this happens, you can take a deep breath and stop. Calm the anxiety in your body. Calm the storms in your heart. Calm the swirling in your mind. Calm the wild fire in your will. Then call in your Wise Woman if you feel caught in the shadow path. See how you can make more conscious choices in the moment.

Through the initiation process, the Wise Woman is activated and can get you back on your Path of Power and back into alignment and integrity with your true self. You'll be able to identify where you get stuck in disempowered behaviors - whether it's fear, self-sacrifice, chaos, or manipulation. You can overcome the fears that hold you back from being your true self. With the gifts of the Wise Woman, you can reclaim your own power, align with your true self, and manifest your dreams.

When you embody the Wise Woman, you live your life with strength, compassion, vision, and conscious action. You are spiritually centered and fully awake. As the Wise Woman, you are master of your own life and destiny. You follow your calling and know your life's purpose. You have a powerful inner light like a compass, pointing to your true north each day of your life. The Wise Woman awakens your true feminine wisdom and helps you embody your true feminine essence. She helps you unlock your creativity and full potential.

Majah's Prayer

Majah's Prayer at the end of the story is important for several reasons. Here it is again so you can refresh your memory:

"Arise, proud bringer of feminine knowledge and wisdom.
Share your beauty with your sisters.
Do not fear that your wisdom will be shunned or dismissed,
We are eager to hear what you bring to us from the other land, the land of spirit.
Your opinion matters to us,
What you think and feel is essential to our survival and well-being.
Take your place around the women's circle,
Trust yourself completely.
Do not hold back if you sense there is untruth here or falsehood or deceit,
We need you to be strong and honest.
We need your insight, expertise, understanding, intelligence, perception, originality, good judgment, creativity, observation, astuteness, cleverness, ingenuity, talent, and skill.
Without your contribution our circle is less colorful, less diverse, less vibrant.
So I urge you sister to value what you bring to the women's circle,
However crazy, however outrageous, however unusual.
For what you bring completes our circle.
And we are proud to know you,
You bless our circle,
You proud bringer of feminine knowledge and wisdom."

Majah encourages you to bring your best and most valuable gift to your community. Why? Because your gift enhances the village of women. Your gift is needed. Your insight is needed. The village needs your skills. And when you bring your best gift forward, you also receive love and support. The community rejoices when you are bold enough to bring forward your true self. What a relief. You don't have to be anything else or anyone else other than WHO YOU ARE.

If you are a strong Warrioress, bring your gifts forward. If you are a Queen with a big heart and abundant love to give your community, bring these gifts forward. If you are a Visionary and have innovative ideas, bring them forward. If you are a Manifestor, create and act decisively for your community. Utilize your leadership skills to help your community. You are not responsible for everyone and everything. You just need to be yourself, *however crazy, however outrageous, however unusual,* and bring forward your particular gifts. When you do, everyone in your village will rejoice and celebrate. They will appreciate your gifts and offer you support.

If your family or friends do not support your gifts, then please find a new group of conscious women who will support your genius and your true gifts.

One thing I have observed working with women for over 30 years, is that most women do not get enough support. You have your passions. You are tremendously capable of loving. You care about life. You care about the world. What you need is support, so that you feel your cup is being filled up internally. You can experience a whole new way of living when your cup is full and you feel seen, loved, nurtured, supported, and cherished.

When you feel surrounded by initiated elders, women who have the capacity to see and value what you bring to the village of women, your life changes profoundly. You feel love and joy. You feel relaxed inside yourself. You begin to understand that you bless the village of women. Your gifts are exactly what the village needs.

Initiating your Inner Wise Woman

How can you live today as an Initiated Wise Woman and step fully into your wisdom and power? Well, the first and most important thing you are already doing is seeking your feminine initiation. You have made a commitment in your heart to walk a path of wisdom, a feminine path to empower yourself to live fully in the present.

Identify your shadow path

Another helpful step on your path of initiation is to identify where you have been disempowered and identify where you need healing. This means identifying which shadow paths you have been engaging in and walking down and making some positive choices to walk in a new direction. When you begin wrestling with the shadow energies you can receive some help to break the hold of the negative patterns, thoughts, and feelings.

Let's begin with the shadow of the Warrioress. Have you been living on the path of fear? Do you feel like a Victim? Do you lose energy when someone confronts you? Do you find it hard to stand up for yourself? If you have been walking down this shadow path then you can begin to face your fears and commit to stop living as a Victim. You can call in your Warrioress and seek the Warrioress initiation. You can work with the element earth to feel grounded and to transform your body so that it becomes a beautiful container to hold you profoundly in strength and truth.

Have you been living on the shadow path of the Queen, the path of self-sacrifice? Do you notice your heart is caged and locked away? Do you find it hard to trust others? Do you end up feeling like a Martyr, sacrificing yourself and feeling bitter and disappointed in love? If you have been walking down this shadow path then you can commit to stop sacrificing yourself and no longer living as a Martyr. You can call in your Queen and seek the Queen initiation. You can transform your heart and unleash unconditional self-compassion into your system.

Have you been living on the shadow path of the Visionary, the path of chaos? Do you spin your wheels and have lots of ideas but never bring your vision to fruition? Do you distract yourself and procrastinate? Do you get caught in negative thinking? If you have been walking down this shadow path then you can commit to stop stirring up chaos and commit to no longer being a Saboteur. You can call in your Visionary and seek the Visionary initiation. You can transform your mind and liberate your vision. You can begin to envision the change you want to bring to your life.

Have you been living on the shadow path of the Manifestor, the path of manipulation? Do you find yourself controlling others or over-controlling your life in general? Do you dominate others in any way? Or have you given away the power of your will to others? If you have been walking down this shadow path then you can commit to stop controlling and commit to stop living as a Manipulator. You can call in your Manifestor and seek the Manifestor initiation. You can transform your will and manifest your true purpose.

Have you been living on the shadow path of the Wise Woman, not seeing your power of choice? Do you mistrust your own spiritual way of knowing? Do you lack confidence in your own spiritual authority? Are you disconnected from your spiritual center? If so you can commit to seeing your power of choice in every situation. You can call in your Wise Woman and seek the Wise Woman initiation.

You can claim your spiritual knowing and sovereignty.

A crucial part of the initiation process is making a commitment to yourself to transform any of your shadow behaviors - any ways you remain a victim, any ways you self-sacrifice to your detriment, any ways you create chaos or manipulate with your will, and any ways you fail to claim your spiritual authority. This commitment from your body, heart, mind, will, and spirit safeguards your initiation process and calls in abundant support for your highest growth and development.

Choose which Feminine Guide to call in

The next step in the initiation process is to choose which Divine Feminine guide you want to call in, depending on the situation. In every situation you can evaluate who to call in: your Warrioress, your Queen, your Visionary, your Manifestor, or your Wise Woman.

Call in the Warrioress when you need to face your fears. Call in the Warrioress when you need strength, boundaries, and grounding. Call her in when you need to take a stand. Call her in when you need to protect yourself or your village.

Call in the Queen when you need to be diplomatic or compassionate with others. Call in the Queen when you need emotional balance. Call her in when you need profound self-love. Call her in when you need to grieve and release emotions. Call her in during an emotional crisis.

Call in the Visionary if you need to cut through some confusion. Activate the Visionary when you need to call in the Winds of Change. Call in the Visionary when you need the powers of transformation and innovation. Call her in when you need to liberate your mind and open to new possibilities. Call her in when you need to break the hold of negative thoughts.

Call up the Manifestor when you need to take decisive action. Call in the Manifestor when you need will power and the power of manifestation. Call her in when you need to get out from someone else's will or control. Call her in when you need to mobilize resources for a project.

Call in your Wise Woman when you need to make a conscious choice or when you need to claim your own spiritual authority. Call her in when you need to center yourself. Call her in when you need to connect with your own inner wisdom.

Become the creator of your Life

The last step in the initiation process is to become the master of your own life. With your Wise Woman on the Path of Mastery, you can create your life exactly the way you want. You can envision your best life according to your gifts, your skills, your talents, and your genius. You can seek healing where you are blocked and feel empowered to get back on your Path of Power and then dream and envision the best world you can imagine.

Your own initiation is set in motion when you make a commitment to living the wisdom paths of the Warrioress, Queen, Visionary, Manifestor, and Wise Woman. This gives you the energy to transform any disempowered paths you may have wandered onto. You now have the power to stop fear-based behaviors or co-dependent behaviors and you can stop creating chaos and controlling others. As you do this for yourself, you can also assist other women who are stuck on a disempowered path.

Affirmations on the Initiation path

In order to embody the Feminine Path of Power, you can create some powerful affirmations as you walk the initiation path. Here are some suggestions:

- "I align my body, heart, mind, will, and spirit."
- "I create healthy boundaries."
- "I love myself profoundly."
- "I clear my mind of all chaos and confusion."
- "I envision clearly what I want."
- "I commit to conscious action."
- "I focus my will."
- "I align with my higher will."

The simplest and most profound affirmation, "I align my body, heart, mind, will, and spirit" covers all five Divine Feminine Guides and reminds your whole self to wake up and align together. As you call in the Warrioress, you align your body. As you call in the Queen, you align your heart. As you call in the Visionary, you align your mind. As you call in the Manifestor, you align your will. As you call in the Wise Woman, you align your spirit.

Your Wise Woman also reminds you that you have CHOICE to call upon any Divine Feminine Guide that matches the situation you are facing. You have the choice to walk the paths of Strength, Compassion, Change, Action, or Mastery.

Tools in your Toolbox

In any given situation, you have a variety of tools in your toolbox you can choose. You can choose your Warrioress' Shield if you need to protect yourself or draw a healthy boundary. You can choose your Queen's Crystal Heart if you need to balance your emotions or employ right speech. You can choose your Visionary's

Sword of Clarity to cut through confusion and envision change. You can choose your Manifestor's fiery Wand to manifest what you need or to lead others. You can choose your Wise Woman's Circle of Empowerment to make a conscious choice so that you can be the master of your own life.

Embodying Majah, your Inner Wise woman

It is very helpful to visualize your inner Majah, your inner Wise Woman as clearly as possible. When you can envision your Wise Woman living inside of you, you can tap into her more easily. One way to envision her clearly is to contemplate the image of Majah on the Sacred Robe and visualize her inside you, residing in your heart or residing in your entire body.

Look at the image of Majah now and imagine her inside you and take some deep breaths. Imagine you are sitting on a throne and relaxing. Imagine you have a huge rainbow headdress. Radiate out your colorful self. Your light is going out in all directions.

Imagine there is a powerful purple flame radiating out of your head. This purple flame can sustain your vital energy. It can burn off anything you do not want inside your sacred space. This purple flame is very powerful and you can "tell it" whatever you want it to do. It is like an alchemical flame that you can direct with your conscious will and utilize for your own sacred purpose.

As you sit on your Wise Woman throne, recognize the power of choice that you have in every situation. Imagine now that you can call in the powers of the Warrioress. Feel your body strong and sturdy. Feel the sacred boundary around your soul. Now feel the Queen within you and your power to command the sacred waters. Open your heart and feel love and compassion flowing from your open heart. Take another deep breath and call up the Visionary. Clear your mind and be still. See how effortlessly you can move the Winds of Change. Awaken your Visionary power to envisioning what you want. Now call up the fire of your Manifestor. Feel your wand in your hand and cast a spell to manifest what you want to create. Feel your core fire and align with your highest will.

And now come back to Majah, your inner Wise Woman. Feel the spirit within you, who is the ultimate master of your life. Feel how your Wise Woman holds the secret of your purpose and destiny. Feel your gratitude for your life. Feel gratitude for all the people you know and love. Call in all the support you need on your journey. Be willing to give generously of your gifts and talents. Feel your body at peace, feel your heart at peace, feel your mind at peace, and feel your will at peace in this moment.

Interviews with Wise Women

The following are interviews with women who have attended my Feminine Path of Power Programs and interacted with all 5 Divine Feminine Archetypes. Here is how some of them relate to their Wise Woman.

Interview with MK

Let's talk about Majah. She represents your inner Wise Woman, the one who unites the clans and all the tools inside you. How do you relate to Majah?

I feel so much closer to her after our last retreat. I feel I have Majah centered within me and I have her power. I feel like I'm on my own Majah throne with the other goddesses around me and I can call on them for their strengths and gifts. I call Majah in when I need help - and it is working! We are all working on this together; I feel all five of the goddesses' support. I feel I can activate Majah on the inside of me and she works with me. What's really cool about this is that rather than her being outside of me, I really feel her on the inside of me.

How do you experience that? How do you feel her inside of you?

I feel a wholeness that I didn't have before. I long time ago, I was in a seminar and as an exercise I remember drawing an outline of my body. I was supposed to draw a picture of my soul and I drew a teeny, tiny person inside my bigger body. I felt at that point in my life that my soul had shrunk to pretty much zero. I was unhappy in my life and unhappy in my marriage and I realized that my soul was so small and shrunken. With the Wise Woman now I feel full. I feel like my soul is big and full inside my body. She's part of me now, not an untouchable. When I first met Majah, the Wise Woman, it felt really hard to reach her and now she is me! She is my inner goddess and she is me.

I love that you now feel full. Do you imagine yourself sitting on her purple throne? Is there a way you visualize yourself as the Wise Woman?

I imagine I'm in a room that is glowing and I feel full. When I visualize it, it is glowing with energy and glowing with colors. Majah's on a throne but she's not higher than the other goddesses. They are all working together and all part of a whole. I get to work with all of them equally. Majah can access the Warrioress, the Queen, the Visionary, and the Manifestor easily. So each of the goddesses are part of me.

I love that description because Majah's path is the Path of Mastery and choice so she gives you that choice in every situation to use one of the Guides and one of the tools – the Shield, Heart, Sword, or Wand - whatever is appropriate for that situation.

Yes, since our retreat I call Majah in when I need to make a decision about what I want to do or where I want to go. Decisions are easier now because I don't worry about what people are going to think or feel. I am just concerned with where I want to go and what I want to do. She helps a lot in my decision-making process.

I can see that your Wise Woman makes it easier and you don't have to dither around, you just know what to do.

Yes. I don't have the chaos going on any more, I got rid of the chaos. I implement what I want to do, and I move ahead. And by the way, the women at our retreat were incredible. I've never experienced anything like that before. I felt like we were all resonating and vibrating. When I left the retreat, I still have that great feeling inside of me.

Yes it reminds me of a beehive - when everyone's resonating and buzzing together, everything runs smoothly. And when you touch into that place inside your self that is resonating like the Majah Wise Woman, you can hum and buzz and resonate with this positive vibe.

It catches. It's contagious. Thank you for all the work you've done because this has just been fabulous for me. I feel like I'm moving along quite nicely!

Thank you so much for sharing your relationship with your Wise Woman.

Interview with Margaret

It feels so important to have access to all the Goddesses and connect in with Majah the Wise Woman because she stands in your sacred center and helps you stay centered. Majah unites and connects all the clans inside you. So how are you connecting with your inner Wise Woman?

That certainly has changed through The Feminine Path of Power program. I am more aware of the place inside me, which is my High Priestess. It feels like a place of integration. Energetically, I feel my Wise Woman as a beautiful light pouring through my crown and creating this whole alchemy throughout my body. It's a super energy field. It's like this yellow and blue light just going through me, like stardust falling down. My Majah Wise Woman holds a place of presence inside me. I can be more present, more integrated, and can listen more deeply.

I call on my Wise Woman to help me discern what is arising within me. I feel it as wisdom bubbling up from inside, like a waterfall of scintillating light. Sometimes I say things to people and I have no idea where it came from, and they experience it as so perfect for them and so amazing. All I do is tune into my deep spirit and get into alignment with my higher self and I feel like a co-creator with spirit. This is the same place I go when I am in prayer, where I hold the needs of the world in my heart and send out the intention of renewal. I feel a sense of healing and renewal and I allow the wisdom of what's needed to really soak into the world.

I'm beginning to understand much more what that unification is when we talk about connecting the spirit world with the physical world in a very practical sense. I can now call upon my Wise Woman and pray for the world in a tangible way. I love Majah's image on the Sacred Robe. I can relate to her. I notice some people want to project their own wisdom onto religious figures, like Mother Mary. But they forget to see they have their own wisdom and they can find answers within themselves. For me, when I look at Majah I feel I have this deep wisdom within me. I can touch into that space. Instead of believing that other people are wiser than me, I can seek the answers within myself. What I need to know is inside of me.

That is the ultimate empowerment, to recognize one's own inner wisdom. And it's like that pearl inside that keeps growing. You described it so beautifully when you said your Wise Woman is like scintillating light or a waterfall of light bubbling inside of you. The wisdom and power are out there in the universe and also right inside of you! Wow, that was a really rich stew we just jumped into. Thanks for sharing your experience.

Interview with Cynthia

Your Wise Woman sits in the middle of your sacred circle and sits in the center of you! She's your High Priestess on your throne. She choses the correct tool you can use in the moment. How do you visualize your Wise Woman and how is she working for you?

I am incorporating her more now, especially after Goddess Camp. I am reminding myself to bring her in everyday so she can guide me in making good choices. I called upon her a lot last weekend with all that was going on with my family. Even talking about her right now I can really feel Majah right here inside me. There's such a sweet wisdom in her. The Wise Woman has such a presence. She's integrated and patient. Majah can just sit there. When the Wise Woman in me can just be calm and sit there then she's in the Matrix or the energy field and everything can just unfold. So I can sit calmly and call her in. She has a centered knowingness. That's her wisdom – she knows that everything is going to unfold in the right place at the right time.

I really love what you're saying here. The 4 archetypes of the 4 clans have 4 tools you can choose from. Your Majah, your Wise Woman can wait, evaluate the Matrix, and then go into action when it's appropriate. That's a really great way to think about the Wise Woman. She waits until the time is right.

Yes, there's such wisdom in her. I feel her so much, Megan, right now just talking about her. I think of her image on the Robe, with her hands out and activated and her rainbow headdress and her beautiful purple throne. When I picture her there's an instantaneous re-remembering of who I am and who we all are as Wise Women - rather than us being in some weird play or drama.

Majah can give you some objectivity about the drama that's happening around you. Remember your Wise Woman is connected to eternal time. She's connected to the timelessness of spirit, and gives you a broader perspective.

Yes, when the drama was taking place last weekend in my family, I was continuously praying for the highest and best for my son and his girlfriend. I could draw on Majah, which I did. At one point I brought out my huge crystal bowl, attuned to the heart, and I put it right in the middle of our barbecue, and I made everyone stand around and I played it. It helped everyone to ground. And then there was a lot happening with their breakup and then my son's girlfriend was not in a good place. I sent my higher self out to meet her higher self. And I just sat there, out in the sun, and waited and allowed her to do whatever she needed to do. And it was amazing. It was exhausting, but it was amazing to see how that unfolded too. I knew what to do. I called in my Majah Wise Woman and knew what to do.

What you've just described, you playing your crystal bowl with everyone standing around it, is exactly what Majah does – she finds a resonance and unifies the field. Her energy unites everyone together in a common field of loving resonance. When we're in our High Priestess self, our Wise Woman self, we can unify the field because we're not attached to the outcome of what happens. The crystal bowl is a perfect example, where it resonates out a vibration of oneness and wholeness. And when people want to attune to that, they can come into greater harmony. If they choose not to, then they'll grate against that attunement, and not come into harmony. But the important thing about Majah is that she's the unifying energy within us that can bring all parts of self into greater wholeness. That crystal bowl is a beautiful touchstone for you to imagine her as the unifying field.

Yes, and I remembered your voice saying, "Bring Majah in to help you decide which Goddess to call in and which tool to use. So I called in my Warrioress to ground, ground, ground, ground, ground. Then I called in Majah for the highest and best, highest and best to come out of the situation.

The other thing I love with Majah is that she gives you a higher perspective – like when you're in an airplane and you're ascending and then you pop up above the clouds. I often think of Majah as the part of us that can pop up above the clouds, and just look around at the landscape and see what needs to be done from that higher, spiritual perspective. Majah gives us a much vaster, bigger, higher viewpoint. Then we wait and see what creative solution might come. When we can live patiently in that space of higher resonance, Majah will think of a solution. Our Wise Woman usually finds a solution that's more unifying - one that will bring harmony and wholeness to the situation. And as you said, it doesn't mean perfection or happiness; it means wholeness.

That's very helpful, because I think there was a sense of wholeness after I played the crystal bowl. One of the things I need to let go of is perfection and what happiness should look like. This is what is deconstructing within me. Happiness doesn't look like a Norman Rockwell painting or a Hallmark movie.

That's right, and if we only have one vision of the way it's supposed to be, we miss other possible perspectives because our inner Majah can take the entire picture into account. Wholeness may look like a breakup, a divorce or a loss - things that we typically think are bad. And yet, from Majah's perspective, the Wise Woman in us may be able to see very clearly that a breakup is absolutely the next step that needs to happen in order for wholeness to arise. Majah sits in repose on her throne. She's not moving. She's not going anywhere. She's simply attracting. She's resonating wholeness, which then will attract wholeness to her.

When I look into Majah's eyes, they are portals. I can see that she just resonates wholeness and attracts what she needs. I can just go through her eye portals and bring her fully into me! All these feminine archetypes are beautiful.

Thank you so very much for sharing your experiences with the Wise Woman.

Interview with Susan

Let's talk about how you relate to the Wise Woman, your spiritual self. She walks the Path of Mastery and Integration. Tell me about your relationship to your Wise Woman.

I've always felt a sense of responsibility to heal myself and to seek out different ways to do this. I didn't feel valued for my gifts in my family as I was growing up. During the Feminine Path of Power, I felt my Wise Woman's strength and her wisdom in new ways. She showed me what I had built inside me already and how I can combine all of the Goddesses to create my life with conscious intention. I can use one Goddess or all or a combination of them. It's just so empowering.

Through the Virtual Journey of Mastery program I did with you, I explored in detail what it means to be the master of my life. The Feminine Path of Power highlighted the importance of embodying my mastery in a feminine way and how important this is in our culture right now.

I see how wounded and distorted the feminine energy is and the need for it to be healed is becoming very clear. You put forth practical steps to heal the feminine energy inside and set an example for a new template for the Divine Feminine to come through. I didn't know she was so strong inside of me until taking the Feminine Path of Power. My awareness of who she is inside me increased. Once I understood who my Wise Woman is and how to connect with her, she became much more alive inside me.

I'm thinking about the image of Majah on the Sacred Robe as she sits on her purple throne. She's open, relaxed, and she's aware and awake. Is that similar to how you feel your Wise Woman inside of you?

Yes, but I didn't know that was my higher self. I thought she was missing. If you asked me in the past, I would say, "Oh, I don't have such a great connection with my higher self. I don't feel my higher wisdom come through." I think it was a real shift in perspective for me to understand all the different Goddesses and how they work in my life. You gave them job descriptions and talked about both the positive and negative sides of each Archetype.

When I learned that about Majah, the Wise Woman, I really began to understand the higher wisdom that I have and what that looks and feels like for me. Now that I have identified my inner Wise Woman, I am much more aware of her and aware of the wisdom I carry.

I think you're speaking to something that many women feel – difficulty in connecting with their higher wisdom. They know it's in there somewhere, but don't know how to connect with it. It's so important to find creative ways to connect with the Wise Woman. As a visual artist myself, I love the visual on the Robe as this helps me picture her inside me. I look at the image and imagine her melting into me. I can feel her in me, sitting on a purple throne and open, awake, aware with this big rainbow headdress and the big, purple flame. That's how I feel, see, and connect with her. What are other ways you connect with your inner Wise Woman?

I feel and sense her kinesthetically. I look at my life and see the ways I display her values and her wisdom. When I listen to what I say and then people mirror back to me that they liked or enjoyed what I said, this makes me feel good. When I see them adopting this piece of wisdom into their own lives, I know my Wise Woman has been speaking.

So your Wise Woman gives someone practical wisdom that has meaning and they can then implement it in their life.

Yes. That's the way I hear the Wise Woman in me. Another example involves my art, which is always informing me. I create my paintings and drawings and then I look at them and question, "Where did that come from within me? How did I do that?" Then my art helps me shift perspective. All of a sudden I see the wisdom of my higher self and my Wise Woman reflected back to me in this art book I'm creating.

Your Wise Woman is also your master magician. She creates magic in your life. That's what you're speaking about - you get to see your magic go out there into the world. It is magical and miraculous what comes from our Wise Woman self.

*Yes, my Wise Woman integrates all my characters together and pulls down the ideas from the "plenum" (*the creative stuff of the universe*). Then my Wise Woman sends the new ideas to the Visionary to create a picture, or to the Warrioress so I can be more brave and fearless. Then we do it all over again.*

Right. Your Wise Woman is the integrative command central. She uses wisdom in a flash of a second to know the right choice in the moment. Wow! Thank you, Susan. It is wonderful to hear how you're integrating all of your Goddesses together and working with them so tangibly. Thank you.

Interview with Kala

Well, let's talk about Majah. She's your Wise Woman who walks the Path of Mastery and integrates the Warrioress, Queen, Visionary and Manifestor together. She gives you choice in every situation. I would love to know how you connect to your inner Wise Woman.

There's been a really intense alchemical process for me as I embody my Wise Woman more and more. When I touch into my higher self, it's as if all parts of me come together. It dissolves any fear, any ego attachments, any otherness, any doubts, and any delusion. On the way home last night after hearing all these really horrific things about our government at this lecture I went to, all I could do was shift as deeply as possible into my Wise Woman. She is my inner refuge. I gather in the world, my struggle, my doubt, my pain, and then I know where to go and how to go. She helps me align and integrate.

Yes, the Wise Woman is definitely the integrator. She aligns all the different parts of you and pulls all your separate bits into one big cauldron and you can stew and bathe in the cauldron, where everything comes together.

Yes and our journey changes in our different ages and decades of life. It sure is easier to go through life when you have sisters and women surrounding you to support you through your life changes. When we hear and see other women's beauty and wisdom it creates a resonance and we gather strength from this. When I came to your seminars and retreats I really experienced this support and I felt seen. I thought, "Oh, I still have to do work on this particular piece in my life." Then I witnessed another woman who had really worked on this and she inspired me to move forward in a way I couldn't have before.

Yes, you're speaking of the resonance that the Wise Woman creates. The Wise Woman, Majah, is really your higher self. When women are connected to their higher selves, we come into more coherence, more attunement, and more resonance. Then, when others walk into the coherent field that the Wise Woman creates, people heal faster, they integrate faster, and they come into a resonance, which helps them vibrate at that resonance, too. The Wise Woman / Higher Self is so, so powerful in that way because she brings us into greater coherence.

Yes. The great lesson of this whole Divine Feminine Path is that we are not separate. We are all particles of the One Presence. That's at the base of the whole thing. We're all rays of one sun. In that loving presence, when all of those elements are really integrated, we can stand in communion and community.

Thank you so much for sharing your relationship to the Wise Woman. You have a beautiful way of describing her!

Interview with Carol

Let's talk about the Wise Woman. She walks the Path of Mastery and she's the one who gives you the power of choice. How are you relating to Majah, the Wise Woman?

The Wise Woman for me is a new and powerful energy in my life. I did not feel that I had choices in my life when I was younger. I didn't feel like a Wise Woman sitting on her sovereign throne. I felt invaded all the time and I felt very powerless. I did not feel my light shining brightly. I didn't radiate out all the colors of the rainbow. So when I envision Majah and I bring her in I can see myself in the middle of my sacred circle and see myself making choices and wise decisions. Calling her in has brought in the "wise" part of my Wise Woman. I remember many, many years ago doing an exercise where I had to write down what I most wanted if I could have anything in the world - I wrote "wisdom". That's what I wanted.

Now I am starting to feel like the Wise Woman who can sit back and choose who and what I want to call in. I can choose to see things clearly and choose to hold my boundaries. I feel like I'm incorporating all of these energies within myself, and then the Wise Woman in me feels lighter because I've got all of these tools. I feel like I have some wisdom.

How do you feel her inside you? Do you visualize sitting on your throne?

Yes, I do at times envision myself sitting on the throne just like Majah, the Wise Woman, with my hands out, my chakras open and my headdress on, which symbolizes to me the sovereignty of my being. I can see that I am an important piece of this huge puzzle, this huge web. I am an important person in the web. So, I visualize myself sitting on the throne and feeling strong, being clear, being compassionate, being a Visionary, and being able to use my wisdom. I want to take my wisdom and first use it just for myself, for my own sovereignty. Because I feel that as I bring these pieces into myself and heal myself, I'm also helping others heal too. My Wise Woman is the one who pulls it all together, who has access to all 4 clan tools.

I love what you've just said about healing yourself first and this automatically heals the world. I think this is really important for other women to understand, that when each woman vibrates her own Wise Woman, together we can literally heal the world.

Right, and that's what I see. And I see such great balance in her and in me when I'm sitting on my throne. I feel a sense of non-judgment. By presenting a non-judgmental attitude and presence, I can make an impact.

Wow, thank you so much. This has been such a rich discussion. I know you are going to help a lot of women. Thank you!

Interview with Ali Marie

I know the Wise Woman pulls everything together and you've been talking a lot about balance between the Warrioress, Queen, Visionary, and Manifestor. So I'd love to hear how you relate to and call up that beautiful Wise Woman in you?

Well, it's interesting because I have one meditation practice that I really love, which is a practice with the angels. And the angels and the goddesses in The Feminine Path of Power have overlapped a little bit which has been kind of cool. Both practices have a lot of similarities. So for me, the Wise Woman becomes the indwelling, very feminine, very present overarching experience of all the Goddesses.

And how do you feel when you call up this Wise Woman and/or your angels? How do you register that inside, can you give an example?

It's a feeling of wholeness and a feeling of having everything I need. It feels infinite and expansive. It just feels like this place of infinite possibility. I can call in any one of the Goddess: the Warrioress, the Queen, The Visionary, or the Manifestor, depending on what I need in the moment. And then when I feel the angels, I feel I'm touching into the Divine.

Oh, that's nice!

Yes! It is my experience of divinity, of the divine realm. I feel like all parts of me come together.

I love your phrase, "infinite possibility", because then you're not blocking any flow that could be moving through you.

Right. It really is about infinite possibility and this constant flowing and allowing. Allowing is really great for someone like me, who's put a lot of blocks around in the past. So when I'm part of that flow and that dynamic, expansive experience, I have a much more satisfying experience in the world.

Thank you! This is great. I'm so grateful for the way you've articulated how all the Feminine Guides fit together for you and bring you wholeness.

Interview with Susana

Let's talk about your Wise Woman. She walks the Path of Mastery and represents your core Self. She taps into your spirit and makes conscious choices. How are you relating to the Wise Woman?

Good question. It depends on what moment you ask me. I go to her like I would a wise elder. I guess I don't quite feel her in my core; it's more like I bow down to her. That's the posture that I imagine. I call on her. I ask for her guidance.

When you look at her image on the Sacred Robe, she is sitting on her purple throne and she has on that big rainbow headdress. When we meditate with her and imagine her melting right into us, can you feel that? Can you imagine her inside you?

Yes. When I imagine her inside myself, she does feel very much at home. It feels comfortable.

You embody this energy very well and you might not even know it! I see Majah in you. I see the Wise Woman in you. You actually embody this energy quite effortlessly. So it may be that you can just take that one step to notice and acknowledge she's inside you. Feel how you embody her. She's the part of you that shows you which Goddess to call in, whether you need the Warrioress to be grounded, the Queen to be heart-centered, the Visionary to be clear-minded, or your Manifestor to create your magic in the moment. Your Wise Woman knows exactly what to do.

Yeah. She does. And it's fast; it's like a flash.

What's fun about embodying your Wise Woman more and more is that you feel this sense of calm, centered confidence. You can sit in repose, like Majah on the Robe. And there's an effortlessness about her that is so fun for us as women to tap into, because normally we're on the go all the time, and making things happen. Why not just sit on our throne and relax, and realize that maybe the world can come to us.

Yeah. That is a novel thought. I like that idea! When I see a woman who embodies this kind of Majah Wise Woman, I admire that in her.

Well, I see you carrying your Wise Woman in this way and really embodying her. Stay conscious and aware of connecting with her inside of you and you will notice your Wise Woman being there more and more.

Okay. That's a good reminder.

Your Wise Woman chooses which of the four tools she wants to use in any given situation. Really she's about choice and free will and connecting in with our spiritual self.

Yes. Well I do find great comfort in her and she is very discerning. My Wise Woman discerns pretty quickly what needs to be done. And this does give me a sense of confidence. I know that I can discern things well, I might not always know in the moment, but give me a little time or let me sleep on it overnight, and I will always have an answer.

Thank you so much. I really appreciate your examples of how you're using this archetype. It's really helpful to get your personal examples.

Interview with AB

Let's talk about your Wise Woman. How do you relate to her?

One thing I want to start with is my amazement at the very beginning of the Majah story, that there could actually be a women's village, a group of supportive women holding space and initiation ritual for other women. This is very new to me. I feel my deep yearning for this when I read the story. Actually, my yearning for this isn't new, but it was so wonderful to see that we could all imagine the world this way and that we are doing this together on the Feminine Path of Power.

The second thing that was amazing was imagining that when a female baby is born, there's recognition that she has a special purpose. There's a special initiation and a special reason for her soul being present for the community. She is honored by a group of elders. I have never had that so boldly stated or embraced. It would make it so much easier to say, "This is who I am." Thank you Megan, for letting me be part of the Feminine Path of Power so I can claim this as my birthright.

You are welcome! Tell me about your relationship to the Wise Woman. I would love to hear!

I am having some big realizations about my inner Wise Woman. I realize now that I am the master of my life. I'm 53 now and I'm at mid-life so what do I want? What's my destiny? I still have my health and staying power ahead of me. I have a right to be seen. I have a right to be respected. I have so many gifts, but what are those gifts? These are questions I am now asking.

You can use your Visionary to envision what you want to create, your Manifestor to make it happen and your Wise Woman to choose exactly how it's all going to look.

I want to tell you a story that shows how I've been using my Wise Woman. In the past 5 months since I moved across the country, I had guests for 37 of those days. I've always had an open house, and had people to stay. This was no problem in my old house as it was huge and 3x the size of our new smaller bungalow. In my old house, my guests stayed in the basement so they were pretty independent. But in our new house, my guests are right there and having so many guests has taken its toll on me.

With all these guests, I did a lot of caretaking, a lot of giving, and a lot of holding my ground. It was an exercise in meditation and in holding my words and trying not to over-verbalize. I really needed to be centered for those different visitors. At the end of all these visits I went to our cottage, which is what we've been doing for 19 years, and nobody wanted to come with me. I went anyway to relax, as that's my happy place. There's no TV, there's no Internet, there's no boats. It's on a very quiet river. I could be naked and I could dance and I could be my wild thing, just being out in nature. That's what replenishes my soul. That's my 5-star hotel!

I actually love being there on my own to get back to a sense of who I am. I journal and I write poetry and I sleep when I want to. It is absolutely fantastic. My husband did visit, which was very nice. He followed my rhythm versus me accommodating and following his, which was something new.

Then, before I was to come home, I received an email saying that a young man, one of my son's friends, was going to be visiting. I didn't know anything about this and I found out that my husband had forgotten to tell me because he didn't think it would pan out. I felt outraged. It was like "the straw that broke the camel's back." I wanted some consideration for me and some understanding of how I would feel with more guests in the house, because I had had it by the end of the summer. We were already going to have another young man staying with us and with our smaller house, there would be nowhere for me to go or escape if I needed my own space.

So what outraged me was my husband's lack of consideration of my needs, but I didn't know how to communicate that. I was just so hurt because my boundary was crossed. But then I realized I was coming at this from the point of the Victim, the shadow side of the Warrioress. I assumed I had no choices and that I was being forced to go back home and cook and clean for all these people. I thought I was being victimized and that no one was thinking about me.

So I made a choice for the first time in my 21 years of marriage. I called up my husband and I said, "I just want you to know I am coming home on Thursday as planned. Friday, I've booked myself in a bed and breakfast in Ojai and I will stay there until the 3 boys leave. Then I will be coming home. Then we'll commence our drive to British Columbia to drop them off at university."

This felt truly amazing. I went to Ojai and I had a facial and I had a massage and I had a pedicure. I ate organic prepared meals and brought them up to my bed and I ate in bed. Then I read a book on co-dependency. I had an AHA! I thought, "Oh, my God. I have been living all these years as if I had no choice. But YES I DO!" I realized how co-dependent I've been and it's like being an addict. Instead of feeling forced into coming home and caretaking and feeling angry that no one was looking after my needs, I realized it was up to me to make the choice. I had a light bulb go on.

Wow, great story! Let's go through the Goddesses and see how you utilized their gifts to help you get out of the Victim and realize you had choice. The most important piece is that called up the Wise Woman inside of you in order to make a different choice. From the Warrioress, you realized you'd been on the shadow path and had succumbed to being the Victim. From the Queen, you saw your journey on the shadow path of self-sacrifice and how you have been a co-dependent - giving with strings attached and depleting your own inner resources.

From the Visionary you intuited that going home would be very chaotic, which describes the shadow path of chaos. Then from your Manifestor you realized you could make something else happen, like manifesting a spa and pampering yourself for a few days until all the people left your house. When you recognized your power of choice and called in your Wise Woman, you could get off every one of those shadow paths at once. This is the power of the Wise Woman.

I could actually make a choice.

Yes. Remember in the Majah Story we read about the women who are downtrodden in the Shadowlands with the "Demonesses" feeding off their energy? When we just keep walking down that shadow path, feeling victimized and depleted, we feel we don't have any choice.

Let me tell you the next part of my story as we drove to British Columbia on the family road trip to drop off our kids at University. Our boys started to say how they didn't want us to expect much communication because they would be studying etc. I told them clearly that they wouldn't need to worry about my expectations because as far as I am concerned, no news is good news. I know in my own heart the amount of work I have put into raising my boys. Plus I am ready to let them fly. I am watching their back, but I am not going to be the hovering kind of mother.

Then I said, "There's something that happens when you go away to university - you have accountability and responsibility. Now that you are adults, you can be accountable and responsible for checking in to ask us as people, 'How are you doing?'" I said it's an accountability of adulthood, where the relationship becomes more reciprocal.

Something powerful happened when I realized I had choices. It's like I gave birth to myself and to my personal power. I spent my whole life mothering and giving my heart, my emotions, and hours of love and care, and somewhere the boundaries got muddled up. I don't know what happened. Now I know I have choice, it's really changed everything.

Right, exactly. This is exactly what happens when you live with your Wise Woman in the center of your life. You can choose healthy boundaries from the Warrioress and openheartedness from your Queen. With the Visionary, it's your time to envision and birth your own life and with your Manifestor you can create exactly what you want and need for you. It sounds like you're good at the envisioning. Now you can spend time figuring out how you're going to manifest who you are in the world. It's your time now.

Yes, it's my time now. I knew that when I had a taste of that Wise Woman, I wanted more of her because it cuts out the drama.

Absolutely. There doesn't have to be any drama because you just allow people to be where they are and who they are and then you take care of your needs. You respect other's boundaries and let them be.

Yes, I noticed how I respected my son's boundaries when we dropped him off at college. I got him what he needed and specifically asked for, no more and no less. At first I wanted to overbuy and over-shop, and then realized I need to have clear boundaries. Without the drama and with clear, respectful boundaries it was a much easier parting with them. I felt a deep sense of confidence and trust that all will be well.

Then on the trip back I had a very honest conversation with my husband. I guess this is also where the Wise Woman came and pulled in all the different Goddess tools. Basically, what I said to him is, "We've been married 21 years. I love you very much. If you want to have a relationship with me, as I want to have a relationship with you, you've got some work you need to do. I'm doing my work. I'll own my 50%. I'm doing my work and I'm trying my best in my best awareness. You're an amazing provider. That's not what I'm looking for now. I'm looking for a relationship of love and compassion and kindness. I will not accept any less. I cannot any longer, out of self-respect, play the games that you and I have been engaging with in our relationship. I cited examples of "not niceness". It's not nice when you're in a conversation and there's a conflict and the other person stands up and says, "I'm not dealing with this now," and leaves. That's not nice. This is one example of what I said.

This is a great example of what happens when you stand in your Wise Woman because then you can access the tools of the Warrioress, the Queen, the Visionary, and the Manifestor all the time. When you stand in your center and you show up as a person who has boundaries, definite needs, an open and compassionate heart, clear mind, and a strong, conscious will, then you ask those around you to also show up with integrity.

Right. What I learned from the Feminine Path of Power is to be conscious and to pay attention.

Thank you so much for sharing this wonderful story of success with your inner Wise Woman. Congratulations!

Conclusion

These interviews show the practical application of internalizing the Wise Woman on *The Feminine Path of Power.* You've seen how these women are consciously utilizing the Wise Woman Archetype and how it is positively affecting their lives and the lives of their children and loved ones.

In the next chapter we meet a new Divine Feminine character named Chiman (pronounced *Chee-mon*). She will take us through the Warrioress Initiation and show us how to walk the sacred Path of Strength.

Chapter 6
The Warrioress: Find your Core Strength

The Story of Chiman, the Warrioress

In this second initiation story, you will journey now with Chiman (pronounced *Chee-mon*) as she trains to be a powerful Warrioress, mastering the Path of Strength and becoming an Earth Clan Woman, powerful in body, focused and strong. You will follow her wilderness adventure as Chiman battles the shadow path of fear, breaks the spell of the Victim, and returns women to the Path of Strength - back to their own potency and power.

Part 1: The Story of Chiman

Once upon a time, a long, long time ago, there was a land where women were honored for their power and strength. It was a sacred land called the Village of Women where each girl child was honored for the unique gifts she brought to the sacred circle. And when each new female soul was still in the womb of her mother she would whisper her name and her soul's purpose to the elders who were eager to hear this good news.

Now in this ancient land there were 4 different clans of women that all female souls were sorted into at birth. There was the Warrioress Clan, those who walk the Way of Strength. And the Queen Clan, those who walk the Way of Compassion. And the Visionary Clan, those who walk the Way of Change. And finally the Manifestor Clan, those who walk the Way of Action.

Now one special day, the elders gathered to hear the good news from a female soul who was about to be born into the Village of Women. As they stood around the pregnant mother who was full of life, the elders asked the unborn soul who she was, what clan she belonged to, and what her soul's purpose was. And this is what she said. "Chiman is my name. I come to the Warrioress Clan. My purpose is to guide lost women back to the Path of Strength." Soon the excitement spread among the Village and especially among the Warrioress Clan who eagerly anticipated the birth of Chiman and the knowledge she would bring to the entire clan.

And so Chiman was born and was cared for and nurtured in the old ways as was the custom in the Village of Women. For all girl children were held and loved and valued and given chores and kept in line and watched over by those who were assigned as their special guardians. And as the years went by and Chiman grew into a young woman, the elders felt that the time had come to initiate her so that she could fulfill her purpose.

And so the elders took Chiman to the Warrioress Initiation ground, away to the far, wild country where the granite mountains stand strong and the red earth smells rich and ripe with life. And as they journeyed further and further and the mountain terrain grew wilder and wilder, Chiman felt deeply at home and felt an inner strength she had never experienced before.

And when they came upon the Warrioress training ground, Chiman saw the sacred encampment; a powerful stone fortress nestled among the granite cliffs and rocks. And standing guard around the walls of the fortress were the Warrioresses, beautiful and strong, who stood with focused attention, holding colorful shields with amazing symbols and holding tall staffs rooted into the earth. And at the entrance to the stone fortress was a huge gateway with the banner of the Warrioress Clan stretched proudly across the top, saying "Earth Clan Women, Powerful in Body, Focused and Strong." And as Chiman crossed the threshold, she felt deep pride in her strong body and was eager to begin her initiation to strengthen and fortify her powers.

The elders in charge of her initiation greeted Chiman, welcomed her to the sacred training ground and invited her to sit around the stone seats that formed a circle in the center of the fortress courtyard. As Chiman gazed around, she saw training weapons of every size, shape, and description. There were shields and swords and ropes and balls made of unknown material. She saw arrows, crossbows, blindfolds, helmets, strange protective clothing, hand-made tools, and other objects she had never seen before and could not imagine how they were used. A jolt of fear and panic surged through her belly but she did not show this as the elders gathered around.

And so Chiman spent her first days learning of the Warrioress powers and the purpose of the Clan. And at night a fire was lit inside the stone circle and the drummers drummed while the storyteller stood in the center, firelight flickering on her robes of dark brown feathers, mud spread on her broad face and graying hair. And the storyteller recited the good, brave and true acts of courage that the Warrioresses had accomplished over the centuries. And here is what the storyteller said….

"Over the years we have walked the Way of Strength. So connected are we to Sacred Earth, we can call upon Her powers and become grounded like a granite mountain, solid, tough, and immovable. We can hold our position when others are in fear and stand firm amidst the storms. Over the years we have become skilled in hunt, battle, confrontation, and strategy of all kinds. And because of our great skill in creating sturdy and protective boundaries, we are always called upon when someone is being attacked in body, in heart, or in spirit.

Yes, the Warrioresses are the great protectors of the people and the land. We are known for being fearless, courageous, bold, and adventurous. Of all our weapons, it is the Sacred Shield that is our greatest tool – for when we have conquered the shield and made it our own, carved our own symbol into it, our shield can banish all fear, our shield can stop harmful attacks, our shield can create any boundary, our shield can provide worthy defense."

And late that night around this very fire Chiman was told a chilling story about the Shadow Path of the Warrioress clan. Yes, it was true, there were some women who had wandered off their path of power and onto a disempowered path that robbed them of their strength and their dignity. This was called the Shadow Path of Fear.

And Chiman heard disturbing tales of women who walked the Shadow Path of Fear – women who are fearful to be themselves, fearful to stand their ground, fearful to speak their truth, fearful to draw limits to protect themselves. And even worse than this, these women are vulnerable to the negative energies that stalk women on the Path of Fear and tempt them to become Victims by blaming others and staying small. And when Chiman heard these stories, something deep within her stirred into outrage for she knew this was exactly what she had come to do, to redeem the Shadow Path of Fear and Victimhood and restore women back onto the Path of Strength.

And when the elders saw the outrage of her energy and the knowledge of her destiny burst forth, they smiled and nodded around the circle for they knew the time of her Initiation had come.

Chiman Part 2: The Wilderness Training Ground

A few mornings later when the sun rose bright yellow in the sky, the elders blindfolded Chiman, put her on the back of a horse and then rode with her deep into the mountain wilderness. Many days later they arrived at the initiation ground and when Chiman's blindfold was removed she found herself in a small valley between two tall mountains. A stream trickled nearby and there were green, leafy trees and wild plants sprouting lush from the rich red earth. The elders spread out into the surrounding territory and seemed to be conversing with the stones, rocks, earth, plants, trees, and animals that lived in this sacred training ground. When they were finished the elders mounted their horses and said, "We leave you now. We will return in 3 moon cycles. The earth, animals, stones, and trees will teach you what you need to know."

And so Chiman was left in this wilderness place by herself, with nothing but her own apprehension and foreboding. During the long weeks of the first moon cycle, Chiman felt scared, lonely, and hungry. She felt cold, wet, and thirsty. She was used to being fed, being warm, and being comfortable. One day it just got too much and in a fit of self-pity, she cried aloud to the surrounding bushes and trees, hoping someone would do something. She longed for someone to rescue her and bring her some comfort. Her cries and moans were suddenly replaced by a loud rustling nearby and to her shock and horror, a large mountain lion stepped into the clearing where Chiman stood, rooted to the spot, and no longer breathing.

The wild cat spoke to her saying, "I hear your cries of self-pity. No one is going to save you but yourself! Let go of the cravings of your body. Do not cry I'm hungry! I'm thirsty! I want a warm blanket! With too many comforts, your body goes to sleep and your senses grow dull. Stop whining like a victim. Rely on your inner strength, use your instincts, awaken all your senses, or die in this wilderness. It is your choice my daughter." And so the wild cat taught Chiman how to stop whining and how to let go of the cravings of her body. The wild cat taught Chiman how to fashion tools, build shelters, and survive in the wilderness land. And her body became strong, instinctive, and alive like the mighty mountain lion.

And it was during the second moon cycle that Chiman learned her second great lesson in the Wilderness. Yes, during the second moon cycle, after mountain lion had returned to the wild places, the stress of being alone with her own thoughts and feelings became too much for Chiman to bear. With no one to talk to and no one to guide her, frustration, confusion, and all manner of feelings exploded within her like a volcano. And energy poured out of her every cell like red-hot lava and she could see she was losing her vital energy as it drained out of her like water through a sieve. And she panicked and ran around, stomping her feet and feeling like a demented, crazy woman because she did not know how to stop this leaking of vital energy from her body. And the soft brown earth beneath her stomping feet rumbled and grumbled and then cracked wide open like a gaping mouth in the ground, swallowing Chiman and burying her up to her neck.

And the earth spoke to Chiman and said, "Do not allow your feelings to sway you off your path of power. Stop and ground yourself. Feel how the earth holds you and contains you and absorbs your negative and fearful energy. You are a Warrioress! You will be called upon to be grounded and solid during times of great instability, when the storms of life are knocking people over like loose stones on a mountainside." And the earth would not let her go until Chiman learned how to ground herself and how to contain feelings that threatened to overwhelm her. And the earth would not let her go until she learned how to stop energy leaking out of her body.

And it was during the third moon cycle that Chiman learned her third great lesson in the Wilderness. Yes, during the third moon cycle, as Chiman sat on the mighty granite rocks during her daily meditations, the stones began to speak to her, saying, "Now it is time for you to meet your Stone Being that lies hidden within the depths." "What is my Stone Being?" Chiman questioned, "And how do I find it if it lies hidden in the depths?"

"We will show you", said the stones. "Pick up the stone sisters you see around you and place them in a circle that you can sit inside. Then find a small stone sister you can hold in your hands." So Chiman prepared her stone circle and sat within it, holding a small stone in the palm of her hand. And the stones said to her, "Now close your eyes and focus on the stone you hold. Feel its sturdiness, feel its weight. Feel its unyielding core. Feel how this stone is like your own inner strength, your own solid inner core."

And as Chiman sat, trying to feel her inner core, she felt herself slowly sinking into the ground as if being lowered into a cave. And the stones descended with her, holding the sacred circle intact around her. And the stones said, "As you focus on your inner core, WHO ARE YOU? WHO ARE YOU?" And Chiman thought for a moment and responded, "I am a woman." "Yes." said the stones. "Yes. This is true, but this is not your core self".

Then Chiman felt herself descending again into a lower chamber. And the stones asked once again, "As you focus on your inner core, WHO ARE YOU? WHO ARE YOU REALLY?" And Chiman responded, "I am a good friend, a hard worker, and a lover of nature." "Yes. But this is not your core self", said the stones. And she felt herself descending again. And again the stones echoed the questions, "As you focus on your inner core, WHO ARE YOU? WHO ARE YOU REALLY AT THE CORE OF YOUR BEING?" "I am a Warrioress, bold, courageous, and strong. I serve the community." "Yes. But this is not your core self", said the stones. And once again she felt herself descend into a lower chamber and the stones asked, "WHO ARE YOU? WHO ARE YOU?"

And in utter frustration Chiman shouted out everything everyone had always wanted her to be, every role she played, every expectation she tried to fulfill for her parents, friends, elders, teachers, and mentors………. "Yes" said the stones, "You are all of these things yet none of these things. You are so much more at the core of your being. Are you ready to descend one final time and meet your Stone Being? Are you ready to discover who you are at the core of your being when everything is stripped away?" "Yes", said Chiman, although she was a bit concerned that at her core there might be nothing, just emptiness. And so they descended to the core chamber and Chiman wondered who she would meet, what her Stone Being would be like.

But as they descended into the final chamber deep within the depths, something very strange happened….. the stone she was holding became very hot in her hands and she wanted to throw it aside, but the stones implored her saying, "NO! Do not let go! Call to your Stone Being to reveal itself!" And when she called for her Stone Being to show itself, the stone suddenly exploded into a shower of blinding light. And when the sparks faded away and she could see once again, Chiman found herself back above ground standing in her stone circle, facing her Stone Being who was a magnificent, dark horse with wild hair and green and gold markings on her body.

And the wild, dark horse spoke to her saying, "You have finally called me forth from the depths of your being. Carve my figure into your shield as I teach you about my magic." And for the rest of the third moon cycle, Chiman carved the figure of the wild, dark horse into her Warrioress shield, decorated with beautiful green and gold markings. And Dark Horse taught her the secret magic Chiman held at the core of her being – the strength, the power, and the stamina she could call upon whenever she needed her Warrioress powers.

And so it was that after the 3 moon cycles had passed Chiman had survived the wilderness, awakened her instincts, learned to ground herself like a granite mountain, and called forth Dark Horse, the inner strength and secret magic she held at the core of her being.

Chiman Part 3: Mastering the Shield

And so it was that at the end of the three moon cycles, the elders returned for Chiman and were pleased to see her Warrioress shield carved with the symbol of Dark Horse. And the elders said, "Each Warrioress calls forth her own magic. You will now be called Chiman Dark Horse and we honor the magic you bring to the Clan. You have faired well my daughter. Now it is time to master the powers of your shield. So as we journey into the ancient forest, bring your shield and all the powers you have awakened in the wilderness." So Chiman held her Dark Horse shield proudly as they walked deep into the ancient forest. For many miles they walked together in silence until they came to a small clearing in the woods. And it was here that the elders left Chiman standing alone waiting with her shield, and this left her somewhat bewildered and somewhat nervous, for she did not know what challenge lay ahead.

After some time standing alone in the forest, 3 elders suddenly appeared in the clearing, wearing full body coverings, and holding strange round balls that seemed to be made of some kind of liquid. Swiftly and without warning, one of the elders threw a liquid ball straight at Chiman. As it flew towards her, it made a sharp, screeching sound, like a terrible scream muted through water.

With reflexes born of her sharpened instincts, Chiman threw up her shield and repelled the strange liquid ball. As it splattered onto a neighboring tree, the tree burst into flame as the poisonous and deadly liquid of the watery ball touched its surface. Terror coursed through her veins as Chiman realized she would die if any of the liquid touched her in any way. She would have to shield herself entirely, deflecting the water weapons with agility and skill.

So when another liquid ball was thrown at her, she deflected it again with her shield, but his time she heard something more than a scream. She heard a vicious, cruel voice, "Who do you think you are? You are nothing." And when another liquid ball was thrown she heard, "I will destroy you. You are weak, stupid, and pathetic." One after the other, the elders hurled the strange balls - and faster and faster they flew at her with an awful force. Chiman realized that if she listened to the insults and allowed the poisonous words to get under her skin, she would falter in her self-defense.

So when the next water weapon was thrown she heard, "You'll never get what you want. You are doomed to failure." And Chiman hesitated for a fraction of a second because she secretly harbored the fear that she would never get what she wanted and perhaps was doomed to failure! And in that fraction of a second when she considered the possibility that this was the truth about her, she lost her focus. And the water weapon almost hit her in the chest but she threw up her shield and blocked the attack at the last moment before contact. And Chiman realized the water weapons could easily destroy her unless she mastered the powers of her shield. And so after several more attacks, Chiman shielded herself, refusing to listen and refusing to take this poison into her body.

And after a few days of this training, Chiman was mastering the art of water weaponry so adeptly that she could name the poisonous attack as the balls flew toward her. And when she could name the poison and speak it out loud - ENVY! or HATRED! or RESENTMENT! The ball would explode before it ever reached her shield. And soon the elders were satisfied that Chiman had become a master at deflecting the insults, emotional attacks, and poison arrows that so often penetrate deep into the emotional body and lodge there for years and years and years. Now she was truly a master of her shield.

Chiman Part 4: Conquering Fear in the Cage of Bones

And after Chiman mastered her shield and trained in the art of water weaponry, the elders took Chiman out of the ancient forest and brought her to the dreaded place where each Warrioress must face her worst fears, the dreaded place called The Cage of Bones. Now the Cage of Bones was frightening because it had no door, no gate, no entry, no exit, and therefore, no escape. And everyone knew it was a cage made of the bones of those who had died of fright and were not strong enough to face their fears.

And so when the elders told Chiman to close her eyes and ready herself for the Cage of Bones, she felt the urge to run as fast and as far as her strong legs would carry her. But instead she remembered to stop and ground herself and when she opened her eyes, she found herself inside the eerie, ghostly Cage of Bones, where bone upon bone was fixed together with yellowing sinew and it smelled of rotting flesh and the sweat of naked fear.

As time passed in the Cage of Bones, Chiman felt her courage falter because each bone came alive and taunted her with a fear she harbored deep within her soul. And with all the bones talking fear talk, she felt trapped by them, trapped in this cage where there was no escape. One bone became her fear of not being good enough, another bone, the fear of not knowing enough. Another bone became her fear to fully speak her truth, another, her fear of losing herself to what others want. Another bone became her fear of being abandoned and cast aside, another bone her fear of being rejected. And soon she felt afraid to fight back, afraid to be right, afraid to be wrong, afraid to be powerful, afraid to be weak, afraid to be seen, afraid to trust herself. And after a few days of living in the Cage of Bones she felt afraid to move or breathe.

And when the elders decided she had had enough, they stood around the Cage of Bones shouting, "These putrid bones have become your cage of limitations! Why do you listen to the bones talking fear talk? Do you believe these lies? When a woman succumbs to her deepest fears, she becomes weak and loses her powers. Chiman, do you wish to be liberated from your Cage of Bones?" "YES!" Chiman cried back to the elders. "Then face your fears! Call out what entraps you and be free!"

And Chiman called out all the fears that entrapped her, all the fears that bound her in her own deathly Cage of Bones. "I fear I am not good enough, I fear losing myself, I fear being abandoned, I fear not being able to cope, I fear being swallowed by everyone's demands, I fear standing up for myself." And as she named her fears aloud, they lost some of their deathly grip.

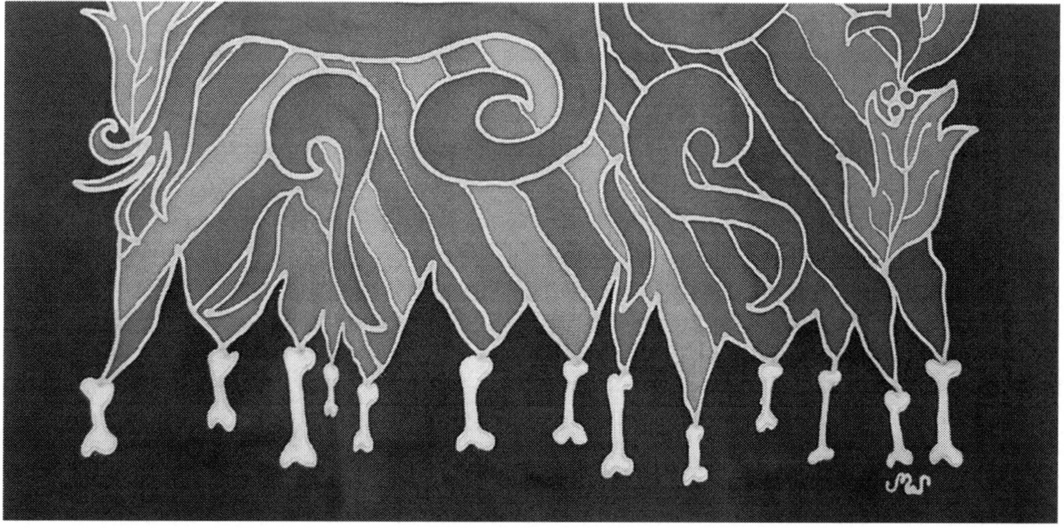

The elders continued, "Do not succumb to fear. Do not listen to the lies of the bones. Fight back. Rise above your limitations, your strength will lift you from the bonds that confine you! We ask you again, do you wish to be liberated from your Cage of Bones?" "YES!" Chiman said with the determination of a true Warrioress. "Then draw deep into your core self. Find your inner strength. Find the courage of your own convictions. Find your truth and conquer your fear!"

And so Chiman concentrated deep within until she felt the solid core of her own self rise into her throat as she yelled, "I will not listen to these lies. I am good enough. I know enough. I can speak my truth. I am powerful. I trust myself. I will not lose myself to what to others want me to be. I will not be cast aside. I will not bow to fear!" And then Chiman chanted the ancient words of power from the Warrioress Clan, "I am focused, skillful, and strong! I am focused, skillful, and strong! I am focused, skillful, and strong!"

Chiman was filled with the courage and bravery of all the great Warrioresses who had walked this path before her. And as she chanted the words of power, the Cage of Bones began to dissolve around her and the dread lifted as each bone disintegrated and crumbled to the ground into a pile of fine, white powder. And as the elders gathered around her, Chiman sank to her knees and collapsed in exhaustion. And the elders carried her back to the Warrioress encampment and brought her to the healing tent for a period of recovery and rest.

Chiman Part 5: The Sacred Boundary Around the Soul

And so it was that after Chiman survived the Cage of Bones, she was taken back to the Warrioress encampment and brought to the healing tent. And as she slept, the Healer placed a small golden crystal inside her body to restore her energy and bring happiness back into her bones. And a few days later when Chiman awoke, the elders gathered round and were pleased to see the golden glow around her body and the flicker of new wisdom in her eyes. She was ready now to learn the greatest secret of the Warrioress Clan – how to activate the sacred boundary around the soul.

So the elders brought her to a special, darkened room inside the fortress that enabled Chiman to see the golden light emanating from her body. She was amazed to see how this gold light radiated from somewhere deep inside and shone out in all directions, creating a beautiful shimmering golden sphere surrounding her entire being. And when she walked, she could see a bright gold line that followed her and a luminescent gold line that stretched out before her, like a path of light leading the way. "This line is your soul path", said the elder. "You can see where you have been and you can see where you are going - only a few steps ahead of you to point you in the right direction. The deeper you commit to your soul's path of power, the farther out the gold line stretches before you."

And Chiman wondered, "Does everyone have a gold line that stretches out before them and lights their way? Does everyone have a soul path?" "Yes, my daughter. But you are only responsible for your own path. You must never interfere with another person's path or lessons. Women have a peculiar desire to want to help other people on their path, to walk the soul path of another. But I am here to tell you my daughter, that if you try to walk on another person's gold line by taking on their emotional burdens, solving their problems, doing their soul work, carrying their baggage or holding their pain for them - as soon as you tread on their gold line, it will trigger an alarm inside your golden crystal. This alarm warns you that you are violating the sacred boundary around another's soul. If you choose to bypass this warning, a toxin is released in your body and you will become violently ill."

Chiman was horrified. "But why? Why does this happen?" "This is to protect each person's sacred boundary", said the elder. "Sometimes women have a crazy moment or a crazy week or a crazy decade when they bypass reason and take on the life lessons of another soul. But we cannot! Each soul has its own unique path and unique lessons to learn. We cannot interfere with another's gold lifeline or we lose our powers and are poisoned by the toxins released into our bodies. So as a Warrioress, you must discipline yourself to walk only on your own gold line. You may walk alongside your friend, sister, brother, mother, father, or child - but never, never step foot on their path of power. That is theirs and theirs alone."

Chiman took this in and pondered it in her heart. Soon she asked another question. "What then, is the golden sphere of light surrounding my body?" And the elder said, "The sphere of golden light is the sacred boundary that exists around your soul. Most women cannot see it as you do now. It is your birthright. You have always had it to protect you but now you will learn to activate it consciously and with power so that it becomes a protective force field around your body, protecting you and all you serve.

Focus now on the true center of your body and radiate your golden light out from this central place. This is a safety zone around your body. You must activate it by centering yourself directly within it and being aware that wherever you go, you are always the center of this circle." So Chiman closed her eyes and imagined herself as the center of the circle and she imagined that wherever she walked, she was still the center of this circle and it made her feel powerful and protected and confident. And as she concentrated with all her might, the golden sphere of light around her blazed brightly and the elder smiled with satisfaction.

"Ah yes, the circle of light is strong with you! You also need to know my daughter that you are in control of whom you allow into this circle and whom you decline. If someone approaches you with harmful intent, you have the right to say "NO!" If someone tries to violate your sacred circle, you have the right to say,

"STOP, this does not feel good to me" or "STOP, this is destructive to me". And if someone approaches you with honorable intent, you can invite them into your circle. Use your powers of discernment. But I must warn you my daughter, sometimes the people you are closest to, forget to respect your sacred boundary."

"And another thing my daughter, it is your duty as a Warrioress to have strong and impeccable boundaries and to protect the basic rights of the human soul" "What are the basic rights of the human soul that I must protect?" asked Chiman. And the wise elder said, "Each human soul has the right to be seen, the right to be valued, the right to be loved and respected. You have a right to mutual exchange in your relationships, where needs are met back and forth, reciprocated and shared. You have the right to negotiate for what you want and negotiate for what you think is fair and just. And when these boundaries are dishonored, the true Warrioress fights with all her skill to protect these boundaries around the soul. The Warrioress does not succumb to the pleas of others trying to move and manipulate the boundary. NO! The Warrioress holds steadfast to the boundary with commitment, conviction, passion, and strength."

And so for the remainder of her initiation training, Chiman accomplished her goal and activated the sacred boundary around her soul. She defended the basic rights of her brothers and sisters. She increased her powers of discernment and walked only on her own path of power. And when others were in fear and lost their focus, Chiman stood firm like the granite mountain. And the elders had never before seen a Warrioress with such strength, such courage, such discipline, such focused power, and such bold fearlessness.

It was no surprise then the day Chiman told her training elders that she was ready to fulfill her soul's purpose and redeem the Shadow Path of Fear and restore women back onto the Path of Strength, the great Path of the Warrioress. So Chiman journeyed to the Shadowland of Fear to help women who had wandered off their path of power. And she met women who had become victims, women who had died of fright in the Cage of Bones, women who had not yet found the Stone Being medicine at the core of their being, women who still lived in fear and did not know the magnificent strength they possessed. And through her great fortitude and Dark Horse magic, Chiman was able to guide women from their disempowered ways back to their path of power, the Path of Strength.

And over the years Chiman became the greatest Master the Warrioress Clan had ever known, for each day of her life she walked the Path of Strength with dignity and honor. And because of this, she was beloved in the community. And stories were written and ballads sung in her honor for her amazing accomplishments: surviving the wilderness, mastering her shield, conquering her fear, protecting the sacred boundaries, and embodying the quintessential powers of the Warrioress.

Walking the Path of Strength

WARRIORESS CLAN OVERVIEW

Archetype: **The Warrioress**
Path: **The Path of Strength**
Essence: **Powerful in Body**
Element: **Earth**
Tool: **Shield**
Qualities: **Healthy boundaries, strong, grounded presence, fearless, defends and protects, skillful in confrontation**
Affirmation: "**I am focused, skillful, and strong.**"
Motto: **"Earth Clan Women, powerful in body, focused and strong."**
Empowerment: **comes through strong boundaries**
Shadow Archetype: **Victim**
Shadow Path: **Path of Fear**

In this story we are introduced to Chiman, our Warrioress Divine Feminine guide. The path she walks in life is the Path of Strength and her tool is the sacred Shield. During the course of her initiation, she learns to face her fears and become the strong, bold, and courageous Warrioress she was always meant to be. What does her story mean for you? How can you follow her lead and become a strong, courageous Warrioress yourself?

As an emerging Warrioress, you need to find your relationship with the Earth Clan. This might mean becoming more embodied and feeling more present in your body. It may mean coming into better relationship with the Earth itself, enjoying nature and the material, sensual world. It might be helpful to go camping or go on a Vision Quest out in nature. Connecting with the Earth element - however you do this - will bring you into a deeper relationship with your Warrioress.

When Chiman begins her initiation, she is taken to the Warrioress Training ground, to the far, wild country where the granite mountains stand tall and strong and the earth is rich and ripe with all kinds of life. In the Warrioress encampment she sees various Warrioresses standing guard with their colorful shields and she sees training weapons, arrows, crossbows, helmets, and other mysterious Warrioress paraphernalia. In the initiation training ground she learns about the Earth Clan Women and how they are powerful in body, focused, and strong.

Chiman learns that Warrioresses know how to call upon the element Earth to be strong like a mountain when they need to hold firm when others are in fear. She learns they are skilled in battle, confrontation, and strategy. Warrioresses are also master boundary makers and can protect themselves and others when under attack. Chiman learns that Warrioresses are fearless, brave, bold, and adventurous and their Shield can banish all fear and provide worthy defense.

She is also told some chilling tales about the shadow path of fear, a disempowered path that some Warrioresses have wandered onto. These are women who have aligned their energy with the Victim and have contracted into a very small version of themselves. This motivates her to start her initiation so she can call women from the path of fear and back onto the Path of Strength.

At the beginning of her initiation, Chiman is blindfolded and taken way out into the heart of the wilderness, where the elders converse with the rocks, plants, and animals and then promptly leave her to fend for herself. Yikes! What would this be like for you? Have you ever been backpacking far from civilization? Have you ever done a Vision Quest where you are out there on your own for days at a time? What's it like for you when all your comforts are taken away?

Maybe you are like Chiman and start to panic and whine. I know I have been in situations where I have been without normal comforts for weeks and months on end. I love a good adventure, but there have been times when my ego kind of falls apart and I feel like a little kid wanting this or that comfort. My Warrioress gets wimpy and I regress into self-pity.

I do remember one successful Warrioress wilderness adventure when I was 16 years old. This was my very first encounter with my own inner Warrioress. I went on a backpacking trip with other teens from my High School and at the end of the 2-week trip each of us did a "solo" for 3 days and nights, in the wilderness of the Sierra Nevada Mountains in California. Our leaders dropped each of us off at various locations with no food or water. We had a sleeping bag and a journal. We were completely on our own to find water and a place to sleep. I vividly remember looking up at the stars at night, feeling totally alone and yet vibrantly alive and joyful. I didn't wimp out or cry or regress. On the contrary, my Warrioress came alive and I felt the power of my instincts to survive. My Warrioress helped me cope and thrive in the wilderness. I will never forget this successful experience, for it forged a powerfully positive relationship with my Warrioress.

A Vision Quest type of experience is actually an important test for a Warrioress, for it calls forth the "Mountain Lion" within us who calls us to be stronger than we thought possible. In the story, Mountain Lion forces her to be a worthy Warrioress by telling her to stop whining and playing the victim and to awaken her instincts, which have gone to sleep. How can you be a good Warrioress if your instincts are asleep, numb, and dulled? So when you let go of your ego attachments to comfort, luxury, security, and your desire to be rescued, you may find you have tremendous inner resources you never knew you had!

Chiman's next initiation test comes after Mountain Lion leaves and she is completely alone with her thoughts and feelings. She is stressed out being alone without guidance or company and she explodes with frustration and confusion and all kinds of crazy feelings. She began to lose her vital energy, which looks like lava pouring out of her and she panics even more. Thank goodness the earth swallows her so she is buried in a pit of dirt up to her neck. Finally she is contained and the earth gives her instructions on how to contain her vital energy and explains why this is important for a Warrioress.

As a Warrioress it is imperative that you contain your vital energy. This means being aware of how and when you are losing vital energy and when your inner container is leaking. You lose vital energy when you play the Victim and when you allow your feelings of fear and negativity to push you off your Path of Power. One way to strengthen your container is to go on silent retreat or keep your thoughts and feelings to yourself without sharing or scattering your energy. As a Warrioress, you must be able to rely on your own inner resources, take your own advice and make your own decisions. You must find the core place inside to be grounded, solid, firm, resolved, and defined. The earth is a powerful element to hold and contain you on the Path of Strength.

The next stage in Chiman's Warrioress initiation is when the stones talk to her and encourage her to find her Stone Being or animal ally. This represents your core inner self, a place you must find and be able to access immediately. It requires you to search your soul and ask the key question, "Who am I? Who am I at the core of my being?" At first you may answer with more surface answers like, "I am a woman, a wife, a girlfriend, and a daughter. Or I am a lawyer, a teacher, a secretary, or an adventurer. Or I am a nice person, a nature lover, a vegan, a slob, or a dentist." When you keep stripping away all the different identities you think you are or what you think people want you to be – you begin to get closer to your core self.

When Chiman drops deep into the chamber way under the earth, she finds her Stone Being and comes into contact with her core self. The stone represents the solid, stable, core presence of your inner Warrioress. Chiman's Stone Being was wild Dark Horse, who possessed a kind of deep magic that he taught Chiman over the course of that third moon cycle. This magic had to do with Chiman's core strength, power, and stamina that she possessed deep inside and that she would need to call upon throughout her life.

You too can seek a symbol for your core self. This will help you connect in a very tangible way to your core essence. It will help you call upon your animal strength when you need to stand your ground or speak up against injustices. This is the core magic you possess deep inside yourself and is worth seeking and owning. Do you think of yourself as possessing deep magic? If not, I encourage you to try on this possibility! If so, you can access your deep magic and your core power when you identify a symbol or an animal that could represent this magic. Then allow that symbol or animal to teach you something about the gift it is bringing to you. What kind of strength is it giving you? What is the purpose of this symbol relative to your Warrioress? How does it help you walk the Path of Strength? Play with your magic!

The next part of Chiman's initiation is mastering the powers of her Shield. She is led into an ancient forest and left alone once again in a small clearing. She is slightly apprehensive because she has no idea what is coming. What is coming is certainly unusual, as the 3 elders appear suddenly in strange protective clothing and hurl water balls at her at top speed. When she holds up her Shield to instinctively protect herself, the water ball explodes on a nearby tree in toxic flames. What could possibly be so toxic?

Chiman soon realizes that these toxic water balls are filled with vicious and cruel voices, voices that may sound familiar to you such as, "Who do you think you are? You are nothing. I will destroy you. You are weak, stupid, and pathetic. You'll never get what you want. You are doomed to failure." These voices, whether they come from within or without, can be intensely toxic if we allow them into our system. They are poisonous to our body, poisonous to our psyche, and poisonous to our spirit. We must have a Warrioress Shield to protect ourselves and deflect these attacks when they fly.

In her initiation, Chiman realizes that if she pays even the slightest attention to the water ball voices, she loses her focus and risks letting this toxin under her skin. It takes the incredible strength of our Warrioress to NOT PAY ATTENTION to these voices. There is an art to not listen, not pay attention, not give the time of day, refuse to look, and refuse to take it in. At one point Chiman hesitates and considers that "She'll never get what she wants and she is doomed to failure." When she gives this cruel, toxic voice a teeny, tiny listen and considers for a millisecond that this might be true, she falters with her Shield. She almost dies!

Imagine you are holding your Shield and someone hurls an insult at you. What can you do as the Warrioress? Imagine you are giving a presentation and your inner critic starts attacking you. As the Warrioress, how do you use your Shield to protect yourself? Imagine being at a party and someone sneers or talks behind your back. How can you shield yourself from this toxicity? You can practice mastering your Shield by presenting yourself with a few scenarios where water balls may be thrown at you. Then take a physical stance, see yourself holding up your Shield. Deflect the insults, the judgment, and the criticism. If you have an actual physical Shield it is even more powerful because then you can hold it and move it around. You can tangibly feel what it is like to protect yourself from oncoming water balls!

When you have mastered your Shield, you can remain strong, shielded, and protected - not defended or rigid. You can handle toxic insults and destructive emotional attacks that fly towards you at incredible speed. If you feel attacked in some way, you can instantly shield yourself from taking toxic energy into your system.

When a woman takes toxic energy into her system such as envy from others, insults, hate speech, criticism, or attacks on her character, it can be powerfully corrosive. The Warrioress knows the wisdom of never listening to these destructive voices. Never. Never. Never. Criticism, attacks, judgment, disapproval, or denigration do not help you grow or become strong. It is better to shield against these cruelties and watch as the toxic energy is deflected away and disperses into the atmosphere.

In the next part of the Warrioress Initiation, Chiman is challenged to conquer her fears in the Cage of Bones. The Cage of Bones is a dreadful place, a cage of sinewy, human bones that has no door, no gate, no entry, no exit and therefore, no escape. This cage is made of the bones of failed Warrioresses, those who died of fright and couldn't face their fears. So as she is trapped within the Cage of Bones, each bone comes alive and taunts her with fears she harbors deep within her soul.

I'm sure you can relate to some of these fears: fear of not being good enough, fear of not knowing enough, fear of fully speaking your truth, fear of losing yourself to what others want, fear of being abandoned and cast aside, fear of being rejected, fear of being right, fear of being wrong, afraid to be powerful, afraid to be weak, afraid to be seen, and afraid to trust yourself. That's quite a list of fears. Maybe you can add your own. Your Warrioress needs to know so she can help you tackle your fears.

Chiman learns in the Cage of Bones that when a woman succumbs to her deepest fears, she becomes weak and loses her powers. So when you succumb to this fear talk, you lose your strength and your power. It is a powerful exercise to name all the fears you have and to see them as your Cage of Bones, a cage that entraps you and limits your life. If fear is your inner structure, the inner skeleton that holds you up, you need to replace that fear structure with the structure of strength. During Warrioress training you learn to rise above these destructive voices and liberate yourself from your own Cage of Bones.

One helpful exercise is to write down affirmations that directly confront each inner voice that disempowers you. So if you fear not being good enough, you can write down the affirmation, "I am good enough." And then say it out loud. This may sound simple, but it is a powerful way to replace fear bones with strong bones. This way you begin to align yourself with the strength of your Warrioress and grow an internal skeleton that has no room for fear. You create an inner bone structure of affirmations rather than fears.

The last phase in the Warrioress initiation is the activation of your Golden Path of Power and the sacred boundary around your soul. You have your very own Path of Power, like a golden rope leading straight in front of you. This Golden Path of Power is your unique path. The more your Warrioress embodies your power and strength, the further out the Golden Path will be, showing you the way to go. Many women however, have a habit of believing they can help others on their Golden Path of Power. But they cannot. Often women jump onto another person's Path of Power, thinking this is the right thing to do, but they are gravely mistaken. Each woman is solely responsible for her own Golden Path. If a Warrioress moves off her path and steps on another person's path, an alarm goes off and she can become very ill if she continues to interfere.

This is obviously a strong warning to stay on your own path and not interfere with the paths of others. I always tell my initiation students that the most loving thing they can do is to come close to the path of a loved one and wave and say hello and offer support without jumping onto the other person's path. You can assess your success or failure here by considering whether you are interfering with another person's path. If you have jumped onto their path (to try and help them), do you lose your power? What is appropriate help you can offer without crossing boundaries? Have you violated another person's sacred boundary? Have you ever become ill because you took on another person's problems or tried to solve their dilemma? Your physical, emotional, and spiritual health is at stake here - you must remain on your own Golden Path and honor the sovereign golden paths of others.

Lastly, Chiman learns to activate the sacred boundary around her soul. She is able to discern a golden light emanating from within, which then creates a protective force field or aura around her body. It emanates from deep within her center and spreads outward, like an inner sun that radiates out in a sphere of light. To activate your own sacred boundary, you can imagine yourself at the center of a circle and imagine that wherever you walk, you are the center of this circle. Then radiate out your inner light so that you can feel a sphere of light around your body.

It's amazing to recognize that this sacred boundary around your soul has always been there. It is your sacred birthright. You have the right to allow anyone into this circle and you have the right to say no to anyone you do not want within your circle. You must learn to use your powers of discernment so that you can decide whom you want in your circle and what kinds of energy you want inside your circle.

These are very important issues as you train to be a Warrioress. When you are able to activate the sacred boundary around your own soul, you will feel safe, protected, and solid and stable in your core self. It is your duty as a Warrioress to have strong and impeccable boundaries and to protect the basic rights of the human soul. You have the right to be seen. You have the right to be valued. You have the right to be loved. You have the right to be respected. You have the right to mutual exchange in relationships. You have the right to negotiate for what you need.

When you complete the journey with the Warrioress you have embodied the powerful energy of strength into your life. You have gained the powers of the Warrioress Clan: strength, bravery, fearlessness, courage, healthy boundaries, and resourcefulness. You can use your Sacred Shield to ward off inner and outer attacks and activate the sacred boundary around your soul to protect your vital life essence. You have said yes to awaken the Warrioress in yourself and in your life. You are on your way to self-mastery.

Warrioress Sacred Robe

When you look at the Warrioress Sacred Robe what comes up for you? Here are some responses from my students:

- *The Warrioress is able to connect with all sorts of animals. She seems to be one with the wilderness. She's really connected to nature and seems to draw strength from the animals.*
- *She looks like a medicine woman to me, deeply connected to her body and to the earth and all the richness and gifts from the earth.*
- *I love the shield she's holding. It's a magnificent spiral and feels like the sun. It feels like she has grounded her power.*

- *She's really connected to all earth creatures, plants and animals. She's got mountains on her robe so she's also drawing her strength from that instinctive animal place and the mountains.*
- *The shield reminds me that she has appropriate boundaries. She defends and protects.*
- *She's present and you can't shake her. She's so solid. She has a dependable, reliable presence.*

Notice your reaction to the Warrioress. Do you feel drawn to her? Do you feel scared, intimidated, or repelled by her? Do you feel connected to the Earth? Have you ever been in the wilderness or out in nature and felt the energy of the Warrioress? Notice your physical responses when you look at the image of Chiman. How do you relate to the Warrioress now in your life?

When do you want to call upon the Warrioress? You call the Warrioress when you need to speak the truth to somebody and you need to stand your ground. Whenever you feel fear, she's the one to call up because she has the courage to help you face your fear. If you're feeling scattered, she can ground your scattered energy. Anytime you want to call in protection for yourself or anyone else, call her in. Anytime you need to hold sacred space, you can call in the strength and good boundaries of the Warrioress.

Interviews with Warrioresses

The following are interviews with women who attend my *Feminine Path of Power* Programs and have interacted with all 5 Divine Feminine Archetypes. Here is how they relate to the Warrioress.

Interview with MK

Tell me about your relationship with the Warrioress.

The Warrioress is my happy place. The first time I walked into the retreat last year and I saw the Warrioress Robe, I knew her very, very well. I feel like I have been protecting others and caring for others all my life. I've also been caring for the earth and the animals. I've been doing that all my life. What I hadn't realized so much is the shadow side of the Warrioress that you pointed out to me, the shadow of fear and being a victim of circumstance. I certainly took care of my mom way too much. And my mom is a perfect example of a person who is overwhelmed by fear.

So it's not so much that I myself have the shadow side of fear but I've been caring for others with fear at the expense of myself. When I went through all the goddesses and began to see how they all worked together, I realized that I have a little bit of shadow in one clan and a little bit of shadow in another clan. Then I could see how I pull on my strength, the natural gift of the Warrioress. So I can see from the Majah Wise Woman perspective that I need to be more than just the Warrioress. I can use the power of all the goddesses and the gifts of all the goddesses. I don't have to perfect one

Goddess to move onto the other clan.

So for me, I like to draw on the Warrioress and be strong and grounded. I can put up boundaries for myself where I feel comfortable, rather than opening up the floodgates and making everyone else feel comfortable. I am looking at it differently now. So people (like my mother) who have fears in their lives, I'm seeing it's not my responsibility to take care of them.

How has making good Warrioress boundaries helped you?

When I catch myself doing what I don't want to do, I step back and ask myself, "Why I am doing this?" Then I realize I'm trying to make the other person feel safe. I have an example of something that happened several years ago, before I knew about The Feminine Path of Power. My mother has a history of having panic attacks and when one comes upon her, she starts sobbing. As her daughter, I've always wanted to take care of her when she gets in this state. Several years ago, after she had some minor surgery, I was with her at her retirement home. She was crying and didn't want me to leave her. I had arranged to stay at my cousin's house nearby. My mother really didn't want me to leave because she was having a panic attack and was crying. I was able to stop and put up a healthy boundary. I was empathizing with her but I wasn't being caught by her anxiety. She was crying and crying and crying and I told her that I was going to stay at my cousin's. "I'll stay here until you stop crying, but I am going to go. I'll wait for you to get it together." And so she got it together. So that's a visual I use now when I want to call up the Warrioress. I can stop and wait and just be myself and allow people to work through their fears or whatever else they are doing. I can't fix their fear.

Do you visualize that boundary for yourself now?

I remember that experience with my mother that weekend and I take that stance and can feel it in my body. I picture a magic boundary around me and imagine that others cannot cross it. It's like holding my ground and not allowing a person to cross that boundary. I've got this boundary around me and I can choose who I let in and who I'm not going to let in. I think to myself, "I'll be close enough to you so that I can support you but my boundary is here." It's an energy field. I don't really have a color associated with it.

I also practice what we did at our Wise Woman retreat when you asked us to stretch our arms out and then move them in a circle around our body so we could see and feel where our boundary was around our body. This way I can stand my ground and hold my ground. I don't have to run in and try to rescue anybody - that's not my job. I'm not going to fix my mother's fear. I can be strong for her. I see that I have the strength and that might help motivate others but I can't make them move out of their fear.

So you're recognizing that other people may be on the shadow path but you don't have to rescue them from that path.

What I did with my mom and my ex-husband was that I always tried to rescue them. I kept supporting them and I gave up my own space by doing that. I am living differently now with my Warrioress.

Thanks for explaining how you are calling up your Warrioress. I'm sure other women can relate to your story about healthy boundaries. Thank you!

Interview with Margaret

I'd love to hear how you connect with the Warrioress. What does she feel like when you call her up inside of you?

It immediately takes me to a place of being held in the earth, as I know the element of the Warrioress is Earth. When I call up my Warrioress, I feel deeply held by Mother Earth. So it's a very anchoring space for me. When I call the Warrioress I feel really deeply connected and truly embodied. I would like to share with you a piece of poetry I wrote after we were "buried" in our sacred Wise Woman ritual. It speaks to my relationship with my Warrioress. (During the Feminine Path of Power ritual weekend we re-enact Majah's journey in the Place of Liberation. This entails being "buried" in the earth, under the stars and surrounded by Redwood trees.)

Burial

Mother Earth, how sweet the softness of your soul
Your embrace so assuring and gentle.
Spacious eternity is my shield.
I belong, I am strong
Revisiting my place of birth
Through the astral realms.
Beyond Mother Earth.
I give to you all that does not serve.
My destiny now pure.
Stillness through chorus rings.
Focused star new message brings.
My ancient mother caressing me,
Loving whisper of voice carried on a cloud of joy.
Gaia heart beat pressing into mine.
Sweet soil, I am united as thine.
Energy pushes amazing grace, mercy and your loving face.
Bring with you my ancestors whole.
Clear night, clear sight,
No longer in need to be seen.
Those days have been.
Now in your full warrior hold
Move to your path that will unfold.
Praying mantis holding still

Eyes fix aligned with will.
Manifest your creation now
Visit Majah, find out how.
Be true, be kind, take your time
Focus, journey, listen masterfully aligned
Mind, Body, and Spirit with thine.

Hmmm. That's beautiful. Thank you for sharing your wonderful poem.

This speaks to how deeply I feel the Warrioress holds me. It also speaks to how I can walk on my own path and know my birthright. In one of the meditations I did with the Warrioress, I asked her to bring me a gift. She brought me the gift of my African shield, which I have sitting next to my altar. It was like this real connection. I can use this Shield like a boundary.

So your Shield is there to protect you and create a sacred boundary?

Yes, and standing with the Shield, I can create with it energetically. I can stand with it and hold my presence. I hold my presence to protect myself and to establish my authority and to be grounded. When I hold my Warrioress Shield, I create a place of deep honesty inside myself and I can be fully present with myself. I don't have to wear a false mask. When this piece of poetry emerged, it peeled off a layer of something. It feels as if I'm weaving part of my blueprint into my life. It also feels as if I've turned a piece of my shadow into a grounded presence within me. Back in my 30s I was much more co-dependent. I was more reactive. Now I feel embraced by Gaia. I feel held by a real positive mother.

It helps to be present with yourself and also to show up as yourself. When you want to call up your Warrioress, do you feel her somewhere in your body? How do you call her into yourself? How do you feel her when she's there?

I often think of the Warrioress Robe when I call her in. Chiman, the Warrioress, is so strong and the colors are strong. It strengthens me and I just sort of plant my feet. I also find it helpful to do some breath work, where I breathe in counting to 10 and then hold it and then breathe out to the count of 10 and hold. I breathe really slowly and intentionally, which brings up my energy and then pushes it way down into my pelvis. This is a very helpful way to call in my Warrioress. If I'm going to go into a meeting, in a real practical sense, I use that.

Thank you. It's really good to hear some practical ways to imagine the Warrioress inside your body and learn some physical body postures to help conjure her up and feel her as an embodied presence inside.

Interview with Cynthia

I would love to hear how you are connecting with the Warrioress. Tell me how you connect with her and how you call her up in your life.

For me, all the Goddess archetypes are interconnected. I just came in from my studio where I did my morning meditation, where I connect the Warrioress, Queen, Visionary, Manifestor, and

Wise Woman with the Tree of Life, my Hindu goddesses and the chakras. The Warrioress is the one that I most need to connect with throughout the day. It's been so crazy lately and my Warrioress helps me feel so grounded. I feel solid with my tools and my Warrioress Shield. When I go out into the world, I just get bounced around with all the energies of life, the energies of the city, and the energies of other people. For my work I go into people's homes, so I'm always interacting with their energies. I try to remember to do the shielding and grounding between each home visit, but sometimes I forget, especially when I'm tired.

I had a profound experience of Chiman, the Warrioress at Goddess Camp. When I was waiting for the ritual, I was sitting in the yurt at the Warrioress altar and looking at the Warrioress Robe. I drew some animal cards and felt the power of the wolf. Then when we were going up into the forest the next night during the ritual, I called up my Warrioress big time. Remember I was the last person to go up into the forest path for that initiation. And when I was standing waiting for my name to be called, I got scared because I am afraid of being alone in the woods at night. When my name was called, I took my staff and I just got into Warrioress position, kind of low to the ground with a solid stance. And I could feel all the animals around me, and I could feel my Warrioress. I could feel her shielding and protecting me. And as I walked up the path, I imagined all the strong animals around me and I imagined my Warrioress inside me. I was totally in that energy. So I walked more solidly up the dark forest path with more confidence. I was thinking to myself, "Just don't mess with me! I'm here, and ready." This was so helpful for me to experience my Warrioress embodied in this way. I so need to ground myself.

I love that story. When you feel the Warrioress in your daily life, how do you feel her presence? What gifts does she bring to you?

My Warrioress brings a sense of groundedness and being in my body, which, as I've said over and over again, is a fairly new experience. I'm a fire clan woman with lots of fire and I'm often not in my body. I'm an escapist! When things get uncomfortable, I'm outta here! So my Warrioress makes me stay present and in my body. Look, I made a Warrioress Shield.

(She shows me the amazing Shield she created herself. A real piece of art!) I love it. Tell me about your Shield. What does it do for you?

It's powerful to hold my Shield and it makes it all very physical and tactile. It helps me ground and it makes me feel shielded and protected. Making my own Shield was a powerful experience because I can now tangibly hold my Shield and take my Warrioress stance.

You said you're going into peoples' homes for your work. If you remember to shield yourself, how does this feel?

When I have my Shield, I am more present, and I don't get hijacked into other people's stories. I also don't take on other people's energies as much. I'm a total empath, which is great, but it opens me to other people's energy really easily. I'm learning how to use my empathy more positively. I know it's unhealthy for me and for others when I take on their energy or get hijacked by their complaints.

So with your Shield, you don't get hijacked into their story and you're also not taking their negative or toxic energy into your field. That's powerful.

One thing that has been so key with my Warrioress is staying on my own Golden Path of Power and not trying to save people who are walking on their own Golden Path of Power.

Yes, that's part of the Warrioress Initiation where you learn that each person has their own path they are walking on and we are not to interfere or jump onto their path to save or rescue them!

Yes, that is key for me, to daily reconnect with this! What happened last weekend was my son was going through some stuff and I was aware of not jumping onto his path and rescuing him. I'm holding a boundary. I've had such a stomachache all week just feeling the energy around his crisis. When a family member is going through some stuff, I take on people's energy. I feel that rawness and all that tension, and then I feel it in my own stomach. All of a sudden I realize I've given my power away. So then I remember my Warrioress and stay on my own path, I can visualize my son on his own path and radiate out love from my own path, my own ground, my own place of truth.

So you can see your loved ones on a separate path and you stay on your path. You can wave to them and offer help, but you don't go onto their path to save them.

The Warrioress is helping me stay focused and have healthy boundaries. I say to myself all through the day, "Healthy boundaries, healthy boundaries, healthy boundaries!" That's a daily, throughout-the-day process for me.

Thank you for sharing your growing relationship with your Warrioress. You are a real inspiration!

Interview with Susan

I would love to hear about your relationship with the Warrioress? What gift is she bringing to you? How do you use her in your daily life?

Yesterday when I actually sat down and created some space to meditate about this, what came up for me was how much I have used my Warrioress throughout my life. In my childhood, my Warrioress and my child were very courageous. The main challenge for me when I was a child was dealing with my fear of my father. Both my child and my Warrioress have very strong wills! That helped me along the way. I had an initial sense that I could overcome this and always could. My Warrioress gave me a strong foundation to learn my truth while I was learning how to create healthy boundaries that were permeable.

My Warrioress had a large role in protecting and shielding my heart, which felt like the vital essence I was protecting. My Warrioress had to work to overcome the journey from just existing to actually living life, just surviving to actually living and enjoying it. It feels like she has been my common sense and has helped to provide stabilization for me along the way.

More recently, I've been practicing speaking my truth verbally to others, so I can help others find their truth in the near future. I look forward to being able to do that. Currently, my Warrioress is helping me be brave and fearless and she's helping me find touchstones for those. I'm working on overcoming my fear of being seen and heard in the world, in order to build my confidence. This enables me to be able to explain and communicate my "Fear to Beauty" process, one of the messages that I'm getting ready to bring to others. This is part of my mission in life.

Can you say something more about your "Fear to Beauty" process?

"Fear to Beauty" is the name of the workshop I am developing. Helping people overcome fears and create the beauty that they want to have in their life and see in the world.

Wow! That's a great way to employ your Warrioress because she helps you and can help other women move off the shadow path of fear.

Yes. Actually, that's what I'm experiencing now. I'm dealing with my own fear and building my courage in order to be able to be seen and heard so I can deliver my Fear to Beauty workshop!

How do you call up the presence of the Warrioress? Do you have a particular practice that you could share with others?

Yes, In order to overcome and push through my fear, I've been doing freestyle dance. I just turn on a piece of music that inspires me and then I just dance it out. It helps me breakthrough. It moves my energy. When I'm in a contracted position, I can move through that, breakthrough that energy, and move it, get myself unstuck and really push myself back out there to have breakthroughs or get over some of the paralyzing or freezing feelings surrounding fear. My Warrioress gets going when I dance.

That's beautiful. I know that the greatest secret of the Warrioress Clan is to activate the sacred boundary around the soul. Can you say something about the difference between having unhealthy boundaries and healthy boundaries? It sounds like you had boundaries that were too "thick" because you had to protect your heart growing up. And now you feel your boundaries are more balanced and healthy?

Yes. Sometimes it's a little bit hard for me to discern which goddess or character I'm pulling in because some of them heal in a similar way – like both my Warrioress and Queen. I had a cage around my heart, the shadow of the Queen. I was frozen in fear in reaction to my father, which is the shadow of the Warrioress. And there was a lot of chaos, the shadow of the Visionary. I put a cage around my heart to protect it and actually protect my essence.

It sounds like your Warrioress was very present in your childhood because it helped you to create a protective shield of your essence.

Absolutely.

Now, in your adult life, what would you consider a healthy boundary?

I know that I have the ability to contract and pull in and cocoon. So even though it may seem like a defense, it is really a healthy boundary for me because cocooning helps me rejuvenate. I actually learned to lead with my heart rather than my mind. It's like an accordion feeling to me. Sometimes I'm really out and open and my heart is leading the way - it depends on how safe I feel. If I feel unsure or afraid, I can pull back in my energy. So I move out and then I pull back in.

I think you're talking about both the Warrioress and the Queen right now. If you want to open your heart and be openhearted towards others, you have the strength of the Warrioress to really ground you and help you to feel safe and the Queen to open your heart. That's how the Warrioress and Queen can work together.

Yes, that's absolutely how I viewed it in my life. I guess I have less of a need to pull the Warrioress in because I don't feel very threatened in my life presently. I feel like I've healed my heart in many ways. So now I feel the ability to expand and contract and the ability to cocoon. This quiets things on the outside, then I set up the boundary, make it permeable where things can come in and out, but I can control that. It's a healthy boundary for me.

I like that you are describing the cocoon as a positive image because cocoon, for some people, might be too much of a boundary. You're saying that you need times when you go inside and you really do need to cocoon yourself. That, for you, is a sacred boundary.

Having a defense system, yeah. Absolutely. It protects my vital life essence. It works for me!

Thanks for the examples. This is really helpful.

Interview with Kala

Let's talk about your Warrioress. She grounds you and helps create healthy boundaries. I would love to hear about your relationship with your Warrioress.

I use nature to ground. I've spent a lot of time in nature and in the mountains climbing and walking in the forests. That's my retreat space, my home territory, and my grounding. My Warrioress and my Shield are very much oriented to nature and all of the meeting points and openings that nature provides.

Your Warrioress sounds like a bit of a wild woman! She creates a sense of being grounded and present and also defends and protects your truth. Do you have a particular way that you call in your Warrioress when you need that kind of strength and grounding?

I imagine myself in nature if I'm in a situation where I don't feel safe. We're in a really strange and challenging time in our global history as Humanity. So we need this grounding even more. We are shattering through a lot of veils of illusion now and this means there's a lot of chaos around.

Yes, there's so much chaos and ungrounded energy in our world right now, it seems like we need the Warrioress even more in our culture.

Yes, I need to stay vigilant of being and staying present, being radically present.

Can you give me one practical example where you use your Warrioress to stay grounded and present in your daily life?

One of the things I do in my work is volunteering at one of the hospitals to pick people up and take them to appointments – children and adolescents mostly. When I'm doing that, I feel like I am just completely present with what is needed in a given situation. This involves me also in the medical field and all the ethical dimensions of it. So I am always discerning what I can and can't talk about, what is my business and what is not, what's appropriate and what's not appropriate. It's important that I keep my clients comfortable but not impose on their business. I did a Masters in Bioethics and we really walk on that razor edge of ethics. So when I'm with people in this context it demands my attention and I need to be very present and conscious.

I love that example of your Warrioress holding very clear boundaries. Thank you for sharing how you are currently working with your Warrioress.

Interview with Carol

Let's talk about the Warrioress. How do you relate to her?

In the home I grew up in, I really didn't know anything about the Warrioress because I didn't know anything about healthy boundaries. I grew up in a very, very, dysfunctional home with a lot of mental illness and violence. My boundaries were violated so much as a child that I really didn't know what healthy boundaries were at all. So once I started working with the Warrioress, with Chiman, I began to understand her energy and to bring her energy into me. I started to understand what healthy boundaries feel like.

When I call in my Warrioress, I have a sacred circle around me. I create my sacred space. I know now that I have a right to hold and preserve that sacred space for myself. With my Warrioress present I can say, "No", if I don't want someone in my space. I have a right to say, "No", and that's a healthy boundary for me. When I make a healthy boundary I honor myself and develop more of who I am as a person. I am coming to know who I am and what makes me happy. I can say what works for me.

When my boundaries were violated all the time as a child, I didn't know who I was. I didn't know the difference between what I wanted and what someone else wanted. With a sacred boundary around me I can start to see who I am, and what I like and dislike. I say to myself, "Hey I'm tired, I can't do that right now." So I'm taking care of myself.

I love that. How empowering for you!

And my Warrioress helps me connect with the Earth, which also feels like a very strong boundary too. When I was young, I really didn't feel like I was welcomed, or belonged on this earth. As I work with the Warrioress, I realize that I am connected to this earth, and I do belong here. I am much more grounded within myself.

That's a great description. Your Warrioress anchors you into the Earth. She walks the Path of Strength, so she gives you strength.

Yes, she definitely gives me strength. I know that strong earth energy has always been there for me, but I had just kind of blocked it out. My Warrioress has actually made me stronger, like an alchemical process has happened. It's not just in my mind, I actually feel stronger!

Right. When your boundaries are violated as a child it becomes difficult to have a healthy sense of self and to stand your ground. Your Warrioress is helping you to take your stand, stand your ground, and to know who you are. She is giving you back your self-esteem.

Yes, she really is, because I feel now that I do have my self-esteem. When my boundaries were so violated I had no sense of self and it was a hard way to go through life. So now I feel like I have that anchor. I have a sense of who I am as an individual. I am a divine spark and I have a mission. I know more what makes my heart sing. I think there are many people out there who had a similar experience to mine. Maybe they aren't connected to their Warrioress and have no sense of personal boundaries. It's just a horrible feeling and it's hard to function in the world that way. I'm seeing the difference now that I can call in my Warrioress. The change in me has been really dramatic. It's been life saving.

Yes. When we're not shown in childhood how to have healthy boundaries then often we fall onto the shadow path of the Warrioress, the path of fear. Can you speak at all about your experience of feeling fear?

Yes. I can say that growing up, I really feared everything. I never knew what was going to happen in my house. Not just people, but even objects could make me afraid. I was actually tortured as a child, so even objects could trigger fear. I experienced the Warrioress shadow side as fear of myself, fear of not knowing who I am, and fear of my own emotions. I didn't have any healthy attachments, and I had fear of being attached to anyone. So, I went through life basically without friends because I couldn't connect to people. I didn't know how to connect in a healthy way. It was always just a scary thing to think about attaching, or speaking to someone, or sharing my heart. I couldn't do that, because it was too scary. I lived in fear, total fear.

So it sounds like your Warrioress has given you internal strength.

Yes, for sure! This Feminine Path of Power work has been so profound. I have been to different therapists and they've been great but working with you and these Goddess archetypes has caused a huge shift in the way I think about myself. I have experienced an alchemical shift. I actually feel a huge energetic shift in the different parts of me. I've been able to face a lot of fear and let it go.

Do you feel the Warrioress inside of you in some way? Do you visualize her?

When I call her up, I actually feel her. It's an energy that is very solid. I feel her connected to the ground. I feel her in my lower body, in my feet, legs, and in my hips and she strengthens me. She takes a stance inside me, not an aggressive stance but a stance that allows me to stand up for what I believe. I take a stand for my sense of self, who I am. When I call the Warrioress in I can feel that energy as a stable groundedness.

It sounds like you're describing her presence in your first two or three chakras.

Yes. Right.

That's great, because I think it's really helpful for a woman to get a feel for how to call her own Warrioress into her body and really feel her presence. You can create a body posture or a stance that feels like your Warrioress. I know when I stand with my knees bent a little and really connect with the ground it feels like my Warrioress is right there inside my body, giving me strength.

Sometimes in situations when I'm caught off guard, I start to feel helpless and I feel that shadowy fear start coming in and I'll call in the Warrioress. And I feel a real sense of protectiveness. I tell myself, "Okay, I see this fear coming in - bring in the Warrioress and wait a minute. Where are my boundaries right now? Where are my healthy boundaries? And what do I think and what do I feel and what do I want? What do I see in this situation?" And it brings me back to a place of strength.

That's great. Love that. Thank you for that description. It's really helpful.

Interview with Ali Marie

How do you relate to the Warrioress and how is she working in your life.

I think for me the Warrioress is probably strongest within me. As I look back on my life, I probably had to be more reliant on the Warrioress than I needed to be. I developed a relationship with her early on. Maybe because I called her in when I was so young, the Warrioress took on more than she needed to. And so now as a result of this work and lots of diving deep, I think that she can relax a little bit. Her role, is more clearly defined and so my Warrioress is able to be present in a much more productive way, in a much more compassionate way, a more balanced way.

Are you saying she was overdeveloped within you? Was she strong in the boundary-making department? How would you describe that?

I think I overdeveloped her from the time I was young, out of necessity. Rather than a boundary, she built a wall. So in my over-reliance of her, I created walls rather than boundaries. I think that's the best way I can describe that. It became more of an impenetrable barrier. It didn't allow for any kind of exchange of vulnerability because that did not feel safe. So my Warrioress built a complete barrier.

Yes, we often talk about the shadow side of the Warrioress as the victim, but you're talking about another shadow side, which is having a boundary with an extra thick wall!

Yeah. And I'm not saying that the victim wasn't there! I think the victim was so much there and that's why I built that wall. That's why that wall went up because of the constant feeling of being a victim. So the two were not necessarily mutually exclusive, they built one from the other. I feel the shadow side of the victim was definitely a prevalent part of my experience for many years. And in response to that, I needed to create a total barrier. So both of those things go together.

Do you feel you're in a better relationship with the Warrioress? Do you have more of a sacred boundary, or a different kind of boundary, or shield?

Much better, much, much better. I have a better understanding of what a healthy boundary is. I am now able to make more clear, responsible, compassionate, and loving boundaries from having the presence of the other Goddesses in my life. So I have more love and other things that allow for a healthier balance and a clearer understanding of what a boundary is. I've learned how to put a boundary in place, how to hold the boundary, and how to allow some fluidity. This means I can still have an open heart and show up in the world and be able to be vulnerable and intimate, and still feel safe.

Oh I love that! How do you call up the Warrioress? When you call her how do you feel her and/or visualize her?

Well, I think for me, the Warrioress is still a central figure. I rarely need to call her up. I often need to call the others to bring balance. She's kind of right there. She's ready. But I call up the others to hold her, and infuse some balance, some wisdom, some love, some light and perspective, those kinds of things, to help her have a more clear role.

Is that because her role was too powerful in the past?

She was too powerful, exactly. So, she's always there at ready.

Thanks for bringing this perspective to our discussion of the Warrioress. You are helping us see that sometimes our Warrioress can be over active. When we build a boundary that is too thick and non-permeable, it is hard to have intimacy and open our hearts. By calling in the other Goddesses, we can bring the Warrioress into better balance.

Interview with Susana

I'd love to hear about your relationship with the Warrioress. How do you call her up and how do you connect with her?

My Warrioress has become more differentiated for me in this process. I've had an on again / off again relationship with my Warrioress over the years! I have a lot of earth in my Astrology chart and in many ways I do ground with her. It is easy for me to ground and be present. However, I also have a lot of fire energy, so I can get fired-up and wound-up easily. Through the Feminine Path of Power I can relate to my Warrioress more consistently, and in a more integrated fashion. She brings in a much slower energy for me.

Before I thought that I couldn't be in my Warrioress energy and the more fiery, fast moving energies at the same time, so I would abandon one for the other. This process has shown me that actually tapping into my Warrioress more often during the day provides a great sense of comfort for me. Whenever I start to get wound up inside, or too fast, or in a rush, I remember to come back to my Warrioress. She provides comfort for me. I connect in with my Warrioress through breath. I breathe deeply, down real low in my belly. Sometimes I project her out around me in a circle, so I'm in a bubble. That's another way I activate her.

And when you're in that bubble how do you feel?

I feel empowered. I feel strong and empowered, and at peace at the same time.

I know you work as a Chaplain in a hospital. How do you use your Warrioress in the hospital?

When I consciously call her in, I breathe deeply and activate that Warrioress bubble around me as I walk through the hospital and as I see patients. Then when I'm preparing to walk into a room, I activate her the most.

We know that the sacred tool of the Warrioress is the Shield. Is that what your bubble is - is it a shield of protection?

Yes, it is. The Shield has been an interesting thing for me to relate to. I haven't quite come to terms with that in a way that feels strong, that feels true and empowered. I prefer to think of my Warrioress with a staff, a tall staff. So when I stand with my hand on a tall staff in that very strong pose, that's when I feel my Warrioress the most.

I like that. And she makes you feel strong in your body. The Warrioress walks the Path of Strength. So much of embodying your Warrioress is feeling strong in your body so that you can hold your ground, or stand your ground and be in command of your day.

Yes. That's true. I do things through the day to activate her again, I bounce on my ball, I get in my body, I stretch, and I do things to get back in my body while working at the hospital. The Warrioress is one of the most natural archetypes for me to relate to. Although I do say I forget her at times, it's almost because she's always there. Whenever I reach for her, she is absolutely there. She's very solid with me.

Thank you sharing with us. You have a strong relationship with your Warrioress and I like the way you use her energy for protection in the hospital.

Interview with AB

I would love to hear about your connection with the Warrioress and how you use her in your daily life.

As I look at the Warrioress, I realize that I have lived more of the shadow side of this one. I have played the Victim. I also realize that I have lived out all of the shadows of the Goddesses. I have a piece of me in each shadow!

I know the Warrioress is about having strong and healthy boundaries so I have been listening to the energy of my heart and not saying yes when I really mean no. What I learned from the Warrioress was the importance of staying quiet inside versus my default reactions. I've come to see that making strong boundaries is actually a feminine energy. I don't need to make an aggressive stance, which is heavy-handed like, "You've crossed my boundaries!!"

I see now that having healthy boundaries is a healthy place to start and that serving and loving and giving and receiving doesn't mean that I am not a strong character or a strong feminine presence. I have a choice and I do have boundaries that I need to speak and actually claim.

Every day I'm trying to be quiet and ask myself what the healthy boundaries are for me today rather than taking on assumed roles. I'm taking time to stand on the ground and to say, "This walk with my dog isn't just for my dog! This is what I need for me to be grounded in my body and find a place on earth."

I just moved across country. In my old house I had a huge backyard with 2 great, big oak trees and a lot of muck. It was easy for me to connect to the roots of Mother Nature. In my new house, part of the change for me is that we're in an urban suburb, and the suburb is more urban than my old city house. Energetically, there's a re-shifting of myself.

So your Warrioress is helping you create healthy boundaries and find new ground in a new city and lifestyle. And yes, the Warrioress is a very feminine energy. Having healthy boundaries is essential for us to define who we are in relation to others. This way we stay open and present to others and not give too much of our life essence away. Thank you so much for sharing how you are calling up your Warrioress.

Warrioress Initiation Conclusion

When you are initiated and embody the Warrioress energy, you will feel bold and courageous. You will feel a deep inner strength that will manifest physically as well as emotionally. You will be surprised at your own resourcefulness and your ability to figure out how to best handle any situation. You will be able to quickly shift from feeling victimized to taking back your power. You will be able to take a stand for what you believe and value, and be able to speak your truth. You will also gain the ability to know exactly how to make healthy boundaries in every situation so you feel safe and protected.

When you embody the Warrioress you feel instinctively alive and profoundly connected to your body and to the earth. You are grounded, courageous, bold, and empowered to face your fears. You can stand your ground, speak your truth, and hold boundaries to protect your vital life essence. As a Warrioress, you become the strength of your community, protecting and defending personal and collective truth.

Celebrate your Warrioress!

Chapter 7
The Queen: Radical Self-Compassion

The Story of Oyuna, the Queen

In the third initiation story, you will journey with Oyuna (pronounced *Oh-you-nah)* as she trains to be a powerful Queen, mastering the Path of Compassion and becoming a Water Clan Woman, full of emotion and big of heart. You will follow her ocean adventure as Oyuna celebrates in the Sacred Grotto, drinks love potions in the Temple of Self-Love, luxuriates in the Tent of Healing Touch, swims with the dolphins, and tells stories by the fire near the cove.

Part 1: The Story of Oyuna

Once upon a time, a long, long time ago, there was a land where women were honored for their power and strength. It was a sacred land called the village of women where each girl child was honored for the unique gifts she brought to the sacred circle. And when each new female soul was still in the womb of her mother she would whisper her name and her soul's purpose to the elders who were eager to hear this good news.

Now in this ancient land there were 4 different clans of women that all female souls were sorted into at birth. There was the Warrioress Clan, those who walk the Way of Strength. And the Queen Clan, those who walk the Way of Compassion. And the Visionary Clan, those who walk the Way of Change. And finally the Manifestor Clan, those who walk the Way of Action.

Now one special day, there was a commotion among the elders who had gathered to hear the good news from a new girl child who was about to be born into the village of women. When they asked who she was, what clan she belonged to, and what her soul's purpose was, this is what she said. "My name is Oyuna. I come to the Queen Clan to dance with the Sacred Waters and guide lost women back to the Path of Compassion."

Soon the excitement spread among the entire clan of Queens who eagerly anticipated the birth of Oyuna and the knowledge she would bring to the clan. And so Oyuna was born and was cared for and nurtured as was the custom in the village of women, for each girl child was held and loved and valued and given chores and kept in line and watched over by those who were assigned as her special guardians. And as the years went by and Oyuna grew into a young woman, the elders of the Queen clan felt that the time had come to initiate her so that she could fulfill her purpose.

And so the elders took Oyuna to the initiation training ground of the Queen Clan to awaken the powers of the Queen that lay deep within her being. And they journeyed far across the wide ocean to the place of the Sacred Waters, where the streams and rivers flow into the lakes and the waters pour into the sea. And in this wet and wondrous land there was every kind of water imaginable. There was cold water, hot water bubbling with steam. There was muddy water, clean water, clear water, and there was moving water, still water, deep water, icy water, fountains, waterfalls, and pools.

And when they arrived at the Queens' training ground, Oyuna beheld the Place of the Sacred Waters, a beautiful tropical grotto lush with green plants of all kinds, palm trees, banana trees, ferns, and bright flowers and long hanging vines covered in luminous green moss. And all around the grotto there were waterfalls pouring down the rocks emptying into a crystal clear cove of sparkling blue-green water. And in the sheltered cove, dolphins played with giant sea turtles and bright colored tropical fish swam to the shore to greet them as they entered the Queen's grotto.

In the sand around the cove, driftwood benches were placed in a large semi-circle, open to the sea. And in the center of this circle Oyuna saw a fire pit with a huge iron cauldron, blackened from the initiation fires that had been lit for generations before her. And at the entrance to the grotto, a long seaweed banner proudly announced the motto of the Queens: "Water Clan Women: Full of Emotion and Big of Heart." And as Oyuna crossed the threshold into the grotto, she felt deep pride in her big heart and was eager to begin her initiation to awaken and embody her powers.

The elders in charge of her initiation greeted Oyuna, welcomed her to the Place of the Sacred Waters, and invited her to sit on a driftwood bench by the cove.

As Oyuna gazed around the lush grotto, she saw many unusual things. She saw underwater diving gear, colorful wetsuits, and mermaid costumes. She saw beautiful life-size statues of women of every shape and size you could imagine carved into the rocky cliffs of the grotto – big women, small women, curvaceous women, thin women, extravagant women, shapely women, and every variety known to woman kind.

And at one end of the lush grotto there was an open Temple of white marble with fountains and pools and places set out for luxurious massage and deep relaxation. And surrounding the entire grotto, sparkling like luminescent gems, were crystal hearts in every size and color imaginable, tucked into the cracks and crevices of the rocks; white and blue, black and green, red and violet, orange, yellow, and turquoise.

And so Oyuna spent her first days in the sacred grotto learning of the powers of the Queens and the purpose of the Clan. And at night in the sand by the cove, the fire was lit under the ancient cauldron, which bubbled with steamy, salty sea liquid. And the drummers drummed while the storyteller stood in the cove, sand and water swirling around her feet, necklaces of white sea shells, pink pearls, and red coral flung around her neck and shoulders, bits of green seaweed spread across her face and graying hair. And the Storyteller recited all the good, right and true acts of compassion that the Queens had accomplished over the centuries. And this is what the Storyteller said….

"Over the years we have walked The Path of Compassion. Our empowerment comes through emotional honesty. So connected are we to the Sacred Waters, we can call upon their powers to flow and cleanse our emotional body, open the floodgates of love and compassion, melt any glacier of grief and misery, bring joy where there is sadness. We feel deeply but we can hold a steady presence when others are swamped with feelings. We are not swayed to and fro by the torrential seas, for we can handle any emotion, no matter how passionate or extreme. We can still the inner waters and achieve emotional balance.

Over the years we have become skilled in diplomacy and right speech. The Queens are always called upon to mediate when people are overwhelmed, irrational or out of control. We teach people to speak kindly and respectfully and teach them to honor the emotional power of words. We feed and nurture all the people with our generosity and love. As Queens we are openhearted, forgiving, tolerant, generous, and kind. Of all our tools, the sacred crystal heart is our greatest ally, for when we have cleansed and purified our crystal heart from all grief, from all bitterness, all anger and resentment, we radiate a love so powerful, it breaks down all barriers and all divisions, it eradicates all loneliness and dismantles the cage that grows around the human heart."

And late that night around this very fire in the Queens' grotto, Oyuna was told a chilling tale about the Shadow Path of the Queen Clan. Yes, it was true; there were some women who had wandered off their Path of Power and onto a disempowered path that robbed them of their happiness and emotional well-being. This was called the Shadow Path of Self-Sacrifice.

And Oyuna heard disturbing tales of women who walk this path, women who sacrifice their own needs and give their life-blood for others, women whose hearts are frozen with grief and loss, women who carry loneliness and sorrow in their hearts. These women are vulnerable to the negative energies that stalk women on the Path of Self-Sacrifice and tempt them to become martyrs, giving and giving, never allowing themselves to be vulnerable and doomed to remain forever disappointed in love. And when Oyuna heard these stories, deep compassion stirred within her heart for she knew this was exactly what she had come to do, to redeem the Shadow Path of Self-Sacrifice and restore women back onto the Path of Compassion.

And when the elders saw compassion flow from her heart and the knowledge of her destiny burst forth, they smiled and nodded around the circle for they knew the time of her Initiation had come.

Oyuna Part 2: Flowing River, Boiling Swamp and Still Lake

A few mornings later the elders invited Oyuna to the Queen's grotto to sit at the shore of the Sacred Cove. One of the elders handed Oyuna a beautiful crystal heart that fit into the palm of her hand and said, "You are ready my daughter to begin your initiation. Take this crystal heart Oyuna, cleanse and purify it through your initiations, utilize its powers when you are in need. And now it is time to learn from the Sacred Waters, let us travel to the place of Flowing River, Boiling Swamp and Still Lake. They have lessons to teach you about the human heart."

And so the elders traveled with Oyuna up into the high country, to the place of the Flowing River. And they climbed high to the source of the mighty river and stood beside the lush green place where fresh water bubbled up from the ground in a great surge. And from here the mighty river flowed down, winding its way to the sea. The elders sat Oyuna down by the river and said, "Observe the mighty Flowing River. It has a natural bubbling up and natural flow down to the sea, a natural free spirit, unencumbered and untamed. This river is like your emotions.

Allow your deep feelings to bubble up from the depths, let your emotions flow naturally and take their course. Be emotionally honest my daughter, acknowledge, accept, and express your feelings."

And for many days Oyuna sat by Flowing River allowing every emotion to bubble up from her depths. And the river whispered her secrets to her "Oyuna, my daughter, dare to be emotionally honest. Whatever emotions you have kept down, whatever you have dared not to feel, let it bubble up. Dare to be emotionally honest." So Oyuna became like mighty Flowing River, letting her emotions flow - joy, sorrow, love, hate, boredom, frustration, envy, sadness, compassion, and every other feeling under the sun.

On the third day, Oyuna saw a vision of what happens to a woman when the sacred rivers are blocked and the emotions do not flow. She saw how the toxins and poisons build up in a women's heart and her emotional body becomes dammed up and blocked. "Why?" she asked the River, "Why does this happen?" And the River answered, "Women are taught to be nice, to be good, to cooperate, and do what others want them to say and do. Women forget how to be emotionally honest and so their sacred rivers do not flow."

"How does a Queen cleanse the toxins and poisons?" asked Oyuna. And the River told Oyuna the secret of cleansing the poisons. "The Queen cleanses her waters by being honest Oyuna. If you are emotionally honest what do you feel? If you are emotionally honest what do you need to say? If you are emotionally honest what do you need to do? Do not be nice, do not be good, go ahead and stir the waters my daughter, you are safe and protected in this initiation space. Do not be afraid of your own heart."

And so Oyuna held her crystal heart and opened to her deepest honesty and stirred the waters. A torrent of emotions bubbled up and the crusty layers of her nice, good, appropriate self fell away and a surge of toxins and poisons poured out of her heart, cleansing her body and soul. "Well done my daughter", said the River. "Now stand up and wade into my flowing waters to be purified and healed."

So Oyuna waded into Flowing River and lay down in the water, allowing the river to flow around her entire body until she was completely submerged in the flow. And Oyuna heard the song of the River, "Flow with your own heart, cleanse and be healed. Flow with your own heart, cleanse and be healed. Flow with your own heart, cleanse and be healed." And Oyuna surrendered to the mighty Flowing River and the song of her own soul.

After some time the elders came for Oyuna and they traveled to the Boiling Swamp, a wide expanse of marshy land with bubbling mud, steaming geysers of angry, blistering water, and a pungent, sulfur smell rising from the wet, hot earth. The Queen elder sat Oyuna down at the edge of the Boiling Swamp next to a huge black iron cauldron. "You cannot enter the Boiling Swamp my daughter until you have built a cauldron inside your heart. Your cauldron must be strong enough to hold the depth of feeling that resides in the human heart. Then you may enter the Swamp. Without a cauldron, a woman gets overwhelmed and may drown in the Swamp.

So Oyuna sat by the huge iron cauldron and imagined the cauldron inside her own heart growing stronger and stronger until it was as strong as iron. And when the elders were confident her cauldron would contain her through Boiling Swamp, they brought her to the bubbling mud pit. And as the mud slurped and gurgled and belched hot muddy water and putrid gases, it activated Oyuna's hot emotions of anger, fury, and outrage.

Memories flooded to the surface of times she was hurt and violated and injustices were done to her sisters. Like a volcano she wanted to explode and lash out, she wanted to take revenge and hurt those who had hurt her and those she loved. She felt hot resentment and boiling anger and just when she felt she might burn from the heat of it, she remembered her inner cauldron. She remembered to place these intense feelings into her strong iron cauldron where they felt contained and safe, boiling away in the cauldron of transformation.

With her inner cauldron strong, she was able to walk through the bubbling mud pit until she came to the place of the steaming geyser, where the hot waters spewed forth from the earth high into the air. As Oyuna stood near the geyser, which was blowing off steam, she felt a welling up of emotional turmoil, a building of chaotic feelings, unintelligible, irrational, and unknown. The Queen elder said, "Do not be afraid of your primal feelings Oyuna. Do not try to understand them by using your mind. Drop into your heart! Activate your cauldron! Allow the primal, crazy, chaotic, terrifying, irrational feelings to come to the surface and blow them off, like the steaming geyser. Do not put a lid on your feelings or the pressure will be too great. Trust that your cauldron will hold you."

Oyuna allowed her primal feelings to burst forth, spewing out like the mighty hot geyser. And she dropped into her heart and felt the chaotic and irrational feelings that she could not explain, did not know where they came from, and did not know where they were going. She blew off her steam and her cauldron held all the intense emotions that surfaced from her primal depths. Now she could walk safely through the Boiling Swamp unharmed and unhurt, confident that her cauldron would hold. And when she came to the other side, the elders smiled with pride and took Oyuna

to the next initiation ground, to the place of Sacred Still Lake.

Now Still Lake was a beautiful, peaceful lake surrounded by lush green meadows. Here Oyuna was told to sit beside Still Lake and calm her inner waters. As she sat, the waters of Still Lake whispered their secrets to her, "There will be times Oyuna when your waters will be stirred. When people are in crisis you will be called upon to hold a steady presence amidst the tempest of emotions and the tidal wave of feelings coming at you from all sides. You must calm your waters and become still and serene. I will teach you. Now breathe deeply and calm yourself my daughter. Invite the stillness of my water to enter your heart and you will feel the balance you seek. Accept who you are. Accept what you are. Return to yourself and your place of equilibrium. Breathe in peace, breathe out calm. Breathe in well-being, breathe out joy. Breathe in serenity, breathe out harmony. Return to yourself. Breathe deeply and calm your heart."

And so Oyuna imagined the still, calm waters entering her heart, calming her body, soothing her soul, and quieting her spirit. And she breathed in peace and breathed out calm. She breathed in well-being and breathed out joy. And she imagined Still Lake residing in her heart and she found a place inside of exquisite balance and delicious equilibrium. And through this breathing by Still Lake, Oyuna attained joy and serenity. She could feel her heart connecting with the universal heart beat of all creation and this calmed her soul profoundly. For many days and weeks she sat with Still Lake until she attained balance and harmony within her deepest self.

And when Oyuna had completed this part of her initiation, the elders said, "You have done well my daughter. From Flowing River, you learned to be emotionally honesty and flow with your heart's natural flowing waters. From Boiling Swamp you learned to contain the full spectrum of intense feelings and learned how to blow off steam. From Still Lake you learned to calm and sooth your heart, achieving emotional balance and inner harmony. Now you are ready to travel to the far North for the next phase of your Queen initiation."

Oyuna Part 3: The Icy Sea of Pain and Sorrow

With her inner cauldron strong and with newfound peace in her heart, Oyuna began the next phase of her initiation. "You have learned much from the Sacred Waters my daughter. Now we take you to the far North, to the Icy Sea of Pain and Sorrow, where you will confront the aching grief that is held in the human heart." And so they traveled north through the cold, wild country and the further north they traveled, the colder the waters became. And the terrain grew icier and more foreboding. Soon the land and sea were covered white with ice and snow and the frozen waters shimmered icy blue.

As they walked through the frozen, barren landscape the elders told Oyuna tales of Queen women who had wandered off their path of power, lost in the cold country of the North; women whose waters no longer flowed because their hearts had been frozen through grief, pain, and neglect; women who had sacrificed their life blood giving to everyone else but themselves. "Why" Oyuna asked, "Why do they do this?" "Because they believe if they just keep giving they will eventually get love in return. But they rescue people and choose lovers who are needy and incapable of loving them in return. And now their hearts are frozen and they are doomed to remain forever disappointed in love. They have forgotten how to be vulnerable and their hearts are closed." Tears poured from Oyuna's eyes as she contemplated their frozen doom and then she gasped as she saw in the icy waters, these very women - frozen solid, stiff and suspended - bitterness, sorrow, and resentment etched on their faces.

A deep compassion welled up in Oyuna and she pleaded with the elders, "What can be done to release these women from the Icy Sea of Pain and Sorrow? How can the waters flow once again in their hearts?" "Ahhh", said the elder, "It would take a very powerful Queen with exceptional heart powers to release these lost Queens from their pain and sorrow. She would need to plumb the depths of grief and loss, facing her deepest pain. She would need to confront the dark ambassadors that live in the Netherworld and find the secret to releasing women from the Icy Sea of Pain and Sorrow." Compassion welled in Oyuna's heart and she cried aloud, "I will do this. I will confront the Netherworld and learn to release grief, pain, and sorrow. No woman should be doomed to be forever disappointed in love. Our Queens will know joy and love in their hearts once again!"

And so Oyuna was led to a small boat and the elders set her afloat to drift in the Icy Sea of Pain and Sorrow. Soon a dark ambassador appeared in the icy water and her name was Arctic Seal of Sadness. She sang the song of the frozen ones, a song of deepest loneliness and defeat. "My body is heavy with sadness and my eyes blinded by tears. My heart has been torn to shreds and lies shattered on the ice and rocks. Will my sorrow ever end, will my pain ever subside, will my longing ever cease? How can I bear the unbearable?"

And then Arctic Seal of Sadness made an unearthly, wailing sound, a sound that penetrated deep into Oyuna's body. And Oyuna's heart was pierced with longing and sorrow and she began to wail along with Arctic Seal. And the wailing vibrated throughout her body from the depths of her toes, through her bones and muscles, up her spine to the ends of her fingers, circulating through her whole being. And she howled and moaned for all the women who have suffered loss and disappointment, rejection and wounding, and longing never fulfilled.

And the wailing sound vibrated powerfully over the Icy Sea of Pain and Sorrow and began to crack open the ice. The frozen women began to stir and awaken and break out of their icy enclosures. They too began to wail and moan and make the sound that released more and more women from their frosty doom. And the women freed from the frozen waters gathered on the edge of the sea and a warm fire was built and the elders held the sacred circle and listened to their stories of sorrow. And through their storytelling they came back to themselves because the sisters held the circle strong and valued each tale in the telling.

But Oyuna's initiation was not over, for she had not yet liberated the frozen hearts that were trapped in the Netherworld of Grief. And the Queen elder said, "To complete this initiation, you must face your deepest grief." So the Queens brought Oyuna to the frozen gateway of the Netherworld of Grief. There she was instructed to hold her crystal heart to help her with the great challenge that lay ahead. There at the gateway, she was greeted by another guide named White Polar Bear, who led her into the Netherworld of Grief. Deep into the Netherworld they journeyed until they came to the place called the Imprisoned Heart. And there in the icy depths, Oyuna was horrified to see a life-size frozen cage, the chilling cage that grows around the human heart when it has been broken through grief.

Suddenly without warning, White Polar Bear growled and pushed Oyuna into the cage of the Imprisoned Heart and locked it shut. "To release the heart from its misery, you must experience all the ways you keep your heart locked and caged! Face your grief Oyuna. There is no way around it. There is no place to hide from it. The way to wholeness lies in going through your grief." Inside the frozen cage, Oyuna's heart contracted with misery as she recalled every memory that filled her with grief and every person who had rejected her when her heart was wide open and tender. She recalled every betrayal, every wound and as she did so, the cage around her heart tightened and trapped her even further and she felt her heart freezing right there inside the ice-cold cage of the Imprisoned Heart.

And White Polar Bear brought forth a bucket of poison ice arrows that she threw into the cage, right at Oyuna's heart. And with each poison arrow she shouted, "You'll never get what you want in love. No one will ever love you. You don't deserve love in return. You'll be rejected if you open your heart. See how your heart has shriveled and hardened. You are doomed to be disappointed in love. You will always feel this longing in your heart. Love will never find you. Love will never fulfill you." And the poison ice arrows pierced Oyuna's heart, which flooded with grief and despair at never knowing love, never feeling supported, never being considered, never feeling held or nurtured in a way that fed her soul.

And just when Oyuna felt she would die of a broken heart, she seized her sacred crystal heart and held it up to her own thumping heart and immediately she could feel the poison ice arrows loosening their grip. White Polar Bear called to her saying "Oyuna, see how you keep your heart caged and locked by holding onto these wounds and betrayals. You are still frozen with grief." Oyuna cried, "But I cannot get rid of the wounding memories. I cannot forget. I hold on because it is the only way I have power over my grief." But White Polar Bear assured her, "There is another way. Surrender Oyuna, Surrender to your grief. Let go and let the waters flow."

And because Oyuna did not want her heart to be imprisoned any longer, she surrendered to her grief. She surrendered to all grief, to all the grief that all women have felt. She began to cry and she cried and cried with tears flowing and flowing and flowing. She surrendered to the crazy, mad grief that threatened to split open her heart. And White Polar Bear held her hand through the cage. And slowly as Oyuna continued to flow freely with her tears of grief, the frozen cage began to melt and the tightness in her chest began to loosen. And as the cage melted, White Polar Bear held her as she collapsed and her whole body shook with grief. And she saw the faces of those who had hurt her, rejected her, wounded her, and betrayed her and she released them from her heart. "I release you from my heart space. I release the grief I hold around that memory. I release my despair. I release this cage around my heart. I free my heart to trust and love." And with this surrender, Oyuna felt a releasing of centuries of held grief, centuries of imprisoned hurts and violations. And she held her crystal heart up to her warming heart and a flicker of compassion flared in Oyuna's heart and her heart began to warm and thaw.

And as Oyuna's warm compassion flowed, the ice around the Netherworld of Grief began to melt and release all the women who had been caged there. And Oyuna showed them how to grieve and how to release the cage that grows heavy and constricting around the human heart. And when all the women walked out of the Netherworld and back to the Icy Sea of Pain and Sorrow, they witnessed a wondrous transformation. The icebergs had melted and the seawater was warming into a beautiful ocean flourishing with new life. The Queen elders brought boats and took all the women who had wandered off their path of power into the Shadowlands of Grief and Sorrow back to their Path of Power, back to the land of the Queens, back to the Path of Compassion.

Oyuna Part 4: The Ocean of Heart Wisdom

After Oyuna's initiation in the far north where she melted the Icy Sea of Pain and Sorrow and surrendered in the Netherworld of Grief, the elders brought her to the deep ocean for the next phase of her initiation. For many days they sailed south to warmer seas until they came to the Ocean of Heart Wisdom. The Queen elder said, "Oyuna, the heart needs special food to grow wise. There is good food and there is bad food, you must learn to tell the difference and protect your heart from poisonous food. Put on this special diving gear and go to the place of Great Octopus, she will teach you how to protect your heart."

So Oyuna dove into the Ocean of Heart Wisdom and swam to the place of Great Octopus where the water was the deepest blue and many octopus friends floated gracefully with their tentacles swaying in the warm ocean current. "Welcome Oyuna", said Great Octopus. "I will teach you how to protect your heart. Because a Queen is naturally endowed with a big heart, she is more vulnerable to the emotional demands of others. She can easily get entangled, hooked, and ensnared into carrying her loved one's emotional burdens. Therefore a Queen must learn to protect her heart and stop poisonous entanglements from knocking her off her emotional balance." Oyuna asked, "How does a Queen become entangled? Teach me to protect my heart!"

Great Octopus spread out her giant tentacles and said, "See my long tentacles Oyuna? These are like the cords of connection that flow back and forth between you and those you love. Sometimes these tentacles are avenues of love and nurturing and give you good food to help your heart grow strong. But sometimes the tentacles grab and entangle you, feeding you poisonous food that is toxic to your heart. Oyuna, hold your sacred crystal heart in your hands. It will glow red hot as a warning when a poisonous tentacle is near. Only take in the good food, the genuine love that feeds your heart."

Suddenly Oyuna was surrounded by the octopus clan as they fanned out their long, suckered tentacles and challenged her saying, "Let's see how people entangle you Oyuna. Let's see how your loved ones ensnare you and knock you off your emotional balance!" And Oyuna heard the voice of her loved one as one tentacle reached out toward her, "I love and support you. I believe in you." This felt like good food so Oyuna opened her heart and felt the love flow in. But then another tentacle reached out toward her and she heard, "Oyuna, you are responsible for my happiness. Take care of me!" And her crystal heart glowed red with warning but Oyuna felt guilty and gave in to the voice and the giant tentacle wrapped around her and she became entangled in the sticky octopus arm.

Then more tentacles came toward her and she heard voices saying, "Oyuna attend to my needs, they are more important that yours. Oyuna take my pain away. Oyuna you are the only one who understands me. Oyuna help me with my problems!" Her crystal heart glowed red hot but Oyuna was confused by their pleading voices. I'm a Queen, shouldn't I help them? But all the sticky tentacles tangled around her arms and legs and wrapped around her so tight that she could no longer breathe.

"Oyuna!" shouted Great Octopus. "See how you believe these voices and give into their unreasonable demands! You are not responsible for their happiness! See how you are seduced by guilt and manipulation! See how you take on other people's pain and sorrow! This does not help others. This is not the true compassion of the Queen. This food is poisonous to your heart. You are not protecting yourself. Do you wish to be free of these emotional entanglements?"

"Yes, please Great Octopus. Show me how to cut myself free of my entanglements." Great Octopus gave her a sharp knife so she could cut herself free. "You must name each tentacle; name where it comes from and how you get entangled by it. Then cut the tentacle and release the poison that flowed into your heart. Then send love and compassion to each person you disentangle from. Only when you can protect your heart will you be free to love as a true Queen."

So Oyuna took the knife and held it to one of the tentacles that bound her heart. "I am not responsible for your happiness! I release you with love and compassion and send you on your way." And with all her strength, she cut the tentacle. Then she took another one and shouted, "Your needs are not more important that mine. I must attend to my needs first." And she cut the tentacle and said, "I release you with love and compassion and send you on your way." She took another tentacle and said, "I cannot take your pain away. I will not take on your emotional burdens. This will not heal you!" Oyuna cut and slashed all the many tentacles that had been feeding toxic poison into her heart for many years and she said, "I release you with love and compassion and send you on your way."

After Oyuna had cut all the tentacles entangling her she collapsed and Great Octopus rushed in to catch her and hold her in a loving, soft embrace. Oyuna fell into her soft body and was caressed by the gently swaying arms of one who understood how to give real love without emotional demands. And Oyuna felt a deep freedom she had never experienced before. She realized she had the power to say no and not feel guilty. She had the power to protect her heart. She had the power to release her loved ones to find their own emotional power within themselves. And slowly after much compassionate holding from Great Octopus, Oyuna felt her emotional balance once again. Great Octopus surrounded her and said, "Well done my daughter. Remember to heed the red hot warning of your crystal heart and always protect yourself from negative energy. Take care of your emotional needs first. This makes a Queen's heart grow strong so that she can give others true love and true empathy. Only this kind of compassion can heal others. You are now ready to go to Starfish, who will teach you how to extend the boundaries of your heart."

So Oyuna swam to the place of Starfish who greeted her saying, "Now that you can protect your heart, I will teach you to expand your heart. If a woman extends her love to everyone and everything but has no boundaries, this can be dangerous. She can be flooded with the pain, sorrow, and the problems of the world and can drown, losing her objectivity and powers of compassion. Oyuna, see the star shape of my body? Imagine this star shape inside of your heart. Each one of my rays is like a ray of compassion, radiating out in all directions. Now Oyuna, imagine extending the circle of love and compassion to your loved ones."

And Starfish saw a wave of compassion emanate out from Oyuna's heart. "Good Oyuna, now extend your circle of love and compassion wider to people in need.... Good, now extend your circle of love and compassion to all beings..... Good, now extend love and compassion to your enemies." Oyuna struggled with this last request, but she tried hard to extend love and compassion even to her enemies, to those difficult people who were very hard to love. As Oyuna sent compassion to her enemies, the starfish rays of love lit up and her chest opened and she felt love for all beings and her heart felt free. Starfish was very pleased with Oyuna's ability to extend her heart. "Well done Oyuna, well done. Now it is time for you to visit Dolphinia, your dolphin sister, to deepen your empathy even more!"

And so Dolphinia joined her in the warm Ocean of Heart Wisdom and presented Oyuna with people who were in very difficult life situations. And Dolphinia said, "In order to learn true empathy, you must step into other people's lives, feel what they feel, and understand their perspective. For when you truly understand their struggles from the inside out, you will gain empathy so powerful, it will banish all judgment from your heart. And when the heart is free of judgment, love knows no bounds and the power of love can be unleashed into the world."

Then Dolphinia swam around Oyuna and swished her magic tail and Oyuna found herself inside the body and heart of a women caught in a very hard life situation. Oyuna felt her pain, lived her struggles, cried her tears, and experienced the depth of her suffering. And with each person she empathized with, Dolphinia encouraged her to drop all judgment, all criticism, and all prejudice. And over time Oyuna felt profound empathy for each person's path and deep compassion for their suffering, but she did not get flooded by it. Over time, Oyuna became profoundly open hearted, forgiving, tolerant, generous, and kind to all she encountered. "Well done" said Dolphinia, "You are now ready to go to Manta Ray and Sting Ray to learn about the emotional power of words."

So Oyuna swam to the place of the Rays where many manta and sting rays flapped their graceful wings through the clear blue-green water. "Welcome Oyuna" said Sting Ray. "It is crucial for a Queen to understand the power of words, for words are a form of energy that can either heal or create destruction within the heart. A Queen must learn right speech. She must learn to speak truth with compassion and deliver words with diplomacy and kindness. Words delivered with kindness can nourish the heart, but words delivered to the heart with malice and cruelty can crush and destroy a tender heart. Witness what happens when a woman receives harsh and cruel words into her heart."

And there before her, Oyuna saw an older woman shouting harsh words at a younger woman who cowered in fear. As the cruel words left her mouth, the angry woman grabbed a stingray and hurled it stinger first. The sharp stinger of the stingray pierced the younger women's heart and she doubled over in pain. Sting Ray said, "Words with the energy of anger, hatred, malice, and cruelty pierce the tender heart and damage the force field that protects the heart. Now witness what happens when a Queen delivers truth with compassion." And Oyuna saw one of the Queens with the same younger woman. Before speaking the Queen centered in on her heart and took a deep, calming breath. As she spoke her words with truth and kindness, Manta Ray delivered the message gently into the younger woman's heart and she received the words as nourishing.

And for many days with Manta and Sting Ray, Oyuna explored the different energies of words and how they affect others for good or ill. And she learned to deliver truth mediated by compassion. She learned to center first on her big heart and breathe deeply and speak with kindness. She learned to mediate between people who were in great conflict, helping them find solutions. She learned the art of negotiation and how to find the right words that are medicine to the soul. And Oyuna never again underestimated the power of words, for she now understood very well how powerfully they can destroy or heal.

And when her initiation with Manta and Sting Ray was complete, the Queen elders gathered in a circle and said to her, "Well done Oyuna. Your heart has grown wise in the Ocean of Heart Wisdom. With Great Octopus you learned to free your heart from emotional entanglements. From Starfish you learned to extend the boundaries of your heart with great love and compassion. From Dolphinia you learned deep empathy and non-judgment. And from Manta and Sting Ray you learned right speech and the emotional power of words. Now it is time for your final initiation in the Temple of Self Love."

Oyuna Part 5: The Temple of Self Love

After Oyuna's time in the Ocean of Heart Wisdom, the elders knew that she was ready to learn the greatest secret of the Queens - how to love the self with profound compassion, compassion so powerful it banishes all self-loathing and casts out all self-hatred so that the heart can do nothing but love. And so back they traveled to the Queen's Grotto to visit the Temple of Self-Love. Now the Temple of Self-Love was an open-air temple on the far side of the grotto, with white marble pillars and lush green vines growing up the sides. And in the center of the Temple was a courtyard with white marble statues of women placed all around. Another space was full of big chairs and baskets of food, mirrors, brushes and multi-colored oils, scented with perfume. And in another place, there were waterfalls, pools and fountains of clear, fresh water flowing and splashing.

A Queen of the Temple approached Oyuna saying, "Welcome to the Temple of Self-Love. Come and meet the Sculptress of the Temple. She will carve your beautiful figure into a white marble statue that will be displayed around the Courtyard of Goddesses in the Temple of Self-Love." So Oyuna posed for the Sculptress as she lovingly carved her statue. At first this was difficult because Oyuna felt self-conscious and embarrassed, for she discovered feelings she held secretly against herself, feelings of revulsion, disgust, and shame. But over time she surrendered to the experience and accepted her body just the way it was. Finally the statue of Oyuna was complete, with every nuance of curve, muscle, roundness, and extravagance of body part, in all its stunning and beautiful naked truth. And the Queens lovingly carried her statue to the Courtyard of Goddesses and displayed it there along with other Queen initiates from times past.

And when it was devotion time in the Temple, Oyuna watched as hundreds of worshipping devotees came to the Courtyard of Goddesses. Many were drawn to her particular statue because they felt she embodied the Goddess that spoke to their heart. And this group of love-struck devotees gently adorned Oyuna's statue with flowers and anointed her with oil. They bent low on bended knee and lay down and kissed her marble feet. They brought offering baskets of fruits and nuts, figs and pomegranates and all manner of delicious fruit to honor the feminine beauty embodied by the statue of Oyuna. And as Oyuna watched her statue being touched, caressed, loved, and adorned, a door swung open deep inside and she felt a self-love she had never known. There were people in the world who loved her body shape, her curves, her roundness, and her extravagant body parts. Strangers found her body type a perfect ambassador of the Sacred Feminine, a succulent representative of the Goddess Herself.

And when the elders perceived her growing self-love and self-acceptance, they led her gently into the Tent of Healing Touch. Here she was helped onto an elegant couch, strewn with billowy pillows, and colorful, soft fabrics. Several Queens attended her, catering to her every need, offering cool water and delicious refreshment. The attending Queen encouraged her, "You must learn to receive Oyuna, receive the healing touch that banishes all self-loathing you carry in your body and soul. As we massage your body and stroke your hair, let go of any shame or self-hatred you carry. Let any resistance melt away as we attend to your needs. Take in the love you so deserve because you are a daughter of the Goddess."

And the Queens rubbed her hands and massaged her body, brushed her hair and washed her feet with the love and tenderness of a mother caressing her child. They sang her sweet songs and soothing lullabies that sank into her heart like soft, gentle rain. And with each song and each loving touch, Oyuna soaked in the love, soaked it into the parts of her that were parched and dry, barren and empty, desolate and bleak. And gently the love she received replaced old feelings of self-hatred and self-loathing.

She began to feel loved and adored, appreciated and valued, cherished and treasured. She found herself saying, "I love my body. I love myself. I am worthy of love. I am worthy of tenderness. I am held and supported. I am honored. I am precious. I am valued. I am cherished and treasured." And the more time she spent in the Tent of Healing Touch, the further she sank into the luxury of deep self-love.

When Oyuna's initiation in the Tent of Healing Touch was complete, the Queen elder said, "Come to the Sanctuary of Healing Waters, a special place in the Temple where you will be cleansed in the Waterfall of Generations and blessed in the Fountain of Abundance." So she brought Oyuna to the Sanctuary of Healing Waters, where a great waterfall poured out of the rocky cliff, splashing and spraying onto the white marble floor.

"This, Oyuna, is the Waterfall of Generations. Your female lineage goes back for many generations, as far back as you can imagine. Somewhere in the line of your ancestors, your mothers and grandmothers may have been ill treated for being women. Some of them suffered, some were punished, and some were harmed, injured, and silenced for being women. This can cause negative energy to tumble down the generational line to you Oyuna. If you choose to stand under the Waterfall of Generations, you can cleanse your female lineage. With your loving intention, the falling water can dissolve any fear or anger your mothers and grandmothers may have held around being feminine."

Oyuna stood under the Waterfall of Generations. Holding her sacred crystal heart, she let the water fall on her head and shoulders and over her entire body. She focused her loving intention on cleansing her female lineage. And she cried to the roaring Waterfall, "Release my mothers and grandmothers from their suffering. Liberate my ancestors of any anger or fear they hold around being female. Dissolve any and all hatred of the feminine or hatred of women that has been passed down my lineage. If I myself in any way disregard, disrespect, degrade, defile, or reject the sacred feminine and my feminine ways of being in the world, cleanse and purify me oh mighty Waterfall of Generations!" And to Oyuna's surprise, she saw her mothers, grandmothers, and great grandmothers dancing for joy under the waterfall with her, their spirits laughing and rejoicing at their liberation and cleansing, as centuries of negativity and suffering washed away in the turbulent waters. And Oyuna's heart burst open with gratitude as the entire lineage was cleansed that day in the Waterfall of Generations.

And the Queens in the Sanctuary also danced with joy because Oyuna had attained a power of love in her heart that was so strong, so magnificent, and so spectacular, it created a magic love potion that flowed like liquid gold through all the waters in the Temple. Now the Queens could drink from the golden waters and love themselves with a profound love that would open their hearts to full capacity and banish all self-hatred forever. And the elders said, "Come with us Oyuna, you are ready to receive blessings from the Fountain of Abundance."

And there, in the center of the Sanctuary of Healing Waters, stood the Fountain of Abundance, a beautiful, shimmering fountain, shaped like a chalice with clear, fresh water spilling out in all directions. And the eldest of the Queens took a golden chalice from the side of the fountain and filled it with the magic water. And one by one, each Queen gave Oyuna a sip of healing water from the Fountain of Abundance and offered her a sweet blessing. "Live from abundance my daughter." "Feel the bounty of your life my sister." "Wholeness lies in total self-acceptance." "Your wealth resides in your generosity of heart." "All your needs are being met." "When you open to the flow of life, life flows abundantly towards you." And on and on the blessings flowed, flowed until the moon rose high into the night sky and the stars sparkled down upon the Clan of the Queens.

And for many days and nights the Queens celebrated in the Sacred Grotto, drinking love potions in the Temple of Self-Love, luxuriating in the Tent of Healing Touch, swimming with the dolphins, and telling stories by the fire near the cove. And over the years Oyuna became the greatest Master the Queen Clan had ever known, for she could command the mighty waters, melt any glacier of grief, bring joy where there was sadness, hope were there was despair. And she lived among the people, radiating deep and profound love to all she encountered. And each day, with dignity and honor, she walked the Path of Compassion, the path of a true and loving Queen.

Walking the Path of Compassion

QUEEN CLAN OVERVIEW

Archetype: **The Queen**
Path: **The Path of Compassion**
Essence: **Powerful in Heart**
Element: **Water**
Tool: **Crystal Heart**
Qualities: **Openhearted, emotionally honest, generous, empathic, compassionate, and diplomatic**
Affirmation: "**I am compassionate, openhearted, and emotionally balanced.**"
Motto: **"Water Clan Women, full of emotion, big of heart."**
Empowerment: **comes through emotional honesty**
Shadow Archetype: **Martyr**
Shadow Path: **Path of Self-Sacrifice**

In this story we are introduced to Oyuna, our Queenly Divine Feminine guide. The path she walks is the Path of Compassion and her tool is the Crystal Heart. During the course of her initiation, she learns to be emotionally honest, emotionally contained and emotionally balanced, and she becomes the big-hearted Queen she was always meant to be. What does her story mean for you? How can you follow her lead and become a compassionate, self-loving Queen?

As an emerging Queen, you need to find your relationship with the Water Clan. This might mean connecting more deeply with your emotions and having more compassion for yourself. It may mean coming into better relationship with Water, soaking in baths and hot tubs, taking showers, and imagining you are cleansing in the healing waters. It might be helpful to go sailing or kayaking or surfing to come into closer contact with the power of the seas, oceans, rivers, or lakes. You may want to drink more water and feel replenished and renewed more often. Connecting with the Water element - however you do this - will bring you into a deeper relationship with your Queen.

To begin her initiation, Oyuna is taken to the place of the Sacred Waters, a tropical grotto with rivers, lakes, waterfalls, fountains, and all manner of flowing water. Here she learns about the Water Clan Women and how they are full of emotion and big of heart. She learns that their empowerment comes through emotional honesty. She also learns that Queens can call upon the mighty waters to cleans emotions, open the floodgates of compassion, and melt glaciers of grief. She learns that Queens are open, tolerant, generous, and kind and that their role in the village is to mediate when people feel overwhelmed, irrational, or out of control.

At the beginning of her initiation, Oyuna is taken to Flowing River, Boiling Swamp, and Still Lake. At Flowing River she honors all her feeling and allows them to bubble up from the depth of her being. For you, this is when you dare to honor all kinds of feelings such as anger, rage, joy, sorrow, envy, enthusiasm, and so on. When you allow all feelings to flow in an atmosphere of honesty and non-judgment, you can continually cleanse your emotions so your system doesn't get blocked with emotional toxins and poisons.

Flowing with your emotions doesn't mean acting them out, it simply means allowing them to bubble up from the depths of your being so that you are no longer repressing them. You may have some inner taboos against feeling certain feelings such as anger, rage, or grief, so they fall into the unconscious never to be found or felt. This can be toxic to your body and soul because your waters are no longer flowing. When you allow yourself to be honest about your true feelings, they can flow once again.

After a few days with Flowing River, Oyuna sees a vision of what happens to a woman when the sacred rivers are blocked and the emotions do not flow. She sees how the toxins and poisons build up in a women's heart and her emotional body becomes dammed up and blocked. When she asks why this happens, the River answers, "Women are taught to be nice, to be good, to cooperate and do what others want them to say and do. Women forget how to be emotionally honest and so their sacred rivers do not flow."

In order to cleanse yourself of the poisons of blocked up feelings, you can challenge yourself to not edit your emotions. You can ask yourself the questions: If I am emotionally honest what do I feel? If I am emotionally honest what do I need to say? If I am emotionally honest what do I need to do? Then you can take the advice of Flowing River, "Do not be nice, do not be good, go ahead and stir the waters my daughter, you are safe and protected in this initiation space. Do not be afraid of your own heart."

This exercise allows all the crusty layers of your nice, good, appropriate self to fall away so that you can cleanse your body and soul. You can do like Oyuna does and imagine lying down in the river and allowing the flow to carry away any and all emotional toxins. You may be blessed to hear the song of the River, "Flow with your own heart, cleanse and be healed. Flow with your own heart, cleanse and be healed. Flow with your own heart, cleanse and be healed." As you surrender to the mighty Flowing River you may even hear the song of your soul.

In the next part of her initiation, Oyuna is taken to Boiling Swamp and is instructed to develop an internal cauldron to hold and process all of her feelings. Whenever you find yourself in the Boiling Swamp of difficult memories and emotions, you can contain the internal heat and chaos by imagining you have a sturdy, solid cauldron inside your body. You may find you have big emotions that need to be contained such as anger, frustration, grief, or sadness. On the other hand, you may not be in touch with your feelings and need to allow them to bubble up to the surface. Either way, your inner cauldron will help you contain and metabolize your emotions, master them, and deal with the intensity of your heart.

Feelings of rage or outrage, fury, anger, and frustration need to be felt and not suppressed. Grief and hurt also need to be expressed and honored. Sometimes we just need to blow off steam! A Queen learns how to manage all her emotions without acting out, repressing, or blocking them. This way she learns to flow with all her emotions so she keeps her waters moving, flowing, bubbling, and swirling.

Oyuna is then taken to Still Lake, where she learns to quiet her heart and still her emotions. She learns to breathe and be tranquil so that she can calm her waters and become internally silent and serene. She invites the stillness of the water to enter her heart in order to feel internal balance. Still Lake whispers to her, "Accept who you are. Accept what you are. Return to yourself and your place of equilibrium. Breathe in peace, breathe out calm."

When you learn to calm your heart as Oyuna does, you can provide a Queenly, calming presence in the village whenever a tempest of emotions and tidal wave of feelings threaten to overwhelm. When you learn to calm your heart you can connect with the heartbeat of creation and experience an exquisite equilibrium. This inner balance and harmony prepares you to be a powerful Queen when others are in crisis or when you need to steer through some rough storms.

Another important aspect of the Queen initiation is surviving the Shadow path of the Queen in the Icy Sea of Pain and Sorrow. In the story, Oyuna travels to the far North to rescue the women who have wandered off their Path of Power and onto the shadow path of self-sacrifice. Here their waters no longer flow because their hearts have been frozen through grief, pain, and neglect. These women have sacrificed their lifeblood giving to everyone else but themselves. Their hearts are frozen and they are doomed to remain forever disappointed in love. They have forgotten how to be vulnerable and their hearts are closed. They have aligned their energy with the Martyr and continually sacrifice themselves and close down their hearts.

I imagine you can relate to being in the Icy Sea of Pain and Sorrow and that at some point in your life, you closed your heart because you were hurt or betrayed. During the Queen initiation it is crucial to sit compassionately with your own grief and discover where your emotions have frozen through grief, pain, loss, neglect, and sacrifice. When you are hurt, your emotions usually contract and stop flowing. When you don't know how to process a loss or a betrayal, your waters often freeze and you can get stuck in a frozen wasteland where it is hard to reach out. It's hard to open your heart and be vulnerable again and you may fall into depression or hopelessness.

Oyuna finds a solution to this dilemma when she encounters the Arctic Seal of Sadness during her initiation. Arctic Seal begins to sing the song of the frozen ones, a song of deepest loneliness and defeat. "My body is heavy with sadness and my eyes blinded by tears. My heart has been torn to shreds and lies shattered on the ice and rocks. Will my sorrow ever end, will my pain ever subside, will my longing ever cease? How can I bear the unbearable?" This is the key to the great thawing process – allowing yourself to grieve, to wail, and to make sounds that match your sorrow and longing. When you can tap way down into your grief and loss, and feel the ancient feelings, your waters start to flow once again.

I remember well the first "grief ritual" I attended. It was designed to give participants the opportunity to let go of any grief we held so that we could be liberated from the icy grip of grief and loss. I already had a lot of experience with crying and grieving because I had been in therapy for quite some time. But I was not prepared for the ancient depth of grieving and the sounds that emerged from my body as I surrendered to the grief process. To prepare for the grief ritual, we had created together as a community a "grieving shrine" where people could come to grieve. When it was my turn to spend time at the grief shrine, (it was night and the drummers were drumming and others were holding space) I knelt down and took some deep breaths. I thought of the grief I wanted to release and then something else took over! I began to cry and wail and make sounds that were completely foreign to me. Was that me wailing? I allowed myself to vocalize ancient, profound grief from the bottom of my toes to the top of my head. It felt as if grief was leaving every cell of my body.

The key to releasing my grief was the sound. I felt like Arctic Seal, putting voice to grief that my mind could not comprehend. It was a total body experience. I encourage you to either set up a grief ritual for yourself or join a group that is ritualizing the grieving experience. However you do it, allow yourself to vocalize your grief, no matter what sounds come out of you. Allow yourself to wail like Arctic Seal and release long buried grief from your system. It will profoundly cleanse you and awaken a new power inside your Queen.

The other initiation test in the great icy north is when Polar Bear pushes Oyuna into the cage of the Imprisoned Heart. Here she recalls every memory that fills her with grief and she experiences how this contracts her heart and builds a cage around her heart. As a Queen you need to release any and all cages around your heart so that it is free and unencumbered. When you hold onto wounds and betrayals, it ultimately hurts you instead of the person you believe perpetrated the crime. In the story, Oyuna must surrender and let go and release all of things that keep her heart caged. When you do the same, you can feel a tremendous relief and cleansing and opening of the heart. This allows space for love and compassion to enter and healing to occur.

The next adventure in the Queen initiation is when Oyuna is taken to the Ocean of Heart Wisdom, where she learns about the kind of emotional food that can feed her heart. She learns to discriminate between good and bad food and to free her heart from emotional entanglements. She begins this part of her initiation with Octopus who shows her how to recognize and take in the good food. Then she is shown bad food that is often sugar coated to look like good food! "You are responsible for my happiness. Take care of me. Attend to my needs, they are more important than yours. Take my pain away." Octopus shows Oyuna how to resist taking on other people's emotional burdens. Queens are naturally big-hearted and often take care of others at their own expense. Queens often get hooked, entangled, and ensnared into taking care of others, when really, people should be taking responsibility for their own path and journey.

When you can distinguish between good and bad emotional food coming your way, you will be more discriminating about what you take into your system and what you do not. Good emotional food is support without strings attached. It is clean, good, nourishing food. When people ask you to carry their burdens or take their pain away, this is often a manipulation and not good food at all! Bad food makes you feel guilty, ashamed, and confused. A strong Queen can say no and desires above all that each person take full responsibility for their lives. She can be there to support, encourage, and love, but not take responsibility for anyone else. This is a crucial lesson to learn in the Queen initiation.

It is also helpful on this Queen's Path of Compassion, to identify the difference between negative entanglements and cords of connection. With cords of connection to others, you can give and receive positive emotional food. Love and support flow naturally and it feels good. When caught in negative entanglements, you often take in toxic emotions, which feel poisonous and make you feel bad. It's shocking when you discover the amount of toxin you have been willingly taking in from other people. Perhaps you believed this was your job, your responsibility, and your duty – to take on other people's emotional burdens. Really take a good look at this in your own life and see the kinds of emotional toxins you have been soaking in, eating, and metabolizing for others. See what it does to your own emotional waters!

As a healthy Queen, you can disentangle from all poisonous tentacles and release these people with love and compassion, sending them on their way to be on their own journey. A Queen refuses to be co-dependent because she knows how toxic this can be for her emotional life. A Queen fiercely protects her sacred waters and no longer takes in any toxins from the outside. It is her birthright to be free and clean from emotional toxins.

Next in the Queen initiation, Oyuna learns from Starfish how to extend her love, empathy, and compassion to all beings, even to her enemies. This comes after she has cut negative entanglements, so she has already learned how to have healthy boundaries and self-protection. So when she spreads love to the world it is not draining her of precious life energy. It is easy to extend love to your beloveds. It's entirely another matter to extend love to your enemies. It feels counter-intuitive; your instincts probably kick in and you want to withdraw your energy from your enemies. However, when you can extend love to your enemies, you release the grip they hold over you and you liberate your heart even more.

When you can radiate out your Queenly heart to the world, it unleashes a kind of pure compassion that is needed in the world at this time. When you practice this, you can imagine your love and compassion as a color and a substance that spreads around the world and has a powerful, positive effect. As a Queen you can have a profound impact on the moods/emotions/feelings of the world around you. You can uplift the mood, change hatred into love, and transform the way people feel about someone or something. Through your positive emotions you can change, transform, shape, and mold the world around you to make it a better place!

When Oyuna encounters Dolphinia in the Ocean of Heart Wisdom, she learns deep empathy and non-judgmental acceptance. You can practice this by identifying someone in your life with whom you feel critical, and find it difficult to accept and love. Then imagine stepping into their shoes and living their life for a day. When you truly understand a person's struggles from the inside out, you gain empathy so powerful it banishes all judgment from your heart. This frees your heart profoundly and leaves a lot more room for empathizing and understanding. Imagine your life when you let go of blame, judgment, and criticism. Imagine how your heart will be open, forgiving, tolerant, generous, and kind.

Next Oyuna meets Sting Ray and learns the power of words to heal or harm. She learns that words have an energy that can heal a person and give them deep support or words can create destruction within the heart. A Queen must learn the art of right speech - speaking truth with compassion and delivering words with kindness and diplomacy. You can practice this in your own life today. Practice speaking words of kindness and see their effect. See how they nourish the heart of the recipient. Notice how cruel words can crush someone's heart. You may have had destructive and cruel words spoken to you and you know how that wounded your tender heart. As a Queen, keep practicing diplomacy and compassion in action!

In her final initiation, Oyuna travels to the Temple of Self Love to learn the greatest secret of the Queen Clan – how to love the self with such profound compassion, it banishes all self-loathing and casts out all self-hatred so that the heart can do nothing but love. In order to love herself profoundly and move through her initiation, Oyuna must visit the Courtyard of Goddesses, where the Temple Sculptress carves a life-size figure of her. The statue then goes on display and Oyuna witnesses devotees worshipping her particular form as a beautiful and viable aspect of the Goddess. This is a Queenly opportunity to love your physical form with profound love and compassion. Imagining other devotees worshipping your statue can be a deep, meaningful, and liberating experience. When Oyuna understands that her body shape, curves, roundness, and extravagant body parts are a perfect ambassador for the Sacred Feminine, a door swings open and she feels self-love she has never known. I pray this door swings open for you too.

Then Oyuna is invited to lie down and to receive in the Tent of Healing Touch. This is one of the keys to loving herself so profoundly that all hatred is banished from her heart. Have you ever allowed yourself to receive a massage or any kind of beauty treatment? Have you allowed yourself to receive love into all the dry, parched places? Have you allowed the quenching waters of compassion to flow into your inner desert? This may be the trickiest part of the Queen initiation. I know when we set up the Tent of Healing Touch at the live Feminine Path of Power retreats it can feel quite scary for some women. It's hard to trust others to care for you when your heart has been hurt and shut down.

When you can receive loving, tender touch and take this kind of Divine Feminine love into the dry, barren, desolate, and bleak places inside you, it can replace old feelings of self-hatred. Feelings of self-loathing begin to drain away and are replaced with strong, abiding self-love. There is no more room for any negative self-talk when love and compassion are filling your heart cavity. During this initiation phase, you begin to hear the self-affirmations Oyuna found, "I love my body. I love myself. I am worthy of love. I am worthy of tenderness. I am held and supported. I am honored. I am precious. I am valued. I am cherished and treasured."

After the Tent of Healing Touch, Oyuna is invited to the Sanctuary of the Healing Waters where she is cleansed in the Waterfall of Generations and blessed in the Fountain of Abundance. The Waterfall of Generations represents your entire female lineage that stretches back for thousands and thousands of years and honors all the women in your family who have been ill-treated for being women. When you receive cleansing and healing for generational patterns of misogyny, persecution, disrespect, and rejection you will feel a tremendous weight off your shoulders. You will feel a deep ancestral healing that will liberate and release oppression, fear, and negativity, from your family line, from your cells, and from your very bones.

In the last part of Oyuna's initiation, she is taken to the Fountain of Abundance so she can drink the magic love potion, unique to the Queens. What's the special cocktail? How do you get this living water for yourself? Well, in the story, Oyuna created the love potion herself by having the courage to love herself profoundly so that she banished all self-hatred and self-loathing from her heart. Oyuna had attained a power of love in her heart that was so strong, so magnificent, and so spectacular, it created a magic love potion that flowed like liquid gold through all the waters in the Temple. So you create the love potion yourself through your Queen initiation by daring to love yourself completely.

I always recommend to my Queens that they intentionally activate the water they drink each day. For you, this means setting aside your purified drinking water and writing the words "Love" and "Compassion" on the glass container you use. Then breathe deeply and infuse your drinking water with abundant love and compassion. Each time you drink, imagine compassion going to every part of you, hydrating, infusing, and informing every cell of your body. You can also buy or create a golden chalice and decorate it as you would a Queen. Drink from your chalice and imagine it is your special love potion.

At the end of the Queen initiation, the Queen elders bless Oyuna. Imagine now that the elders are blessing you and take in their beautiful words. Write them down and put them on your bathroom mirror if it helps you soak them in. Make up your own blessings too, ones that are exactly right for you! "Live from abundance my daughter." "Feel the bounty of your life my sister." "Wholeness lies in total self-acceptance." "Your wealth resides in your generosity of heart." "All your needs are being met." "When you open to the flow of life, life flows abundantly towards you."

When you complete the journey with the Queens you have embodied the Path of Compassion and successfully invited this powerful love energy into your life. You have gained the powers of the Queen Clan: emotional honesty, emotional balance, compassion, generosity, openheartedness, and self-love. You can use your Crystal Heart to cleanse grief, anger, disappointment, and toxic emotions. You have said yes to awaken the Queen in yourself and in your life. You are on your way to self-mastery.

Queen Sacred Robe

When you look at the Queen Sacred Robe, what comes up for you? Here are some responses from my students:

- *She's all about movement to me, watery, fluid movement. I guess that means she can go with the flow!*
- *To me she's also about flow and flexibility. I sure need to be more flexible and flowy in my life.*
- *For me she is full of abundance.*
- *She is like the wonderful hostess, like she's throwing a party and everybody wants to come to her party. Look at all those sea creatures! She's very inviting.*
- *I'm having a hard time with her. She looks to me like she gives away too much. I want to protect myself from her. It feels like people could take advantage of her because she's so flexible.*

Notice your own reaction to the Queen because you are interacting with your own emotional body when you have your unique response. How do you relate to the water element? Are you drawn to Oyuna the Queen? Perhaps you don't like her because you have experienced people taking advantage of your big heart. Maybe you have experienced giving too much away. How do you relate to the Queen now in your life?

When would you want to call upon the Queen? Call on the Queen when you are in need of some self-love and compassion. When a situation calls for diplomacy and right speech, call in the Queen. If you need to intervene when people are overwhelmed or feeling irrational or out of control, call in the Queen. The Queen can speak kindly and respectfully. Call in the Queen when you need to nurture people, taking care to avoid dipping into your reserves of love.

I always call in the Queen when I am speaking or teaching so that my words are healing and nurturing, rather than sharp or shaming. I also call in the Queen when I need to move through intense emotions such as grief, frustration, sadness, or anger.

Interviews with Queens

The following are interviews with women who attend my *Feminine Path of Power* Programs and have interacted with all 5 Feminine Archetypes. Here is how some of them relate to their Queen.

Interview with MK

Let's talk about the Queen on the Path of Compassion. What have you learned about the Queen, about the Water Clan and about yourself?

Well I love the water. I'm always in the water and I swim a lot. I gravitate naturally to the ocean. So at first, I really related to the Queen and to her shadow path because I give a lot of love but I don't take a lot of love for myself. I got beat up in this area with my ex-husband, so I closed myself off to it. So when we first studied The Feminine Path of Power I thought I was good with the Queen. It wasn't until this summer when I started a new relationship that I was blown away with how much I was missing with my Queen. I had closed her off. I knew she was there but I had simply closed myself to receiving love. And I wasn't going to go there.

When I walked away from this last retreat I wrote down for the Warrioress one of my fears - that I'm not good enough. So with the help of the Warrioress I set the boundaries that I am good enough. But when we got to the Queen, my negative belief was – I'm not worthy of love. I could give love; especially to all the people I've had in my house living with me. I make sure that everyone else is okay, but my enjoyment in helping other people and the love I gave to others was good enough. I accepted that as good enough for me because I couldn't think about taking love in for me.

My relationship with my ex-husband didn't help this whole Queen process. I always supported him and only took the love when I could get it. And I was aware that there was always something tied to that love, like if he gave me something I would need to give something back. One example is that I love horses and one Christmas he gave my daughter and I horseback riding lessons. I was so excited because he really nailed it. So we did our six lessons and I loved it so much I signed up for six more. And he was so mad at me that I would take the time away from my professional work and my family work to go horseback riding. So there were always strings attached to the love. And in this new relationship I'm in, there are no strings attached to the love that's being offered to me. The first weekend we were together he said he loves me more than I love myself, and that I was going to have to start learning to love myself more!

Do you think it felt safer to love others rather than letting love in for yourself?

Yes, definitely because I have control then. This new relationship is helping me let go and receive because I've known him for many, many years and that helps me trust again. I don't feel like he has an agenda. He just wants to be with me and this makes me so happy!

That helps to open your heart again?

It does. It makes me better all the way around. It makes me more loving. Another thing I changed in my life is that I moved my personal altar from my living room to my bedroom. So in my bedroom I've been putting up thank you notes people have sent to me over the years. And I read them now and I feel so much love coming towards me, love I didn't let in before. So I am re-reading the cards and letting in more love this time.

That's so beautiful! Why do you think it's so hard for us as women to let love in?

For me part of it is the era in which I grew up. My mom was the classic mom who was going to be the caretaker and that's what she did - and that's what my grandmothers did so that's what I saw. And even though I lived through the women's liberation movement, where we were taught to stand up for ourselves, love wasn't really a part of that. "You're going to go into the workforce and you're going to be strong." I really don't know why it's so hard to love ourselves and let love in but we sure do a good job on ourselves not letting it in!

Well, many women I know can relate to what you said about giving love to others and getting a lot of satisfaction out of that because it's wired into our DNA. And yet it's so hard for us to let love in. It hurts too much and doesn't feel safe to let love in because we've been let down, hurt, or disappointed.

Yes, we had many experiences early on that shut that down. The fun thing in my new relationship is that we can tell each other pretty much everything. In the past I was always protective. The other thing my new man has said to me is, "You're so beautiful, I can't believe another man hasn't snapped you up." And I honestly felt that I wasn't that beautiful and why would anyone want to be with me? He says that every woman is beautiful and every woman has something. I am noticing how shut down my heart has been and probably a lot of us feel we are not worthy of love. The magazines show us something we can't relate to. We don't look like those women and we don't dress like those women. They tell you what love should look like so you start looking on the outside rather than going inside, looking at what makes you feel good on the inside.

Yes, good points. I know another challenge with the Queen is offering yourself unconditional love and compassion. How is that going?

It's improving. I'm not beating myself up as much, getting down on myself for little things I haven't done. Like if I don't do yoga today, that's okay. I just let it go rather than beating myself up. I'm accepting myself at a much deeper level. Like if I forget to bring a pair of earrings to wear at work because I was doing other stuff, it really doesn't matter and I can let it go. Happiness is coming through me on my face and not so much how I decorate myself on the outside.

So you feel it's getting easier for you to give yourself unconditional love and compassion?

It is and I have to work at! It's not easy, so I take baby steps. I remember a conversation I had with my ex-husband years ago about giving our children unconditional love. He didn't believe in unconditional love. "What if they screw up and you can't love them anymore." Are you kidding me? That's your child. I would put my life down for my child. No, he wouldn't do that! So what I'm trying to do with unconditional love is recognize if I can love my children this way then I can love myself this way. So it's a work in progress.

Well it's nice to shoot for that! Remember the love potion of the Queen? On the Sacred Robe she is holding the cup of compassion, so we can drink in and soak in that unconditional love on a daily basis.

Yes and I can do things for myself and not wait for other people to do them for me. Like giving myself a hot bath or the other day I walked to the farmers market and bought myself lavender spray. I love that!

That's a great practical way to love yourself and embody your Queen. Thanks for sharing your growing relationship with your Queen!

Interview with Margaret

Let's talk about your Queen. She walks the Path of Compassion and she's a Water Clan woman. How do you relate to your Queen?

The gift of my Queen is her compassion. I imagine myself sitting with my Queen's crown on my head. The crown helps me to gather my emotions, my self-love, and my compassion. With my Queen I can be openhearted and generous from a genuine place. When I call in my Queen, I sometimes get a lump in my throat because she is so very loving and gentle with my inner child. Then sometimes I feel the shadow side of the Queen, when I definitely don't give myself compassion but rather criticism. Then this inner character feels and sounds like my inner critic. When the inner critic runs loose, I go down a negative pathway of wanting to accomplish something, but I just procrastinate and start feeling bad about myself. My inner critic turns on and I feel an inner attack. I get stuck between being creative and courageous and feeling fear. So when I call my Queen, she talks to my little girl saying, "You sweet little girl, you're okay." I call on my Queen to balance that inner critic.

That is a sweet way of nurturing your inner child with your Queen. Why do you think it's so hard for us to receive unconditional love? When we're so willing to give it to others, why is it so hard to take it in ourselves?

I believe we have received a lot of messages, either spoken or unspoken, to not be kind to ourselves. We're told to serve others before ourselves. So we over-reach in our civic duties as women. We also often suffer from lack of self-worth. We feel we aren't worth that kind of self-love. "I'm not good enough. I don't deserve to have all this for myself. I need to give it away!" As women we get a lot of negative subliminal messages about our body image, and messages about how we relate, both in our emotional and intimate relationships.

So instead of weaving our own beautiful feminine fabric, our own beautiful tapestry, our weaving starts to have knots. What we really need is healthy mirroring and the encouragement to love ourselves. But we get negative messages from our collective and our families that we shouldn't love ourselves first. We have to unravel the negative messages wired into our nerves, into our synapses!

Do you feel that the more you call the Queen into your life the more able you are to give yourself unconditional love and compassion?

Yes. This has truly accelerated over the past 2 years. It has been phenomenal, truly phenomenal. I would say that this work started without really naming it, in the last 8 years. But now, I am really experiencing this self-love and self-compassion. I am choosing to really love myself. And I'm not just being a "Queen for a day" because now I know I am truly worthy. I can choose self-worth. I am feeling a huge acceleration of this. I can transform all that inner negativity and just say to my inner child very gently, "I know you're suffering. I am here for you."

That's so beautiful. As you're talking I'm getting an image of the sacred water of the Queen going into all those parched places inside, into the places where you haven't really accepted love before, and it's really going in.

Yes, with the Queen I always get a sense of greater creativity and lightness. I just feel lighter and filled with more love. I was up in the mountains this past weekend and I drove six miles just to find a river, because someone told me there was a nice place to see the river. So I got to the river and I just skipped my way over to the river and jumped on the rocks and put my hands and feet in the water. There was a little waterfall and I was just happy. "Hello River. I'm here." I felt so connected to the water and this place just brought me so much joy. Normally I wouldn't have done this just for myself. If my kids had wanted to go see what was there, I would not hesitate for a minute. But to go to the river just for me, just because I wanted to do it, was a great experience. It felt really good to be that kid for myself.

I like how you're talking about the Queen in a playful way. When I look at the Queen robe, she's flowing and playing with all the sea creatures and allowing the dance of life to come to her. And that's what you're talking about. Instead of blocking yourself to the flow of love, you are going with the flow of love. This river of love flowing through the universe is consistently nourishing us. When you're playful and open like a child, you can receive love in a much deeper way. Many women have shut down their hearts and don't want to be vulnerable. What you're talking about is the playful interaction with the Queen.

Yes, I am being much more playful and loving with my Queen and it is a wonderful feeling.

Thank you for sharing your relationship with the Queen.

Interview with Cynthia

I would love to hear how you're relating to your Queen and how you relate to the Water Clan.

I have a lot of affinity for Oyuna, the Queen. To embody my Queen, I'm bringing in the healthy boundaries and the groundedness of my Warrioress first because I've lacked healthy boundaries for so long. I've given away so much compassion and been sucked dry. So now with the Queen, I practice self-compassion, self-care, and self-love. It's so huge to love myself first. The more I can offer it to myself, the more love I can take in, the more compassion I have for others.

In what ways do you love yourself with profound compassion as a Queen?

In the morning, I do meditation. I ground with my Warrioress. Then I take the Queen's tool of the Crystal Heart. Once I've grounded, then I bring energy up through the chakras, and I get to the heart. I imagine my Queen's Crystal Heart reflecting light throughout my body. I've learned to hold myself with my hands on my shoulders. There are meridians there so when you press and hold your heart and shoulder you actually calm down. I've been holding and gently rocking myself and this is a beautiful practice to activate my Queen.

Just the other day, I said something to someone without the intention of hurting, but I think it hit a button and they got triggered. And then I felt terrible. I was trying to ground, ground, ground in front of my Warrioress altar. And then I had a hit to go over to Oyuna, the Queen. She offered more of a healing way to solve this problem. I could open my heart and just feel joy! And all of a sudden, I felt this radiation of the light within myself. It was very interesting and unexpected as far as a cure was concerned. I turned to the Queen and she said, "Just go to your heart and feel joy." It wasn't even about forgiveness. It was just about allowing myself to feel joy and it cleared my feelings of self-blame.

That's the power of the open heart, the Queen's heart. When you can be in your radiating heart, it just banishes negativity from your system!

Yes. I had a direct experience of my Queen in this way. It is interesting what words or images work for each of us individually. For me in that moment, it was to feel and resonate with joy. I also like to feel the Queen's fluidity. When I meditate with my Queen, I feel the watery and cleansing nature of her. I visualize swimming with the dolphins. And again, I feel that joy and freedom. This joy is all encompassing. So all that other stuff I get stuck on just washes away. There's no room for it. I love swimming, and I love being in water. It represents freedom to me.

Yes, and when you have healthy boundaries with the Warrioress, your Queen can empathize without taking other people's emotions into your system. If you don't have good boundaries, you could be taking on the watery, emotional stuff that other people want to put onto you.

Yes and when I do that, my system gets swamped. It floods. In fact, when my boundaries aren't good, I have taken on other people's emotions and literally fallen to my feet - physically fallen. Sometimes I take on emotions without even knowing it and then suddenly I can't breathe or I'm nauseous because they're nauseous. I literally feel what other's feel and I take it on unknowingly and then I get into trouble. I'm such an empath, which I know is a gift of the Queen, but sometimes I get flooded.

I think many women, like you, are clairvoyant, clairsentient, and/or clairaudient. These are intuitive ways of knowing and connecting with the world. This makes you so porous because you naturally have a big heart, and you're connecting naturally with people. Now it sounds like you've gotten that more in balance, so you can be more in the joy and the flow of the water, rather than taking on other people's emotional burdens.

Yes. I'm still breaking through some of the old mental brainwashing or belief systems I was brought up with. I was taught I was supposed to give and give and it's way more important to help others than myself. It's selfish to help myself. So I'm taking baby steps into this other Queen way of being. I'm allowing more and more love in!

I think many of us can relate to these old beliefs you mentioned. As you allow your Queen to transform your old belief - that it is better to give than to receive - she can show you a more nurturing way to live. She can fill up your cup first so your heart is filled with love and joy. Thank you so much for sharing your deepening relationship with your Queen.

Interview with Susan

Let's talk about your Queen. She represents compassion and self-nurturing. Her shadow is the path of self-sacrifice, when we give too much of our heart away and we self-sacrifice rather than being openhearted. Tell me about your Queen and what your relationship is with her.

I feel like the challenge in my childhood was that my heart was locked and caged as a defense system. Then my heart was frozen in fear and felt shattered by my relationship with my father. And because there was a ruling Queen in my family - my mother – my own Queen got overshadowed. My Queen had natural tendencies toward openheartedness and compassion for the earth and for plants and the animals.

I always felt a strong sense of love and compassion in my life so I knew my Queen was alive and well. But she was out of balance with emotions and didn't have expression of her full range of feelings because of my childhood trauma. My heart was very shielded because I was protecting my vital life essence. The cage around my heart offered protection until it felt safe to open and heal, which happened to me about four years ago.

What you have shared here probably resonates with a lot of other women. It's a common experience for many of us that we can only open our hearts when we feel safe enough. We need to trust that we're not going to be crushed or rejected, and then we can open our hearts wide.

Yes, I had to actually set up my own safe environment, a safe container for myself. My parents didn't provide any safety for my heart. When I related to my mother, I feel like my mother broke my heart. When I related to my father, my heart froze in fear. I was paralyzed with fear itself.

Oh no! You got it from both your parents!

I did. I actually felt like I had to draw on my love and compassion from nature, and my innate sense of high emotional intelligence. I was able to develop my emotional honesty and truth in my heart space. I feel like those two things really helped me. I also really wanted to heal my heart so it could be whole again.

Together with my Queen, I have dismantled the cage around my heart and uncovered what it protected. It was very much a surprise to me to see and actually feel the beauty of my own heart and to recognize it. In some ways, my heart was really untouched by my childhood trauma and the brokenness I felt after all those years. My emotional waters that had been frozen and shattered like ice, began to melt and thaw. I realized that under the deep freeze, my heart and life essence were still there, very much intact.

I see. So even though your emotional, watery heart got frozen, your essential heart was still there, untouched in some ways by the trauma you sustained in your childhood. Now that you are unfreezing your heart, you can come back to the essence of it.

Yeah. Now it is like this big, flowing river of love, now that I've taken down the cage. It transformed from ice being shattered and broken, frozen and fragmented, into this river of love. The ice turned back to water, its true essence.

That's such a great way of talking about it. I know the Queen walks the Path of Compassion. Have you experienced the compassion of your Queen?

It's interesting because in the past, I felt like I wasn't a compassionate person. Then I learned that I had a different view about compassion and I realized I was a very compassionate person. When I met my husband, he helped me see that about myself. I started to understand my definition of compassion.

A lot of it had to do with my beliefs and perceptions. I believed that a compassionate person gives money to charity. It was a narrow definition - you give money and that gets passed on to others. I just had that materialistic view of what compassion was. I didn't feel like that fit me, so I concluded I wasn't a compassionate person.

I began to really see that I could be compassionate in a non-action way. In fact for me, it was healthier to just be compassionate without any action. So my Queen's energy was spent healing my own heart and keeping the love for myself. I used to think that was selfish, but it was the right way for me to use my Queen's energy.

You're speaking about the power of self-compassion and when you validate this as a legitimate activity, you allow yourself to bathe in this gift of compassion! Giving yourself unconditional love and compassion is the supreme gift from your Queen.

Yes, I definitely defined compassion as something I did for others and not for myself. For a large part of my life, I wasn't ready to give back and I didn't have it to give. I was busy healing myself and giving myself love and compassion and attention and learning so I could become healthy and whole. Now is the time for me to share my love and compassion with others. I just stored that up. I'm ready and I think I have a lot to give.

Can you give an example of how you give yourself compassion now in your life? What does that self-compassion look like?

Of course, after all my work with you I am now giving my inner child lots of treats, like I indulge her with ice cream. It's very tangible and physical. So I eat an ice cream or I'll paint my toenails. It has a lot to do with things that feed my inner child, I think because that's my creative part. My inner child is important to me and I want her to be loved and spoiled a little bit and happy.

After doing the Tree of Life Training and The Feminine Path of Power with you, I'm more focused on self-love, compassion, and nourishment for myself first - and then others - because I know that that is the priority. Lately I've been creating "sacred selfishness", where I prioritize my day and do my things first. When I start to shift that, and feed myself first, I see how much more available I am for other people and to do other things.

If at all possible I do my art first. I'm seeing how that really changes my energy and gives me the ability to be more compassionate. I'm feeling an amazing sense of balance between my personal life and responsibilities and my mission responsibilities. That's what I'm noticing for myself right now.

Wow! That's really powerful. It's helpful to hear how you extend compassion to yourself because I know a lot of women want to have tangible examples. I love that you are taking your child out for an ice cream and painting your toenails! When we extend compassion to ourselves, we can also extend self-forgiveness and we can love every part of ourselves, even our inner critic. We can extend our Queen's compassion to every part of ourselves.

I do have another example of how I use my Queen. I am focusing on being non-judgmental towards myself. When I judge myself, I recognize now that I'm actually abandoning myself. Of course, abandonment was a theme for me in my life. Sometimes when I do my art and I look at it, I start judging it, saying things like, "I don't like it. It should be better." When the critical voice starts, I'm really focusing on loving what shows up and then learning. What I'm learning is that each picture is just a component of the whole body of work that is coming. When you put it together in a book, then each part makes up the whole. It's an important part, but it's not the only part. This helps diminish my self-judgment.

Thanks for sharing that. Almost every woman I know suffers from inner critical voices. It's great to have examples of how you are tackling that inner critic.

It feels really good. I never felt good enough so this is a good change. I have been through times when I lacked self-confidence, felt insecure, and felt invisible and powerless. I know where it's coming from because my mother was very critical and judgmental. I learned to then tell myself, "I'm not good enough. I don't meet the expectation." My Queen is really helping me move into non-judgment.

Yes, you are now giving yourself the love and compassion to be exactly who you are! You have a generous Queen! Thanks for sharing your growing relationship with your Queen.

Interview with Kala

Let's talk about your Queen. She is connected to the Water Clan and walks the Path of Compassion. She transforms and cleanses your heart so that you can love yourself and love others. Tell me about your relationship with your Queen.

I love to live so close to the ocean here in California because I can easily call in my Queen. When I am at the ocean and the sun goes down and dips beneath the horizon, I have that sense of disappearing into the unfathomable. I can throw myself into the ocean, into the depths of being. When I go to that place where the ocean and the sky meet, I can fill myself with that beautiful resource. It's like I can fall into that ocean of love and not leave anyone behind. When I melt into this love I am one with everyone. I am saturated in the presence of love.

So when you are by the water, you get replenished and you get to bathe in that beauty. The Queen provides you with personal regeneration and also you get to feel connected to all of life.

Yes, I feel each one of us is a little drop of the whole ocean. As we become immersed in compassion, then we can be compassionate towards ourselves and towards others.

Do you have a particular self-compassion practice that you'd like to share, in addition to sitting by the ocean?

One practice that is really helpful for me is centered on a little mantra that I found along the way. I sit every day at noon and say it. It's a translation from a Sanskrit mantra and it's really simple. It just says, "More radiant than the sun, purer than the snow, subtler than the ether is the self, the spirit within my heart. I am that self; that self am I."

That's lovely. Thank you for sharing that beautiful prayer. We know that the shadow side of the Queen gets us into co-dependency and self-sacrifice. Have you ever found yourself on the Shadow Path of the Queen?

Well, I've done something a bit different with my Queen. Years ago I got very into the Vajrayana Buddhist practice called "consuming the world", where I was trying to figure out all the world's problems. The practice involves things like "eating all the world's genocides" and transforming them into the bliss of space. So this is not about being co-dependent but about using my Queen's compassion for the world. My mother is a holocaust survivor. She wasn't actually in the camps because the family escaped, but when she was eight she came to America and grew up as a little refugee. She helped me a lot at one point and I wanted to give back, so I found a way to clean that karma and do this compassion practice.

It was like throwing my pebble in the pond. In doing this, I realized how every little ripple in the pond was then connected to the whole of human history, the whole of modern spirit and psyche, and social justice, and racism, and the feminine and masculine, and everything else. This journey of cleansing and clearing has taken years and years and has gone way beyond anything I had anticipated.

It sounds to me that your Queen has been very active in a more collective sense. You have dedicated a lot of energy to showing compassion for all of humanity, for all beings. This shows that women can give love and compassion to themselves and are also equipped to give love to the world. The world needs our Queens to be very active in these days. Thank you for sharing your Queen's big heart of compassion for the whole world.

Interview with Carol

Let's talk about your Queen. She walks the Path of Compassion and allows your sacred waters to flow. How are you relating to your Queen?

I can relate to the Queen, and I love my Queen now. In my childhood, I had no compassion for myself and this attitude also followed me into adulthood. This has a lot to do with my lack of healthy attachments and relationships. I always condemned myself if things went wrong in my relationships. I always beat myself up and I had no compassion for myself. I tried to adapt to the horrible situation in my childhood, but I ended up feeling it was my fault, which I know now is what children do when they are traumatized. I felt that I was guilty so there was no self-compassion for me. I actually thought that I was the most awful person in existence and that there was no hope for me.

So when I was introduced to the Queen, this was a big one for me. So instead of feeling bad about myself, or blaming myself for things, my Queen comes in with self-compassion and love. She encourages me to have great compassion for myself. She shows me how my old patterns of self-protection were survival mechanisms I used in my childhood. I was protecting myself in a healthy way and I don't have to beat myself up about it. So now I can call the Queen right into my heart and I can change.

Because I've been doing a lot of the work with the Queen, I have water cups all over my house. I have cups and jars that I drink water out of and I have written on them words like "love", "self-compassion", "peace" and "joy". Love and self-compassion are important words for my Queen and I write them on my water containers. I know, through the work of Dr. Emoto, that positive words actually change the composition of the water. So when I drink from these love cups, which are my daily drinking vessels, I am actually drinking in that love and compassion of the Queen.

I love that. What a wonderful way to embody your Queen!

And the Queen is watery too. She represents my emotions. When the Queen flows, all the fluids in my body flow. She's helps me flow through life in a more easeful way.

Oh, that's a great way to put it.

Yes, then when I do get stuck, when I start condemning myself, I call in the Queen. She has that great, deep compassion for the little child within me that was hurt so badly and was so scared and was scapegoated and always felt guilty and felt she had to fix everything. And the Queen will come in now and she'll comfort me, and help me to understand what happened in my family. She reverses my feelings of guilt. I don't have to believe that everything was my fault. My Queen will come in and tell me, "No, it's not your fault. I love you unconditionally." And so, that old pattern breaks.

Before I had my Queen, I would go deeply into that bad place to the point where I'd be so depressed and felt like the burdens of the world were on my shoulders. I used to feel like I had to win everybody's love because I didn't think I was worthy of love. Now my Queen tells me I am worthy. She makes my life flow easier. I don't get stuck in that self-condemnation. She comes in and she eases that stuck-ness so I can move and flow on.

I love your Queen of compassion! One thing I do know about you is that you have raised four beautiful children. I know you have had great compassion for your children and for others, but it's been harder to harness that love for yourself. Can you speak to this? I think many women can relate to feeling this kind of generosity they are willing to give others but not so much for themselves.

Right. I wanted to raise kids that were happy. I love my kids and that was the one thing I wanted in my life, because I had such a bad experience in my own family growing up. I have always had great compassion for other people. I wonder too, if part of it was growing up in a dysfunctional family, I always wanted to help. I wanted to fix my family. Even though I wasn't getting what I needed, I still had great compassion for my mom, my dad, and my sister. I got caught in a pattern of helping everyone else and having such great compassion for everyone else and wanting to fix everything, I forget about myself.

So even though you were traumatized as a child, you could still find an abundance of compassion to give your own kids as they were growing up. Your Queen was intact and willing to generously give to others, but you weren't able to access your Queen for yourself. Now your Queen is helping you to turn all of that lovely compassion on yourself.

Right. And something I learned from the Queen and from you Megan, is that the great compassion I have for everyone else, I can give to myself. That was a big revelation to me. What about me? What about me giving compassion to myself? My Queen now says, "Hey, you're a being who deserves love just like everyone else." That was a big revelation for me, because I didn't think I deserved any love. I had images of myself as this little child all by herself and undeserving of love. I learned through my trauma and family conditioning to think about everyone else but me.

So you've turned that all around with the help of your Queen.

Yes, so when I do feel unlovable at times, I'll call in my Queen. She tells me I am loveable and that I am worthy of love. When I can give myself this great compassion it allows me to have more of a true compassion for others.

Thank you so much for sharing so deeply and so openly about your struggles with feeling unworthy and how you are changing that all around with the loving help of your Queen.

Interview with Ali Marie

I would love to hear about your relationship with the Queen. She helps you open your heart and walks the Path of Compassion.

The Queen is a huge one for me at this time because my relationship with her is developing into something very profound. The Queen is becoming more prominent within me, and that is so healing for me. She is bringing a much-needed balance to my life. I'm now able to open up, and feel that open-heart space. I feel an internal source of love that just really flows. I've always had a sense of loving myself so if you ask me, "Do you love yourself?" I would say, "Yes." But how do I put that into practice? I've not been able to articulate any practice of self-love and now I can. After learning about the Queen, compassion practices are coming alive in my life. They're really more concrete actions that I'm taking everyday and I'm finding that I'm really guided and held by them.

In the Queen Initiation we talked about the love potion and I still have my water bottle with my heart on it. I think of that water as my love potion. And so, that's one example of how I call in my Queen. I have also been holding my own hand or hugging myself. I feel my Queen when I physically touch myself in specific ways, like touching my shoulders or kind of holding myself. These little things that I do, little actions that I take throughout the day, I feel my Queen very present. My internal dialogue has changed and become so much more loving. I call myself 'Sweetheart' and really look at myself in the mirror and practice these loving actions, loving words, loving thoughts throughout the day - particularly in the hardest parts of my day.

That's really beautiful. And it feels like it brings such a sweet balance to your Warrioress, so that when your Warrioress and Queen work together you can have this permeable boundary and feel safe and then also have love for yourself and others.

Yes. I really needed those two to get connected. I really needed the Warrioress and the Queen to get to know each other because that changes everything. That wall comes down and turns into a healthy loving boundary.

Do you feel people in your life are noticing a change?

Yes. I would have to say that definitely. These changes represent the culmination of years of work, but in our Feminine Path of Power with the visuals of the Goddesses on the Robes and time that we've spent together has helped to bring those into a culmination. I'm having a fuller experience and I do think that it is very apparent particularly to the people who are closest to me who are really aware of the differences and my openness. This new self-love and openness has become a really big part of how I am in the world.

Do you have a particular practice of calling in the Queen or feeling her inside somehow?

I think my favorite thing to do is meditation. This is one way that I connect to my Queen and all the Goddesses. One of the best ways for me to connect with the Queen is bathing and showering and anything involving water. Those water rituals are very therapeutic and very healing for me. It allows me to connect a little more to my Queen. I really connect to the water - I talk to the water, I feel helped by the water and it becomes a living experience.

Why do you think it is so hard for most women to come into good relationship with the Queen?

We are not taught tangible practices to connect with our Queen. I just don't think we're given the tools to know how to do that. I think we also get very, very confused and tripped up in the idea of selfless action being the highest goal, so it's hard to prioritize self-love. Even early on as little human beings, we have to reach outward for what we need. We have to extend outwards for the things we need to be okay in the world and then we're never taught to look inside for what we need. We have what we need all within ourselves!

When I call in my Queen and cultivate a loving relationship with myself, a flow of love starts to happen and it extends outward so naturally. So loving myself first means I really don't need it from someone else. I have what I need within. I have that fullness of love and compassion that extends through me and from me and then flows outward. Trying to grasp it externally is not sustainable for me. There will never be enough love if I'm looking for it from an external source. It has to come from within - where it already is. I need to find that Queen and find that compassion from within my own self.

Thank you, that was really well articulated. And I would agree, I think as women, we're taught to turn our Queen outward. We are taught from the time we're very young, to give that compassion away to others. And then it's reinforced through our spiritual teachings that say compassion and selfless action towards others is the highest good. What gets left out is the most important piece - the Queen is there to give love to you first.

Right, and loving myself first is the only sustainable way to go. It doesn't mean that I don't show up for other people. On the contrary, when I am so full of love and feeling that flow of unending love, eventually that love wants to go somewhere. It flows out to others. It just extends very naturally and organically, without my needing to grasp for anything. I can be more present with and for other people.

Yes, the inner Queen says things like, "Fill up your chalice first, so that when it's overflowing, the overflow goes to everyone else." I often think about the Queen as an inner fountain that's always on, so I have this source of love inside myself and it never runs dry. Then, when the fountain is flowing I can naturally give it to others.

Right. I love that. That image is perfect for me. I can see that getting in balance with the Warrioress is an absolute must, because, otherwise, if my fortress is too big with the Warrioress, I can't let love in from the outside. With too big a boundary, then the flow of love stops. When I honor my Queen, I become part of the flow. But when the walls are up this impedes the flow.

Yes, thanks so much for sharing your relationship with your Queen. I love how you are balancing your Warrioress and Queen so you can have safe, healthy boundaries and also a big heart full of love!

Interview with Susana

I would love to hear about your Queen. She walks the Path of Compassion and belongs to the Water Clan. How do you relate to your Queen?

The Queen, she is another one that is always there for me. I do need to water her at times! Sometimes I forget to nurture her as well as I would nurture my own garden. She's one that I continually bring more attention to. I find that she is naturally activated around water. So I activate her when I go swimming or I water the plants or run cold water on my feet when it's hot outside, like it is today. I find those are ways I can bring her into my heart, but I do think I ignore her more than I would like to admit.

And is that because you find that you're not giving yourself enough love and compassion, or self-care?

I would say that's true, yes. I am doing more of that actually. I'm scheduling massages and finding good practitioners near me. This good self-care is a continual journey for me. I would say I'm better, and I would say I haven't quite had the breakthrough with her that I've had with the Visionary.

What's it like for you when you do remember to call in her love and compassion?

What's it like? Yummy. Yummy and Delicious. And very special.

How do you feel that yummy-ness? How does your Queen show it?

When my Queen is really present, I experience her as *soothing. I feel her like a humming vibration. I also feel my Queen through music, when I play my harp. I listen to beautiful music in my office, when I'm writing or answering emails. I feel my Queen as a vibration around me all the time. The ways I decorate in my home or office, I surround myself with the vibration of my Queen. I do create a sanctuary in the places where I spend a lot of time.*

That's really beautiful. I was just reading about Doctor Emoto's work on water and the effects of positive thoughts and feelings on water crystals. So I love what you were saying about creating beauty and harmony in your environment, because this must have a huge effect on your internal waters. It helps you emotionally. You create an emotional sanctuary!

Yes. I believe I do. Every space I go into, I create a healing sanctuary. My colleagues laugh at me - in a wonderful way – because I do create beautiful spaces. I spend a lot of time at work in the hospital so it's important to me to have a nice space. That's a way I nurture myself and yes it's very important, the environment I'm in. In the hospital, we are moving office space and going into this new set of suites, and I'm going have a gorgeous office with windows on two sides. It's going to be absolutely lovely. My colleagues just said, "Well Susana, would you pick out the carpeting and the wall paint, and just let us know what we need to do." So they laugh at me about creating these sanctuary spaces but then they also trust me to create the beautiful space.

So you're saying that your Queen is an incredible harmonious interior designer! When you can create a good atmosphere, the good vibe helps people integrate. It helps them come into equilibrium and harmony with themselves. I think that's a huge gift of your Queen.

Yes. I agree with you. Thank you for helping me to see that. That is how she manifests in my life and I think that's so important. When I go into a hospital room to see a patient, if they've got the TV blaring and they're not watching it, I mute it so that we can talk. I'm working on bringing the relaxation channel, which is a 24-hour ambient relaxation channel on television sets, into rooms throughout the hospital. So I have been the spearhead in bringing that to the hospital because I feel that would make such a difference. If the TV's show some beautiful nature scenery with lovely music playing, this is a wonderful option for people to have.

Wow, your Queen is a Temple Priestess! She creates an environment where people can come into the flow of life. Your Queen is watery and sensitive to what I call the "ocean of love" that is flowing through the universe all the time. And when you create an atmosphere that harnesses that flow and that love, you're creating an amazing environment for people. Your Queen is really active.

Yeah, I guess she is. She's bigger than just me - that's interesting. She goes out there into the world and creates these environments around me. Wow, that's neat.

Your story helps people to understand how they can express their Queen. This is one beautiful way to express your Queen, to be very tuned into the beauty and harmony of your living and working environments.

Yes. It's very important, that. And there's so much you can do, just in little ways that can make a difference.

Thanks for sharing your Queen with us and inspiring us to let our Queen do some interior decorating. With a little help from our Queen we can create a healthy emotional environment for people to connect and feel good.

Interview with AB

I would love to hear about your relationship with the Queen. How is she working in your life right now?

I really like the Queen. I have been working for a long time on opening my heart and being self-compassionate versus self-deprecating. I don't know why I've been so hard on myself. It certainly wasn't my mother's overt judgment, for she was my main female figure, the main Queen in my life growing up. She would actually get quite upset if we weren't kind to ourselves. I've been working on forgiving myself and trying to release and grieve so that I can have some self-love and nourishment.

I called in my Queen during my grieving process when I moved recently. I didn't expect to be so shaken up when I moved. I'm rebuilding my whole life and grieving my female relationships, women that I saw on a daily basis. I miss seeing my next-door neighbor and having a cup of coffee with someone that's known me most of my adult life. Because my husband did so much traveling, I have extremely strong women in my life and my homeopathic practice was predominantly women that I cared for.

When I look at the Queen Robe and I stand in her place, I call her in to ask for respect in my household here and to help me find direction now that I've landed here in a new place. I've been looking also at the Martyr, the shadow side of the Queen. I could see her in others, now I can see her in myself!

Another thing I love about the Queen is she gives me permission to be emotional. Rather than being told I'm too emotional, actually, no, I'm not too emotional. I'm just learning to be responsible for my emotions and not take on anyone else's. As we studied the Queen in the Feminine Path of Power, I got for the very first time how I assume people are feeling certain feelings when really I'm just putting those feelings onto them. For example, if I say to my son, "You seem to be really frustrated. Can we talk about it?" He often isn't feeling frustrated. I've projected my emotions onto him, and it leaves very little room for either one of us to stand in our personal power.

So you're noticing where you've been projecting, and you're taking back your projection in order to have a cleaner way of relating to people. Thanks so much for sharing your journey with the Queen.

Queen Initiation Conclusion

When you awaken the powers of your inner Queen, you feel emotionally centered and balanced. Your heart is cleansed of debilitating grief, anger, bitterness, and disappointment. You trust your emotional intelligence and intuition.

As a Queen you hold an emotional container for yourself, your loved ones, and your community. When you embody the Queen, you are loving, compassionate, and emotionally balanced. You know how to master emotions and nourish your heart. You are emotionally honest and your heart is true. You are openhearted, generous, and empathetic. You know that self-love and self-nourishment are the keys to happiness and successful relationships.

Celebrate your Queen! You are on your way to self-mastery.

Chapter 8
The Visionary: Unlock your Creative Vision

The Story of Pujai, the Visionary

In the fourth initiation story, you will journey with Pujai (pronounced *pooj-eye*) as she trains to be a powerful Visionary, mastering the Path of Change and becoming an Air Clan Woman, powerful in mind, full of vision. You will follow her high mountain adventure as Pujai flies with Falcon, hangs upside down in the trees, learns the art of Swordcraft, masters the Winds of Change, confronts the Veils of Illusion, and awakens her visionary powers in the Dream Dome.

Part 1: The Story of Pujai

Once upon a time, a long, long time ago, there was a land where women were honored for their power and strength. It was a sacred land called the village of women where each girl child was honored for the unique gifts she brought to the sacred circle. And when each new female soul was still in the womb of her mother she would whisper her name and her soul's purpose to the elders who were eager to hear this good news.

Now in this ancient land there were 4 different clans of women that all female souls were sorted into at birth. There was the Warrioress Clan, those who walk the Way of Strength. And the Queen Clan, those who walk the Way of Compassion. And the Visionary Clan, those who walk the Way of Change. And finally the Manifestor Clan, those who walk the Way of Action.

Now one special day there was a commotion amongst the elders who had gathered to hear the good news from a new girl child who was about to be born in the village of women. When they asked who she was, what clan she belonged to, and what her soul's purpose was, this is what she said. "My name is Pujai. I come to the Visionary Clan to dance with the Sacred Winds and guide lost women back to the Path of Change." Soon the excitement spread among the entire clan of Visionaries who eagerly anticipated the birth of Pujai and the knowledge she would bring to the clan. And so Pujai was born and was cared for and nurtured, as was the custom in the village of women, for all girl children were held and loved and valued and given chores and kept in line and watched over by those who were assigned as her special guardians. And as the years went by and Pujai grew into a young woman, the elders of the Visionary clan felt that the time had come to initiate her so that she could fulfill her purpose.

And so the elders took Pujai to the Initiation training ground of the Visionary Clan, off to the high country, to the tallest peaks of the Great Mountains, where the wind blows clear and free and the giant trees thrust upward to the heavens. Higher and higher they climbed while eagles, hawks, and falcons soared overhead, guiding them to the summit of the tallest ridge. And Pujai breathed in the clear, fresh air and she felt deeply at home and felt an inner clarity she had never felt before. And when they came upon the Visionary Training ground, Pujai beheld the Sacred Site.

Nestled among the mountain peaks in a great clearing, she saw a great Crystal Palace, with a huge transparent pyramid and many surrounding towers and domes with clear windows open to the sky. There were outdoor courtyards overlooking the great expanse of land below with sweeping panoramas of the mountain peaks, valleys, and giant trees. Great birds circled around cawing and crying their welcome. And at the entrance to the palace a large banner hung overhead that read, "Air Clan Women, Powerful in Mind, Full of Vision". And as Pujai crossed the threshold, she felt deep pride in her sharp mind and was eager to begin her initiation to awaken and embody her powers.

The elders in charge of her initiation greeted Pujai welcoming her to the Visionary Palace and invited her into the great crystal pyramid at the heart of the sacred dwelling. She sat on a crystal bench and gazed around this most unusual place. The floor beneath her feet was completely transparent and revealed an upside down pyramid reaching deep down into the ground with huge milky white crystals giving off a faint glow. And above her in a perfect mirror image, an enormous translucent pyramid thrust upwards toward the sky.

Hanging on the walls of the pyramid were hundreds of swords in every size and shape imaginable. There were long silver swords with encrusted jewels, pirate swords, broad swords, daggers, black oriental swords, Egyptian swords, Viking swords, and dragon swords. And in several places Visionary women gathered around steaming cauldrons gazing into the rising mist, swaying and muttering quiet incantations. And she saw bird costumes and feathery headdresses, crystal crowns, diamond tiaras, and diadems with precious stones and jewels.

So Pujai spent her first days in the Crystal Palace learning of the Visionary powers and purpose of the Clan. And at night outside in the courtyard, Pujai sat with the elders under the moon and stars, gazing out over the vast expanse of the Great Mountains. And the drummers drummed while a fire was lit under an ancient, steaming cauldron. And the great Storyteller stood bathed in starlight, a large falcon on her arm, steam swirling around her body as she swayed to and fro. She held a silver sword and wore a wild feather headdress with a large luminescent diamond hanging down on her forehead. And the Storyteller recited all the creative changes the Visionaries had implemented over the centuries. And this is what the Storyteller said.

"We are the Air Clan Women, powerful in mind, who envision new ways, new ideas that breathe life back into the village. We are skilled in shape-shifting, attitude changing, and knowing when things need to die to be reborn. The Visionaries are called upon when things need to change, when energy gets blocked and the wheel of life is stuck in its turning. Our power lies in our objectivity, discernment, and creativity. We listen to our dreams and visions, attuning to sacred wisdom.

We are the Seers, the Knowers. We can see the way ahead when others are stuck in old ways of doing and being. We harness the power of the wind to transform outmoded beliefs, rigid dogma, and fixed attitudes. Of all our tools the Sacred Sword is our greatest ally, for as we cut through confusion and falsehood, we become clear-minded, sharp-witted, confident, and true to our inner core. We train our minds so that where others see limitations, we see limitless potentials. We liberate our minds so that we are free to create, imagine, and envision infinite possibilities."

And late that night under these very stars, Pujai was told a chilling tale of the Shadow Path of the Visionary Clan. Yes, it was true; there were some women who had wandered off their Path of Power and onto a disempowered path that robbed them of their clarity and focus. This was called the Shadow Path of Chaos. And Pujai heard disturbing tales of women who walk the Path of Chaos, doing so many things they have a tornado of energy circling around them, constantly distracted, scattering energy in a hundred directions. She saw how they deceive themselves and make every excuse why things aren't changing.

These women are vulnerable to the negative energies that stalk women on the Path of Chaos, and they sabotage themselves through confusion, procrastination, and holding on to old ways that don't work. When Pujai heard these stories, her mind cleared and a vision appeared and she knew exactly what she had to do; she must redeem the Shadow Path of Chaos and restore her sisters back to the Path of Change.

When the elders saw her intuition open and the knowledge of her destiny burst forth, they smiled and nodded around the circle for they knew the time of her initiation had come.

Pujai Part 2: Trees and Falcons

A few mornings later the elders invited Pujai into the crystal pyramid to begin her training. One of the elders said to her, "Wait outside in the great courtyard Pujai, your training will begin soon." So Pujai stepped outside and gazed out over the Great Mountains and the forests of giant evergreen trees that surrounded the Visionary's Palace. Suddenly she heard a bird's cry overhead and as she looked up, three enormous she-falcons swooped down and snatched Pujai up in their giant talons. The falcons carried Pujai effortlessly, like a feather on the wind, and flew her to the ancient forest, heading straight for the tallest tree.

And there the falcons hung Pujai upside down in the tree. Disoriented and confused, Pujai cried out, "What are you doing? I'm supposed to begin my Visionary training today!" The falcons laughed and said, "This is your training my daughter. Your training begins here, upside down in this tree. To walk the Path of Change, you must begin by changing your perception. You think you see the world as it is. This is not so!"

And the falcons flew around her diving upside down so they could look her right in the eyes. "We are shape-shifters, trickster falcons, we muddle your mind and confuse your mind so that we can re-train your mind. Look around you Pujai, what do you see?" "I see the whole world upside down, everything looks completely different! The ground is now the sky and the sky is the ground. The trees grow downward and the animals walk on the roof of the world. Everything I know to be true is now reversed. My mind is a jumble!"

"Your mind is LAZY! You see what you are taught to see and you think this is real. Suspend your judgments. Let go of the conditioning that has limited your thinking and colored your vision. Open to a new way of perceiving and knowing!" And so Pujai hung upside down for a long, long time. Many days perhaps, she lost track of time. The wisest of the magic falcons taught her to let go of her early conditioning and look at people afresh, look beyond their external appearance and really see into their heart and soul. And Pujai was horrified at how many judgments she made simply based on how people look. She saw how upside down collective thinking really is when women base their self-worth on popularity, money, status, and some crazy limited definition of beauty. "This is a reversal of true reality Pujai," cried Falcon. "When you can see right through to the soul, you see that self-worth is based on the treasures and talents a woman possesses inside. A true Visionary can see through, see beyond, see around, and see underneath the surface of what is really happening in any given situation."

"You have learned well my daughter", said Falcon. "Now climb onto my back and fly with me to gain your next power – the power of objectivity." And so Pujai flew with Falcon and they flew far and wide around the Great Mountains. It was amazing to see how big the world was. When they flew over a large lake whose waters were stirring and churning with the wind Falcon said, "This lake is like the water of emotions that most people get caught in. You are a Visionary and have the power to rise above the waters. Do not become entangled in other people's emotions and do not take things too personally. You must train your good mind to observe emotions and notice how stormy feelings can cloud the mind. Rise high above the waters so that you can be objective. The Visionary needs neutrality to be effective."

As they soared high above the landscape Pujai practiced detaching her mind, observing and being objective, seeing the world from a much higher perspective. And as they flew higher and farther, Falcon taught her to expand her vision, to widen her focus and not get stuck on one part of the landscape that fascinated and drew her attention. She learned to scan the environment, get an overview and take in the entire landscape as a whole.

Falcon taught Pujai to expand her vision of herself. "You are bigger and broader than you ever imagined. You are not just a small human body. Your mind can expand and extend to the farthest reaches of the earth and beyond. Your small concerns about whether people like you or approve of you are petty emotional squabbles that Visionaries have no time for. With your powers of objectivity and detachment you can concentrate your powers on the bigger picture and the broader perspective in any given situation. The village needs you to transcend emotions and your own concerns. But never disconnect from your heart Pujai. Staying connected to your heart anchors your flight and tempers your reason."

After many days of flying, Pujai mastered neutrality and detachment and Falcon returned Pujai to the branches of the tall trees. "You are a woman of the Air Clan Pujai", said Falcon. "The trees will now teach you how to truly breathe." And so from the majestic trees she learned to sit very still and attune her breath to the slow breathing of the trees. "Breath is life", they whispered to her. "Breathe deeply and take in the life force." And she breathed slowly and quieted her mind and became receptive to the soft whisperings of the wind. And she found that there were gentle voices in the wind that carried deep wisdom.

The trees also taught her to reach upward toward the sun and sky "Look up Pujai, in the sky you will find many sources of guidance. Reach up to the heavens as we do with our branches and leaves. Receive the abundance of love and guidance from the skies. Attune yourself to the sun, moon, and stars, for you will receive intelligence from the sources above. Some call it Spirit, others call it Divine

Intelligence, but whatever the name, this spirit brings wise guidance into your mind and heart." And so for many weeks Pujai remained in the trees, listening to the wisdom in the wind and opening her mind to guidance from Spirit.

When her tree training was over, Falcon was very pleased with her progress and said to her, "Pujai, you have done very well my daughter. You have gained many powers. You can change your perceptions, see beyond appearances, practice objectivity, and still your mind to receive wisdom and guidance from Spirit. Now you are ready to learn the art of Swordcraft and wield the sacred tool of the Visionary Clan.

Pujai Part 3: Learning the Art of Swordcraft

After her adventures with the falcons and trees and equipped with her powers of objectivity and openness to Spirit, Pujai began the next phase of her initiation. Back now at the Crystal Palace, the elders invited Pujai into the great crystal pyramid to learn the art of Swordcraft. The Swordcraft elder handed Pujai a beautiful silver sword, with a carved handle, and jewels encrusted down the blade. "The Visionary's sword is her sacred tool. It has a handle, blade, and point. To master the sword you will learn to *handle* situations, become sharp as a *blade,* and get to the *point.* When you master handle, blade, and point you will gain your next Visionary power – clarity of mind. Are you ready to begin training in the art of Swordcraft?"

When Pujai answered yes, the Swordcraft elder showed her first how to get a handle on any situation. She gripped the handle of the sword and readied herself. The elder presented Pujai with many confusing situations, everyday events that happen in the village, conflicts between people, problems to be sorted out, arguments to be resolved. "How do I get a handle on all this?" cried Pujai. "To get a handle, the Visionary asks questions. We ask how, why, when, where, and who? What is really going on here? What would happen if we try this? Who will be affected if we do that? And we must keep our mind free and clear of judgment and stay open." So Pujai practiced clarifying each situation, asking many questions, and keeping her mind free and clear of judgment.

And when she could handle situations with ease the elders taught her to use the blade to make her mind as sharp as a knife's edge. "The blade of the sacred sword represents your quick mind and sharp intuition. It is your weapon against falsehood. You must learn to slash through the veils of illusion and falsehood to get to your truth. Your veils of illusion keep your mind foggy and unclear and prevent you from trusting your own truth and knowing." And the elder opened a door in the side of the crystal pyramid and led Pujai into a darkened passageway. "Take your sword of clarity and confront your veils of illusion my daughter."

Pujai stepped into the darkened tunnel and the door was shut. She walked a few steps and was confronted with a dark veil named DO NOT QUESTION, which hung before her, blocking her passage. A strange scene came to life on the veil and she saw herself as a young child when authority figures were telling her what to do and what to think. She had to swallow their opinions and was not allowed to ask questions or have her own viewpoint or opinions. When she could not ask questions, her mind seemed to freeze. This seemed outrageous to her present day self and suddenly her mind cleared and she raised her sword and sliced her blade through the veil of illusion saying, "I can question authority! I have my own mind and opinions!"

When that veil fell she approached another veil named CONFUSION. And Pujai recalled many times in her life when she was confused and her mind was muddled. And she saw how cluttered and scattered her mind was when she had too many things to do and too many people to sort out. She lost her own mind and was confused about her own needs. Each time she was swamped by confusion she sabotaged her own growth and her own ability to change and move on with her life. Why was she giving her power away? Suddenly large, sticky cobwebs appeared all around the veil of Confusion and as the cobwebs threatened to darken and bewilder her mind, Pujai raised her sword and sliced this way and that, clearing the cobwebs and slicing the veil saying, "No! I clear my mind of chaos and clutter. I will not succumb to the cobwebs of confusion!"

When that veil fell to pieces she approached another veil named SELF-DOUBT. And she saw herself trying to make an important decision but other voices crowded her out of her right mind. She listened to this person and that person; she read this book and that book. Too many sources of information flooded her mind and she began to doubt her own counsel and her ability to make good decisions. She was distracted from her own truth and intuition. And Pujai raised her sword and sliced her blade through the veil of Self-Doubt saying, "I will listen to my intuition and to my own counsel. I banish all self-doubt and I trust myself completely!"

And when that veil of illusion fell away, Pujai came to the end of the dark passage where the Swordcraft elder was waiting for her. "Well done Pujai. You have confronted your veils of illusion. The blade of your Sacred Sword is sharpening. Your mind is becoming clear. Some women never make it through this passage. Their sword of clarity is not strong enough to cut through confusion and self-doubt. They are trapped by the veils of illusion and fall onto the Shadow Path of the Visionary Clan, called the Path of Chaos. Pujai, come with me to the place below the palace. I want to show you what happens to your sisters when they succumb to the Shadow Path of Chaos." And so Pujai followed her elder down to the place below the Palace. Down and down they went, down to a huge underground city where many women lived in their own illusions, in their own little worlds, not recognizing the dungeon-like prison surrounding them.

Here Pujai saw a woman dashing around and doing so many things there was chaos all around her. And she was scattered and distracted, losing things and forgetting things. She had lost her focus of mind. Where was her sword of clarity? And she saw another woman procrastinating and delaying decisions so she never made any changes. And Pujai saw another woman who stirred up chaos in her relationships, gossiping and betraying confidences. And each woman had a shadowy figure swirling around her like a dark cloud, confusing her mind and making her forget who she was. And the elder said, "The women who live in the Shadow Path of Chaos attract a hungry creature called Saboteur, who sabotages their plans and goals. And the women feed it by remaining confused and chaotic, never changing or moving on with their life. They have forgotten how to be Visionaries and how to walk the Path of Change."

Something deep within Pujai stirred and a blazing determination seized her. She knew she must release her sisters from Chaos and restore them back to the Visionary's Path. And Pujai cried out to all the women, "Take up your swords my sisters! Take up your sword of clarity! Stop sabotaging yourself. Trust yourself. Trust your mind, trust your intuition. Hold up your sword and meet Chaos head on!" And Pujai ran towards them brandishing her Sacred Sword. And as she slashed it this way and that, the reflected light shone all around the Place Below. The light illuminated the women and they seemed to come back to themselves. Their minds cleared and they woke up and shook themselves out of their confusion. "Take up your sword my sisters, your sword of clarity and meet Chaos head on!" And the sisters held up their swords and facing their Saboteur, they slashed and sliced and cut until the dark creature disappeared in a cloud of smoke.

Pujai Part 4: The Wheel of Mindspinning

The Swordcraft elder was very proud of Pujai for releasing her sisters from the Shadow Path of Chaos. But her initiation in learning the art of Swordcraft was not yet over. There would be one more initiation test, one more test of Pujai's skill with the sword. The elder escorted Pujai back up to the Crystal Pyramid and said, "Now you are ready to face the Wheel of Mindspinning." And the elder of Swordcraft showed Pujai a huge wooden wheel with great spokes, spinning in midair. "This is the Wheel of Mindspinning, the wheel that turns when your thoughts go round and round, when you get obsessed with a problem and can't get it off your mind. The wheel has an energy all its own, it spins and spins and we feed it with our emotions of regret, anger, and longing. The Visionary walks the Path of Change Pujai, how will you bring change to this wheel of obsessive thinking?"

The elder touched the spinning wheel with her sword and suddenly, a miniature Mindspinning wheel magically jumped into Pujai's head. She found herself thinking about a difficult problem and she began to fixate on it, thinking and re-thinking the details of the problem. Her mind spun round and round, reviewing the situation over and over. As time went on and on, Pujai could not sort it out. She could not make a decision about what to do. She was seized in the grip of compulsive thought, compelled and mesmerized. When she tried to think about something else the problem kept jumping into her mind. She felt crazy and mental, spinning round and round.

"Pujai, make a decision to get off the wheel. You may be tempted to stay on the wheel of obsessive thinking, but remember the great force of the wheel. It locks you into old patterns of thinking and locks you into the prison of the past. When the mind spins like a whirlwind, it plunges you into massive confusion. If you truly walk the Path of Change, release your mind from its prison of obsessive thinking, invite change, do something different. Use your sword of clarity and smash the obsessive wheel!"

Pujai held up her sacred sword and focused on the sharp tip, the apex of the sword. This helped to focus her spinning mind and direct the energy of her thoughts. She then quieted her mind, cleared it of all confusion, and focused on her desire for change. "I want to get off the wheel. I want to get off the wheel of Mindspinning." she said. She pushed away the obsessive voices distracting her from her goal. She tuned out all sound and random thoughts that invaded the sacred space of her quiet mind. Her single pointed desire was to get off the wheel and stop her mental spinning.

As she focused and directed her thoughts, the point of her sword began to glow and the glowing spread down the blade, to the hilt, to the handle, to her hand and arm and soon her entire body was filled with a powerful intention to change. Pujai raised her sacred sword, pointed it directly at her target, and smashed the blade straight through the wooden wheel. The spokes cracked and the wheel crashed down in pieces onto the floor of the crystal pyramid. Her mind stopped spinning and Pujai came back to herself, back into her right mind, calm and centered.

And the elder of Swordcraft led Pujai to a big soft chair where she sat down to rest. The sun was setting now and Pujai could see through the crystal ceiling of the great pyramid that the light of the day was fading quickly into night. "Well done my daughter, you have learned the art of Swordcraft. You have mastered the handle, blade, and point of your sword. You have gained clarity of mind, one of the greatest Visionary powers. Rest now, for soon you will begin your training with the Winds of Change.

Pujai Part 5: The Winds of Change

After learning the art of Swordcraft and gaining clarity of mind, the elders knew Pujai was ready to master the Winds of Change. And so the elders invited Pujai outside onto the courtyard overlooking the Great Mountains. And the Visionary elder said, "We can control the sword Pujai, but we cannot control the wind! We can only learn to work with its energy." And the elder held up her Sacred Sword and pointed it into the sky calling, "Winds of Change come to our aid!" And suddenly the wind whipped around them, spiraling and circling and dancing. And the playful wind invited Pujai to move her body and dance with the breeze as it caressed her body and swooped her gently this way and that. And the elder said, "The Winds of Change invite us into the great dance of life and remind us that all life flows in cycles around the great spiral of Life, Death, and Rebirth. Move with the wind, be flexible and supple, feel where the wind is blowing you and flow with it. Do not resist change. The way to wholeness lies in embracing change."

The elders showed Pujai how to dance with the wind and how to keep the cycle of life flowing. And when things got rigid, tight, and stiff, they showed her techniques to get energy moving once again. They taught her to use the wind of her own breath to move stuck energy in her body and cleanse her mind of negative thoughts. Pujai discovered her wind-breath could make awesome sounds, beautiful tones, and vibrations of song that push out toxins and bring healing to her body and soul. The elders were pleased to see how well Pujai shifted energy when it needed to change, how she loosened things up and kept the Life - Death – Rebirth wheel turning. "Well done Pujai, it is time for you to befriend the Great Winds the Visionary can use as her allies."

And so the elders took Pujai up to the tallest tower, up to the highest point of the Crystal Palace, to the place called the Stormtower. And there, high in the Stormtower, the elders called upon the Great Winds. They called forth the mighty hurricane and Pujai learned she could call upon hurricane force winds when something big needed to change, like when the entire village needed a change of attitude. And they called forth the powerful tornado and Pujai learned to call upon tornado's wind of destruction when old ways and old laws and old structures needed to be utterly destroyed. And they called forth gales and squalls and typhoons and cyclones each with its own strength and purpose.

"Focus your mind Pujai. Choose your powerful wind wisely and know exactly when to call it in. The Great Winds must be controlled to move with purposeful action for change, purposeful destruction of what is no longer needed. When the storms of life hit the village and old ways need to die, the Visionary guides the people through death into the rebirth cycle of the wheel. Fresh ideas can then blow into the village, minds are opened and insight is given."

And when Pujai could control the Great Winds and bring rebirth into the village, they left the Stormtower and the Crystal Palace and journeyed deep into the Great Mountains for the next phase of her initiation. For many days they journeyed until they came to a mountain pass, to the place called the Stone Gateways. "The Stone Gateways are the blockages within your mind that block you from change. They are made of your negative thoughts and fixed ideas about yourself that no longer serve your highest good. Thoughts have energy Pujai, and negative thoughts carry negative energy that is toxic to your body and soul. When you face each Stone Gateway you will confront a barrier within your mind that obstructs your growth, blocks your way forward and obscures your vision. You must identify the blockage and blast through the stone and break apart your negative thought patterns."

Pujai approached the first Stone Gateway, which was called DEATH VOICES. And suddenly she heard crazy voices in her head, horrible thoughts she said to herself, "I can't do this. I can't do that. I can't do what I want to do because I'm not smart enough, not good enough, not pretty enough, not creative enough." And on and on they went. And the Death Voices made her shrink from engaging fully with life. And she found herself retreating into her own mind, becoming numb and falling asleep under death's spell. How can she blast through this Stone Gateway? What Wind of Change will she call in to assist her? She must focus her mind and not succumb to the Death Voices holding her back from life.

From deep within her being she found the voice that said, "I choose life! I choose life! I will not be paralyzed by these negative thoughts holding me behind this stone wall!" And as she chose life and full engagement, the parts of her living under death's spell woke up and pushed the poisonous Death Voices out of her body. And Pujai called in the mighty tornado that stormed in and snatched up the negative thoughts embedded in the stones and tore the entire Stone Gateway to pieces. Pujai cried, "I let go of the negative thoughts that block my progress. I release the poison held in my body. I now move forward with my life!"

And she took a deep breath and moved forward to confront the next Stone Gateway, which was called POPULAR BELIEF. And suddenly all thoughts were wiped from her mind and she did not know what she really believed. She had lost her own mind and she heard voices in her head that sounded like proclamations delivered from on high, "There's no such thing as women's intuition. Women should be seen and not heard. Women are the source of evil. Women are unclean. Women do not have spiritual authority. Women should look a certain way, dress a certain way, act a certain way."

And Pujai's mind was tossed this way and that as she searched for the truth. What is true? What is right? She felt disempowered, uncertain, and fearful of trusting her own truth. So she jumped onto the bandwagon of popular beliefs and opinions. This Stone Gateway was blocking Pujai from connecting with her own beliefs, her own mind, and her own power; she was sinking under the weight of Popular Belief.

"Pujai," cried the elder, "You must not get seduced by popular beliefs and opinions. They will crush your powers of discernment and rob you of your feminine wisdom. These beliefs are based on fear and fueled by fear. Align yourself with your own deepest wisdom. Attune yourself to Divine Truth and Divine Intelligence and regain your powers of feminine intuition." So she called in the soft whisperings of the Spirit wind and focused deep inside to connect with her own wisdom. And here is what she knew to be true, "I have strong intuition. I am seen and heard. I have great wisdom and spiritual authority. I look, dress, and act in a way that is true to who I am."

And armed with this powerful truth, Pujai called in the mighty hurricane, the Wind of Change she knew could tear down the wall of Popular Belief. And as the hurricane tore the stones to shreds, Pujai cried, "I let go of any beliefs I hold that are untrue about me and based in fear. I release the poison that has been in my body. I now move forward with my life!

The elders gathered around Pujai saying, "Well done my daughter. You have learned how and when to call in the Winds of Change. You can shift energy when it gets stuck and you know how to keep the Life - Death - Rebirth wheel turning. You understand the poisonous nature of negative thoughts and you have confronted the barriers within your mind that obstruct your growth and block your way forward. You are now ready for your final initiation Pujai; you are ready to awaken your powers of vision and free your mind for liberation.

Pujai Part 6: Freeing the Mind for Liberation

After Pujai mastered the Winds of Change, the elders brought her back to the Crystal Palace for her final Initiation. They brought her to a special place, high in one of the many towers, to the place called the Dream Dome. The Dream Dome had glass walls and a glass ceiling that opened up to the wide expanse of sky and heavens. "You are ready to learn the greatest secret of the Visionary Clan Pujai, how to free the mind for liberation and develop your great powers of vision." And the elder pointed up to the heavens, which Pujai could see through the transparent dome. "The potential of the universal mind is infinite, but our human mind is limited and must be released from its prison. Experience now the prison bars of the limited mind."

The elder had several buckets of paint and as she spoke to Pujai she painted these words onto the walls. "This is the way we have always done things." And she splashed the words onto the glass wall of the Dream Dome. "There is no such thing as the dream world. Dreams are only brain cells firing off at night." And these words she painted on the ceiling, obscuring the light shining in from the sky. "The world is one-dimensional. The only reality is what we experience on the physical plane." And she painted these words over the walls. "See the shortcomings in traditional methods of thinking Pujai? Visionaries know there are many planes of reality. We know dreams carry real healing from another place."

Then Pujai picked up a paintbrush and splashed these words onto the Dream Dome, "I am not worthy. I am unlovable. I don't deserve happiness." Yes, Pujai these are your conditioned thought responses that limit you and entrap you in untruthful, mindless chatter." And the elder splashed new words across the dome, "Our worth is only based on wealth, status, family, and class." And the Dream Dome was feeling more and more oppressive as it was being totally covered by collective thinking and rigid ideas. And they painted the Dome with all the dogma and philosophies that keep women small and trapped, imprisoned and disempowered.

And when the Dream Dome was completely darkened, Pujai felt trapped within the bars of her own making, whenever she believed these false ideologies and creeds. She felt the walls squeezing in on her. And just when Pujai felt her mind might be trapped forever, the elder shouted, "Free yourself from the oppression of limiting thoughts and beliefs. Free your mind from its prison!" And when Pujai got mad enough she kicked the sides of the Dream Dome hard, kicking and smashing the glass walls, shattering the ceiling until the entire Dream Dome crashed down all around her. It was nighttime by now and the stars were sparkling in the night sky.

"Well done Pujai. You have freed and liberated your mind. Explore all the limitless possibilities within your reach. Gaze into the heavens. Each star is a possibility, a new thought, a new idea, a new star to follow. We Visionaries train our minds so where others see limitations, we see limitless possibilities, where others become stuck in finite beliefs, we see infinite potential." And the elder reached out and touched Pujai's forehead lightly with the sharp point of her Sacred Sword, drawing out a diamond shape pattern between her eyes. "I am activating your Inner Diamond. Open your mind and receive the Inner Sight."

Suddenly Pujai's mind burst open and her forehead became very, very hot. She gazed into the heavens and the night sky was like a blank canvas and now she could paint anything she wanted. She was free to create and innovate, to think unedited thoughts, and let her mind wander around the universe. The Dream Dome was opened fully and she let her imagination fly, fly as far out as possible. And she learned to interpret dreams and to understand the images and symbols that come from the dream world. And she received dreams and visions that brought healing medicine to the village of women.

Now the Inner Diamond was very special and each point of the diamond had a unique power. The elders taught Pujai how to activate the diamond by focusing first on the top point of the diamond. Here she took time to breathe, quiet her mind, and align with her deep inner self. Then she activated the side points of wisdom and understanding and finally she activated the base point of knowledge. When Pujai was able to control her Inner Diamond with wisdom, understanding, and knowledge, the elders gave her a beautiful cauldron to increase her powers of vision.

"This is the Cauldron of Inspiration Pujai. As you stir the cauldron, let it bubble with possibilities. Inhale the steam and mist. Be inspired and follow where the breath of spirit leads you." So Pujai stirred her Cauldron of Inspiration and inhaled the swirling mists. And she felt a powerful creativity enter her mind and heart. She felt the joyful energy of the new spirit that wanted to be born within her. And the fresh wind of renewing spirit blew through her and she began to write and sing and dance and paint and drum. And she felt joy and ecstasy, delight and bliss.

And after many days and nights working and creating in the Dream Dome and playing with her Cauldron of Inspiration, the elder told Pujai, "You are ready now to focus your powers of visualization and learn to envision the changes you want." So they returned to the Crystal Pyramid and Pujai was instructed to sit in the very center of the pyramid so that she was directly aligned with the apex of the pyramid above and the base of the pyramid stretching below under the translucent floor. "Pujai, this Crystal Pyramid is designed to help focus your powers of visualization. You have the power to visualize and then create exactly what you want. With the power of your imagination and the strength of your intention, you can bring about the changes you desire. But your motivations must be pure or the magic will fail. Think about a situation where you feel stuck. Imagine how you want it to change, imagine the possibilities. Now focus your intention and picture it differently. Visualize precisely the change you want."

So she thought about one of her relationships and how she did not feel the open channel of love she used to feel. She thought of many reasons why the channel was no longer flowing but that didn't make it change. Then she considered the possibility of the channel opening once again and she visualized exactly what she wanted - an open channel of love flowing between her heart and the other person's heart. She said out loud, "An open channel of love is flowing between us." And she pictured this with vivid clarity on the screen of her mind. And she felt an open channel of love flowing once again. "Well done Pujai! As Visionaries we are trained to always consider possibilities, for without possibilities we cannot create. With openness to what is possible, we can create something new. Creativity requires envisioning that a situation can, indeed, change."

"How can this happen so quickly? How does the change actually happen in the present, in the here and now?" asked Pujai. "It depends on your desire for change and the strength of your intention. It also depends on your understanding of time. You think you know what time is Pujai, but you do not. Time is only an idea in your mind. I will teach you how to use time to become a true Visionary." And the elder showed Pujai that when we are stuck in a situation, we are energetically living in the PAST. When we clearly envision the changes we want, we tap into the FUTURE. When we invite the future possibility to live in the PRESENT, we can create changes in the here and now.

So Pujai practiced using her imagination to move out of the stuck energy of the past and form a clear picture of her desired outcome. Then she invited the future possibility to live in the present. She practiced envisioning for many, many months until she could clearly direct her imagination to envision the future and create change in the present. And through her initiations, Pujai gained all of the powers of the Visionary Clan: objectivity, clarity of mind, inner sight, creativity, and the power to envision change.

Over the years, Pujai became the greatest Master the Visionary Clan had ever known, for she was a master shape-shifter and attitude changer. She could wield the sword of clarity and command the mighty Winds of Change. And she trusted her intuition and trusted her dreams and visions. And with her loving and wise guidance, Pujai brought change into the village of women. Not change for change's sake but for the evolution and growth of the whole community. And she inspired them with new thoughts, new hope, and new beliefs. And each day with dignity and honor, she walked the Path of Change, the path of a true and faithful Visionary Woman.

Walking the Path of Change

VISIONARY CLAN OVERVIEW
Archetype: **The Visionary**
Path: **The Path of Change**
Essence: **Powerful in Mind**
Element: **Air**
Tool: **Sword**
Qualities: **Clear mind, objective, innovative, cuts through confusion, and envisions new ways of being and doing**
Affirmation: "**I create, transform, and regenerate.**"
Motto: **"Air Clan Women, powerful in mind, full of vision."**
Empowerment: **comes through clarity of mind**
Shadow Archetype: **Saboteur**
Shadow Path: **Path of Chaos**

In this story we are introduced to Pujai, our Visionary Divine Feminine guide. The path she walks in life is the Path of Change and her tool is the Sacred Sword. During the course of her initiation, she learns to be clear-minded, objective, discerning, and ready for positive change. Pujai liberates her mind and becomes the creative, imaginative, intuitive Visionary she was always meant to be. What does her story mean for you? How can you become a creative Visionary?

As an emerging Visionary, you need to find your relationship with the Air Clan. This might mean clearing out any internal clutter or mind chatter that keeps you confused and foggy. It may mean coming into better relationship with the Air element itself, learning to breathe more deeply and more slowly. It might be helpful to go on retreat to the high mountains, to practice meditating, and opening your third eye. Connecting with the Air element - however you do this - will bring you into a deeper relationship with your Visionary.

To begin her Visionary initiation, Pujai is taken to the highest peaks of the Great Mountains, with tall trees, circling birds, and fresh air. There is also a beautiful crystal palace with a transparent pyramid and lots of clear domes and towers reaching to the sky. Here she learns about Air Clan Women who are powerful in mind and full of vision. As she observes the initiation training ground, she sees the crystal pyramid with another upside down pyramid in the floor, filled with crystals. She notices various swords and cauldrons and bird costumes, all reminding her that she is an Air Clan Woman herself, ready to train her mind to be a powerful tool of liberation and creative envisioning.

At the training ground, Pujai learns about the Air Clan and their important role as change-makers and shape-shifters in the village. Visionaries must change attitudes and perspectives when things in the village need to shift and new ways need to be envisioned. They move energy when life gets stuck. She learns that a Visionary's power lies in her ability to be objective and creative and to see limitless possibilities, when others see limitations. She learns that the Visionary's tool, the Sacred Sword, is used to cut through confusion and falsehood so a Visionary can be clear-minded and true to her inner core.

Pujai is excited to begin her initiation, but then she hears about the shadow path of the Visionary Clan and how some women wander off their Path of Power and succumb to the path of chaos. This sounded horrible, as it robs women of their clarity and focus, scatters their energy, and causes them to sabotage their success. She had seen this shadow phenomenon before and had some experience with this negative energy and this made her even more determined to go through her initiation so she could help restore her sisters back to the Path of Change.

To begin her initiation, Pujai is invited to wait outside the crystal pyramid. She then receives a big surprise! She is taken by 3 She-Falcons to the high forest and hung upside down in the trees. Here she learns to see the world from a whole new perspective. Everything is turned upside down in order to scramble her mind. What would it be like to hang upside down in a tree and see everything differently? What if the sky became the ground and the ground became the sky? What if everything you believed was actually reversed? What if reality is only a matter of perception, the way you see and perceive the world around you?

It is a strange phenomenon that you see only what you are trained to see. Your mind does become lazy because of the way your mind is conditioned. If your mind is taught to focus on negative outcomes, then you will see and even create negative outcomes. If your mind is conditioned to believe people reject you, then you will read the signs and signals coming from others and conclude they are rejecting you. But what if you saw the world with new eyes? What if you read the signals differently with new eyes, new thoughts, and a new brain?

During your Visionary training you learn to see differently, see beyond, and see through. The Falcons encourage Pujai to see the world afresh, without judgment and limitation. It is shocking when you realize how automated your conditioned responses really are. The next time you go to a store, notice how your conditioned mind makes immediate judgments when you see people. In that moment, shift into the Visionary and look beyond external appearances. See through to that person's soul. What do you see and feel? A true Visionary can see beyond and through to other realities.

Next Pujai is taken for a highflying ride with Falcon and learns to rise above emotions. They soar above the landscape and see the world from this larger, more objective perspective. A Visionary must not get caught up in other people's emotions and dramas and not take things personally. This Visionary discipline creates more and more objectivity and internal spaciousness so you can detach in a healthy way and see clearly. This kind of neutrality allows you to transcend your emotions and your own personal concerns. As a Visionary you need this impartiality to be able to vision for the community and for your own highest good. Worrying about what others think and feel can weigh you down and sabotage a project. It's important to remember, as Falcon warns Pujai, to keep your mind connected and anchored to your heart. This way your objectivity is tempered with your compassion.

At the end of her upside-down-in-the-trees and flying-with-Falcon initiation phase, Pujai is taken to the tallest tree and taught how to truly breathe. She learns to slow her breathing down and attune to the slow breathing of the trees. Have you ever noticed how you breathe? Most people don't really take in enough breath. They breathe in a shallow way and don't take in enough life force through their breath. Do an experiment today and notice whether you are taking deep breaths or shallow breaths. Then deepen your breath and breathe more consciously.

If you have some trees around, take time to sit under a tree and breathe in, imagining the life force rushing into your body. Or look out your window at a tree and imagine breathing in the oxygen released by the tree and as you exhale, imagine the tree breathing in your carbon dioxide and transforming it into oxygen. Feel this miraculous circulation of life force that occurs every moment in our relationship to trees. All of this breathing is preparing you to be an Air Clan Woman.

As you breath more consciously, your mind is more open to receive guidance from spirit. Pujai is instructed to look up at the branches of the tree and feel how they are open to the sky, sun, moon, and stars. In the same way you can attune yourself to the wisdom and guidance coming from above, from the heavens, from spirit, and from your higher wisdom. When your mind is still and you are breathing in the life force of conscious breath, you will be amazed at the kind of inner guidance you can receive.

In the next phase of Pujai's initiation, she learns the Art of Swordcraft. She is taken back to the great crystal pyramid and handed a jewel-encrusted sword, in order to master the handle, blade, and point. To master the sword she learns to *handle* situations, become sharp as a *blade,* and get to the *point.* When she masters handle, blade, and point she gains the Visionary power of clarity of mind.

To be able to *handle* her sacred Sword, the elders present Pujai with confusing situations in the village and she learns to ask the right questions to unravel what is really going on. She asks how, why, when, where, and who? What is really going on here? What would happen if we try this? Who will be affected if we do that? When you clarify the confusion, ask the clarifying questions, and keep your mind free of judgment, you can make swift decisions and handle most situations with ease.

To become sharp as a *blade* Pujai is instructed to take her Sword and slash through her veils of illusion, which fog her mind and prevent her from knowing her truth. She is taken to a dark passageway where she encounters three Veils of Illusion: DO NOT QUESTION, CONFUSION, AND SELF-DOUBT. When she confronts the DO NOT QUESTION veil, she observes times in her life when she followed authority and swallowed her own opinions for the sake of conforming and fitting in. Do you relate to this Veil of Illusion? Are you ready to question authority and value your own opinions? In order to sharpen your *blade*, have the courage to trust and value your own knowing and your own authority. Cut through this Veil!

The next Veil called CONFUSION is a common one for women, because we get confused about our own needs. It's usually due to the fact that we care for so many people and need to consider their needs, that we forget our own needs in the process. A Visionary must prioritize and be crystal clear about meeting her needs first so she doesn't get swamped by others' needs and sabotage her own projects. Consider cutting through your own Veil of CONFUSION, clear and still your mind, and you will know exactly what to do. When you clear your mind of the chaos and clutter, your intuition and crystal clarity will emerge and you no longer need to be confused.

The last Veil of SELF-DOUBT can be tackled when you stop listening to everyone else and begin to go inside and trust your own knowing. How often do you make decisions based on the latest popular book, the opinions of your friends or family members, advice from radio or television? When too many sources of information and "expert knowledge" flood your system, you can't hear your own thoughts. You forget to take your own counsel and trust that you can make the right decision for you. When Pujai takes up her Sword of Clarity and slices through this Veil of Illusion she banishes all self-doubt and commits to trust herself completely.

The elders then show Pujai what happens when women get stuck behind their Veils of Illusion and get trapped on the shadow path of chaos. They are full of questions, confusion, and self-doubt and remain in their own world of illusion. Pujai saw how each shadow woman was connected to the negative energy of the Saboteur, who sabotages her plans and goals for the future. These women have forgotten how to be Visionaries, forgotten how to envision the future and move forward and change.

When you feel caught in this shadow place, you can call on Pujai and your inner Visionary to take up your magic Sword and begin cutting all the sticky cobwebs of confusion, illusion, and self-doubt. When you take your Sword of Clarity and meet chaos head-on, the veils of illusion begin to dissolve. You begin to trust yourself more. You begin to trust your good mind and sharp intuition.

Take a look at the ways you are sabotaging yourself in your life right now. Are there projects left undone and incomplete? Are you making excuses why you aren't following your desires and ideas? Are you procrastinating and delaying decisions? Are you forgetting to write down your dreams when you wake up? Are you stirring up chaos in your relationships? Imagine now taking your Sword of Clarity to stop the chaos and get back on your Visionary Path of Power. Slash this way and that and cut away the cobwebs of confusion!

After mastering the *handle* and *blade* of her Sword, Pujai is then taken to the Wheel of Mindspinning, to master the *point* of her Sword. The Wheel of Mindspinning represents the wheel that turns in your mind when your thoughts spin and spin around in an obsessive way. I'm sure you know this experience well, when you compulsively ruminate over a problem. This kind of obsessive Mindspinning never resolves anything because your mind is in a particular state; it's like a racecar that loops endlessly around the same track. When your brain and nervous system get stuck on the same circular neural pathway, your mind cannot create a new solution or find a new neural pathway to travel down. Compulsive thought is mesmerizing and compelling. It seduces you into "autopilot" mode and you believe you can't stop it. However, your Visionary must intervene.

Pujai is told that she needs to make a decision to get off the wheel because she is locked in the prison of the past. Take a moment and consider how you might be locked in the past. Is your mind conditioned to respond in a particular way based on past experience? Your Visionary can quickly shift your orientation from past to future as you envision the change you want to make. Then grab your Sword and point it at the spinning wheel in your mind, push the obsessive voices aside, and quiet your mind. There in the still point of your mind, you will be able to focus and direct your thoughts towards your desired change. Then you can point the tip of your Sword and break apart your Mindspinning wheel. Keep practicing!

In the next phase of her Visionary training, Pujai learns to call in the Winds of Change, in order to flow easily with the changes of life and shift energy when it gets stuck. The Visionary elders first call in the playful wind, which invites Pujai into the great dance of life and reminds her that all life flows in cycles around the great spiral of Life, Death, and Rebirth. As she moves and sways and dances with this wind, she learns to be flexible and supple and she learns to feel where the wind is blowing and flow with it. The elders warn her to not resist change because the way to wholeness lies in embracing change.

This is an important Visionary lesson because all of life is constantly flowing through cycles of life, death, and then rebirth. When you resist change, energy gets stuck and you're no longer in the flow. You may feel a build up of toxins, negative thoughts, and old patterns pulling you backwards. When this happens to Pujai, the elders show her how to use breath and sound to move stuck energy out of her body. This is a wonderful technique to push toxins out of your body and cleanse your mind of negative thoughts. Next time you feel stuck energy in your body, in your behaviors, routines, or emotional patterns, try breathing, moving and sounding and visualize the stuck energy flowing once again.

Pujai then goes to the Stormtower to call in the Great Winds of hurricanes, tornadoes, gales, squalls, typhoons, and cyclones. These mighty winds are needed when big attitudes need to change, like when an entire family system, village, community, or nation needs to shift to a more inclusive or progressive way of living. When old ways, old laws, old institutions, and old beliefs need to be dismantled or destroyed, the mighty Winds of Change need to be called in. Is there anything in your life that needs a hurricane wind? What collective attitudes need to change with a tornado force wind? What life structures no longer serve you or the ones you love? As a Visionary you welcome death. You allow whatever needs to die, to die. This is the only way to usher in rebirth, renewal, regeneration, and restoration.

In the next phase of her initiation, the elders bring Pujai to the place of the Stone Gateways, where she confronts the barriers in her mind that block change and obscure her vision. These Stone Gateways are made of negative thought patterns and fixed ideas that no longer serve your growth and evolution. The first Stone Gateway to confront is called DEATH VOICES, which are those crazy internal voices that erode your self-esteem. They cast a death spell over you as they tell you you're not good enough, there's something wrong with you, you're too this or that or not enough of this or that. When you really see how paralyzing these DEATH VOICES are, you can call in the Wind of Change that feels right to you and destroy the Stone Gateway. When you fully engage with your life and wake up the parts of you that have fallen under death's spell, you can wake up fully and demolish those old beliefs and voices.

POPULAR BELIEF is the next Stone Gateway Pujai must face. These are the fixed ideas in our culture that are embedded in our brain like a virus or faulty program. "There's no such thing as women's intuition. Women should be seen and not heard. Women are the source of evil. Women are unclean. Women do not have spiritual authority. Women should look a certain way, dress a certain way, and act a certain way." These beliefs are based on fear and fueled by fear. They crush your powers of discernment and rob you of your feminine wisdom. These entrenched lies need to be extinguished. What kind of wind will break the spell of this cultural brainwashing?

As a Visionary, you can call in the hurricane to tear this barrier to shreds. It helps when you align with your inner wisdom, attune to Divine Truth, and call in your feminine intuition. You can also practice the Visionary antidote, "I choose life!

I will not be paralyzed by negative thoughts or collective beliefs holding me behind this stone wall! I let go of the negative thoughts that block my progress. I let go of any beliefs I hold that are untrue about me and based in fear. I release the poison held in my body. I now move forward with my life!"

You can also say these affirmations to yourself, "I have strong intuition. I am seen and heard. I have great wisdom and spiritual authority. I look, dress, and act in a way that is true to who I am." When you confront the barriers within your own mind that obstruct your growth, you can liberate yourself from negative voices and negative collective ideas that are false and devolutionary. A Visionary can do this easily when she masters the Winds of Change.

For her last initiation sequence, Pujai is taken to the Dream Dome to learn the greatest secret of the Visionary Clan - how to free the mind for liberation and develop her great powers of vision. The elder points up to the heavens, which Pujai can see through the transparent dome and says, "The potential of the universal mind is infinite, but our human mind is limited and must be released from its prison. Experience now the prison bars of the limited mind." They then proceed to paint onto the walls all of the collective conditioning that hijacks the mind and imprisons the infinite possibilities of our imagination.

Think about the rigid thinking and collective ideas that have covered up your Dream Dome? What conditioned perspectives, dogmas, creeds, and false ideologies have kept you small and disempowered? "This is the way we have always done things. The world is one-dimensional. I am not worthy. I don't deserve happiness. Women don't have spiritual authority." Make a list of any rigid beliefs, thoughts, and dogmas that have kept you small, imprisoned, trapped, and disempowered. When you really feel and see and recognize with every fiber of your being how your mind has been hijacked and brainwashed to believe these crazy ideas, you will get angry enough to break down your Dream Dome.

When you are willing to liberate your mind, you can begin exploring the huge potential of your mind to imagine new thoughts, new ideas, and new ways of doing and being. After smashing down her Dream Dome, the elders activate Pujai's Inner Diamond, her third eye. When your third eye awakens, you begin to the see the world very differently. You see far beyond conditioned thinking, collective ideas and dogmas, and you begin to see the world as a playground of limitless possibilities. Your mind can reach up to the stars, up into the heavens, and you can create, innovate, think without editing or censuring, dream, and let your imagine fly. When you open your second sight you can learn to interpret dreams, see into the future, receive visions, and bring healing medicine to yourself and the village.

With her Inner Diamond now open and awake, Pujai has access to Wisdom, Understanding, and Knowledge and she is ready to gaze into the Cauldron of

Inspiration. As she stirs the cauldron, bubbles of new possibilities come forward. She is filled with inspiration, creativity, joy, and bliss. You might want to get a cauldron yourself and fill it with steamy liquid. Then inhale the spirit bubbling up and let yourself imagine what you want to do and be. What do you want to create in your life right now? What is your biggest dream for yourself? Pretend there is absolutely nothing in your way and allow yourself to be inspired. What new fresh spirit wants to be born in you? This is a really fun exercise because you are practicing your Visionary powers of dreaming, creating, and envisioning. The only way to make a change is to first clearly visualize what you want.

And this is precisely what Pujai learns next – how to focus her powers of visualization so she can envision the changes she wants. This is the last initiation in her Visionary training. She is taken to the Crystal Pyramid and shown how to sit in total alignment with the lower and upper pyramids. This represents an alignment with your own spiritual center. You can do this by imagining you are sitting in the middle of a crystal pyramid aligned with the apex above you and the base stretching below you. You can hold crystals too if you have some. Then it's important to charge up your intention and your motivation. This is the fuel to make the magic happen.

You can then practice this sequence of visualization: Think about a situation where you feel stuck. Set your intention. Identify what you want, your heart's true desire, and your vision. Declare it out loud. Purify your motive and dedicate the change you want to your highest good and your soul's higher purpose. Open to what is possible. Visualize the change you want. Imagine it clearly, already changed, already happening in real life. Bring the future possibility into the present. Feel the good feelings now that it has already changed. Strengthen the good feelings.

Pujai learns that the key to effective envisioning is to manipulate Time. When you are stuck, your mind is focused on the past and therefore you are energetically living in the past. When you envision the change you want, you tap into the future possibility that resides outside of linear time. Now you are living energetically in the future. Your mind is liberated from the past. When your mind is liberated, it can then manipulate time and invite the future possibility to live in the present. You then anchor the visualization by infusing the scene with powerful, positive feelings. This floods the new scenario you have created with love, happiness, joy, gratitude, and appreciation. As a Visionary, you have the power to envision the future and create change in the present. Dream big!

When you complete the Visionary initiation you will gain the powers of the Visionary Clan: objectivity, clarity of mind, inner sight, creativity, and the power to envision change. You will be able to wield your Sword of Clarity and command the Winds of Change. You will be able to inspire growth and evolution for yourself, your loved ones, and your community. You will be able to usher in the changes needed to breathe new life into the culture. You have said yes to awaken the Visionary in yourself and in your life. You are on your way to self-mastery.

Visionary Sacred Robe

When you look at the Visionary robe, what comes up for you? Here are some student responses:

- *To me she's saying, "Look out, here I come!" She's like a tornado.*
- *I like her third eye. Her intuition is open and she has clarity from that place, clarity of mind.*
- *I feel like she can cut through any of my delusions and illusions and just move forward.*
- *For me, I like her powerful presence. She seems very focused and clear, like she has clarity of mind and purpose.*
- *She looks like she doesn't waste your time. Like there's only this moment and I need to be clear.*

The Visionary certainly has very different energy from the emotional Queen. It's not the Visionary's job to feel feelings like the Queen or to be grounded like the Warrioress. Her job is to use the energy of her mind to bring clarity, change, and innovation.

Notice your own reaction to the Visionary. Are you drawn to her or repelled by her? When you look at the Visionary, it stimulates your own mental body and intuition. Maybe you have always trusted your intuition. Maybe you have been shutting it down. How do you relate to the Visionary now in your life?

On the Robe, you can see the Visionary's third eye has been activated. The yellow diamond on her forehead is awake and shining its light. The Visionary is open to her knowing, her intuition, and her psychic capabilities. The Visionary truly embodies the feminine way of knowing. With her activated third eye, she can look up at the stars and the vast cosmic landscape and bring new inspirations and new ideas to change the village. She can also move energy when people are stuck or when she herself feels stuck in old ways of doing and being.

Notice as we go through the different feminine guides, that each one builds upon the others. For example, in order to be effective, the Visionary needs to be grounded like the Warrioress and needs a balanced heart like the Queen. If the Visionary is not grounded or emotionally balanced, she may use her powers unwisely and call in destructive Winds of Change.

When do you want to call upon the Visionary? You call in the Visionary when you're stuck and when you need to move energy - out with the old and in with the new. When you start a creative project, call her in. When you want to be liberated from an old belief or an old pattern, call in your Visionary. When you want to remember your dreams or take seriously the knowledge that is coming to you, honor the Visionary. When you need to be clear-minded, or when you need to cut through chaos and confusion, call upon the great Visionary.

Interviews with Visionaries

The following are interviews with women who attend my *Feminine Path of Power* Programs and have interacted with all 5 Feminine Archetypes. Here is how some of them relate to the Visionary.

Interview with MK

Let's talk about your relationship with the Visionary and with the Path of Change - clearing your mind and opening your third eye. How is the Visionary working in your life?

Well, the Visionary is working pretty well because change is happening all around me! After the retreat last summer, I went into chaos and had so much on my plate. And as a mom, I had a lot going on and it made it hard to rise above the chaos and see where I was going. When you're a mom you're trying to get your kids to different places and you're making sure they are succeeding, and you're working and you have so much to do. You are just trying to survive. So I really connect with the Visionary's shadow side right now, which is the path of chaos. And I can relate to the Visionary's winds of change. They are blowing!

I've been talking to a friend for years about the changes that are coming on a global scale. And now it's popping up in my own life. Like when I got the notice from my landlady that she was going to turn our house into two flats. I had to stop and evaluate whether I was going to stay or move. The change in living situation was forced upon me from the outside. At first I was angry and then I realized that it is her property and she can choose to do with it what she wants. And I can decide how I want to react to that. So in embracing the change, I can clear out the people I no longer want in my life so I can really choose who I want to live with.

And I've been clearing out the basement of all of the stuff of my parents and grandparents and great-grandparents that has been stored there for generations. I've been the keeper of all of that stuff and so I spent the spring going through it all box-by-box and sending stuff to my other relatives. I told them if they don't want it, then donate it. So I finally got it all out of my house and I feel a real clearing. So the Visionary is helping me do a lot of clearing in my life right now. I feel lighter and I feel like I can look ahead of me without all of these old anchors. Now I am free to do what I want to do.

Wow that's such a great example of the Visionary, letting things go that needed to die, giving them all away, and clearing out your clutter. This is the perfect Visionary path isn't it? You really can't envision for your own life until you have let go of a lot of the clutter.

Right, because it's always in the back of your mind. I did have some jewelry from my grandmothers and decided to give one of the rings to my daughter. I thought she might want it because she's getting married. So she picked out one of the diamonds from my grandmother's ring (who is one of my ancestors that I call in when I do ritual), and she took the diamond and had an engagement ring made out of it. And that to me is what needs to go forward, a treasure from someone in the family that can be passed down and something beautiful can be made of it. And from my Dad I have his navy dog tag on my key ring so he is always with me. It was powerful to do that shifting through all the stuff from my ancestors. I don't need my mom's wedding dishes, I just need these little things I can carry with me, because the small things don't weigh me down.

I love what you're saying because all these boxes were anchoring you in the past and weighing you down. The purpose of the Visionary is to move energy for change and look up to spirit for a new way forward. When we are clear of the clutter we can focus on envisioning the changes we want for ourselves and for future generations. The Visionary has a future orientation – envisioning what you want for your future.

Yes, envisioning and seeing it clearly so that you can go there. If you can't visualize it, it's hard to get there. You have to visualize it and then create it.

Part of the Visionary training is about opening your third eye. I know a lot of women want this to happen but don't know how to do it to. Have you been able to open your third eye and open up your vision for yourself?

I am practicing opening my third eye and it makes sense to me that I need it open to envision. I get flashes of it. Rather than getting too literal about my third eye, sometimes a vision comes through to me that feels like it's in my mind and then I can visualize it clearly. So that's been how I experience it. I sometimes get tripped up about the physical third eye, like I should be seeing something, but really it's in the middle of my brain and because so much is going on in the brain, I can access visions from there.

And what do you think about this notion that women's visions are going to save the world? I heard the Dalai Lama say that women's Visionary powers of intuition and spiritual knowing are going to help solve the world's problems.

That makes so much sense because the masculine way just keeps screwing it up. One thing I'm interested in is working with children and women who are in difficult situations because I went through that myself. So the answers must be something different, something more feminine. We have power as women and mothers and caretakers, of people and the earth. The feminine choices we make seem so much better than what men are offering. I really like the way you talk about this because the Feminine is coming through. We've had the feminine wisdom in the past and so it can come through again. We can get back to the Divine Feminine because it hasn't been lost. And I feel like that's what's happening inside of me. My feminine power went away and now it's coming back.

So to bring in the other Goddesses, when you put in healthy boundaries with your Warrioress and you love yourself profoundly with your Queen, then it's easier to activate your Visionary and bring your feminine vision into your life and into the world.

Yes!

That's really exciting! Thanks for sharing your relationship with the Visionary and how you are moving with the winds of change.

Interview with Margaret

Let's talk about the Visionary, the Air Clan Goddess. She has clarity and combats the Path of Chaos. She represents the Path of Change and opening the third eye. How do you relate to the Visionary path?

I think immediately of the Visionary as my spiritual guide. I have a meditation I do regularly, the Merkabah meditation where I imagine myself inside a glass pyramid. Within this Merkabah pyramid (similar to the crystal pyramid at the Visionary training ground) I am just receiving and listening. I am also connected to ravens so I allow them to hang me upside down in the trees like the falcons do in the Visionary story. I imagine the ravens coming to get me and hanging me upside down in the pine trees as if I were in the mountains at 10,000 feet. Here I take a look at the world and see it from a different perspective and I can easily cut through all the crap!

When I respect myself and respect what is arising within me, it brings me more clarity, so I can start cutting through the crap and start getting a clearer vision. When this vision is intertwined with self-love and I can put that inner critic aside, it's like this whole wide spaciousness opens up and I can get a bigger perspective. In a very practical sense, when I'm sitting in a meeting, I can sit in a specific place where I can take in the whole space. I have a need for spaciousness, so I'm honoring the part of me that needs that big space around me.

I love that. That's such a cool way of thinking about your Visionary. So you can step back and take a bigger look at the bigger picture instead of being bogged down by the details of a meeting.

When I call in my Visionary, I invite a vision and some insight. When something is pushing up within me that I'm not quite aware of yet, I find my desire to hike up a hill. I hike up to get a better perspective on the problem. From up high, I can observe and take it all in and even think in new ways. When I'm at the top I then get grounded with intention. I really get a sense of being closer to the Visionary. I pay attention and see what's being invited for a new place of transformation.

I really like your visual of climbing up the hill to get a bigger picture of the vista. How do you feel about the Visionary as the goddess of change?

I used to get thrown off by change. I would feel that something was much more of a crisis than it was and then react from that place. Change seemed very painful and would stir up a lot of fear. Now I am able to stay calm, even in a whirlwind. I don't have to be caught up in it. Growing up in South Africa I think of all the dustbowls that would get stirred up in the wind and chaos. And here in the USA, in the mid-west, we have tornadoes that stir up the ground, and whirl up branches, rocks, sucking up everything in its path. Now when I think of the Visionary's winds of change, I visualize the wind just passing. I can stay calm and centered through this kind of storm now.

What I hear you saying is that you feel more empowered now rather than being taken over by that swirling energy. And you don't have to scatter your energy by talking to a lot of people during a perceived crisis. If you hold it inside and allow the winds of change to move around and inside you, it will pass more quickly. And you can actually use those winds of change for something positive.

The other thing that is really powerful about the Visionary is that she helps us open our third eye. When women have opened intuition and spiritual knowing in the past, bad things have happened: we've been accused of witchcraft, we've been scapegoated and ostracized and even killed. So we may have some resistance to opening our intuition! What happens for you when you feel your third eye opening?

I feel I am being invited to journey deeper into myself, like a shamanic journey experience. I do actually feel a physical sensation of opening and I feel some heat in the middle of my forehead. It usually starts as a pinpoint of blue light and opens out to a huge, wide view of the cosmos, like the pictures from the Hubble telescope. I see this huge astral field. It is so illuminated. And very often I see an eye actually looking back at me.

That's helpful to hear. I know a lot of women want to open their third eye but they're not sure how to do it or what it looks like. It's nice to get a visual of what it's like for you personally, so women can start to visualize for themselves.

In the past, I've also experienced colors of the rainbow rising in layers when I open my third eye. Now I go to a place of being deeply open and it's happening faster using meditation practices, especially your Light Grid Meditation, which takes me there very quickly.

Thank you so much for sharing your experience with the Visionary. Your vivid examples are really helpful.

Interview with Cynthia

Let's explore the Visionary. She is all about breaking through our paradigms that have brainwashed us into certain patterns that are clearly unhealthy for us. The Visionary clears our mind and frees us to envision the changes we want. How are you relating to the Visionary, the Path of Change?

Every morning I call her in and imagine a crystal here in my brain, here in the pineal area, the third eye. I start grounding with my Warrioress, I get heart-centered with my Queen, and then I imagine activating this crystal in my brain and then I go up and out and touch the stars. I feel really connected. I also sometimes grab my Visionary Sword. I made this Sword so I can actually hold it. I can move with it.

So you like to grab your Sword and swish it around in the air? I bet that makes you feel like you're cutting through the clutter.

Yes, I like to slice with my Sword any negativity that's coming at me, anything that's keeping me from love. In the past I would sometimes disconnect from my spiritual practices and get amnesia! I want to stay connected as much as possible now. So my mantra now is, "Connect, connect, connect!" Sometimes I'm unaware that I'm not in alignment and unaware that I am not being present. I blame it on the traffic, on my clients, on an outside crisis. And then, in my gentleness and in my self-care, I remind myself that this is all part of my initiation. "Just move back into your practice. Bring yourself back and reground. Cut the confusion. Get present."

That's really interesting because in the Visionary initiation, we talk about the cobwebs of confusion, like when our mind gets foggy. When you're in confusion then you can disconnect or dissociate. So when you remember to come back into your body, and then connect your mind to your heart, and then connect to your lower chakras, you're back in alignment. I see this all the time with women – we get "confused" - but actually, we know exactly what's going on most of the time. We can see intuitively with our third eye and we see the truth. What a gift to the world when we can stay in our mind and be clear, and then be able to communicate that truth. This is one of the gifts of the Visionary.

Yes, sometimes when I see something and I bring it up – if it's not validated right away, I abandon my own felt truth. Then I go back into my own cycle of "I know nothing."

Exactly. And when we move off of our clear vision, then our feminine vision, our feminine solutions, and our feminine creativity isn't getting out there in the world. The only way to fight this invalidation of the truth is to stand our ground, be heart-opened, and then to speak the truth from the Visionary space. So it's helpful to connect with the Warrioress, the Queen, and then the Visionary.

Right, right. I do see that. So I can say from my perspective - this is what I'm seeing, and this is how I see it - and not back down from that. Not say, "You have to see it this way," but "This is what I'm seeing."

Yes! Because that validates your truth and then you're not disconnecting from yourself. You're staying inside your crystal clear mind. It's your crystal clear vision. The reason why this is so important is that when you trust your own perspective and vision, then you can clearly envision what you want for yourself. That's why it's important to stay connected to your Visionary.

It's so hard to stand in my truth sometimes. It's hard to envision what I want next. Should I stay in my job even though it's draining? Should I have more money coming in? What am I supposed to be doing? Am I confusing myself just to keep safe?

It's helpful to remember that the Visionary envisions what you want in the future. She lays out a pathway for you to follow and then you can envision it into your future. The Warrioress and the Queen can be very present-oriented, and I think they really should be. The Visionary thrusts us into envisioning for the future. When we can get some clarity around that, it doesn't mean that it's going happen tomorrow. What it does mean, though, is that you're laying out a path for yourself to envision what you want. Then you can take tangible steps forward - one step at a time.

I think sometimes I'm afraid to envision because I don't want to be let down. I don't want to be disappointed. Disappointment is just so hard to take. So then I don't envision anything for myself and I stop trusting myself.

That's why the Visionary is all about clearing the mind so that you can trust yourself completely. It takes a lot of courage to envision exactly what change you want for yourself.

I've been thinking a lot about courage lately and what I should do next. It's like stepping off a cliff! When I feel afraid, I think, "Oh no, that's not the direction I should be heading." And then I say to myself, "Wait. You keep getting pushed in this direction. Just do it." I can always say no. And that's the courage. It's like feeling the fear, and doing it anyway. But the clarity has to come so I know that I am stepping off the right cliff.

When your Visionary envisions your future, you can open your mind as far and wide as possible. You can think of the craziest possibilities, because you haven't yet taken the step or put it into action. That's why the Visionary can be a fun place to be, because you allow your imagination and your creativity to fly! The point of the Visionary is to let your clear mind be a tool of consciousness; a tool of creative thinking that might bring in new pathways that you've never even considered.

This really makes me laugh because as you're talking I can hear my Protestant upbringing voice saying, "Oh no, I'm not worthy. How can I ask for what I want for me?"

These beliefs limit your creative thinking.

I'm finally allowing myself to have a few comforts. Like when I come to Berkeley to stay for school, instead of staying at a place with no heat or a place that uses a bucket for the toilet, I'm allowing myself to stay in a place that is lovely and nurturing. Can I dare allow myself to have some comforts and not feel bad? Maybe I get to experience a really yummy, comfortable bed and feel safe. It was like this paradigm shift in my head.

Yes, like a revelation, and that's what the Visionary's all about. The Visionary is constantly pushing us to have new revelations, new thoughts, new ideas, and to not be afraid of new paradigms. The Visionary breaks down old paradigms that no longer work. One of the reasons we hold on to our old belief systems and old paradigms is because we think we should. Do we dare to break through the ceiling of this old belief system? The Visionary says, "Absolutely. Tear down all the boxes of belief that limit your mind. All of them." What are we left with? We're left with infinite possibilities, which means we get to choose which path we want to take, rather than the "should" path.

It feels like my whole life is being deconstructed. Is that normal for the Visionary? It feels very confusing.

It's disorienting. And this is very normal during the Visionary initiation.

There's part of me that's trying to hold on, and there's part of me trying to bust out of the old system. It's been like this for such a long time now - it's like "Come on already!"

It takes a long time to get to those unconscious belief systems that are limiting us, and then when you hit them, it's pretty mind-boggling. And it is totally confusing when those old structures come down. The Visionary energy is designed to clear out your mind, so that you can be clear-headed and use your mind as a tool for higher consciousness.

Well, I'm totally in the deconstruction phase. I'm coming apart and sometimes freaking out. It does get kind of confusing!

Yes! And I have to say that that is happening to many, many women because we weren't initiated when we were young. And because the old paradigms are shifting so dramatically in the wider culture, many of us are going through a complete disorientation and reorientation, which happens naturally in the initiation process. It feels dramatic now because we've been living under these old paradigms for so long. I want to give you some support around this disorientation phase because this is part of the initiation process. We get deconstructed so that we can be reconstructed into our radiant, divine selves! Thanks for sharing your experiences of the Visionary!

Interview with Susan

Let's talk about your Visionary who helps you to be clear-minded and also helps you tackle chaos and confusion. I'd love to hear how you're connecting to your Visionary.

For me, the challenge with my Visionary was to cut through the chaos as a result of my father being a dry drunk. Initially, my Visionary was the strongest and the first to step forward. I led with my clear-mindedness because it brought me the change and the transformation I needed to be able to make the journey from just being dysfunctional to being functional. I used my already detached position to be objective.

Once I learned how my Visionary works for me, I could cut through the confusion of my misguided upbringing. I had the power of my mind and I used it to learn about my inner child and to understand my dysfunction and my co-dependency. I called in my Visionary by reading and reflecting and envisioning a life that was better for me. This really changed my internal landscape.

When I learned about coming out of my illusions and changing my beliefs, I was excited to explore this with my Visionary mind. I now have Visionary tools that give me a higher perspective and help me make quick decisions and let go of things that need to die in order to transform.

Currently, I'm using my Visionary to create some space to envision my book. I'm also opening up my creativity and my creative process in general. Ultimately, I'm hoping for this to breathe a breath of fresh air and new life into the community.

You're describing well the Visionary cycle of death and rebirth – after letting go, you get to experience regeneration and fresh new life blowing in! When you publish your book, you'll be able to see how it breathes new life into the wider culture.

Yes.

Would you say your Visionary is actually your strongest archetype because your mind power has always been strong?

Yes, I led with my mind for a very long time. I had to honor my mind. When I moved to leading with my heart, it was really important for me to honor my mind. It's a great tool. It's just amazing.

I like the way you are using this great tool of the mind and connecting it up with your heart, your Queen. You're talking about how your Visionary and your Queen work together.

Yes. Now I can use my mind for other things. It was nice for my hard-working mind to have a reprieve. When my mind and heart connect, it's really powerful. It's going to bring the manifestation of my book and creative outlets that other people can use. I'm working on creativity, boundlessness and fearlessness and when these start to come together, it's going to be very, very liberating for me. I can feel it, and I'm looking forward to that.

I know that part of your book is about creating artwork. Can you say a little bit about how your Visionary envisions for your artwork? It will be helpful for other women to understand how you envision. How do you use your Visionary when you do your artwork?

My Visionary is not visual. I feel things rather than see them. When you say the word "Visionary" I always think seeing something with your eyes. What was so challenging for me about envisioning is that I don't "see" the way others do in meditation. Others see a real orange or they see the peel coming off the orange and smelling it etc. I just sense it.

My creative Visionary process now is looking at pictures of animals - my book has a lot of animals in it. I'll be attracted toward an animal and then I'll just feel into that. I'll read a little bit about it. I'm pulling in my mental capacity. Then I actually do find a picture that inspires me. Then I'll draw from there. Then the creativity comes in when I add color. Then the feeling comes from my story, in what I write about.

What you're saying is that you're a kinesthetic Visionary, not so much a visual Visionary?

Yes.

I think that's really helpful because it's true that when a lot of women hear the word Visionary, they think they're supposed to be a visual artist or something. It doesn't necessarily mean that at all. Each woman needs to find her own way of visioning, her own way of being creative and innovative. We have to find our own way of using our visionary capacities. You just described it beautifully how you have a unique way of working with your Visionary.

When you say kinesthetic, it reminds me of a wind sculpture I have in my backyard. The wind moves it and because of the way it is constructed, it moves very easily. What I connect with the most is the movement of the sculpture.

Yes. The Visionary is ruler of the air clan and she moves the Winds of Change. She keeps us moving with the cycles of change. The Visionary is connected to motion and represents the Path of Change. The Visionary helps us to be flexible with all the changes that are going on in our lives and in the world so that we can move effectively with the changes that are occurring. I love that visual of having a sculpture that easily moves because that speaks of the flexibility of a Visionary.

Yes. I just developed my new website and one quote I put on it is, "May the Winds of Change blow through you."

Thank you, that's beautiful.

Interview with Kala

Let's talk about your Visionary. She is concerned with change and moving you gracefully around the life/death/rebirth wheel so that you experience renewal and rebirth. The Visionary helps you let go of old beliefs and open to the new beliefs that are blowing into your life. The Visionary also clears your mind so that you can experience spaciousness and open to your intuition and to new possibilities. How do you relate to your Visionary?

The Visionary is so beautiful for my creative work. I love the Visionary's Sword. I also love that she is connected to space and to the stars. I've been involved in math and astronomy, so I feel at home with the Visionary. When the sun goes down and the telescopes open and we leap out somewhere between the galaxies, that's awesome. That's my passion, really.

The Visionary shows me that we're all created out of this incredible dance of space and geometry. It's elegant and it's beautiful. Then we add consciousness and all the creatures of nature and all the birds and the animals and the trees. Everything is born out of this incredible dance of compassion, wisdom, and creativity. That's ultimately where divinity is. We are constructive co-creators and we need to make sure to not obstruct our own process or the process of nature or the process of spirit, which all become one and the same.

That's a beautifully poetic way to speak of the Visionary's gift of creativity. The Visionary is also connected to our mind. Do you have a Visionary practice that you could share to clear away the mind clutter, to clear your Visionary space?

I started meditating when I was 16. Every morning for about 5 or 10 minutes I would concentrate on one of the virtues: Beauty or Wisdom or Patience, or Discipline, those kinds of things. I would focus on one of those qualities and then write about it. This helped me to focus and to really get inside the virtues. From there, I began to look at how the virtues show up in the world. I saw that we needed to all get along together. Later when I was a teacher, my meditation practice helped me as I taught emotional intelligence and mental clarity for kids. I also taught kids peace education - peace and conflict studies.

My father was a Doctor and I learned early on that you have to use your mind intelligently and sometimes be dispassionate and more objective. So I learned to be detached and compassionate at the same time.

Yes, our Visionary helps us to have a clear mind with some healthy detachment so we can do particular tasks without getting too emotionally involved. This is really helpful at times. Our Visionary gives us a bigger picture and a higher perspective so that we can view life from a larger worldview.

Yes, it seems important that we as women can have really clear, powerful, detached minds and incredible hearts at the same time. It doesn't mean that we don't have compassion. When I think about what is happening in our world today, especially in politics, I know we can get past all this drama and corruption. There's something so much deeper and so much more powerful and I know all the chaos and conflict will pass.

From the Visionary's perspective, we know that our thoughts can affect what happens in the world, for good or for bad. So let's do group meditation and change the craziness that is going on in the world now.

What you're speaking to is the importance of our Visionaries getting together and envisioning this new world we desire. One Visionary can envision a good life for herself and a good life for the planet, but we need all of our Visionaries to get together so that we can dream into this new world. The Visionary walks the Path of Change. If we want change to happen, we have to envision it together.

Our consciousness greatly affects our physical world and everything we do.

Exactly, very well said! Thank you so much for sharing your experience with the Visionary.

Interview with Carol

How are you getting on with the Visionary? She walks the Path of Change and she is the Air Clan Goddess. How are you relating to the Visionary?

The Visionary - she's a mighty force. I relate to the Visionary in that, as far back as I can remember I wanted to change patterns in my own family. I wanted to be an agent of change. I wanted to be on the Path of Change and help transform this world to make it better. So I had that in my mind - I wanted to be able to change things that were harmful or hurtful. I wanted to clear my lineage patterns so that my children could benefit from those changed patterns and changed energies.

Sometimes I get stuck on the shadow Path of Chaos and feel a lot of confusion. Once again, this goes back to the attachment patterns in my family. I was confused a lot as a child. There was so much confusion and there were so many lies being told all the time. There was substance abuse in my family so we had to hide and pretend. My mom was addicted to drugs and my sister and I were told we were crazy when we told the truth about what we saw happening. We were told it wasn't happening. My mom would try to convince us we hadn't seen her taking the drugs. So we had to pretend it wasn't happening. It was confusing and chaotic as a child.

We weren't allowed to talk about the trauma that was happening in our family, so it was like everything was supposed to be fine. And yet, there was just so much confusion when I tried to see what was really going on. And so I'd end up thinking, "I'm crazy. Am I crazy?"

Well, the truth was being distorted and so it must have been very confusing for you. It sounds like your whole family patterning was about the shadow side of the Visionary, which is to confuse you and convince you to not speak the truth. And so you got confused in your mind rather than clear in your mind.

Right. Which affected me a lot growing up. I literally blocked out everything that had happened until a certain age. Then as I got older, I started remembering things. But even remembering what happened to me as a child brought such confusion. So trying to work it through in therapy, I questioned whether these things really happened to me. "I'm making this up, I must be making all this up, did this really happen?" I was also confused about my feelings for my mom, my dad and my sister. I had some anger towards my parents but I wasn't supposed to feel anger. So I felt confused and bad. So the Visionary brings in that clarity for me, which is really important.

My Visionary has helped me literally cut through the smokescreens and the confusion. I call her in and she helps me see exactly what's going on in a situation now. I still have a little bit of a struggle discerning other people's intentions, but my Visionary is helping me be more discerning. It's easier for me to see the truth about a situation or see the truth about a person. It doesn't mean I'm bad or a bad person when I simply see the truth about something.

Right, you're just seeing clearly. It's your intuition and your clear seeing.

Yes, it's such a treasure and such a great gift for me to be able to see clearly.

So when you do see clearly, when you feel like your Visionary is strong in you and you trust yourself, what does that feel like?

It feels amazing. Once again, I feel a very strong sense of self. I stand my ground as a Warrioress. Then I bring in my Queen who has compassion and then my Visionary says, "Okay, so I'm seeing that this person is perhaps angry or is not being honest." I can feel the energy, like maybe this person is somehow trying to deceive me. My Queen helps me not feel guilty. My Visionary can see clearly when she is relaxed and supported by the Warrioress and Queen. One of my gifts is clear vision - to be able to see things and discern clearly. And this gift was really distorted in my family growing up. So I feel more confident about being able to walk through this world and know what's going on rather than being confused. It feels so liberating.

I love what you said about liberation because the Visionary initiation has a lot to do with liberating your mind to think for yourself, to see clearly and to stand in your truth. You are liberated to see clearly those people who are deceptive and who have negative motivations. You can just see them for who they are and not be confused about it.

I don't have to be confused about it. They are where they are, and there's no judgment. Or, if somebody loves me, I can discern that clearly too. And you're right, it is total liberation, because I felt like I was a slave to my mind, to the old mental patterns, and to the chaos from my past. And to be able to see clearly is an amazing liberation that I'm still learning to rejoice in and accept.

And what about your Visionary's abilities to envision what you want for yourself? How's that going for you - having your own visions for your life?

Yes, so that is another big part of the Visionary. When I can cut through all the chaos, which keeps my mind cluttered all the time; I'm starting to see the things that I want to do. I've taken up drumming each morning. I've been going out and singing and playing the drum. It is opening up a whole new sense of being for me, a whole new sense of strength. Something is opening up for me even just the singing and the drumming.

Oh, that's powerful.

Yes! My Visionary wants me to come from my heart and use my true gifts. My Visionary can see my gifts and my dreams and my desires. I'm also reading books now by John Bowlby, who writes about attachment theory. And the Visionary is coming into play because as I read these books, I can see my own attachment patterns and it helps to free me. I'm starting to see that I can help other people. The vision is coming. It's pulling together.

That's beautiful. And it sounds to me like your drumming and singing is a Visionary practice as it helps to open your third eye. I love that you're practicing that.

Yes. Every morning, I'm going out and doing that. And I feel like it sets my day. I know I am a part of this ancient lineage. I am. I belong to this Earth. It brings me clarity of mind. I am a woman who can drum and sing and call together a circle of people. That's what I see coming. My vision gets stronger by pulling all the Goddesses together. I call in my Warrioress, Queen, Visionary, Manifestor and Wise Woman and my vision is getting stronger for what I want to do.

I'm so happy for you that your Visionary is strong and helping to liberate so many past patterns. She is weaving new patterns to support who you are now! Thank you for sharing so generously.

Interview with Ali Marie

Let's talk about the Visionary and the Air Clan. How do you connect with and relate to your Visionary?

I relate to the Visionary very naturally. I think though that I'm still learning to build more of a trusting relationship with my Visionary. I feel like I've been dangling upside down in a tree, which is part of that story! I've been hanging out upside down and getting a new perspective. I feel like I've been doing that for a while and I find it's uncomfortable. So, there's some resistance to opening to that greater vision. I feel she has a lot more to teach me.

Yes, we're hanging upside down in the trees with the Visionary so that we can be liberated from our conditioning and from the way our mind is taught to work in our culture. We are encouraged to be overly busy, to accumulate mental clutter and to be in chaos. The shadow side of the Visionary is the Path of Chaos. Sometimes our minds think in very obsessive-compulsive ways and we ruminate too much over things. When really our mind is an amazing tool for higher consciousness. And the Visionary initiation trains you to clear the mind and open to new perspectives. With your Visionary you can expand your mind, open your third eye, and connect with spirit.

Yes. I definitely have had an over-busy mind. I have a lot of natural tendencies in that air element. Not only have I experienced a busy, busy mind but also the worries of the mind. I had that even when I was very little, when I was a young girl. My mind was always going - and there have been a lot of gifts from that. I've been learning how to let go of what isn't useful and build the strengths of my mind.

One thing that I can get tripped up on a lot is going into judgment. I get stuck in thinking things are right or wrong. Then I want to make sure I don't do the wrong thing. Then I don't want to make a move at all because I don't know which is the right step and which is the wrong step. I'm trying to move away from judging and labeling. I trust that I'm going be carried by my greater vision. I trust that my Visionary will offer me something bigger than my limited perspective. Does that make sense?

Absolutely. Many of us are stuck in the "right-wrong" paradigm and it is very constricting, limiting, and paralyzing. So I agree that trust is the key. There's something profound about learning to trust your Visionary's intuition.

Yes, I think that's a big part – trusting!

Yes, you mentioned at the beginning of this Visionary conversation that you feel some resistance to really opening to new vistas. What feels scary about opening up your vision?

I feel like there are things that are currently unknown to me that are still blocking me. Like there still are things I need to let go of. And I don't know what those are. There's more to be explored in my relationship with my Visionary and I want to build more trust with her.

Well, as you say, if we're stuck in a right-wrong paradigm, we don't know what's beyond that. It takes a lot of courage with the Visionary to leap into the air, to leap into that unknown place, because if you really expand your mind and move beyond the right-wrong worldview, where would you be?

Yes, if I let go of the right-wrong game, I can see I would feel a lot more freedom. One thing that is helping me expand my Visionary is bringing in more joy, humor, and laughter. I am feeling a new sense of carefree-ness. There's a sense of youthfulness and having that be part of my Visionary. Living with a sense of fun is the opposite of living a right-wrong paradigm. When I feel the internal pressure of - I better not make a mistake, I better not do the wrong thing - I shift to hold a sense of joyous adventure. When I can hold it in a different light, this has been useful.

I love that you are moving to a place of non-judgment and more playfulness. I also feel what is so potent about your Visionary is her Sword of Clarity. So whatever you have to cut through, whether it's confusion or a right-wrong paradigm or perfectionism, you can just take that Sword and cut through so that your mind can be clear.

Yes, that really helps! And perfectionism - that's a big one for me. This is where the Queen really helps because my need to be perfect or be perceived in that light is intricately tied to the idea that I'm not worthy of love somehow. So when I connect that to the Queen and love myself fully then the perfectionism dissipates. The need to be seen in that perfect light in order to be worthy of whatever it is I need lessens and disappears. I still need a lot of Queen energy even with the Visionary.

That makes sense because the Visionary is about the Path of Change and letting things die and the only way you can do that is when you feel held and safe and loved by your Queen. I can really see how they all work together. How do you connect with your Visionary? Do you use meditation as a tool to help clear out the clutter of your mind?

I do. I have a lot of tools for that. I do a lot of different kinds of sacred writing and meditation and prayer and all of those things – and the busyness of my mind has greatly diminished. I can see the cycle of worry, when it starts to spin, and I can cut through that. So that has definitely improved.

If women could clear their minds and really tune in to their Visionary, what kind of feminine visions could awaken and bring solutions that are different than masculine solutions or visions? Maybe our feminine vision and feminine spiritual knowing could change the world.

Yes. I start to see that more and more, which I think is a beautiful movement. We are starting to shift and a whole new perspective and paradigm is opening up. In the past, when I didn't have as much of a relationship with the Queen and I had a stronger relationship with the Warrioress, I would immediately turn to my body in order to move out of worry or that spinning out place of the mind. When my mind was spinning with anxiety or worry, I would go directly to my Warrioress instead of the Visionary. I would go for a run or I would do yoga or I would immediately move into the body, which can be useful tool, but I've over-done that too. I used to exercise for hours in a day, which is crazy. I didn't know I could turn to my Visionary to help me cut through the confusion when my mind was spinning out of control. So I need the Visionary to be stronger and I still need the balance of the Queen to bring me self-care. If not, I go into self-abusive or self-hurtful behavior. It's so important to have all the Goddesses, all the archetypes working together and balancing each other.

Right. So connecting your mind to your heart, to your body and so on.

Yes, exactly. Because I had ignored the Queen for so long, bringing the Queen in has brought balance to my life.

That's beautiful. I get excited when we talk about the Visionary in this way because it helps to unlock our old paradigms so that we, as women, can envision something new. Not only for ourselves but also for the world. What your saying is that in order to really embody the Visionary, we must be well grounded in our Warrioress and have self-compassion from our Queen. Then it's much easier to start clearing your mind and get a clear vision for who you want to be.

Yes. I've really been experiencing a lot lately knowing my heart's desire. Again, it's that connection between the Queen and the Visionary. I have been motivated by many, many factors in my life to do this or that or take a job or whatever, build a career. There have been different motivating factors, but knowing the call of my heart and allowing that to be the source of my inspiration, allows me to be fully who I am. When I allow my heart to sing, I show up fully. You know what I mean? I can express the highest version of myself by knowing and hearing my heart.

Yes, then you can be clear about the visioning that you want to do. Thank you so much for sharing your experience with the Visionary and how you are using all the Goddesses to work together so you can express your best self!

Interview with Susana

Let's talk about your Visionary. How do you relate to her?

It's funny, when I started the process, I liked the Visionary, but I did not really understand her. I was drawn to her, but I didn't really have an idea of what she was about. But now, I relate to the Visionary the most. I have a lot of third eye stuff happening at the moment. I've been experiencing a lot of openings and a lot of dreams. In my dreams I've seen these bulbs emerging on my head, like small horns growing and it reminds me of my third eye opening and extending. I've also been dreaming about receiving operations, like I'm being worked on at such a deep level. So it really feels my third eye is opening up and it's really quite wonderful that I'm becoming more acquainted with my Visionary.

She's coming alive right now for you.

Yes. That's a good way of saying it. She's coming alive for me. My Visionary represents the Path of Change - and clarity. I'm breaking through a lot of chaos and muddy thinking. I would call that "lower thinking" as opposed to thinking with my higher mind. I am discovering how to tap into my higher mind and not simply believe all the things of the lower mind - like my old patterns, old reactions and ego responses. I really thought that's all that the mind was, just instinctive reactions and responses. Now I am coming to see that my lower mind thoughts are just thoughts. They're not real - not any more real than I need to make them. This has been a revelation to me!

Can you describe what you mean by the lower mind?

The lower mind for me is a lot of my programming and conditioning, like collective beliefs and negative talk, "Oh you're not good enough." Or the perfectionistic talk, "You have to be perfect in order to do anything. You have to do it right." These kinds of monologues in my mind, which I was reacting to, were coming from my lower mind. I didn't even realize these programs were running. I have all these tapes and I didn't recognize they were running as much as they do. These lower mind thoughts just grab hold and I ruminate on things, spin on things, think about things over and over and over again and it never gets me anywhere. For example, I might ruminate for weeks about an assignment I need to write and I don't write one page because I'm stuck spinning things around in my mind. When I'm in that lower mind place, it takes up a lot of energy.

This sounds like a huge transformation, moving away from attaching to your lower mind and connecting to your higher mind as a tool of consciousness.

Yes, it is a huge transformation. It's more about relaxing than it is about striving. I feel this same kind of ease now when I play my harp. I'm a beginner harpist and I don't really know how to read music. I've been striving for the last two years to learn where the fingers go, and chords, and notes, and something has shifted now where my hands are doing things that my mind is not thinking of first. My hands are moving before I can think because that lower mind thinking is too slow.

I'm also seeing my Visionary at work when I plan something out that seems to be so arduous and then I just say, "Oh, let go of the plan," and things happen and unfold very easily and naturally. I would call this the magic of my higher mind. When I get so wound up in the details and lose the bigger, energetic picture, my Visionary kicks in. She allows me to be more present. I'm not thinking of what to do or how to do it so much. So in my work, I'm finding I'm more present and freer to try all kinds of things. My Visionary helps to free my mind for creative thinking.

Now you are using your higher mind more frequently. You mentioned you feel your third eye is opening? Can you give some examples of how that feels to you - maybe some dreams or visions that are coming to you as your third eye is opening?

Yes. I'm so intrigued about these images of the Merkabah that come when I close my eyes. (A Merkabah is the sacred geometric form surrounding our physical body creating a protective aura of light. Some traditions say it is a spiritual vehicle or "chariot", which is the Hebrew translation of "Merkabah".) *So I've been learning how the Merkabah concept is found in so many traditions like the Kabbalistic Tree of Life, mandalas, and on the Flower of Life. So my visions of these sacred geometric forms are leading me to do some research. My dreams are showing me that I have nodule balls that almost look like a young stag's horns, these little nubs that are growing out of my head. Curiously, they're more like balls, and they're full of fluid, in the dream that's the way it seemed. And they were on both hemispheres of my brain, on my head. And then two nights ago, I had a dream that I was having surgery done. Some type of surgery that I didn't really know what it was, but it was not in a regular operating room. So it feels like some kind of reconstruction or opening is happening and it's happening in my brain, my mind.*

Reprogramming comes to mind, because that's what you were talking about. When you let go of the old belief systems your mind begins to expand – like your new horns in the dream. And when you are willing to replace old programs, then your mind is more spacious for a new kind of programming to come in – new beliefs and new thoughts that are far more suited to you and your vision and purpose in this life. You can get closer to your original blueprint when your slate is wiped clean of the old programs. You have a fresh, clean slate and you can program in positive thoughts, feelings, and self-confidence. You can connect with your own Soul's program. I love that the fluid balls/horns are budding out from the left and right hemispheres of your brain. It's like your brain is re-wiring!

Yes, I would say that's very true. So it feels like I'm in a discovery process right now. When you ask about the Visionary, I don't even have an image of a goddess or anything at the moment. Instead of seeing my Visionary I am seeing sacred geometry! I do have a lot more clarity. Now I can just walk into a hospital room when I'm at work and after a short conversation, I have a good sense of what is happening. I "see" a 360-degree picture. And then I give my reports at my Chaplain meetings in a very clear and concise, direct way. This skill is getting more honed. Where other people seem to take two and three visits, I'm finding I can grasp the whole thing in a relatively short amount of time.

That totally sounds like the Visionary to me, when you are clear-minded and able to read the energy in the room and come to a conclusion fairly quickly. I think this is the gift of your Visionary.

Yes it is. It's nice. It makes things pretty quick. And that doesn't mean I don't stay with patients as long as I need to stay there, but I can read the dynamics and the energy pretty quickly. And my vision is clear, that's the other thing. I can quickly look at my own assumptions, my own projections - what I bring to the interaction. I notice that there's not as much of my own "stuff" as there was before, and it's much clearer.

There is not as much distortion or interference.

Yes. And I can see other people's distortions and interferences easier, too. I think, "Oh, that's interesting. No wonder they have that problem with that person." Or, "Gee, that's certainly an interesting distortion." I can see clearly how a person's attitude colors everything they experience in their life.

Yes. With the Visionary, you can pop up above the clouds, like when you're flying in an airplane, and then you can see this huge vista. I often think about this gift of the Visionary, your ability to rise above collective thinking. With your Visionary you can clear away the distortions and connect in with the vision that's much, much bigger. And it gives you objectivity, clarity, and swiftness in terms of interventions, like choosing to say something or do something in the moment. It's almost like TIME takes on a different quality with the Visionary.

Yes, that's very true, time does seem different, and that's a relief. I was feeling so bound by time or the lack thereof. Now I feel more spaciousness.

This makes me wonder what will happen when more women can find this level of spaciousness and can tune in to their feminine visions. How might we change the world? How might our feminine visions and feminine solutions transform the world? When we're free to collectively dream together, our feminine dreams can make a huge impact.

Yes. Historically, I do think that women have a tendency to be more inclusive in their visions, to see the good of the whole, and be more 360 in their visions. However even as I say that, I can't help but wonder if that's from an old paradigm. Maybe both men and women have been under an old paradigm. When I talk with men who have risen above collective thinking, they seem to have similar visions and solutions as the women do. I think women's voices have not been heard in quite a long time though, so perhaps our voices are bringing more balance now.

Your Visionary is certainly active in your dream life and you are honoring what is emerging from your own unconscious. So thank you for doing this because you are bringing forth your feminine dreams and visions! Well it sounds like the Visionary is very, very active for you right now. That's exciting.

Interview with AB

The Visionary walks the Path of Change and is connected with the Air Clan. She is the one inside you helping you move with this wheel of change and all the transitions you are going through. It's a powerful time for you to get clearer with your Visionary and see how she's going to help you to envision your future. The shadow side of the Visionary is the inner chaos that we get ourselves into, through procrastination or distraction or negative thinking. She helps you clear away all the clutter to see what's actually going on. Can you give an example of how you use your Visionary, like when you want to create something or envision something?

I have a colleague in my old city that I jived with in terms of my work. We have great synergy and would get together for brainstorming / envisioning sessions. One time we created a day retreat for women. I wanted to do the expressive arts piece and she wanted to do some journey dancing and we also got a yoga teacher. We would just sit down and envision it - this is what we need, this is our target audience, this is who we know. Let's put it out there and boom! We did it.

Now my Visionary is visualizing a peaceful home versus so much action. I do feel I have some self-sabotage going on though that I would like to explore, as I know this is the shadow side of the Visionary. I'm asking myself what do I want to do now? Where do I want to volunteer? Do I want additional training? I'm spinning my wheels and getting a bit chaotic. I would love to do equestrian work, volunteering for horse therapy. Or I thought about doing a community garden. I want to continue with my homeopathy work – so many things.

One of the beautiful things about the power of your Visionary is that you can go into meditation and clear your mind and be in spacious, clear, still mind for as long as you can. In that spaciousness you might find that a creative solution arises on the screen of your imagination. It is really nice to quiet the clutter and the looping around certain thoughts and just get really clear and breathe fresh air into this transition time. You are now feeding your mind with different possibilities. That's a beautiful gift of the Visionary. You don't have to go into action yet. That's when you call on your Manifestor. The Visionary helps you clear your mind so you can connect in with your Blueprint, your own soul's destiny and magical journey. That happens through connecting with spirit and being quiet and spacious without any distractions.

Does every human being have a Blueprint? Do I have one?

Absolutely. Part of your particular Blueprint was being a really good mother, and you've completed that part of your Blueprint. As you told me, for 19 years of your life, you've been diligently working on being the best mother you could be. Now you're in a period of change. This is where the Visionary comes in. Now you get to explore different parts of your Blueprint.

That's a very cool way of seeing that.

What you're discovering is that you have choice every single day of your life, to make choices that are good for you. When you do that you connect more with your Blueprint because you're no longer on the shadow paths of victimization or fear (the shadow of the Warrioress), self-sacrificing and co-dependency (the shadow path of the Queen), distraction or sabotaging (the shadow path of the Visionary), and manipulating or controlling (the shadow path of the Manifestor). When you connect in with Majah your Wise Woman, you can jump off of those shadow paths and call in the positive aspects of each one of those archetypes.

I love that.

Then you can envision your life however you want, now that you have fulfilled your role as a mother, giving your heart to nurture other souls. It is now your time to nurture yourself in a very profound way. You are mothering in new ways, with better boundaries and less drama. Your intentions are clearer (your Visionary) and you have the power of choice (your Wise Woman). When you're clear and have integrity, everything goes much more easily in your life.

Way smoother. My biggest take-away from this is my not owning other people's emotions and learning that I need to give myself what I need rather than expecting others to fulfill those needs. That's a huge awakening.

Yes, when we do this it makes us more self-contained and then we're less needy and less controlling. It radically shifts the way we relate in our relationships. When we don't give ourselves what we need, we often become very unhappy and expect others to cater to us. It's so disempowering to carry around a list of "shoulds" and expectations we place onto others. This is the shadow path of the Queen, when a woman walks down that self-sacrifice path and becomes a Martyr. Then a woman engages in guilt, unhappiness and a life of "shoulds".

The shift into this other way, where you have choice and you can empower yourself, is so radical when you've grown up with a lot of guilt and a lot of the shadow. This gives me an opportunity to show up as myself and know that in every situation, I can make a powerful choice for myself. It's much clearer and cleaner. I can see that I need to call in my Visionary and sit quietly and meditate and allow her to open up my third eye and just be intuitive.

Yes. Allow your Visionary to guide you to into your next phase of life. Your Visionary feels comfortable with change and can envision your wildest dreams. Dream big!

Visionary Initiation Conclusion

When you have awakened the powers of your inner Visionary you are profoundly clear, discerning, and objective. Your mind is liberated from limiting thoughts and beliefs so that you can be creative and innovative. You will invite change because it will not frighten you. As a Visionary, you breathe new life where things need to be reborn, renovated, resurrected, and transformed.

When you embody the Visionary you are clear minded, creative and able to envision change. You know how to cut through confusion and illusion and master your thoughts. You can envision new ways of doing and being and guide others towards necessary transformation. You encourage change and new direction and breathe life back into yourself, the village, and the community. You are on your way to self-master

Chapter 9
The Manifestor: Manifest your Best Life

The Story of Salima, the Manifestor

In the fifth initiation story, you will journey with Salima (pronounced *Sah-lee-mah*) as she trains to be a Manifestor, mastering the Path of Action and becoming a Fire Clan Woman, powerful in will, ready for action. You will follow her hot desert adventure as Salima connects with the fire in all living things, tames her wildfires, learns to shine her big light, and masters the art of Wandcraft, ready to manifest her dreams into the world.

Part 1: The Story of Salima

Once upon a time, a long, long time ago, there was a land where women were honored for their power and strength. It was a sacred land called the village of women where each girl child was honored for the unique gifts she brought to the sacred circle. And when each new female soul was still in the womb of her mother she would whisper her name and her soul's purpose to the elders who were eager to hear this good news. Now in this ancient land there were 4 different clans of women that all female souls were sorted into at birth. There was the Warrioress Clan, those who walk the Way of Strength. And the Queen Clan, those who walk the Way of Compassion. And the Visionary Clan, those who walk the Way of Change. And finally the Manifestor Clan, those who walk the Way of Action.

Now one special day there was a commotion among the elders who had gathered to hear the good news from a new girl child who was about to be born in the village of women. When they asked who she was, what clan she belonged to, and what her soul's purpose was, this is what she said. "My name is Salima. I come to the Manifestor Clan to walk the way of Action. My purpose is to reconnect women to the Sacred Fires and activate the Clan's deepest and most powerful secret." Soon the excitement spread among the entire clan of Manifestors who eagerly awaited the birth of Salima and the knowledge she would bring to the entire clan.

And so Salima was born and was cared for and nurtured as was the custom in the village of women, for each girl child was held and loved and valued and given chores and kept in line and watched over by those who were assigned as her special guardians. And as the years went by and Salima grew into a young woman, the elders of the Manifestor clan felt that the time had come to initiate her so that she could fulfill her purpose.

The elders took Salima to the Initiation training ground of the Manifestor Clan, far away to the land of the Sacred Fires, far away to the dry, hot desert lands. And they journeyed for many weeks through the mountains and canyons, highlands and lowlands. The further they traveled, the hotter and dryer it became and the sun beat down upon their backs and parched the earth and rocks. And Salima felt deeply at home and felt an inner strength she had never felt before. Deep into the hot lands they traveled until they came to a mighty desert stretching out in all directions as far as the eye could see. There were flat open lands, high desert plateaus, sandy dunes, and mysterious rock formations streaked with the colors of the setting sun. There were desert shrubs and thorny trees dotting the landscape with snakes and scorpions slithering and crawling on the desert floor.

And here, in the midst of the desert, Salima beheld the sacred camp of the Manifestor Clan, with its large circle of desert tents, vibrantly colored in tones of bright red, vivid orange, and brilliant purple. Torches marked the outer circle of the encampment and guarding each round tent stood a proud Manifestor woman, who held a sacred wand in each hand and wore a Cape of Living Fire. Salima marveled at the dancing flames that licked and flared but did not burn the Manifestor women. As Salima entered the protected inner courtyard of the sacred tents, she saw overhead the banner of the Manifestor Clan which read, "Fire Clan Women, Powerful in Will, Ready for Action." And crossing this threshold, Salima felt proud of her strong will and was eager to begin her initiation training.

As Salima looked around the courtyard, she saw many wondrous things. She saw a great circle of torches surrounding the inner courtyard and fire pits with roaring flames. There were wands of every kind and shape imaginable, with colored sparks shooting from each wand tip. There were capes of fire ablaze with orange and yellow flames. And in another place, a living, breathing sun, floated in the air, flaring and blazing with light and heat. Next to the sun was a huge map of galaxies and star constellations seen in the night sky, sparkling and dazzling against the pitch black of deep space. Wandering around the courtyard were various snakes, scorpions, and lions roaming freely and communing with the Manifestor women preparing for the initiations to come.

And so Salima spent her first days in the desert encampment, visiting the desert tents, learning of the purpose, powers, and mission of the Clan. And at night inside the circular courtyard, Salima sat on the desert sand and the torches were lit and the fire pits glowed, the drummers drummed and in the center of this circle, the Storyteller of the Manifestor Clan stood bathed in firelight, shadows flickering across her face. She wore a gown of brightest orange, a blazing headdress, and a Cape of Living Fire. And this is what the Storyteller said...

"We are the Fire Clan women, powerful in will and masters of the Sacred Fires. We tame the fire and focus the fire, radiate the fire and command the fire. As masters of fire, we can manifest at will with purposeful direction. We follow the Path of Action, seeing what needs to be done and mobilizing all resources in the village to act and move forward. We inspire, motivate, and lead. We empower others to act. Our power lies in aligning our strong will with universal will, a higher will that considers the highest good for all concerned.

Of all our tools, the Sacred Wand is our greatest ally, for it focuses our will for determined action. Manifestor women master the power of destructive will so that we do not use our power to dominate and control others. We purify our will and shed our attachments to all things getting in the way of manifesting. We have the courage to shine our big light and inhabit our full power without apology."

And late that night in the fire drenched courtyard, Salima was told a chilling tale of the Shadow Path of the Manifestor Clan. Oh yes, it was true: there were women who wandered off the their Path of Power onto a disempowered path that severed them from healthy will and responsible action. This was called the Shadow Path of Manipulation.

And Salima heard disturbing tales of women who walk the Path of Manipulation, women enflamed with a passion to dominate and control others with their will. They manipulate others like puppets and use them to get their way. These women are vulnerable to the negative energies that stalk women on the Path of Manipulation. They are outwardly successful but inwardly lonely and isolated, secretly feeling invisible and powerless. And when Salima heard these stories, her desire blazed and her passion flared and she knew exactly what she had to do: release her sisters from the Shadow Path of Manipulation and restore them back to the Path of Action. And when the elders saw her intuition open and the knowledge of her destiny burst forth, they smiled and nodded around the circle for they knew the time of her initiation had come.

Salima Part 2: Tame the Fire

A few mornings later, the elders in charge of her initiation invited Salima to begin her training. They took her out into the hot expanse of desert, where the elders had built various fires all around. There were small fires and bonfires, contained fires and wildfires; there was sunfire and moonfire, starfire and galaxyfire. And there was a special place of Magic fire where plants, rocks, animals, and humans burned with a mysterious inner fire. And the elders introduced Salima to the Desert Master, a giant scorpion, who was guardian of the Sacred Fires and the elder in charge of fire taming. "Salima!" said Scorpion, "To become a true Manifestor and Master of the Path of Action you must first learn to tame the fires. Fire is will. If the power of your will is untamed, it burns like wildfire and becomes destructive. Tame the fires Salima and you tame your will!"

Scorpion led Salima to a small, contained fire, surrounded and protected by a boundary. She pushed Salima into the fire to see how she would respond. Salima was surprised to find that the contained fire did not harm her and she felt no fear. This fire seemed manageable for it was contained, restrained, subdued, and controlled. Then Scorpion brought her to a wildfire burning out of control. It crackled and snarled and roared out furiously in all directions. Scorpion said, "Imagine that this wildfire is heading straight for the village. Feel its destructive power. A wildfire is not contained and has no regard for the human life it is about to swallow. It will destroy everything in its deadly path. Do you feel fear now?" Salima did indeed feel a thrill of fear coursing through her veins. Scorpion said, "You must have the courage in the face of untamed fire. Overcome your fear. Contain the wildfire Salima, use your intelligence, your wits, your skill."

So Salima set to work containing the wildfire, visualizing the village it would soon destroy. She grabbed a large shovel and began to dig piles of dirt from the desert floor to create an earthen circle around the fire. She was building a firewall, a barrier of earth that began to contain the fire within its boundary. Slowly, by the sweat of her brow, she contained the wildfire so that it burned only within the firewall.

Scorpion was pleased, "Well done, you have limited and bound the destructive wildfire. You have overcome your fear. As a Manifestor, you will be called upon to contain wildfires as they erupt in life - from emotional fires of conflict and war to creative impulses gone wild and unchecked, to power hungry people controlling for their own gain. You must act quickly and contain the wildfires before they get out of control. This is your first lesson, containing the power of fire."

Scorpion then took Salima to the mysterious rock formations where the Manifestor women were experimenting with different uses of fire. "Come and learn about the true nature of fire and its many uses both positive and negative." In one place, Salima saw women stirring large cauldrons, bubbling and steaming with potions and medicines. Raw meat cooked over a fire that transformed it into safe and edible food. Another fire consumed wood and coal to create energy. A hearth fire warmed those standing around it. A blacksmith's fire helped to soften metal into useful tools. A goldsmith's fire purified the gold by burning off the dross.

And Scorpion said to Salima, "As you see, fire has many positive uses. Fire can warm and sustain life. Fire can be transformative, changing the core nature of a substance. Fire can be cleansing, creating pure gold without impurities. Fire gives us food, light, heat, energy, purification, and cleansing. But it can also bring pain, devastation, and ruin. You must tame the fire to make it a positive force in the world." And Scorpion put Salima through a series of tests where she tamed negative fires into positive ones. She harnessed fire for energy, she melted and shaped metal into tools. She purified gold by burning off impurities. And she felt the power of the tamed fire to cook food, sustain life, transform, cleanse, and purify.

When Salima mastered containing and taming the fire, Scorpion brought her to the place of the Magic Fire, where the rocks and plants, animals and humans were aglow with a mysterious inner fire. Scorpion said, "The Magic Fire reveals the hidden fire living at the heart of all things. Every piece of creation is imbued with an inner fire Salima. This is a deep mystery little understood but revealed to the Manifestors during their initiation. We share this inner fire of consciousness with all our brothers and sisters of Creation. It is the creative fire that gives life to all things."

Salima stepped into the Magic Fire and it flickered and flamed around her but did not harm or burn her. She felt the fire in her body come alive and all her senses felt awake, aware, conscious. And she saw the inner fire glowing inside everything around her. And she felt the deep mystery of her connection to all things, to the rocks, the trees, the animals, the sun, moon, and stars.

And she heard the Magic Fire whisper to her, "The fire at the core of your being is your conscious will, your will to do, to act, to create, to make something happen, your will to manifest. When you will something to happen, the fire moves through your body at lightning speed, commanding action from your arms, legs, mouth, senses, emotions. Feel the power of your will Salima. All creative action lies within your power to command." Salima practiced willing things to happen. She connected with her inner fire and remembered her connection to all things. This helped her make wise choices. "If I am connected to all things, then I must consider others in my decisions. I must tame my will and temper my desires."

"Yes!" said Scorpion. "The secret to taming your own will is to remember your connection to the great web of life, surrendering to the bigger picture and the best outcome for everyone. You have done very well my daughter. You have learned to tame the wildfire and contain its destructive energy, you have learned the positive uses of fire, and you understand your connection to all Creation. You are ready now for your next initiation, focusing your fire and learning the art of wandcraft."

Salima Part 3: Focus the Fire

After her adventure with the desert fires and able now to tame the fire, Salima began the next phase of her initiation. Back at the encampment of desert tents, it was time now for Salima to focus and claim her will and receive her Sacred Wand. The special teacher assigned to Salima was a giant female snake, who slithered forward and said to her, "The sacred tool of a Manifestor woman is her wand. To receive your wand, you must focus and claim your own will and posses it confidently."

Snake pulled back the tent opening and Salima saw 3 large steps leading up to a mysterious black snake door. "These are steps to test your strength of will. The snakedoor is a portal to the wandcraft chamber. To reach the snakedoor and the wandcraft chamber you must climb each step slowly and deliberately, learning the lesson of each stair. Each step helps you to focus your will by shedding your attachments to all things getting in the way of manifesting your own will. You must overcome 3 obstacles in order to claim your own will: the first obstacle is Willessness, the second obstacle is living under Another's Will, and the third obstacle is Willfulness. I will teach you to shed your skins and release all attachments to false will so that you can claim your own will. And now, confront your obstacles and we shall see the strength of your will!"

Salima climbed the first stair and she was suddenly transported to the land of Willessness. She felt empty, lazy, blank, as if she had no will, no desire. She was on a slippery slope to despair and torpor. Her body felt heavy, lifeless, the flame in her heart and mind was rapidly diminishing. Snake hissed at her, "Salima, wake up! Part of you is attached to doing nothing, forgoing your own will, and giving into apathy and depression. Shed your skin, shed your attachment to willessness!" And Salima woke up and was horrified at her lack of will to do anything, to have no dream of manifesting or acting or doing or creating. And she fought through the depression by focusing on her inner fire. As it flamed inside her body, she freed herself from the land of Willessness and came back to her full senses. "Well done!" said Snake. "You may pass to the next stair."

Salima climbed onto the second stair and was suddenly transported to the land of Other People's Will. She felt under the spell of people in her life who had influence and power over her. She felt her mother's will, her father's will for her life. She found herself under the spell of her peers and was thrown this way and that by what they felt she ought to do. She felt fuzzy, unsure of her own will and desires. What did she want? What everyone else wanted? What did she want to manifest? She had forgotten completely.

Snaked hissed, "Salima, wake up! You are forgoing your own will and allowing others' will to triumph over yours. You are allowing others to make crucial decisions for your life. Shed your desire to relinquish your will. Be brave, be courageous. Take back your will. You must create your own life!" And Salima fought the impulse to surrender her will to others by focusing on her inner fire. As it flamed inside her body, she freed herself from the land of Other People's Will. "Well done!" said Snake. "You may pass to the next stair."

Salima climbed onto the third stair and was suddenly transported to the land of Willfulness. And she felt inflated with a desire to want whatever she wanted regardless of how it affected others. And she wanted to push, manipulate, and control. Her inner flame was going wild, flaring and scorching whoever got in her way. Her willfulness filled her heart, her mind, and her body until she was almost completely engulfed and consumed with her own inflated self-importance. Snaked hissed,

"Salima, wake up! You are too attached to your own way, to your own power, to your own importance. Do not be tempted to have everything your way. This is foolish and takes all the magic out of life. Reign in your willfulness. Cleanse and purify your desires! Shed your skin of willfulness!" And Salima shed her desire to manipulate and control. This calmed her inner fire and she freed herself from the land of Willfulness. "Well done!" said Snake. "You may pass to the next stair."

Salima climbed onto the next stair and she was transported to the land of Free Will. A golden light flared suddenly throughout her entire body, so that she was glowing from the inside out. She was alive with the fire of her own will. She felt a deep happiness, a deep satisfaction, a deep confidence in her own desires and choices. Snake spoke to her, "Salima, free will is achieved when you fully desire to know your true self. Your core self knows your highest will, the purpose for which you were born. Go inside your deepest self and call forth your own will, your deepest desires." And Salima closed her eyes and focused on her deep core self and a warm flame spread up her spine, like a heated rod.

"Good Salima, excellent. One of the great secrets of wandcraft is that each Manifestor possesses a wand of fire in her body. The Firewand runs up and down the central column of your spine. To activate the Firewand, align with your own powerful will, not anyone else's will for you but your own. Seek the desires of your core self. What is your will Salima? Declare your intentions for your life!" And Salima said, "I will be truthful to who I am. I will be a woman of integrity in all my actions. I will do no harm. I will create my own life." And the Firewand glowed red hot in Salima's body and she felt the heat surge up and down her spine. "Yes, well done Salima, your Firewand is activated and fired with your own power. Now step through the snakedoor, through the flaming portal to the fire of purification."

And she traveled through the flaming portal and entered a pool of fire that burned off all impurity, all unwanted dross. And as she cooked in the fire of purification Snake asked, "Will you use your power wisely?" And Salima said, "Yes. I will." "Do you willingly and consciously shed all that prevents you from aligning completely with your own will?" "Yes, I do."

And the fire of purification rose higher and higher and all that was false within her burned away and Salima shed all skins that veiled her core self. Her willingness to let go and surrender to the fires of purification quickened the process and soon she emerged out the other side and found herself in the inner chamber, beyond the snakedoor, surrounded by the Manifestor elders. And they pointed to her chest for they could clearly see her Firewand bright and glowing. "Reach into your center and pull out your wand Salima, you are ready to receive your Sacred Wand." So Salima reached into her core and pulled out her Sacred Wand, and it felt warm and wonderful in her hands.

Salima Part 4: Learning the Art of Wandcraft

Back in the inner chamber beyond the snakedoor, Snake hissed, "Salima, you have received your wand and posses your own will confidently. Now, through wand training, you will learn to direct your will with purposeful action." Salima looked around the inner chamber and saw a series of targets set up for wand practice. "In order to hit the targets perfectly you must gather your will into a focused beam of light. Focus on what you want to manifest. Set your intention. Be precise!" And Salima concentrated and gathered her will. She focused on exactly what she wanted to manifest. Suddenly she felt a snake inside her body coiling up her inner Firewand, slithering up her spine, heating up her inner core, gliding down her arm, and shooting out her wand hand in a shower of sparks. And Snake said, "Now with your sharp ray of light, send your power to a particular target."

One target was a project to carve out some much-needed time for herself. Salima knew this to be a worthy cause and focused her will toward this target. When her ray of light hit the target dead center, she saw exactly how to manifest this and she felt empowered to take action and do it. Another target was a project to help the village. Salima knew this to be a worthy cause and focused her will toward this target. When her ray of light hit the target dead on, Salima saw the project come to life in the village. She saw herself directing the action of the project and the people to a conclusion of success.

Snake said, "When you set your intention with purposeful direction, you hit your target. But you must take seriously the profound effect this has, for every cause has an effect. If you target something or someone who is not ready to receive, even though your intentions are honorable, you can cause great damage." And Salima saw how her wand affected different targets. Some exploded when her beam of light hit, some targets melted, some became hard as rock and did not respond to her will. Salima practiced hitting her targets, cleansing her motivations, using discretion and discernment, and seeing the consequences of her actions.

"Well done Salima. Some women never make it through this initiation. Their will may be strong and focused but they seek to manifest only for themselves. These women have fallen onto the Shadow Path of Manipulation. Come with me to the place below the chamber and I will show you what happens to your sisters when they succumb to the false power of control and manipulation."

So Salima followed Snake down to the shadow place, where she saw women who were trapped by their own selfish desires. They walked with purposeful direction but they pushed people aside to get what they wanted. They were ruthless and controlling. They appeared confident and successful but Salima could see a hole in their core self that left them lonely, isolated, and powerless. Other women were in the grip of a greedy hunger called envy. They had lost connection to their inner fire and so they wanted the light of others. They compared themselves constantly, believing that others have more light, better light, the right kind of light. They could not see their own light as good and beautiful and powerful and so they tried to extinguish and destroy the light of others. Shadowy creatures hovered nearby, tempting them to misuse their will power and manifest only for their own self-gain.

Something deep within Salima stirred and a blazing determination enflamed her fiery inner core. She knew she must release her sisters from the grip of Manipulation and restore them back to the Manifestor's Path of Action. And Salima cried out to the women, "Take up your wands my sisters. Reconnect with your own inner light. Stop focusing on the light of others. Contain your wildfires of envy and selfish desires. Stop controlling and manipulating others with the great gift of light you possess!" And Salima ran through the shadow land with her wand held high, its beacon of light blazing this way and that. And it's firelight filled the empty holes in the bellies of the women and they came back to themselves and could once again see the shining light in their own inner core self, flaming and burning and blazing.

The women took up their wands and focused their own free will power into a laser beam of light that hit the creatures of Manipulation, exploding them in a shower of hot, red sparks. And Salima led all the women out of the shadow place and up to the Sacred Encampment, where they reunited with their Manifestor sisters and enjoyed a time of recovery and rest.

Salima Part 5: Expand the Fire

After learning the art of wandcraft and releasing her sisters from the Shadow Path of Manipulation, the elders brought Salima to the high desert where she was greeted by her next teacher, a magnificent Lioness. "Welcome Salima, you have learned to tame your fire and focus your fire, now I will teach you to expand, radiate, and enliven your fire." Lioness then told Salima to lie down on the high desert ground and gaze up into the sky. "Observe the fiery sun. Feel its intensity. Feel the sun radiating and generating its own light and heat every moment of every day. The sun has an inner core of tremendous power. At the center of the sun, colossal explosions are bursting and flaring each moment in a great dance of life."

Then the mighty Lioness did something unexpected, she leaned over and touched Salima's heart and suddenly the sun was within her very own chest, blazing its powerful fire in rhythm with her beating heart and breath. She could feel the sun within her, radiating its own light and heat.

"Salima, this inner sun is your power center. Let your power flare out in a great solar wind, expanding as you breath in and out, in and out. Breathe in to your power center. Breathe out and magnify your fire. See your sun expanding, expanding. Radiate your sunfire out from your chest, out beyond your body, out and out. See how big your fire can be." So Salima practiced for many days under the blazing sun, breathing in to her power center and breathing out, magnifying her fire. She practiced expanding her sun and radiating her sunfire out from her chest. And when Salima could expand her sunfire at will and inhabit her full power with confidence, Lioness held up a magnificent Cape of Living Fire. "Come Salima! Step into your full power with no apology, no excuses, and no hesitation! Claim your Cape of Living Fire!" Lioness cloaked Salima in her cape of fire for she was ready to embody her radiance and claim her full power.

Late that night when the sun set and a tiny sliver of moon rose and the stars began to twinkle against the inky black of the night sky, Lioness told Salima to lie down and gaze up at the stars. "Each star is a sun in its own right Salima. There is enough room in the universe for every woman to be her own star and possess her own big power. We are all part of this star family and must learn to live in harmony together."

Then Lioness touched Salima's heart and suddenly she was transported into the starry heavens and each star was another Manifestor sister in her Cape of Living Fire. And when each radiated out her big light it did not diminish anyone's light but encouraged others to be in their full power. Salima was astonished at this empowerment of the sisterhood and was amazed that each woman could stand in her own power and be a star in her own right. And Lioness said to her, "A Manifestor feels her nobility and feels confidence in her own fire. When you possess your own authority and know who you are and why you are here, you are a light unto others, empowering them to find their own light."

After returning from the starry heavens and learning the lessons of sunfire and starfire, Lioness took Salima to the Land of Creativity, where she could radiate and expand her fire through creative expression. The Land of Creativity was a place in the desert transformed into a giant sandbox where she could play and create. She could build sand castles or cities. She could draw in the sand, make beautiful designs or play with the toys and sand tools. She could throw sand in the air to see what patterns emerged, or dig holes or bury herself. Lioness said, "Salima, have confidence in your own creations. Experiment, explore, become like a child, creating and destroying and creating again. Jump into the great sandbox of life and play!"

But when Salima attempted to play and express her creativity she came up against some blocks to her spontaneous expression. The first block was Paralysis. Salima felt paralyzed to even begin a project in the big sandbox. She looked at all the sand and all the toys and all the fun to be had and simply froze. She heard inner voices saying, "I don't know what to do. I can't." Lioness roared a fierce, fiery roar and blew fire back into Salima's heart. "Do not be afraid Salima, just start, just begin. Put one foot in front of the other and begin a project, anything will do. Get the creative juices flowing." So Salima picked up some toys and began playing like a child and her creative fire radiated out in all directions.

A while later in the great sandbox, Salima hit another block called Perfection. She heard inner voices saying, "My creations must be perfect the first time I try. I don't want to start over or destroy what I've already done. It must be perfect!" And Lioness roared a fierce, fiery roar and blew fire back into Salima's heart. "This is nonsense, Salima. All creative Manifestors create and destroy, experimenting many times until the spirit of the creative project comes to life. Do not kill the spirit by trying to be perfect!" So Salima bypassed perfection and allowed herself to experiment, fail, create again, and play. And her creative fire radiated out in all directions.

Then she hit another block called Cynicism. She heard inner voices saying, "You're not creative. What could you possibly contribute? Who do you think you are?" Lioness roared a fierce, fiery roar and blew fire back into Salima's heart. "Salima, every woman is creative in her own way. What do you desire to create? A work of art? A book? A happy family? A loving relationship? Create what inspires you. Do what fires you into action." So Salima pushed through her cynicism and fired up her true heart's desire and went into creative action. And her creative fire radiated out in all directions.

And through her play in the great sandbox, she discovered that creating, destroying, and experimenting were the keys to successful manifesting. "Well done Salima. With the help of the sun and stars, you have claimed your Cape of Living Fire and have confidence in your inner radiance. You can expand your fire through creativity and play. You are now ready for your final initiation on the Path of Action, learning to command the fire."

Salima Part 6: Command the Fire

Salima was now ready for her final initiation and so she was taken to the legendary desert terrain called Firerock, a place with mysterious rock formations streaked with the colors of the setting sun. To get to the center of Firerock, they wandered through rock valleys and narrow gorges, up giant boulders and down steep cliffs until they arrived at the initiation place. There Salima was introduced to the Great Elder of the Manifestor Clan, the oldest and wisest of all the women. And although she was old and stooped, her Cape of Living Fire was vibrant and shimmering, full of radiance and power.

And the Wise Old Elder said, "Here at Firerock you will learn to command your fire Salima, leading, guiding, and acting on behalf of the entire village of women. To become a strong and trustworthy leader, you must command your inner fire. You will be thrown into situations that demand action, where your life and other's lives are in danger and you cannot hesitate by thinking too much or feeling everyone's feelings. You must master the Path of Action, mobilizing resources and acting swiftly, clearly, and cleanly.

As a Manifestor, you carry the flame of illumination. You carry the fire that awakens people from their slumber and apathy and ignorance. You direct the fire to show people the path ahead. And when people are scared and immobilized by doubt and uncertainty, the sacred fire you command dispels their fear and brings hope. With your sight you can perceive the larger situation, seeing where others cannot see, illuminating where others are in darkness or forgetfulness. You must show them the way."

Then the Wise Old Elder led Salima and a small group of Manifestor women through the winding pathways, valleys, and treacherous ravines of Firerock. Further and further from camp they wandered as nightfall was fast approaching. Salima was soon lost and disoriented and as the darkness descended, she felt a thrill of dread run through her veins. The Wise Elder said, "You are in charge now Salima. You must bring these women back to the camp at the heart of Firerock through your own cunning leadership. No one has a wand but you. You are the only carrier of the Sacred Fire. Command the Fire! Live the Path of Action!"

In that moment Salima knew only this: they were lost, it was dark, she had the wand, they needed a leader, she must act! So she focused her considerable will, embodied her power with confidence, held her wand aloft to illuminate the scene, and went to work on a plan of action. First, she identified the goal to make it back to Firerock camp as quickly as possible. Then she set her intention to arrive safely, avoiding danger and protecting the entire group.

Then she delegated responsibilities, assigning each woman a task according to her greatest gift. The best climber negotiated the rough terrain. The most confident athlete guarded the back of the group. The best tracker listened for wild animals so she could protect the group. The best stargazer determined the directions. And as Salima commanded her inner fire, she was gifted with extraordinary sight. She could see the right way to go. And the women felt inspired, motivated, and hopeful and with her wand of illumination, Salima led them swiftly and safely back to the camp at the heart of Firerock.

The Wise Elder was very pleased. "Well done, Salima. You have proven yourself a successful leader, mobilizing resources and inspiring the group to pull together and manifest the task at hand. You are now ready to learn the greatest secret of the Manifestor Clan: how to manifest feminine values, feminine dreams, feminine knowledge, feminine leadership, feminine truths, feminine perspectives, and feminine solutions. Successful manifesting requires commanding your will through your wand of fire to manifest these feminine values into real life.

Many women desire these things and think about these things, but do not have sufficient will power to actually make them real. Our secret formula is this: ANCHOR, ALIGN, ACT. First you must ANCHOR your will, grounding your wand of fire right here, right now in the present. Then you must ALIGN your will to the higher will, the best outcome for all concerned. Only then can you ACT. Anchor, Align, Act. Anchor, Align, Act. This is our magic formula."

And so Salima learned first how to ANCHOR. After activating the Firewand in her body, the Wise Elder showed Salima how to ground the energy from the top of her head, down her spine, down her legs, and straight into the ground. "It's just like grounding a lightning bolt, Salima. Your fire energy must anchor into the ground the way a tree roots itself deep into the soil of the earth. Otherwise, your energy will be scattered, ungrounded, unfocused, and highly dangerous. Visualize your Firewand solid and grounded in your body, creating your core strength from your feet, up your spinal column. Anchor yourself!" So Salima practiced anchoring her will and grounding her wand of fire right here, right now in the present.

Next the Wise Elder showed Salima how to ALIGN. "Now that you are anchored, align your whole being: your body, your heart, your mind, and your will. And now you must align your own will with the higher will, the universal will that considers the big picture and the best outcome for the good of the community." And so Salima practiced aligning her whole self - body, heart, mind, and will - and then aligning to universal will. This centered her profoundly and enabled her to know what to do and take responsible action.

"Well done! Now that you can anchor and align, you are ready to ACT responsibly with wisdom, understanding, and knowledge. Salima, to act is to manifest, to make it real in the real world. So when the timing is right, take action. Speak your feminine truth. Speak up when you see an injustice. Trust your feminine perspective and bring it forward. Offer a feminine solution to an age-old problem. Teach others about feminine knowledge. Lead with feminine dynamism. Manifest feminine dreams and visions and make them real!" And Salima practiced responsible action and brought forth the powerful feminine values that were so needed in the village and in the world.

And through her initiations, Salima gained all of the powers of the Path of Action: a focused will, self- confidence, responsible action, and the ability to empower, inspire, and motivate others. And over the years, Salima became the greatest Master the Manifestor Clan had ever known, for she was powerful in will and Master of the Sacred Fires. She could tame the fire and focus the fire, expand the fire and command the fire. She possessed her own free will to do, to act, to create, to make something happen. She could manifest. And with her inspirational leadership, Salima encouraged all the women of the village to bring forth their gifts so that feminine dreams, visions, solutions, and perspectives were made real and came into being. And each day, with dignity and honor, Salima walked the Path of Action, the path of a true and faithful Manifestor Woman.

Walking the Path of Action

MANIFESTOR CLAN
Archetype: **The Manifestor**
Path: **The Path of Action**
Essence: **Powerful in Will**
Element: **Fire**
Tool: **Wand**
Qualities: **focused will, manifests desires, inspires and motivates, mobilizes resources, sees the big picture and empowers others**
Affirmation: "**I guide, implement and manifest.**"
Motto: **"Fire Clan Women, powerful in will, ready for action."**
Empowerment: **comes through focusing the will**
Shadow Archetype: **Manipulator**
Shadow Path: **Path of Manipulation**

In this story we are introduced to Salima, our Manifestor Divine Feminine guide. The path she walks is the Path of Action and her tool is the Sacred Wand. During the course of her initiation, she learns to tame, harness, and radiate her inner fire and become the action oriented Manifestor she was always meant to be. What does her story mean for you? How can you follow her lead and become a confident Manifestor?

As an emerging Manifestor, you need to find your relationship with the Fire Clan. This means connecting more deeply with your will and learning to focus your will towards concrete objectives. It means coming into better relationship with the element of Fire, lighting candles, creating a hearth fire, and exploring what you can do with heat. It might be helpful to go to the desert or to sit in the sun and connect with its power and heat, or sit under the stars and imagine your own inner star. Connecting with the Fire element - however you do this - will bring you into a deeper relationship with your Manifestor.

When it was time for Salima to begin her initiation, she is taken to the Land of the Sacred Fires, to the mighty desert, where the sun beats down on the sand dunes and there are mysterious rock formations and a wide expanse of sky for gazing at the nighttime stars. The initiation training ground consists of many beautifully colored desert tents with Manifestor guardians who have Sacred Wands and Capes of Living Fire. Within the desert encampment, Salima sees wands, fire capes, floating suns, maps of stars, and desert creatures such as scorpions, snakes, and lions.

Here at the training ground, Salima learns about the Fire Clan Women and how they are powerful in will and ready for action. She learns that Manifestors are masters of fire and that they know how to tame, focus, radiate, and command fire with purposeful direction. She learns that Manifestors are leaders who can mobilize resources and light the way for others. Manifestors purify their will so that when they do manifest, they are aligned with a higher will that considers the good of the entire village. The Fire Clan tool is the Sacred Wand, which focuses a Manifestor's will for determined action.

Salima was excited to begin her initiation, but then she heard about the shadow path of the Manifestor Clan and how some women wander off their Path of Power and succumb to the path of manipulation. She was disturbed that some women are enflamed with passion and dominate and control others with their will. They manipulate others like puppets and even though they look successful, they are internally miserable and lonely. This stirred something deep inside and she knew she would have a part to play in bringing these women back to their Path of Power and right use of will.

To begin her initiation, Scorpion takes Salima out to the desert to tame her fire. Here she sees different kinds of fires – small fires, large bonfires, wildfires, sunfire, moonfire, galaxy fire, and the fires within all living things. In order to become a true Manifestor she must learn to tame her fiery will so that it doesn't burn out of control. She experiences how a controlled fire is manageable because the will is constrained and restrained. But when Scorpion shows her the bonfire, she can see how destructive it is and how it can destroy everything in its path. When she builds a firewall to contain this out-of-control fire, she understands she will be called upon in the village to tame the fires of conflict and war and the creative impulses gone wild and unchecked.

Take a moment and reflect about your own fire and how you are using your will. Are you using your will in a wildfire kind of way and being destructive with your will? Are you aware of your fire burning out of control? Another great exercise is to observe the wildfires of will out there in our society. There are many examples of hate crimes, shootings, violent movies, threats, and corporate greed, which all point to unchecked wildfires. In many ways, our western culture condones this shadow aspect of the untamed will, which can show up looking like grandiosity, narcissistic entitlement, and manipulation. Somehow we have normalized this behavior and yet it is very destructive to the fabric of society. You can counter this shadow aspect by being honest about your own use of will and by building a firewall around your destructive tendencies in order to harness your willpower for better use. A Manifestor is dedicated to right use of will – in oneself and in the wider culture.

Salima's next initiation involves learning about the positive uses of fire and connecting with the Magic Fire in all Creation. There are so many uses of fire, but the main use of fire is to transform. Salima is amazed at what fire can do: cook food, create medicine, generate energy, forge tools, and burn off unwanted dross and impurities. When Salima worked with the fire to transform all of these substances, she experienced the power of fire to cook, sustain life, transform, purify, and cleanse. Take a moment and reflect on the many uses of fire in your own life and connect with this fire of life throughout your day. This increases your awareness of and connection with the element Fire and invites your Manifestor to use your own fiery will more consciously.

Salima's next adventure is with the Magic Fire, the mysterious fire that lives at the heart of all things. She is taken to a place where she can see the Magic Fire glowing within the rocks, the trees, the humans, the plants, the sun, moon, and stars. As she steps into the Magic Fire, she is able to see and understand her connection with all other living beings. This deep connection must be considered when we manifest because when we realize we are all connected, we will manifest respectfully, taking others into consideration.

Consider that this Magic Fire is living at the core of your being and animates your will to do, act, create, and make things happen. Now imagine that every living thing is imbued with this Magic Fire and that you are intimately connected to this larger web of fire. Will you manifest differently? Will you choose more wisely, knowing that your choices affect and influence all other beings? This may seem like a big responsibility and indeed it is! As Scorpion says, "All creative action lies within your power to command." So when you remember your intimate connection with all life and consider others in your decisions, you temper and tame your will and manifest with mindfulness.

After her adventures with the desert fires, Salima is taken back to the encampment to learn to focus her fire and claim her Sacred Wand. Her new teacher, Snake, shows Salima the steps she must conquer to focus her inner fire so that she can claim her own will. There are 3 steps to test her strength of will. Step 1 is overcoming will-lessness. Step 2 is detaching from other people's will. Step 3 is overcoming will-fullness. She must climb each step slowly and deliberately, learning the lesson of each stair. Each step helps her to focus her will by shedding her attachments to all things getting in the way of manifesting her own will. She must overcome 3 obstacles: the first obstacle is Willessness, the second obstacle is living under Other People's Will, and the third obstacle is Willfulness.

Imagine now being transported to the land of Willessness. Have you ever felt a lack of will and desire? Have you felt depressed, lifeless, empty, or blank? When you lose your dream and your will to manifest, the light inside you starts to flicker and go out. What is draining you of your life force energy? It is crucial as a Manifestor to awaken out of your willessness and lethargy and fight any depression and apathy. A Manifestor acts and creates and makes things happen. If you find yourself in the land of Willessness you can focus on your inner fire and fan that flame back into life.

When Salima went to the next stair, she was transported into the land of Other People's Will. Perhaps you can relate to this place, where you feel under the spell of someone - under his or her power. Perhaps you are influenced by the will of your mother, father, partner, teacher, or peers. When you forgo your own will and allow others to make crucial decisions for your life, you may end up manifesting someone else's dreams. If you feel fuzzy or foggy about what you want, desire and need, then it may be time to be brave and courageous and take back your will. When you create your own life and make your own decisions, even if others don't like it, you get to manifest your own dreams. I guarantee you will be a lot happier when you free yourself from Other People's Will.

On the next stair Salima is transported to the land of Willfulness. This is an entirely different territory, where she feels an inflated desire to greedily get what she wants without concern for anyone else. Have you ever been there? Maybe you remember a time when your inner flame went a bit wild and you scorched people with a controlling will. Or maybe you disregarded how your decisions were affecting others. Have you ever manipulated to get you wanted? Where in your life do you push to get your own way?

This isn't about beating yourself up - it's about being a true Manifestor, reigning in your willfulness, and letting go of your attachment to getting your own way. When you can calm your inner fire of willfulness and shed your desire to push, control, and manipulate, you can shift how you use your fiery energy. Listen to the words of Snake, "Wake up! You are too attached to your own way, to your own power, to your own importance. Do not be tempted to have everything your way. This is foolish and takes all the magic out of life. Reign in your willfulness. Cleanse and purify your desires! Shed your skin of willfulness!"

When Salima was able to let go of the seductive and tempting power of willfulness, she stepped into the land of Free Will. Here in this land, Salima calls forth her own free will, her deep inner core self that knows her highest will and the purpose for which she was born. Salima begins to feel a warm flame flickering up and down her spine. Snake tells her this is her Firewand, which reflects the values of her own will and core self. Here in the land of Free Will you can find a deep happiness, a deep satisfaction, and deep confidence in your own choices. Free will is achieved when you fully desire to know your true self. When you begin to call forth your own will for your life, you discover what you came here to do and find your true purpose.

When Salima is ready to activate her Firewand, she declares her intentions for her life. "I will be truthful to who I am. I will be a woman of integrity in all my actions. I will do no harm. I will create my own life." If you feel ready to activate and receive your Firewand, say these declarations out loud. Then you can imagine stepping through the flaming portal into the pool of fire, the fire of purification. This purifying fire is designed to burn away everything that is false within you. It helps you shed everything that veils you from your core self and prevents you from aligning completely with your own will. The reward for sustaining the fire of purification is to receive your Manifestor's Sacred Wand. All you have to do is reach into your core and pull out your Firewand.

For the next phase of her initiation, Salima learns the Art of Wandcraft in a special initiation chamber set up for target practice. Here she learns to direct her will with purposeful action. This requires her to focus her intention on what she wants to manifest and hit her target squarely in the center. In order to hit her target perfectly she must gather her will into a focused beam of light. She must also be clear that her manifestation is for a worthy cause rather that random selfish desire.

If your Manifestor wants to do some target practice, set your intentions clearly. Imagine this project or desired outcome as a target with a bull's eye in the center. Focus your will. Feel it as fiery snake energy moving up and down your spine. Imagine reaching in and grabbing your Firewand and holding it in your hand. Imagine your core fire coiling down your arm and shooting out of your wand hand. With a sharp ray of light, send your willpower to your particular target. Now see your project coming to life. See yourself directing the action of the project to a conclusion of success. Take your time. See it coming to life and manifesting. This is a great way to learn the Art of Wandcraft and practice hitting your target.

After learning the Art of Wandcraft, Salima travels to the Shadowland of Manipulation and meets women who wander off their path and succumb to the false power of control and manipulation. Even though they look outwardly successful, they have a hole in their core that leaves them powerless. And even though it might feel good to control others, it ultimately pushes people away and leaves them lonely and isolated. This is such a horrible trap. The most striking fact about these women in the Shadowland is that they have lost touch with their inner light.

Have you ever succumbed to the false power of control and manipulation, believing it would get you what you want but leaving a hole in your belly? Have you ever been caught in a cycle of envy, wanting the light of others? Do you ever compare yourself with others, feeling that your light is inadequate or less than? It's time to reconnect with your inner light!

What is the appropriate use of our light? Manifestors are supposed to use their light to bring enlightenment and light the way for others. Manifestors use their light to illuminate the Path of Action. So it's important when you feel seduced onto the shadow path, to stop focusing on the light of others and stop manipulating others with the great gift of light you posses.

After releasing her sisters from the shadow path of manipulation, Salima meets Lioness in the high desert and learns to expand and radiate and enliven her fire. The mighty Lioness tells Salima to lie down and gaze up at the sun and feel its tremendous heat and power. Salima learns that she has her own inner sun, which is radiating and generating its own light and heat every moment of every day. She then learns to radiate out her own sunfire by breathing in and out of her power center. She practices expanding out her fire as far as possible so that she learns to inhabit her full power with no apology. When she can do it without hesitation, she receives her Cape of Fire.

How do you feel when you embody your full radiance and claim your full power? What feelings come up for you when you think about inhabiting your full power? What holds you back from radiating out your power in full force? I often hear women say that they keep their light small for various reasons: they don't want to incite envy, they don't want to make others uncomfortable, and they don't want to extinguish another person's light. But as a Manifestor we are invited to radiate out our light as far as possible and put on a blazing Cape of Living Fire!

One important lesson Salima learns from Lioness is that there is room in the universe for every woman's light. Salima learns this when she lies under the night sky and sees the millions of stars, each one representing a sun that has the right to shine its own light. What a blessing to recognize that we are part of a great sisterhood of empowerment and we are meant to encourage each other to proudly shine our light because there is room for everyone. In the words of Lioness, " A Manifestor feels her nobility and feels confidence in her own fire. When you possess your own authority and know who you are and why you are here, you are a light unto others, empowering them to find their own light." We are meant to share power with other empowered women.

The next phase of Salima's initiation takes place in the Land of Creativity, where she learns to break through blocks and have confidence in her own creations. Here the desert sands are transformed into a giant sandbox and Salima is instructed to jump into the sandbox of life and play, create, and explore like a child. When she does this, she encounters 3 roadblocks to her creative exploration and expression: Paralysis, Perfection, and Cynicism.

Paralysis occurs when you freeze when faced with a big sandbox/blank slate/empty canvas. Has this ever happened to you? Do you ever feel paralyzed to create or express yourself? Perhaps you were told you weren't creative as a child. Maybe you have an inner voice like "I can't or I don't know what to do." If paralysis is stopping you from exploring your creativity, you might benefit from following the advice of Lioness, "Do not be afraid, just start, just begin. Put one foot in front of the other and begin a project, anything will do, and get the creative juices flowing."

This can actually be a really fun activity. When you allow yourself to play in the sandbox of life, you can experiment with lots of different creative mediums. I suggest going to an art store and allowing your playful Manifestor to pick out some pens, pencils, paints, finger-paints, paper, canvas, and anything else that looks enticing and fun. When you move past paralysis and get messy with creative projects, you will begin to experience the fun of creation. Watch what your Manifestor wants to create.

Then there is that horrible block of Perfectionism! You know, that inner voice that tells you your creations must be perfect and must be done "right" the first time? When you go into creativity mode, it's helpful to give yourself permission to experiment and even destroy and start over if needed. A Manifestor creates and destroys many times until the spirit of a project comes to life. You kill the spirit when you want things to be perfect. If you struggle with perfectionism, allow yourself to experiment, fail, create again, and play in the big sandbox of life. Think of a child in the sandbox who builds a sandcastle and then destroys it only to play again and construct a new one.

I found when I started my Sacred Robe project that I had to practice and experiment many times before I figured out a silk painting technique that worked for me. I made lots of mistakes and messes and destroyed many pieces of white silk until I came up with a method that made me happy and satisfied. I learned through this process that creating and destroying and not being perfectionistic, allowed the spirit of each Robe to come alive. I learned that if I forced myself to create the perfect drawing of the Robe on the first try, I was actually stopping the flow of the creative process. Each Robe figure wanted to come alive so I needed to leap over perfectionism and draw and re-draw, paint and re-paint, so that the spirit of the Robe figure could live and move and breathe.

The third block Salima encounters is Cynicism, those cynical, critical voices that say, "You're not creative. What could you possibly contribute? Who do you think you are?" As a Manifestor, it is crucial to shift your perception of creativity. Every woman is creative – she creates her own life. As a Manifestor, what kind of life do you desire to create? You can create a happy family, or a loving relationship, or a project, or a book, or a loving community. This isn't about being an artist or defining creativity in a narrow way. If you can push through your cynicism you can go into creative action and manifest what your heart desires.

In the last phase of her initiation, Salima learns to command her fire so that she develops the Manifestor leadership qualities necessary for effective, conscious action. In order to learn how to be a trustworthy leader, Salima is taken to Firerock, a treacherous landscape far from the desert encampment. Here Salima must learn to command her inner fire and become a strong leader. The elders take her and a group of women deep into Firerock, through winding pathways, steep valleys, and hazardous ravines. As darkness falls, Salima is then instructed to bring the entire group of women back to the camp at the heart of Firerock. Salima must be a cunning leader and figure out what to do – for they are lost and it is dark! She is the only one with a Wand, the only carrier of the Sacred Fire.

And so Salima goes into conscious action. She focuses her will, embodies her power with confidence, and holds her wand aloft to illuminate the scene. She then sets her intention to arrive safely back at camp. She then delegates responsibilities according to each woman's greatest gift. She finds the best climber, the best tracker, and the best stargazer. When she commands her inner fire, she knows the right way to go and she inspires and motivates the group. She is a wonderful model of a conscious Manifestor in action.

As a Manifestor you may be thrown into situations that demand action where your life and other lives are in danger. In these situations you will have to mobilize resources quickly without hesitating and thinking too much and feeling everyone's feelings. You will already be grounded and have healthy boundaries from your Warrioress training. You will be emotionally balanced from your Queen Training and you will be clear-minded from your Visionary training. This gives you a wonderful foundation to be an action-oriented Manifestor.

Another aspect of the Manifestor is guiding others by motivating and inspiring them when things need to get done. As a Manifestor, you can bring the light of hope and dispel fears in angst-ridden or difficult situations. As a Manifestor, you carry the fire that awakens people from their slumber, apathy, and ignorance. You direct the fire and show people the path ahead. You can perceive the larger situation and see what others cannot see, illuminating where others are in darkness or forgetfulness.

When Salima successfully leads the women out of Firerock, the elders know she is ready to receive the greatest secret of the Manifestor Clan – how to manifest feminine values, feminine dreams, feminine knowledge, feminine leadership, feminine truths, feminine perspectives, and feminine solutions. The key to manifesting is summed up in the Manifestor magic formula: Anchor, Align, Act! As Salima learns, a Manifestor must anchor her Firewand into the earth, like grounding a lightning bolt. The energy of your fire, your will, is so powerful. If this life force is not anchored and grounded properly, it can easily become a wildfire and either burn you out or burn down the village. If your energy is scattered or unfocused when you want to manifest, it can be dangerous and will not get you the desired results. So after you activate your Firewand, you must make sure to anchor your fire into the earth.

The next step is to align your entire being – your body, heart, mind, will, and spirit – to your higher self and the universal will that considers the highest good in any situation. So dedicating your manifestation to the highest good for all involved centers you profoundly and prepares you for responsible action. If you do not have a practice to align your will to your higher will, you may want to find one very soon.

I can offer one that works well for me. Try sitting in quiet meditation. Light a candle and focus on the flame. Imagine this flame as your core will, creating fires in your belly, in your heart, and in your brain. Then imagine the fire of your will circulating as light and fire all around your body. Now imagine your higher will, your spiritual self, hovering right above your head and invite this higher will to come right into your body. Now your higher will is activated. Picture what it is you want to manifest. Now check in with the universal will, however you imagine this. Ask, "Does my will match the universal will for this project?" And wait to see what comes to you. Just relax and open to any messages that might come. You are aligning to your higher will and to universal will.

The last step of the magical formula after anchoring and aligning is to act consciously and responsibly with wisdom, understanding, and knowledge. Acting means speaking your feminine truth, standing up for what's right, doing what needs to be done, offering a feminine solution, leading with feminine dynamism, manifesting your dreams, and making them real. When you act consciously in the world, you have the opportunity to actually see and experience the effects of whatever you are manifesting. You can see the ripples of joy go out or the ripples of satisfaction reverberate. You see your creations in action and you can see how you are influencing the world around you with your positive intentions. The Anchor, Align, Act secret formula really works. Have fun playing with your manifesting abilities.

When you complete the journey with the Manifestor you will use your will wisely to take conscious action in your life. You have gained the powers of the Manifestor Clan: confidence, leadership abilities, focused will, wise use of will power, and manifesting abilities. You can use your Sacred Wand to manifest what is needed for yourself, your loved ones, your community, and the world. You have said yes to awaken the Manifestor in yourself and in your life. You are on your way to self-mastery.

Manifestor Sacred Robe

When you look at the Manifestor robe, what comes up for you? Here are some student responses:

- *She looks very focused to me. She's very focused with her fire.*
- *She makes things happen. Her wands can actually create things. She can cast her positive spells!*
- *I love her cape of fire. She looks like she's in command.*
- *It looks to me like she's holding the light up for others. Like she's illuminating the way.*
- *She looks like a leader, a way-shower. I would follow her.*
- *I'm having a hard time relating to her and to my will. I can relate to my body, my mind, and my heart, but I'm having a hard time feeling my will.*

Notice your reaction to the Manifestor. Do you feel drawn to her? Do you feel intimidated or repelled by her? Do you feel connected to Fire? Have you been able to manifest some things in your life? Or do you feel you want to deepen your relationship to your fiery will so you can manifest more assertively? Notice your physical responses when you look at the image of Salima. How do you relate to the Manifestor now in your life?

Most women can relate to the heart or the mind or the body, but sometimes it's really hard to understand what the will actually is. In order to manifest something in the world, you have to know what your will is, and in order to know what your will is, you have to make sure you are not under anyone else's will. An essential component of the Manifestor initiation is to identify who's will you might still be under and to then get clearly aligned with your will only.

Once aligned with your own will, you are free to manifest who you really are and what you came here to do. The ultimate purpose for developing your will, your sacred fire, is to manifest what your soul came to do for the highest good of all. This isn't about using your will to manifest a new car or house (although there's nothing wrong with that). The Manifestor initiation is really about finding your highest calling and then manifesting that into the world for the highest good of all.

When do you want to call upon the Manifestor? You call on the Manifestor when things need to get done in the village. Call in the Manifestor when you need to lead a project. Call her in when you need to mobilize resources and delegate responsibilities. She can be called when you need to inspire and motivate others or yourself when you have a big task ahead of you. You can call in the Manifestor when you need to act and move forward. There's a time for ideas and a time for feelings, and then there is a time to act, decisively and swiftly. That's when the Manifestor comes in very handy.

Interviews with Manifestors

The following are interviews with women who attend my *Feminine Path of Power* Programs and have interacted with all 5 Feminine Archetypes. Here is how some of them relate to the Manifestor.

Interview with MK

I would love to hear about your Manifestor. She represents your inner fire and your will to manifest your dreams and put them into action. The Manifestor walks the Path of Action. How do you relate to the Manifestor?

The first time I walked into the group room at the retreat and saw the Manifestor Robe, I was a little suspicious of her. I'm not so sure about her! It was my immediate reaction when I saw the Manifestor so I've been working with this energy, getting more familiar with her. This reservation comes from my experience with my ex-husband, who was always trying to manifest things just for his own benefit, not the greater good. And I was a supporter of this implementation. So I wasn't sure how to relate to her when I first met her because I didn't want to manifest in that same way.

Even when I took the Manifestor weekend retreat, I came up with a giant action plan of something that I was going to do. What I am learning to do now is pull back in and say, "Wait, I need to manifest for myself first." Before fixing the entire world, I have to manifest me first. I have to manifest what my vision is and step into that using all of the tools of all the clans. The Manifestor is the goddess I am still working on the most.

Well, your primary relationship for many years was with someone who was misusing the Manifestor power and not thinking about the good of the whole, which is a crucial part of the Manifestor training. You witnessed the danger when people manifest for selfish gain rather than for the good of the whole.

One of the interesting things about this new relationship I'm in is that he is a great model of what a true Manifestor looks like. He's a doctor and we were at a conference this last weekend and one of the nurses said about him, "He's the doctor that you send your friends to. He spends time with his patients and really asks how they are doing and he'll spend 45 minutes to an hour if that is what is needed." That's real manifesting! He figures out how he can really help his patients. So it's a really interesting contrast for me because my ex-husband was also a doctor. So there are a lot of parallels here for me to reflect on. And I am also reflecting about where my fire is and what I want to do. As I was going off to our Feminine Path of Power retreat, my new man said, "That's amazing that you're doing a women's workshop. You are more of a woman than any woman I've ever met. It's so great that you're spending time on your yourself that way."

What's interesting to me is that you chose two different men who both chose to pour their energy into becoming doctors, which means they both have a lot of drive and fire and a lot of focus. They wanted to manifest something - being a healer, being a doctor. They say that whoever we are attracted to says something about us. Something in you chose these fiery, manifesting men. And this new choice you've made (an upgraded for sure!) also says something about your own drive to manifest something important. You have that fire in you because you're attracted to the fire in these other people. In the first go around with your ex-husband, you felt and lived what it's like to be with someone who is manifesting fire in a way that isn't very constructive. And now you're with someone who is choosing to use his fire to heal the world.

Yes, thank you for pointing this out. That is so powerful to reflect on.

This is an example of how to use our will (our fire) to manifest things in the world that make a difference to people. I think we shut down our will power when we look around us in the world and we see people misusing their power. What's happening in our world today is that many people are harnessing their will towards destructive ends. So the trick with the Manifestor is to use our will in a way that is healing for the world and is in direct alignment with our higher self. This way we can channel our fire into the world in constructive ways.

That's our challenge as women, to use our fire in a feminine way and to figure out what that looks like. We must be connected to our own will power and not under any one else's will, even the men that we are attracted to. So if we have projected our fire onto our men or onto anyone else, it's so important for us to get that back and generate our own will, feeling the fire inside ourselves every day. One aspect of the Manifestor initiation is learning to radiate out our fire as far as we can, without worrying about dominating others.

Yes, you often see the shadow side of the Manifestor where you see people who are manifesting out there but they're plowing over other people. I don't want to do that. We used to have a neighbor who had her own flower business in the city and she was very selfish and uncaring about others and my ex-husband would applaud her for getting stuff done for herself because that is what he was doing, getting things done for himself and not thinking about others. I don't want to be that kind of Manifestor. I want to be the Manifestor who thinks about the good of everyone. That works for me. Rolling over people isn't who I am and I don't want to do that.

Well, that's because you are a positive Manifestor! That's your strong intention. Thanks so much for sharing about your relationship with your Manifestor and your observation about good and bad Manifestors. This is really helpful.

Interview with Margaret

Let's talk now about the Manifestor. She belongs to the Fire Clan and she has her magic Wand. She is the part of you that can manifest what your heart desires.

I'm really feeling my Manifestor lately. There's a power to my manifestation. I focus on my goals. I set the path and I focus. I'm more trusting now that if I need something, I'll know what to do to get it done. I feel my deep intention of going to my Manifestor and seeking the answer. It's like being the student and the teacher all at once and then manifesting. It brings out the fiery nature of my will. I feel confident that I can manifest what I want and need.

I go inside to a place of great inspiration and then I manifest. I tune into whatever is calling me and it brings my will into action. When I manifest, I allow my conscience to be my guide. I get riled up when I hear about Social Justice issues. I have a sense of justice and when my buttons get pushed, I want to manifest for others when I hear their rights are violated.

I also need to be attuned to what's around me and what's inside me. I sometimes use a spiritual practice to train my consciousness so I can go inside and find the answers, because I am not just manifesting things physically, but spiritually as well. When I get a new idea, my Manifestor also gets all fired up and I can then spring forward into action.

I like how you include desire, inspiration, and enthusiasm, because you need these to be creative and to manifest something new.

Yes. I call in my spirit guides and they help me to manifest what I need. I also listen deeply to my inner voice, to my guidance and what's going on around me. So it really increases my awareness. When synchronous or serendipitous things begin to happen, it's not a mistake or a random event, it is a result of my manifesting. I'm trying to be more aware that I am manifesting all the time. The more aware I am, the more I connect to the synchronicities happening all the time.

You're right; we are manifesting all the time. So when you're in alignment with your higher self and your inner guidance, your Manifestor is in tune with you and everything around you. This increases your synchronicity, attracting what you want and need into your life.

Yes. If I am quiet internally I can hear the answers. And when I have the answers, it really does change how I am in the world and how I relate to others and the world around me. I am becoming more intentional with my manifesting. Instead of being judgmental, critical, and negative towards myself, I can create a different story about myself and manifest my life in a positive way.

That's why it's so important to be grounded with your Warrioress, heart-centered and emotionally balanced with your Queen, and clear-minded with your Visionary. Then you're in alignment and attunement with yourself. So it is crucial when you're manifesting to be in attunement with yourself because if not, whatever you manifest is distorted and may not be in alignment with what you want and need. Thank you for sharing how you are working with your Manifestor right now in your life.

Interview with Cynthia

I would love to hear about your Manifestor. How are you connecting with her?

Well, I can tell you what happened to me last night with the Manifestor. I had a rough night. At 3:00 in the morning I woke up thinking, "I need to get some body work. I need acupuncture. My physical being is hurting and needing support. My body needs to be supported to hold all these changes." It was really nice to get that clear message, and then I sat at my altar and asked for help. I started to think how to manifest this. "I know a lot of massage therapists, but they're not the right massage therapists. I need someone that does some energy work and is really grounded themselves and has a good touch, and then an acupuncturist." It was so fun to get clear on that. That was a clear message this morning. When I align with my higher self, it seems easy to manifest.

You're describing your Manifestor beautifully. You ground, your heart is open, your mind is clear, and then you know exactly how to focus your will into what you want to manifest. It's so beautiful how you're naturally aligning all the clans. Then when you manifest, you know that you're going to get the right person to help you.

Yes, and it was really fun this morning to do that. You've talked about this alignment in all your Feminine Path of Power teachings. When I go into Manifestor mode, typically I haven't called in the other Goddesses. So I'm ready to take action and I just start calling everyone or sending out e-mails, getting names etc., but that all seems really tiring. If I ground, open my heart, clear my mind, and THEN focus my will to manifest, that person will somehow come to me. I don't have to exhaust myself. The person will come to me!

I love that. I know that you are a fire sign Astrologically so you're naturally a Fire Clan woman. This means you'll have a tendency to impulsively jump to action. So now instead of jumping to action, you are taking the time to balance and align all your Goddesses inside first. This is the core of the Manifestor initiation, to be in full alignment with yourself first and then focus your will into outer action.

Yes. And it felt really good to do that this morning. I am experiencing the wisdom of what you've been talking about. I'm finally embodying the teachings of the 4 Clans! It's powerful putting that into practice. I just said to myself, "What do I want to manifest? What do I want to manifest?" I want to manifest coming with you to Crete, that's very clear. I want more clarity though about other things because once I have the clarity, then I usually can make things happen.

You've just said something important about the Manifestor, which is that normally we're taught to push with our will to make things happen. There's another kind of fire magic we may not be accustomed to, which is, "When I'm in internal alignment, then the world comes to me." So rather than me going out to the world and pushing and trying to make it all happen myself, I can relax and align all my inner Goddesses and then align my will with my higher will. When aligned, we attract the help of the universe so that we don't have to generate and push and make it all happen ourselves. This is the incredible magic of the Manifestor; that we use our will and our fire to focus, and then we receive help.

*Yes, it's like the Matrix movie. I was super stressed and then I "woke up", like the guy in the Matrix (*this is Neo, who literally wakes up and realizes he's been asleep on so many levels, giving his energy to another "program" that is not his own*). I could see clearly! I had this night of stress and turmoil and was thinking, "What the hell is going on? And what am I doing? And what's my purpose?" With my Manifestor I went inside, got into alignment with my deep self, and then I got the clear message, "Get a massage and get acupuncture and you will feel better." I can manifest easily from this place.*

And what you're manifesting is one stepping-stone on your path. That's all you need to do, just manifest the very next step that's going to give you support. You don't have to manifest the entire path and your entire destiny all at once!

Right, and I also got clear yesterday that if I got the whole path right now, I would implode! I like that perspective of the Manifestor, that she shows us the next stepping-stone on our path. That's do-able! I can manifest finding an acupuncturist.

This kind of manifesting follows the feminine way of organic timing, rather than pushing, pushing, pushing, which is a much more masculine way of manifesting. The feminine way is more attuned to organic timing and is less stressful!

Yes and so is the gentle self-love that I can give myself. Astrologically speaking, I'm half Pisces and half Aries. I'm so fiery – that's my masculine Aries, and then I'm so watery – that's my feminine Pisces. I'm just this split, and it comes out in my body too. It's like the masculine side and the feminine sides are trying to balance. Sometimes I put on the brakes and sometimes I move ahead. When I bring all my energies into alignment, I can feel this feminine energy integrating me. I don't waste so much energy. I can direct it more and focus it more so I'm not so exhausted.

Exactly, that's exactly right. That's why it's so important to align with yourself first, and then align with your higher self, and then point your wand to manifest. That's the secret to balancing your masculine and feminine energies within yourself. Then when you do manifest, it's a clear manifestation.

Yes, and doing this one step at a time, just moving slowly on the path is so key because it keeps me healthy. And I can see how people who have these amazing abilities, when they don't align properly, it can be detrimental to oneself and to the planet even.

Yes, absolutely because many talented people burn out easily. When we are in alignment with our higher self, we manifest with ease and joy so that the "fruits" of consciousness we offer the world are full of goodness and light. When we are really clear and intentional about our manifesting, we can create a healing field of resonance and everything comes into greater harmony. We come into sync with the universe.

Right. This is part of the Matrix concept, or "the Divine Choreography" as I call it that keeps the flow of the universe going. If we're doing that one step at a time, it keeps the flow healthy.

Thank you so much for this rich dialogue about the Manifestor!

Interview with Susan

Let's talk about your Manifestor. She walks the Path of Action and is connected to the Fire Clan and your will to manifest your dreams. Tell me about your relationship with your Manifestor.

I feel like my challenge growing up was always a lack of confidence and security. I felt invisible and powerless. I now feel at the core of my Manifestor is my great focused will. I always had a strong will. I feel especially powerful when I combine my Manifestor with my Visionary. I can now pull back and see the bigger picture with my Visionary and this helps me to know exactly what to manifest.

I also feel that both my Visionary and Manifestor work really well with my main animal totem, which is the red-tailed hawk. My hawk gives me the ability to see the big picture. Along my life's path, the Manifestor has been very busy too. I've manifested health and love and material wealth and inner wholeness and happiness and a successful career in my life.

When I look around in stillness and see all the things and feel all the things that I've created in my life, it's pretty amazing. I see my home and my relationship with my husband and the career I had and the calling I'm working on now.

The calling that you're working on now, is it more in tune with your essence, your mission?

Yes, they're intertwined. Absolutely. What I'm working on now is calling in my Warrioress to gain the power, the bravery, and the fearlessness to be seen and heard. This is helping my Manifestor to get my work out into the world. When I'm invisible and I'm quiet, it's a safe place for me. Now I'm being called out there and I'm going to be more visible. I'm working on claiming my power.

Right, because a big part of the Fire Clan Manifestor initiation is connecting to your big fire inside and then radiating out that fire to illuminate the path for others.

Yes. I'm now applying this to my mission to help empower others to look inside their own internal landscape and see what they want to create or change. I also want them to see the beauty in themselves and see the beauty that they want to create in their lives and in the world. I'm currently using my Manifestor energy to inspire and motivate me to live as if everything I want already exists. This helps me to bring what I want into manifest form.

You're addressing something about the shadow path of the Manifestor. Normally when we speak of the shadow archetype it's focused on the Manipulator, the active shadow of the Manifestor. You're bringing up the less active side of this shadow path, which is being invisible. So rather than expressing the Manipulator, you're speaking about going invisible, which a lot of women can relate to. "If I just stay invisible and I'm not shining my big light out in the world, then people won't notice me. I can just disappear and be invisible."

I'm safe.

Yes, exactly. You are now moving from the shadow of invisibility to shining your big light out there in the world. And to do this you need your Warrioress to banish your fear, your Queen to offer self-compassion, and your Visionary to offer a bigger perspective and clarity.

Absolutely, yes. I'm actively using all of them on a daily basis to help me with the step-by-step plan to manifest my mission and also to guide me in my short, medium, and long-term goals. I know I need to manifest little step-by-step plans, and also prepare for speaking in front of a lot of people. I'll be speaking to small and larger groups and I'm building the potential for the success of that.

What you're saying is that the Manifestor in you is helping you to build stepping-stones for today, for the next couple of months, and then for the years to come. I think that's really important for women to understand that calling your Manifestor doesn't mean you suddenly use your magic wand and your entire mission is right in front of you. It's more realistic to say that we manifest our destiny and mission step-by-step.

Yes, my Manifestor is using my Warrioress and my Queen and my Visionary to manifest what I need. And I am going at my own pace. I'm also aligning my will with the higher will. That's still new for me. It works best when I bring in my Queen to extend love and compassion to myself, which means loving my art and not abandoning myself. I'm working with all of the goddesses to be able to own and share my gifts with other people.

When I was going through the Feminine Path of Power, I was reading the material and dancing and doing my altar and focusing on the Manifestor. I was just beginning to work on my book, so I thought, "During this Manifestor initiation, I'll focus on something I want to manifest." Then when we got into the Manifestor material together, all her fire just burned away everything inside me. My Manifestor burned so hot in me that it burned away everything. What I realized was that what I was manifesting my entire goddess group - the Warrioress, the Queen, the Visionary, and the Manifestor - inside of me. I was being upgraded to be able to function at a higher level with all of my characters.

This made all the difference in the world; it was like night and day. Rather than choosing one thing I wanted to manifest, I manifested MYSELF! I awakened and brought together my inner team of goddesses. With my upgrade, I can now function on a much higher level.

Wow, you manifested an upgrade! Well done! I look forward to seeing what you manifest! Thanks for sharing so generously about your Manifestor.

Interview with Kala

Let's talk about your Manifestor because she is the part of you that walks the Path of Action. She is connected to the Fire Clan and your will to take conscious action in the world. We say in the *Feminine Path of Power*, that it's helpful to be grounded with your Warrioress, openhearted with your Queen, clear-minded with your Visionary, so that when you act with your Manifestor, it's in alignment with your true self. I'd love to hear about your relationship to your Manifestor and how you manifest in the world?

Since we are talking about the Fire Clan, I've always been fascinated by different Goddesses of fire, like Sekhmet (Egyptian Solar Goddess). *I also love the image of the Shiva-Shakti dance* (Hindu God and Goddess), *their meeting ground in the ring of fire and the dance of life, and all of that. This interest took me to many different places in the world in my quest to find the fire - my fire and the divine fire. What I discovered, especially in the Shiva-Shakti dance, is that within their embrace, there is extreme motion and extreme stillness at the same time. I manifested this fire into the world on a daily basis when I was teaching and working and creating and writing, and going many, many places in that quest. My will was very involved in answering the big questions of life. What are the world's problems? How do we heal them? What do we do? To solve these big problems we must come from the heart.*

I used to ask my kids when I was teaching, "OK, did everybody wind your heart up this morning to make sure that it's still going and that you can make it through the day? Please raise your hand if you did." And nobody raised a hand. "So what do you think is beating our hearts? Isn't that incredibly awesome?" So I would play with my children as I was teaching these big concepts. We would tune into the heartbeat of the universe.

So when you manifest something in the real world, you're tuning in to the heartbeat of the universe. Some people call this, "as above, so below." We tune into the realm of Spirit and then manifest onto the Earth plane. I love that you have manifested much of your heart's desire through the path of teaching kids. This is so down to earth and so necessary to pass on what we know to the next generation.

I've been teaching kids and adults for most of my life. I always had a group of Buddhist students that I would be teaching, both in the schools and in the communities I was part of. My very favorite thing to do is to inspire creativity. When you inspire, it's like you set off a spark. The flint and the heart meet and sets off a spark, it sets off a light, it sets off a photon. You light a match in the world. That's like the whole universe lights a star, or you light a star in your heart of inspiration and you take direction from that.

Thanks so much for sharing how you have manifested through your practical teaching. That's really inspirational.

Interview with Carol

Let's talk about the Manifestor. She is your fire goddess. She helps you focus your will and gather your energy together. So, talk to me about your relationship to the Manifestor.

The Manifestor - I have been able in my life to manifest many things I've wanted. Many years ago I got involved with a ministry, because I really wanted to be helpful to others. So my daughter and I moved from Michigan, out here to Oregon with three other women. They had children too and so we had six little girls altogether. I was the coordinator of the group. And we made that happen.

We came out here to Oregon with no jobs, only a little bit of money, and found a place to live. I needed a job and drove by a restaurant that was looking for waitresses. I'd never been a waitress, and I just happen to drive by so I got out and asked about the job. They hired me on the spot. So, it seems like I have been able to manifest things that I needed in my life. So I know how to do it and I love the Manifestor. I have a strong will when I know what I want. It comes down to having clarity of mind with my Visionary, self-compassion with my Queen, and the strength of my Warrioress.

The Manifestor teaches me how to tame my wild fires and focus my will. I was just this morning sitting at my altar with my Manifestor's Wand, which is a stick that fell off my tree in the front yard. And I thought about all the times that I had believed, and really made things happen out of nowhere. I have felt my Manifestor's strength and it is refining within me.

Yes and a big part of the Manifestor training is aligning your will with your higher will. And I imagine that helps to tame the wildfires when you're anchoring your will to your higher will.

Right. And what I've learned is that it is really important when I'm focusing my will to remember that I am manifesting for the good of all. Not that I've ever wanted to do harm to anyone or anything. But I've had to realize that maybe some of the things that I have put my will to may not have been the best. I need to make sure I align with my higher self. My higher self knows what's best for me and it knows what's best for everyone in the bigger picture.

The Manifestor is an energy that I feel - she's magic. I love magic! I love being able to speak things into being and see them come to pass. I had given up on this kind of magic in my life. For years I just felt like I was at the mercy of outer forces. This new teaching on the Manifestor and the Visionary have revitalized, clarified, and cleared things in my life. When I make that inner alignment I feel so much more confident. It totally renews my confidence in myself, knowing that I can manifest what I want and need. Aligning with my higher self and watching my dream's come true on this Earth, on the material plane, is truly magical.

Well, I love what you're saying about the magic wand and getting the magic back in your life! You remember now that when you connect with your higher self you can create magic, which really is creating something out of nothing. You have your Visionary idea and when you bring it into manifest form you use your magic wand and manifest something that you know is in alignment with your higher good.

Right. And I think before I just saw it as something I could do when I set my mind to it. I'd write things down that I needed and go to garage sale and find all of them. I didn't really see it as my magical manifestation power! Now I can say, "This is who I am as a magician. I take my magic wand, focus it with my higher will and say, "And so it is." And watch it come to pass.

Oh, that's so great. I love that. Thank you for sharing your magical Manifestor!

Interview with Ali Marie

I would love to hear about your Manifestor. The Manifestor has a special connection to all the other archetypes because once you're grounded (Warrioress), open hearted (Queen), have a vision for yourself (Visionary), then you can manifest with your own will on the Path of Action. So tell me about your relationship to the Manifestor.

Well, I think I've always had a pretty powerful relationship with the Manifestor. I have always had a strong Manifestor and at various points in my life she has moved into controlling and manipulating. When I was building my Manifestor altar, I ended up putting symbols from the Warrioress, Queen, and Visionary with the Manifestor because they all need to be working together. In order to have a healthy relationship with the Manifestor, they all need to be present. When they are all in balance, I have a healthier relationship with the Manifestor. In order to manifest my heart's desire, I need to be in an ongoing dialogue with all of them.

When you connect with your Manifestor, do you have a good way to access your will?

Well, that's definitely changed. I have moved from a place of being really willful into a place of comfort with my own will. I'm also experiencing my own willingness to be with the many expressions of my will. I have been connecting my will to a greater will. So instead of being very willful, I know my own will in a much more balanced way – feeling my inner passion. I really want to get to know who I am in the presence of other people's will. Rather than just willful, pushing for what I want to happen. Does that make sense?

Oh yes, you are talking about the difference between being willful versus being willing to align with your higher will.

Yes, this has been an evolutionary process and continues to be my spiritual practice because I can easily go in that other direction. I am being more aware and balancing my Manifestor's will with the Warrioress, Queen, and Visionary.

In the Manifestor training we learn to harness our will and focus on what we want to manifest. We learn to anchor our own will with a higher will. We learn to consider what is good for the whole and this is the key to the Manifestor initiation. So it's not about just my will, it's about seeing what is good for everyone and seeing the bigger vision.

Yes, when I think about it that way, some of my anxious drive has been removed. I don't need to force or plow through or force through. When I have vision and I have trust, I have what I need and I can allow myself to surrender to the process. So rather than a forcefulness that comes from me, I can become part of a larger flow. I can be balanced and I can give and receive. That's very different.

Exactly. Yes and part of the Manifestor initiation is tuning into the fire of consciousness that resides in all things. When we connect with all Creation and recognize we are all part of the same universal flow, we can manifest in a more conscious way.

Yes I can really feel that! It's so good to feel I am in the right place at the right time and I am connected to the universe. Then what I manifest is good for me and good for the world. I have a much greater awareness of that.

Thank you so much for sharing your ongoing process with your Manifestor.

Interview with Susana

Let's talk about the Manifestor. She's your fire goddess. She walks the Path of Action and she brings the Warrioress, Queen, and Visionary all into alignment. How do you connect with your Manifestor?

Well, I certainly have known the shadow path of this archetype, maybe more than all the others. I have been overly willful and manipulative at times, not even knowing I was being this way. I wouldn't have even labeled it as manipulative, but certainly it was as I look back. I also relate to feeling empty and hollow inside even though I had everything in my external life that should have made me happy and successful. I know the Shadow of the Manifestor well!

I also know how incredibly powerful she can be. My Manifestor hasn't always been connected to the other three goddesses. And this is where your Feminine Path of Power has been so helpful Megan. After reading all the initiation stories, I see her connection to the other goddesses. Understanding my Manifestor and embodying her in relationship to the other three is a great gift. And in ways, I trust her much more now, in relationship to the others.

You said you have experienced the shadow side of the Manifestor, which is the Manipulator. Are you in relationship now with the positive qualities of the Manifestor? How might she re-emerge for you?

I don't quite know yet. She's being remade, reinvented. And I don't quite know how my Manifestor is going to re-emerge, but I have no doubt that my upcoming ordination will help. I'll be stepping into a bigger version of myself. I'll be manifesting a more public role. I've been asked to play the harp at a big public meeting where I will be more visible. I will be seen much more in the public eye. My Manifestor will be part of that.

Well, your Manifestor shows your leadership qualities and will guide you to use your will to inspire and motivate others. She holds the light of your magic wand and she illuminates the path for others. You're being asked, and invited to step more into your Manifestor.

Yes I am, in a very integrated way. It feels very whole and grounded now. Whereas other times in my life I have stepped into that role, but it I always felt a bit fragmented and on shaky ground. I didn't feel as authentically integrated as I do now.

Your Manifestor has to be grounded with the help of your Warrioress, openhearted with the help of your Queen, and clear-minded with the help of your Visionary. Then your Manifestor can align with all three to manifest clearly what is needed. It sounds like you have been a successful Manifestor in your life.

Yes, I have been. I can even remember as a young girl, like when I was 13, I would have these visions of living in a beautiful, tropical place. And I think I'd lived in Hawaii a year and a half when I was walking on a path one day and all of a sudden, the vision I had at 13 was right there in front of me. "Oh my heavens! I manifested my tropical place!" I can see how I have done that in my life, not always consciously. That was an "a-ha" moment. I'm well aware now that we're manifesting all the time. And I guess that's always been a reality to me.

Your Manifestor is going to be a lot more active now as you move into more leadership roles as a Chaplain in the hospital and as a trainer/supervisor of Chaplains. As you train and supervise, you'll be using your magic wand quite a lot. You'll have to lead and mobilize resources, motivate others, take more responsibility, make decisions! You're going to be using your Manifestor in many different ways.

Yes, I will be. My Manifestor has kind of been working behind the scenes and now she'll be out front and center. I don't quite have a clear vision of her at the moment. But she is emerging!

Thanks very much for sharing your journey with the Manifestor and how she is working in your life in practical ways.

Manifestor Initiation Conclusion

When you have awakened the powers of your inner Manifestor you will use your conscious will wisely to manifest your dreams and desires. You will be able to mobilize the resources you need and you will inspire, motivate, and empower others to manifest their highest good. You will feel enabled to shine your bright light, radiate your full power, and create a world where you can manifest the life you love!

Imagine honoring the flame of fire and consciousness at the core of your being. Imagine respecting the divine spark in every plant, animal, and every piece of creation. Imagine being in command of your will. Imagine accessing your will to manifest what you want. Imagine your inner fire inspiring you and others. Imagine lighting the way for yourself and others. Imagine a world where we manifest peace, hope, love, and sustainability. Imagine your life lived in moment-by-moment conscious action. This is the strength of the Manifestor, who walks the Path of Action.

When you embody the Manifestor, you focus your will and prepare for action. You are master of the element of fire and know how to control your will with purposeful direction. You see what needs to be done and you inspire, motivate, and lead so the dream can be accomplished. You are able to align your powerful will to the universal will and consider the highest good for all concerned. You have the courage to shine your big fiery light and inhabit your full power without apology.

Conclusion: Divine Feminine Initiation

For thousands of years, women have been gathering in circle to be initiated into the Divine Feminine Way. The Feminine Initiation Path has taken many forms throughout the ages and has been embodied in many ways, depending on the era, culture, land, religion, mythological story, and particular Goddess worshipped in that place. Each Priestess tradition provides unique initiation rituals, teachings, and practices that reflect that culture's core mythology, so there are many variations.

Despite the differences, the commonality in all the various Priestess traditions is the desire to awaken a woman's natural powers of body, heart, mind, will, and spirit. These qualities are universal for all women, transcending barriers of time, culture, and religion. This discovery of the universal themes inspired me to create a modern day sacred path for women to awaken the Divine Feminine within.

In many ways we find ourselves bereft as modern women, without core feminine stories or Goddesses to worship. We feel deprived of a common core mythology that speaks to us today and the ancient initiation rituals seem dead to us - inaccessible and arcane. *The Feminine Path of Power* was created to bring these ancient practices alive for us today, with timeless initiation stories that all women can relate to regardless of their background, race, culture, religion, or experience.

You have now met all 5 Divine Feminine Archetypes, the heroines featured in the 5 initiation stories: Chiman, Oyuna, Pujai, Salima, and Majah. You know that each Feminine Guide initiates you into a particular element - Earth, Water, Air, Fire, and Ether/Spirit - and helps you cultivate your sacred relationship to body, heart, mind, will, and spirit. This is a step-by-step initiation pathway designed for you as a modern woman, with your particular difficulties, trauma, dilemmas, concerns, worries, and challenges.

You have also learned that each pathway has a shadow side that confronts your own challenges with fear, self-sacrifice, chaos, and manipulation. The feminine initiations show you a way forward, through old patterns and traumas, back into the light and onto your Path of Power. Instead of being crushed by the Victim, Martyr, Saboteur, or Manipulator, you can choose to walk on the paths of Strength, Compassion, Change, Action, and Mastery.

When you complete initiation training, you feel empowered and aligned in body, heart, mind, will and spirit. You feel strong and grounded. You feel integrated and emotionally balanced. You trust yourself and your good instincts and intuition. You have the ability to love yourself profoundly. You feel like a master of your own life and destiny. You know your own will and make mature choices. You take responsibility for your life. You are able to flow with the changes and seasons of life.

When you embody the **Warrioress,** you walk the Path of Strength and connect with the Earth Clan. You feel instinctively alive and profoundly connected to your body and to the earth. You are grounded, courageous, bold, and empowered to face your fears. You can stand your ground, speak your truth, and hold boundaries to protect your vital life essence. As a Warrioress, you become the strength of your community, protecting and defending personal and collective truth.

When you embody the **Queen,** you walk the Path of Compassion and connect with the Water Clan. You hold an emotional container for yourself, your loved ones, and your community. When you embody the Queen, you are loving, compassionate, and emotionally balanced. You know how to master emotions and nourish your heart. You are emotionally honest and your heart is true. You are openhearted, generous, and empathetic. You know that self-love and self-nourishment are the keys to happiness and successful relationships.

When you embody the **Visionary,** you walk the Path of Change and connect with the Air Clan. You are clear minded, creative, and able to envision change. You know how to cut through confusion and illusion and master your thoughts. You envision new ways of doing and being and guide others towards necessary transformation. You know what needs to die to be reborn. You encourage change and new direction and breathe life back into yourself, the village, and the community.

When you embody the **Manifestor,** you walk the Path of Action and connect with the Fire Clan. You focus your will and are prepared for action. You know how to control your will with purposeful direction. You see what needs to be done and you inspire, motivate, and lead others so the dream can be accomplished. You are able to align your powerful will to the universal will and consider the highest good for all concerned. You have the courage to shine your big fiery light and inhabit your full power without apology.

When you embody the **Wise Woman**, you walk the Path of Mastery and you connect with Ether or Universal Spirit. You live your life with strength, compassion, vision, and power. You are spiritually centered and fully awake. As the Wise Woman you are master of your own life and destiny. You follow your calling and know your life's purpose. You have a powerful inner light like a compass, pointing to your true north each day of your life. The Wise Woman awakens your true Divine Feminine power and helps you embody your true feminine essence.

The Wise Woman, Majah, represents the magic of your higher self. When you are connected to your higher self and align with your Warrioress, Queen, Visionary, and Manifestor, you come into more coherence, more attunement, and more resonance. Then, when others walk into this coherent field, they heal faster and they integrate more easily. They step into that magical resonance of oneness and wholeness. When we are all attuning to the note of coherence and oneness, something truly magical happens. We create a life that is more loving, more creative, and more conscious. We are less selfish and more generous. We have greater clarity and we trust our intuition. Life comes into greater harmony and balance. The Wise Woman is so powerful because she brings us into greater unity and helps us dream into a better future.

The Feminine Path of Power is an initiation path open to all women of all ages. It is designed for you to awaken your feminine powers and be a part of this great village of women. I invite you to seek your initiation. Join us now in the great awakening that is happening all around us.

"Arise, proud bringer of feminine knowledge and wisdom.
Share your beauty with your sisters…………
For what you bring completes our circle.
And we are proud to know you,
You bless our circle,
You proud bringer of feminine knowledge and wisdom."

If you are ready to be fully initiated, you are welcome to join our *Feminine Path of Power* community. Come to an initiation weekend or participate in our online Priestess program. Join our tribe. We would love to know you.

Step into your full feminine wisdom and unleash your feminine gifts into the world. You have so much to give and you bless our circle, you, proud bringer of feminine knowledge and wisdom.

Blessings to you dear sister and friend…

About the Author

My mission is to help women find their passion, heart, and purpose through teaching, healing, and traveling. When we feel more embodied, empowered, and connected to Spirit, we heal ourselves and we heal the world.

Rev. Dr. Megan Wagner, PhD.

Megan is a therapist, spiritual teacher, ritual leader and Interfaith Minister. She is a leading expert in Psycho-Spiritual Healing and Initiation. She has authored 8 books, many inspirational meditations and sacred chants, and 33 Sacred Robes of her own design and creation. She uses a variety of healing modalities including therapy, astrology, meditation, drumming, chanting, storytelling, and ritual.

Megan is Founding Director of the Feminine Path of Power and Tree of Life Wisdom School, and Director of Spiritual Psychology at The Chaplaincy Institute, Interfaith Seminary. She creates transformational experiences for women to release trauma and increase joy, vitality, and a deep connection to spirit.

Megan provides Certification courses for Tree of Life Training, Spiritual Psychology and Ritual Leadership. She also leads Personal Mastery programs around the world and hosts a Podcast 18-Minute Enlightenment with her colleague Diane Wilcoxson. She lives in the San Francisco Bay Area, California, USA.

My Education, Training, and Experience:

Education
BA Stanford University
MA Marriage and Family Therapy, Fuller Theological Seminary, Pasadena
MA Theology, Fuller Theological Seminary, Pasadena
MMsc Metaphysical Science, University of Sedona, Arizona
PhD Transpersonal Counseling, University of Sedona, Arizona
Ordained Interfaith Minister, The Chaplaincy Institute, Interfaith Seminary, Berkeley, CA
Pranatherapist, Damanhur School for Spiritual Healers, Damanhur, Italy

Therapy Training: I have been practicing as a therapist and spiritual guide since 1985. My training includes Marriage and Family Therapy, Jungian and Archetypal Psychology, Psychodynamic Counseling, Transpersonal Counseling, Astrology, and Inner Alchemy.

Kabbalah Training: In 1988, I began my Kabbalah studies with Kabbalah Master Z'ev ben Shimon Halevi (Warren Kenton) in London, England. I found in the Kabbalah a holistic psycho-spiritual system that made perfect sense to my scientific mind, and spoke deeply to my soul and spirit. For over 25 years I have been studying, practicing, and teaching Kabbalah as a universal path of internal development and spiritual awakening. I run the West Coast Kabbalah School in the San Francisco Bay Area with my partner, Jim Larkin.

Astrology Training: During my 9 years in London I studied Psychological Astrology with Liz Greene and the tutors at the Center for Psychological Astrology. I use Astrology in my counseling practice to help speed up the healing process. The astrological birth chart is an important key to unlocking your Blueprint, your life's purpose, and highlighting your gifts and challenges. It helps deepen your compassion for self and others and improves your relationships.

Initiation Training: While in London, I trained with shamanic practitioners and ritual experts from West Africa and Central America. They taught me so much about rites of passage and ritual as a way to move people through the healing process. During this training, I was in the midst of my own deep inner healing and I was hungry to learn about initiation and rites of passage because they spoke to my own "breaking open" experiences. I wanted to know how the great Initiation traditions held people through the transformation process. These amazing teachers taught me about initiation, ritual, chanting, and drumming and how to hold sacred space for group initiations.

Drumming and Storytelling: While living in London, I learned to drum from the West African tradition of Djembe drumming. The Djembe (*jem-bay*) is a beautiful drum made of wood and goatskin and is designed for ritual, ceremony, and celebration. The word *Djembe* roughly translated means, "gather together in peace". Soon I began to travel to Gambia, West Africa to learn from master drummers there. I also began to do ritual work using drumming and chanting to help people shift quickly out of their pain and suffering and into their radiance and power. When I tell stories, I accompany the storytelling with drumming because it supports the flow of the story and allows deeper access to the imagination.

Sacred Robes: As a child, I was exposed to many different kinds of art, from folk art to fine art, to shamanic art, fiber art, you name it. I tried batik, printing, collage, sculpture, painting, drawing, woodcutting, and many other artistic forms. (I wanted to be a fashion designer when I was a small girl.) Later, I became fascinated with sacred art and how it is used to induce altered states of consciousness. My interest in sacred art has inspired numerous trips to international centers of art and culture and for years I have researched how sacred art aids in awakening and healing the soul. All of these experiences led me to create 33 Sacred Robes for ceremony, ritual, initiation, and healing. Many people who wear the Robes have experienced deep healing, powerful shifts in their energetic field, chakra clearing, and spontaneous awakenings.

Alchemy: Since 1988, I have been studying and practicing Inner Alchemy. Alchemy is an ancient tradition that speaks to the transformation pathway of body, soul, and spirit. Alchemy is an Initiation tradition that uses the analogy of "turning lead into gold" to speak of the developmental process of growing, maturing, and opening to the gold in your life – truth, joy, and spiritual connection. While living in England, I did extensive research at the British Museum, British Library and Oxford's Bodleian Library on Alchemy and also world mythology, shamanism, and the western mystery traditions.

Interfaith Ministry: Since the age of twelve, I wanted to be of service to humanity and to Spirit and to be an agent of change in this world. This calling has transformed over the years as my understanding of ministry, Spirit, and human evolution has shifted and deepened. In my mid-twenties, I attended four years of Seminary training and decided that ordination in a more traditional form was not right for me. After a long search, when I was forty, I met a creative visionary named Gina Rose Halpern, a pioneer in Interfaith Ministry. She invited me to teach at her cutting edge Interfaith Seminary, The Chaplaincy Institute, and soon I was ordained as an Interfaith Minister. I am so grateful to now serve the world by teaching holistic healing, feminine spirituality, and traveling the world embracing the sacred spiritual teachings and healing arts from diverse cultures.

World Travel: I have been traveling since the age of three, climbing mountains, skiing, backpacking, camping, and visiting as many countries as I can. I have traveled extensively in England, Scotland, Wales, and Ireland, Europe, Hawaii, Mexico, Thailand, Indonesia, Malaysia, and also in West Africa, Morocco, Israel, Turkey, Greece, and Japan. My great love is taking groups of like-minded companions to sacred power places to facilitate personal and planetary healing.

Megan's Training Programs & Resources

The Feminine Path of Power: Online and Live
Tree of Life Training
Spiritual Psychology Certification
Ritual Leader Certification
Personal Mastery Journeys – online and live
Sacred Journeys - global adventures
Guided Meditations
Initiation Myths
Sacred Chants
PODCAST: 18-Minute Enlightenment
33 Sacred Robes

Feminine Path of Power Audio Companion

The complete book offered in a 3 volume digital set narrated by Megan Wagner. She guides the listener through this Divine Feminine Initiation Path and brings the women's myths alive through drumming and storytelling.
Volume 1 – The Feminine Path of Power and the Wise Woman
Volume 2 – Initiation into the 4 Clans: Warrioress, Queen, Visionary, & Manifestor
Volume 3 – Nine Interviews with Wise Women

Books by Megan Wagner

Awakening with the Tree of Life: 7 Initiations to Heal Body, Soul, and Spirit
The Story of Majah
The Story of Chiman
The Story of Oyuna
The Story of Pujai
The Story of Salima
The Story of Ariadne

Websites:
www.MeganWagner.com
www.TreeofLifeTeachings.com
www.AncientFuture.Today

My own experiences of initiation

I had my first spiritual awakening at 12 years old, when I met a Spiritual Master on the inner planes and my heart opened to deep and profound love. This experience gave me a glimpse into the spiritual dimensions of life and I made a decision to walk a path of truth and love. Then, when I was 19, I began seeing light (auras) around people and perceived subtle energy when I meditated or sat quietly in sacred space. This made perfect sense to my mystical side and very little sense to my scientific mind. This propelled me on a search to understand what it was all about so I continued my research into spiritual awakening.

I quickly discovered that spiritual awakening, as positive as that may be, often stirs up the psyche in a tumultuous way, so that one must attend to the upheaval of emotions and unhealed trauma from the past. This includes both personal trauma and ancestral trauma that has tumbled down the generations. The emotional upheaval is designed to clear any psychological distortions we carry (blaming others, inner judgment and criticism, lack of love) so that our deeper, more loving nature can emerge.

When this storm began to churn inside me, it was clear that I needed to listen to and have compassion for my unprocessed emotional trauma that was agitated when I began awakening to my deeper, spiritual nature. This is part and parcel of the initiation journey. I also learned that unhealed negative emotions and early trauma greatly hindered my ability to connect with my inner child, my true self and my spirit.

I spent my college years pondering all of this. And then at age 21, when I was attending Stanford University, I had a vision to create a Holistic Academy, to educate, train and provide healing for the integration of body, soul and spirit. In order to accomplish my dream, I felt the logical next step was to study both theology and psychology. So for graduate studies, I attended Seminary and also trained as a therapist. And so I began my professional journey at the tender age of 23.

I remember calling out to the universe as I began therapy training, "I want to awaken fully. I want to know the truth. I want to understand the inner workings of the psyche." In retrospect, this was a rather strong intention to put out to the universe. It may come as no surprise that my life began to crack wide open. This began a 15-year disintegration process in which every structure of my life turned upside down and began to come apart. I descended into the depths of my emotional trauma, did shadow work and wrestled with my family lineage. I questioned everything that had ever had meaning to me. My initiation had begun.

In the midst of my therapy training, I began to have severe migraine headaches 2-4 times per week. Besides excruciating pain, the migraines triggered powerful Kundalini awakenings and spontaneous shamanic journeying, which felt very scary at the time. I had many visions, frightening dreams and general anxiety. I knew I did not have enough internal containment to handle all that was happening and I felt, as a young 28 year old, that I was dying. At least it felt as though my soul was dying, if not my migraine-sick body.

During this difficult time, through a series of miraculous events, I had the opportunity to move to London. I left everything familiar - leaving country, family, friends and professional connections. I hoped to have a fresh start and receive help for my migraines, Kundalini surges and general trauma from my past. As soon as I moved to London, I found a gifted therapist and began a 4x per week classical Jungian Analysis. Within the first month, the migraines disappeared completely and I felt hope that I could heal and pull my life back together.

During my 10 years in London, I continued to dis-integrate but with a lot of emotional and spiritual support. My ego attachments, early conditioning, and old patterns were dissolving in order for a bigger, more expanded version of myself to shine through. I know now that this is a very common experience during profound initiation: our ego dissolves, old coping strategies no longer work, and it feels as if everything is falling apart.

In addition to my therapy, the most important support I received in London was from my weekly Kabbalah group. As soon as I moved to London, I found a master Kabbalah teacher through an extraordinary synchronous experience. (You can read about it in the introduction to my book, *Awakening with the Tree of Life*.) Being part of an ongoing Mystical School was deeply transformative and life altering. It literally changed the course of my life; for I knew from the first moment I walked into my teacher's London flat that I would one day teach this path to others. It also provided me with step-by-step initiation training from a living tradition that was thousands of years old.

During my time in London, I also studied Alchemy at the Bodleian Library in Oxford and the British Library in London. This led me to original alchemical texts and images, which spoke deeply to me about my own awaking process. Alchemy is an initiation tradition, which outlines very clearly the different stages of awareness that emerge as a person dissolves their ego desires and habitual conditioning and is reborn to their spiritual nature through the transmutation process. I also studied Astrology and Jungian Psychology to gain a deeper understanding of Inner Alchemy and how to transmute "lead into gold" – changing our instinctive reactions into mature, compassionate responses to life.

I began reading myths and fairy tales from different cultures that spoke to the psycho-spiritual initiation process. I could relate to the characters with their struggles and triumphs. I began to appreciate how instructive these stories were for our own healing journey, showing us how to awaken long buried inner characters and hidden treasures that bring us closer to our true self.

I also studied the sacred arts from various spiritual traditions. I experienced how sacred art can transport us to other times and places and other dimensions of reality. Contemplating sacred icons, shamanic drumming, chanting and other types of sacred experiences can quickly shift us into altered states of consciousness so we can change trauma patterns and old beliefs more easily. I began drumming, chanting, meditating and painting to journal my process of awakening. I also began traveling to sacred sites around the world so that I could embody the deep wisdom from these different lands and traditions.

I was hungry to learn about initiation and rites of passage because they spoke directly to my own "breaking open" experiences. I wanted to know how the great initiation traditions held people through the transformation process so that they could truly change into their higher nature. In London I found some gifted initiation/shamanic teachers who taught me about initiation, ritual, chanting and drumming and how to hold sacred space for group initiations. My favorite experiences were with my female initiation teachers because it was through them I felt a deeper calling to create a Divine Feminine Initiation Path that would make sense to our modern problems, challenges, and traumas.

After my 15-year dismemberment experience was over, I realized I had, in fact, activated my own initiation so that I could live out my calling to guide others through the process. My desire now is to share this Divine Feminine Initiation Path with you and to create circles of embodied, initiated women to transform themselves, their families and their communities. The time has come. Life is asking us to wake up fully to our divine nature, co-create a better world together and realize there is nothing but love.

APPENDICES

Appendix A – Clan Powers and Shadows

WARRIORESS CLAN

Archetype: **The Warrioress**
Path: **The Path of Strength**
Essence: **Powerful in Body**
Element: **Earth**
Tool: **Shield**
Qualities: **Healthy boundaries, strong, grounded presence, fearless, defends and protects, skillful in confrontation**
Affirmation: "**I am focused, skillful, and strong.**"
Motto: **"Earth Clan Women, powerful in body, focused and strong."**
Empowerment: **comes through strong boundaries**
Shadow Archetype: **Victim**
Shadow Path: **Path of Fear**

QUEEN CLAN

Archetype: **The Queen**
Path: **The Path of Compassion**
Essence: **Powerful in Heart**
Element: **Water**
Tool: **Crystal Heart**
Qualities: **Openhearted, emotionally honest, generous, empathic, compassionate, and diplomatic**
Affirmation: "**I am compassionate, openhearted, and emotionally balanced.**"
Motto: **"Water Clan Women, full of emotion, big of heart."**
Empowerment: **comes through emotional honesty**
Shadow Archetype: **Martyr**
Shadow Path: **Path of Self-Sacrifice**

VISIONARY CLAN

Archetype: **The Visionary**
Path: **The Path of Change**
Essence: **Powerful in Mind**
Element: **Air**
Tool: **Sword**

Qualities: **Clear mind, objective, innovative, cuts through confusion, and envisions new ways of being and doing**
Affirmation: "**I create, transform, and regenerate.**"
Motto: **"Air Clan Women, powerful in mind, full of vision."**
Empowerment: **comes through clarity of mind**
Shadow Archetype: **Saboteur**
Shadow Path: **Path of Chaos**

MANIFESTOR CLAN
Archetype: **The Manifestor**
Path: **The Path of Action**
Essence: **Powerful in Will**
Element: **Fire**
Tool: **Wand**
Qualities: **focused will, manifests desires, inspires and motivates, mobilizes resources, sees the big picture and empowers others**
Affirmation: "**I guide, implement and manifest.**"
Motto: **"Fire Clan Women, powerful in will, ready for action."**
Empowerment: **comes through focusing the will**
Shadow Archetype: **Manipulator**
Shadow Path: **Path of Manipulation**

WISE WOMAN
Archetype: **The Wise Woman**
Path: **The Path of Mastery**
Essence: **Powerful in Spirit**
Element: **Ether**
Tool: **Circle of Empowerment**
Symbol: **The Rainbow**
Qualities: **Spiritually centered, wise, fully awake, confident, self-responsible, integrates and aligns with your life purpose**
Affirmation: "**I choose responsibly, I am Master of my life.**"
Motto: **"I am a Wise Woman, aligned in body, heart, mind, will, and spirit."**
Empowerment: **comes through choice**

Appendix B - The Feminine Path of Power Vows

A vow is a promise you make to yourself, your life, your allegiance to Spirit and to those whom you wish to serve. Our Community has found that repeating these simple vows each day is an amazing way to embody our feminine power and essence. It helps us to show up in the world with confidence, strength, compassion and creative vision. I invite you to say these vows each day and see how they can change your life.

"I commit to Healthy Boundaries, Compassionate Heart, Clear Vision, and Conscious Action."

The Vows are based on each of the Archetypes and the qualities gained through mastering each path. The Wise Woman gives us the choice each day to be as conscious as possible and to choose responsibly. So when you say the vows, you can say it from the voice of your Wise Woman.

"Healthy Boundaries" - This is drawn from the Warrioress and the Path of Strength. As a Warrioress, you want to call in healthy boundaries each day so you can have a strong and grounded presence wherever you go.

"Compassionate Heart" – This is drawn from the Queen and the Path of Compassion. As a Queen you want to activate your compassionate heart so you can be openhearted and emotionally balanced each day.

"Clear Vision" - This is drawn from the Visionary and the Path of Change. As a Visionary you want to have a clear mind and clear vision so you can transform your life and bring in necessary change.

"Conscious Action" – This is drawn from the Manifestor and the Path of Action. As a Manifestor you want to focus your will into conscious action each day to make healthy decisions that are good for you, your loved ones and your community.

Appendix C - The Circle of Empowerment

The Circle of Empowerment is a *Feminine Path of Power* tool belonging to your Wise Woman that helps you make quick, effective decisions by seeing your choice in any given situation. You can choose the Warrioress, Queen, Visionary or Manifestor depending on the circumstance. Don't you wish you had a magic wand or magic toolbox, ready with the perfect response, decision, action or creative solution? The Circle of Empowerment is that magic tool.

How can you use it? Well, your kids, your boss, your partner and your friends present you with new dilemmas every day and you my wonder – how can I respond from my place of truth? What's the best choice here? How can I be most effective? The Circle of Empowerment is a tool that offers choices in how to respond to daily situations – do I need strength, compassion, change or action in this situation?

When you learn the principles of each Path of Power, you will know immediately that one situation calls for strength and healthy boundaries, another calls for deep compassion and love, another for clarity and creative transformation and another calls for action.

Look at the image below and check out the 4 quadrants and the circle of self-mastery in the center.

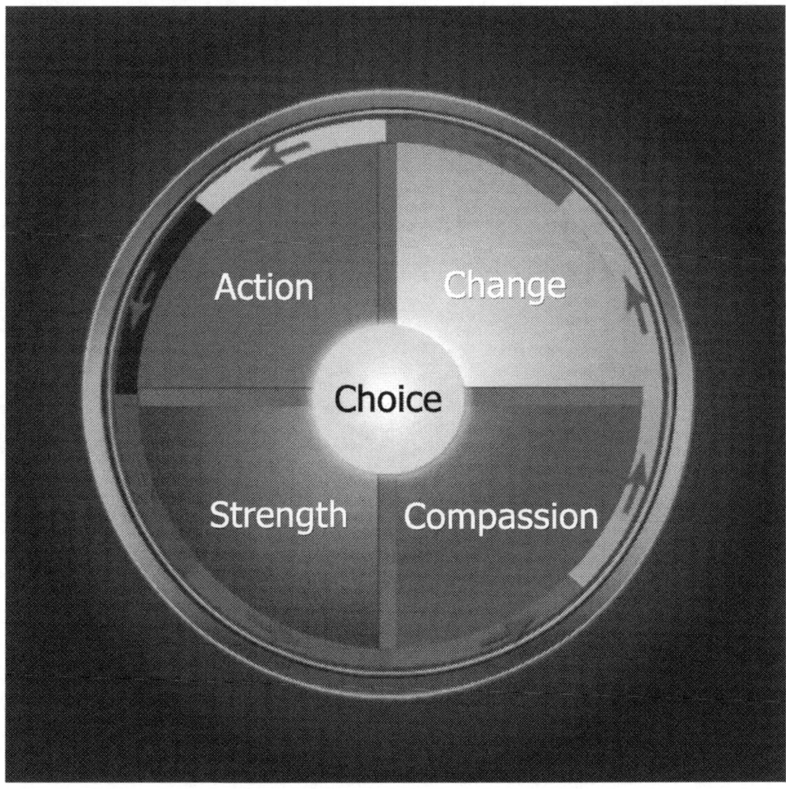

The Warrioress quadrant - Imagine being in the quadrant of the Warrioress, the Path of Strength. Feel the energy of strength and healthy boundaries. The Warrioress helps you feel grounded and present. Whenever you need to stand strong, be awake and present and not check out or stress out, call in the Warrioress!

The Queen quadrant - Imagine being in the quadrant of the Queen and the Path of Compassion. After grounding yourself and creating healthy boundaries, now you can open your heart without getting flooded or overwhelmed with emotions. Whenever you need to contain your emotions or feel deep compassion for yourself or someone else, call in the Queen!

The Visionary quadrant - Let's move now to the quadrant of the Visionary and her Path of Change. You have grounded your energy with the Warrioress. The Queen has given you compassion and balanced your emotions. Now you need to get clarity of mind so you can envision what you want to change. Whenever you need to change direction or change an attitude call in the Visionary. When you need to be creative and envision new ways of doing and being, call in the Visionary!

The Manifestor quadrant - Imagine being in the quadrant of Action, the Path of the Manifestor. You have grounded your energy, balanced your emotions and cleared your mind. Whenever you need to call up your will and manifest something, build something, do something, or take action, call in Manifestor! She will help you manifest what you need for the highest good of all involved.

The Wise Woman in the Center - Imagine standing inside the circle where it says Choice. This is the place on the Circle of Empowerment reserved for your Wise Woman. As you stand in the center of your circle, remember you have choice in each and every situation. You are not powerless, but powerFUL. You can choose the Path of Strength, Compassion, Change or Action. You can master your body, heart, mind, and will and make a responsible choice in every moment. Whenever you need to make an important decision, call in the Wise Woman, stand in the center and choose the best course of action for the situation. Call in your Wise Woman and feel a deep sense of self-mastery.

AKNOWLEDGMENTS

I would like to thank all my women mentors over the years. To all the strong women in my family – thank you. To my first teachers in women's initiation, Sobonfu Some and Erica Helm Meade – thank you. To all the bold, courageous women who have held our women's initiation tradition through the centuries - thank you. To all the women storytellers – thank you!

I would like to specially acknowledge and honor my friend and companion Karen Bandy - sacred dancer, healer, plant alchemist, altar creator, and ritual Goddess extraordinaire. Karen has helped me with all the *The Feminine Path of Power* weekends, initiations, trainings, and ritual preparations over many years. Thank you for all the fun, laughter, tears, excitement, dancing, creating, and hard work! I would like to additionally thank both Karen and her partner Craig for watching Jake when I was writing the initiation stories and to Craig especially for digging many graves.

Also, deep gratitude for my friend and ritual companion Jessica Jacobson, who assists in many rituals and always brings fun, laughter and unexpected surprises to our ritual gatherings. Thanks Jess! And a big thank you to Sequoia, medicine woman and gifted plant medium, who created all the Feminine Path of Power Essential Oil blends. Thank you, the oils are fabulous and gloriously inspired.

I am filled with gratitude for all the Goddesses who granted me interviews for the book: MK, Margaret, Cynthia, Susan, Carol, Kala, Ali Marie, Susana, and AB. I also want to thank all the women who have joined us in any and all of our women's initiation rituals over the years. Thank you for recreating the women's circle. Thank you for speaking your truth. Thank you for solving the world's problems. Thank you for being brave enough to bring your feminine wisdom forward.

Thank you brave women for jumping into the initiation rituals when you had no idea what would happen. Thank you for being buried under the star-filled night, walking up the dark path into the forest, being blindfolded and led on journeys, receiving love from the water nymphs, tearing down the old belief systems, kicking open the boxes of possibilities, cutting the emotional cords that bind you, being crowned a Queen, surviving the Cage of Bones, trance dancing, staring into the steaming cauldron, using your magic wand, declaring what you are letting go, grieving at the ancestor shrine, talking with your tree, and allowing the Goddesses Robes to speak to you.

I also want to acknowledge all the Priestesses, Goddesses, and Wise Woman of the ages who have embodied the Divine Feminine and carried the torch of higher consciousness through very dark times. Thank you for knowing that we would carry on the Women's Initiation tradition in modern times. Thank you for the wisdom, knowledge, and instructions you left us. In deep gratitude, thank you.

COPYRIGHT

 Published by Veriditas Publishing, Redwood City, California, 94064.

Awakening The Feminine Path of Power: Divine Feminine Initiation Path
1. Divine Feminine. 2. Self Help. 3. Psychology. 4. Spiritual.

ISBN 978-0-9974452-2-0

Made in United States
Troutdale, OR
01/22/2025

28225783R00173